The Digital Word

Technical Communication and Information Systems
Edward Barrett, editor

The Nurnberg Funnel: Designing Minimalist Instruction for Practical Computer Skill, John M. Carroll, 1990

Hypermedia and Literary Studies, edited by Paul Delany and George P. Landow, 1991

Rhetoric, Innovation, Technology: Case Studies of Technical Communication in Technology Transfers, Stephen Doheny-Farina, 1992

Sociomedia: Multimedia, Hypermedia, and the Social Construction of Knowledge, edited by Edward Barrett, 1992

The Digital Word: Text-Based Computing in the Humanities, edited by George P. Landow and Paul Delany, 1993

The Digital Word:
Text-Based Computing in the Humanities

edited by George P. Landow and Paul Delany

The MIT Press
Cambridge, Massachusetts
London, England

This book was printed and bound in the United States of America.

Library of Congress Cataloging-in-Publication Data

The Digital word: text-based computing in the humanities / edited by
    George P. Landow and Paul Delany.
        p.   cm. — (Technical communication and information systems)
    Includes bibliographical references and index.
    ISBN 0-262-12176-X
    1. Criticism—Data processing.   2. Criticism, Textual—Data processing.
3. Hypermedia systems.   4. Hypertext systems.   5. Literature and technology.
I. Landow, George P.   II. Delany, Paul.   III. Series.
PN98.E4D54   1993
001.3'0285'5—dc20   92-33742
                                                                    CIP

Contents

Series Foreword

Technical Communication is one of the most rapidly expanding fields of study in the United States, Europe, and the Pacific rim, as witnessed by the growth of professional societies and degree-granting programs in colleges and universities as well as the evolving status of documentation specialists in industry. The writer, and writing, are no longer mere servants of science and engineering but rather partners in the complex matrix of forces that go into the construction of knowledge and information. And the audience is not a passive but an active player in this transaction. Furthermore, computational science has delivered a powerful tool for the creation, presentation, exchange, and annotation of text—so powerful that we speak not in terms of a text but rather of a hypertext, of seamless information environments that integrate a variety of media.

The MIT Press Series in Technical Communication and Information Systems will present advanced research in all aspects of this rapidly expanding field, including hypertext and hypermedia systems, online documentation, information architecture, interface design, graphics, collaborative writing in distributed networks, the role of the writer in industry, scientific and engineering writing, training and education in technical writing. Only in addressing such a wide range of topics do we begin to understand the complexity and power of this field of expertise.

Edward Barrett

Foreword

Two years ago we completed work on the predecessor to this volume, *Hypermedia and Literary Studies.* That collection had as its central concern the linking of units of text, graphics, or sound into structures that had only become possible within the symbolic space of modern computers. However, most such hypermedia structures are bound within a single computer or local-area network. One way to imagine text-based computing is as a more informal hypertext on a much larger scale. The compact node or block of text in hypertext now becomes a chapter- or book-length file; and the links between blocks can easily be the distance between continents, rather than schematic lines on a single workstation screen. In our minds, the concept of text-based computing is inseparable from the recent impact on the humanities world of wide-area networks and the explosive growth in their traffic—currently about twenty to twenty-five percent per month for the Internet. The individual scholar's workstation can now become a node where texts are continually received, reconstructed, and sent on to other points on the network. This participation in an information network need not reduce the importance of such functions as textual search and analysis performed on the scholar's desktop, but we see connectivity as central to text-based computing in the nineties.

The area that we explore here can be comprehended within the larger realm of the knowledge infrastructure that defines what are variously called post-industrial, postmodern, consumer, information, or media societies. Whatever the preferred terminology, all such models recognize that a shift has taken place from processing things to processing their representations, that new technologies give us unprecedented power to generate and distribute information, and that individual knowledge workers face the problem of orienting themselves within a globally linked infosphere or cyberspace. At the same time, many of the essays in this collection emphasize the continuity between recent developments and the bias imparted to the humanities by such previous (and still central) media as conversation, pen and paper, or print. Each editor has done much of his work within traditional paradigms, and both of us expect to continue such work, even as we remain attentive to new revelations of the Digital Word.

George P. Landow would like to thank Brown University's Computing in the Humanities Users' Group (CHUG) and all those visitors who have attended its sessions for the invaluable support and encouragement they have provided. In particular, he would like to express his obligation to Elaine Brennan, Steven J. DeRose, David Durand, Elli Mylonas, Allen H. Renear, Tim Seid, and other passionate advocates of Standard Generalized Markup Languages and the Text Encoding Initiative. He also thanks for their practical assistance and encouragement Paul D. Kahn and the past and present members of the Institute for Research in Information and Scholarship. He owes a particular debt of gratitude to James H. Coombs, who has done so much to advance the cause of humanities computing at Brown.

Paul Delany gives special thanks to the Social Sciences and Humanities Research Council of Canada; their new program of continuing support for humanities researchers has been invaluable in the production of this volume. At Simon Fraser University, Ross Saunders, Nick Cercone, and Bill Krane have encouraged efforts to combine humanities and computing disciplines. Academic Computing Services, especially Lionel Tolan, Doug Davey, Rick Sharpe, and Margaret Sharon, have helped with problems large and small; Rory Gibson, campus NeXT consultant, put Digital Librarian to work. Paul Lawton discussed fine points of translation on the train from Paris to Toulouse, and Jacques Virbel took over on arrival. Heyward Ehrlich, finally, provided a tutorial at Dublin Castle on why text-based computing may not progress so rapidly as we might hope.

Our joint debt is to the contributors who have taught us so much about this exciting new field; to Terry Ehling, our editor at MIT Press who encouraged us to produce this sequel; to Georges Borchardt, Inc.; to Jody K. Gilbert, who wrestled with many different formats and consolidated them in Pagemaker 4.2; and to Noah M. Landow who created the index, designed the bookjacket, and generally helped with matters of design. Our greatest debt is to our copy editor, Ruth M. Landow, who gave this gathering of essays by authors from different countries and different disciplines much of whatever consistency and grace it may possess.

The essay by James H. Coombs, Allen H. Renear, and Steven J. DeRose is reprinted from *Communications of the ACM* 30 (November 1987): 933-97. © 1987, Association for Computing Machinery Inc. and is reprinted by permission. Christinger Tomer's essay previously appeared in the *Journal of Computing in Higher Education* and is reprinted here by permission. Other essays drew on previously published work as follows: by Sue Stigleman in *Database*; by Alan T. McKenzie in *Profession 91*; and by Nancy Kaplan and Stuart Moulthrop in *Computers and Composition*.

George P. Landow
Paul Delany

July 1992

Part I

Introduction

Managing the Digital Word: The Text in an Age of Electronic Reproduction

Paul Delany
Simon Fraser University

George P. Landow
Brown University

A computer in the eighteenth and nineteenth centuries was a human being. Using only pencil and paper, computers spent their days calculating tables: logarithmic tables, ballistic tables, navigation tables, tables of functions, and many more (Shurkin 42). In 1823 Charles Babbage persuaded the British government to finance the development of a "difference engine," a machine that would do more swiftly and accurately what human computers were doing already. When the computer was reborn during World War II—this time as an electrical rather than a mechanical device—one of its first uses was to plot tables for the trajectory of artillery shells.[1] From Babbage's first speculations until about thirty years ago, it seemed obvious that the computer was really a glorified calculator—in current slang, a "number-cruncher."

Project Whirlwind, in the early 1950s, pioneered the idea of displaying the results of computation—in this case, the position of planes being tracked by radar—on a cathode ray screen (Williams 375-76). When the use of keyboards for input followed a few years later, the essentials of text-based computing were in place. But first, people had to change their ideas about the kind of machine with which they were dealing. Jacques Vallée tells how, when he went to work for a French oil company in 1967, he suggested to his boss that it might be useful to retrieve information about service stations under the name of the manager as well as under the station's registration number:

> If all you know is that the name of the manager was DUPONT in 1961, you have to call two secretaries into the office, give them pencils, and let them read the entire file until they find DUPONT. So why can't the computer itself look for DUPONT? Ah, but no, Monsieur Vallée, that

would be using the computer for a name search, don't you see, and that would be, how shall we say, "linguistic"? Computers are primarily for numerical operations, Monsieur Vallée, and everybody (except, perhaps, a few visionary young expatriates returning from America with wild ideas) knows that computers can perform only numerical operations. There follow, for good measure, a few quotations from Kierkegaard regarding destiny and some allusions to the concept of the Self in Sartre and Monsieur Martin rests his case.

Now I try to explain to him that I haven't looked up Kierkegaard in a long time, but inside a computer a name is represented by a number anyway, and for the machine to search for D, U, P, O, N, T is exactly the same thing as searching for 02, 35, 61, 72, 55, and 64. In fact, the poor computer absolutely cannot tell the difference. (Vallée 60)

Vallée lost that argument; but in due course people grasped that computers could do things like organize information into databases, communicate with one another, and manipulate words as swiftly and effectively as they could manipulate numbers. Word processing came into general use in the 1970s on machines designed for that purpose only; in the next decade it shifted over to personal computers, where it was one of many possible functions. But text-based computing, as we use the term in this book, is much more than just word processing. It exists in a whole new environment, created by the computer's ability to revolutionize the world of symbols as much as it has already done the world of numbers. We are dealing here with a new kind of mental space whose topography and boundaries still remain imperfectly mapped. The French term for the discipline of computing, *l'informatique,* suggests that the computer is a powerful manipulator of every kind of human knowledge that allows formal representation.

We shall first discuss the underlying theory of text-based computing, that is, how the computer breaks down the traditional text, recodes it, and projects it into an electronic "virtual space" where it can be reshaped into whatever form suits the user's needs. Second, we enumerate the special qualities of electronic text as opposed to print. Third, we consider how the text-based environment combines several functions: the creation of text bases made up of digital words, the circulation of those words over networks and their storage on magnetic or optical disks, and the manipulation of digital texts at individual workstations. We conclude with some thoughts on how text-based computing may transform the traditional activities of humanities scholars.

Three very general points need to be made in advance because they underlie all the work described in this volume. First, the term *text-based computing* marks the shift in emphasis from handling a single document in the early phase of word processing—what has been called computer-assisted typing—to a complete *textual environment* that brings together networking, mass storage, search and analysis programs, desktop publishing, scanning, and large high-resolution monitors with multiple windows.[2] Second, the elements of this environment have only come together as market products affordable by humanities scholars in the past five years. We believe that the most fundamental change in textual culture since Gutenberg is now under way, but in the early days of this change it would be presumptuous for us to predict how text-based computing will affect society fifty or a hundred years hence. Finally, there is an even greater revolution in progress, one that will both absorb text-based computing and extend its possibilities. The underlying causes of this revolution—continuing geometric growth in computing power and universal access to fiber-optic networks—will support the merging of several key technologies: telephones, sound recording, movies, radio, television, print, and the computer. Under the rubric of "multimedia" or, more speculatively, "cyberspace" (Benedikt), these technologies will restore to texts a sensuous dimension that they lost with the development of writing and printing. Texts will be linked with graphics and sound as a matter of course; as **Kaplan and Moulthrop** suggest,[*] the idea of "composition" will expand from the proper ordering of words to the interweaving of visual, aural, and textual meanings.

These diverse media can become unified only when pictures, sounds, and words have first been translated into the homogeneous medium of digital coding. The conversion of traditional written language into invisible bits of electronic data is the "In the beginning . . ." of the whole endeavor described in this volume, so the nature and the consequences of that recoding will provide the starting point for our discussion.

Virtual Text, Virtual Authors, and Text-Based Computing

Since its invention, writing has received praise for providing unchanging records of language that allow one person to share information with other people in other times and places. Although as Plato has Socrates complain, writing causes vital changes in the people who use it, most civilizations have willingly accepted those changes, which include just the effects that one might expect from a technology that externalizes human memory: people increasingly rely on something exterior to themselves while increasingly devaluing the importance of individual memory. Why clutter one's mind with minutiae, the argument goes, when one can easily consult a written record?

---

[*] References to other essays in this collection are everywhere printed in **bold**.

Printing then adds to written language one feature—the combination of multiplicity and fixity—that has had enormous effect on Western culture and that is ultimately responsible for your reading this volume. As J. David Bolter, Elizabeth Eisenstein, William M. Ivins, and Marshall McLuhan demonstrate, Gutenberg's invention produced what we today understand as scholarship and criticism in the humanities. Writing permits us to create a record that another person far distant in time and space can read. Printing permits us to create a record that *many* other people far distant from us and from one another in time and space can read. The difference between writing and printing may not, therefore, appear particularly interesting or important at first consideration, but the simple fact of multiplicity has had a double effect on literary scholarship. First, multiple copies of a text preserve that text by dispersing it. No longer primarily occupied by the task of preserving information in the form of fragile manuscripts that degrade with frequent use, scholars working with books reconceived their cultural role, transforming it from one of relatively passive custodianship of the text to one that required a far more critical attitude toward it. The cost and conditions of print technology also led to standardized orthography, emphasis on the vernacular, and new conceptions of originality and of authorial property. Nonetheless, the most important impress of print upon our conception of scholarship lies in the way multiple copies of a text permit individual readers separated in time and space to refer to the same information.

Despite the enormous cultural benefits of print technology, it has several major deficiencies. As Vannevar Bush and Theodor H. Nelson, two pioneer theorists of hypertext, point out, printed text presents the reader with fundamental problems, all of which come down to the fact that preserving information in a fixed, unchangeable linear format makes information retrieval difficult. No single arrangement of information proves convenient for all who need that information, and since print, like writing, fixes text in a specific physical form, it causes difficulties for all who do not wish to concentrate on the features emphasized by that particular form. Since the invention of writing, those who work with texts have developed devices to increase the rapidity and convenience of locating information in texts. Manuscript culture, for instance, gradually saw the invention of individual pages, chapters, paragraphing, and spaces between words, and printing added pagination, indexes, and bibliographies (McArthur). Such devices have made scholarship possible, if not always easy or convenient to carry out.

Electronic text-processing marks the next major shift in text-based information technology after the printed book. It promises (or threatens) to produce effects on our culture just as radical as those produced first by movable type and later by high-volume steam-driven printing technology. The characteristic effects of the digital word derive from the central fact that computing stores information in the form of electronic code rather than in the form of physical marks on a physical surface. The letters we encounter on our computer screen seem to be the same letters that we find in our paperbacks, scholarly editions, leather-bound tomes, and flaking, disintegrating, acid-impregnated nineteenth-century books. But they are in fact the temporary, transient representations of digital codes stored in a computer's memory. All the effects of text-based computing on the humanities derive from this one fact. The shift from ink to electronic code—what Jean Baudrillard terms the shift from the "tactile" to the "digital" (115)—produces an information technology that simultaneously combines fixity and flexibility, order and accessibility. As **Virbel, Lancashire, Robinson, Zimmermann,** and others demonstrate in this volume, such translation of the print text into electronic form permits us to relate to the text, literary or otherwise, in radically new ways.

These possibilities come into being because all texts that the writer encounters on the computer screen are virtual texts. Using an analogy to optics, computer scientists speak of "virtual machines" created by an operating system that gives users the illusion of working on their own individual machines when they in fact share a system with as many as several hundred others. Similarly, all texts the reader and writer encounter on a computer screen exist as a version created specifically for them while an electronic primary version resides in the computer's memory. One therefore works on an electronic copy until both versions converge when the writer commands the computer to "save" the current version of the text by placing it in memory. At this point the text on screen and in the computer's memory briefly coincide, but the reader always encounters a virtual image of the stored text and not the originary version itself.

In fact, when one describes electronic word processing, such terms and such distinctions no longer make much sense. As Bolter explains, the most "unusual feature" of electronic writing is that it is "not directly accessible either to the writer or to the reader. The bits of the text are simply not on a human scale. Electronic technology removes or abstracts the writer and reader from the text. If you hold a magnetic tape or optical disk up to the light, you will not see text at all. . . . In the electronic medium several layers of sophisticated technology must intervene between the writer or reader and the coded text." The question then arises, Just what is the text in electronic textuality? Electronic texts intrinsically have "so many levels of deferral that the reader or writer is hard put to identify the text at all: is it on the screen, in the transistor memory, or on the disk?" (Bolter 42-43).

By placing emphasis on some underlying intellectual form, the digital word makes it difficult to identify any particular physical embodiment of a text with "the text itself." The essentially semiotic nature of electronic text leads directly to the ability to manipulate it, to amass large quantities of it in the form of text bases, and to send it over electronic networks. It also forces one to consider carefully just what constitutes the digital text. The authors of "What Is Text, Really?" argue that "text is best represented as an ordered hierarchy of content objects (OHCO)":

> The essential parts of any document form what we call "content objects," and are of many types, such as paragraphs, quotations, emphatic phrases, and attributions. Each type of content object usually has its own appearance when a document is printed or displayed, but that appearance is superficial and transient rather than essential—it is the content elements themselves, along with their content, which form the essence of a document. When mnemonic names for these objects are specified, a document is said to include "descriptive markup." (DeRose 3, 5)

The chapter by **Coombs, Renear, and DeRose** and that by **DeRose** argue the case for the universal adoption of a markup system called Standard Generalized Markup Language (SGML). Such markup adds to the text a description of its own logical structure, allowing the digital word to move easily from computer to computer and from one operating system or word processor to another. It is undoubtedly true that the SGML format provides a disciplined and uniform way of handling electronic texts; unfortunately, it is also true that people tend to do things in the way they find most convenient rather than according to discipline and uniformity. In the days of mainframe word processing, one had to enter a command like <p> to mark the start of a new paragraph in the printed output. If one did not mark up the text properly, one's output would be a mess. But with the widespread adoption of WYSIWYG (What You See Is What You Get) word processors on personal computers, one can start a paragraph in any way that shows the desired result on screen: for example, by using preset margins and styles, by using the tab key, or by using the space bar. This is the style of word processing that most people now practice, though Coombs, Renear, and DeRose are quite right to argue that such habits are sloppy and even, when it comes to compatibility, antisocial. We do not have space here to explore other implications of the SGML debate but will leave the subject with one further comment. In the world of texts circulating over networks, many texts will arrive at the individual workstation in the form called by the French *en vrac*—that is, like hay being tossed into a cart loose rather than in bales—and the receiver's situation becomes What You Get Is What You Must Deal With.

Such desirable features as manipulability, near-instant transportability and transferability, and the capacity for easy reconfiguration are intrinsic to digital computing. Nonetheless, as "What Is Text, Really?" makes clear, today and for some time to come the digital word does not always represent fully electronic text—text originally created in electronic form and intended always to be read only on a computer screen. As successive drafts of this introduction went back and forth over the Internet between Providence, Rhode Island, and Vancouver, British Columbia,[3] some of the versions were read on screen, revised by one or the other author, and sent back without ever having been printed. But people who work with electronic texts usually feel the need, at regular intervals, to print out what they are working on and mark up the paper copy. Part of this need comes from the discomfort many users experience when working only with the amount of text visible in a scrolling window. Suppose you had an assistant who brought you documents with great speed, but handed you the pages individually and never let you hold more than one! The convention of scrolling derives from the limited processing power and screen size of early personal computers. A word processor that displayed two full pages at once and moved through the document by "page turning" rather than by scrolling might make it easier to keep the entire cycle of composition on screen.[4] It is also possible, though, that the current generation of scholars still has habits engrained by print and that scrolling may seem the "natural" way to compose and read for those who are now growing up with computers.[5]

Whatever the future holds, almost all the essays in this volume demonstrate that today electronic text exists largely as a supplement to, rather than a replacement for, manuscripts, typescripts, and books. Thus the chapters by **Coombs, Renear, and DeRose** and by **DeRose** concentrate on the most efficient means for producing electronic text that ultimately appears in the form of printed articles and books, and those by **Robinson, Lancashire, Zimmermann**, and **Miall** discuss the latest ways of using electronic technology to investigate individual texts originally created for the world of print. In contrast, **Clear, Delany,** and **Virbel** concentrate on the individual digitized text as it forms a part of a continuous interaction with a larger text base (see also Brennan).

For the time being, then, scholars will still rely heavily on books, and one can guess that continuing improvements in desktop publishing and laser printing will produce a late efflorescence of the text as a physical object. Nonetheless, these physical texts will be produced (or rather reproduced) from electronic texts. In the long run as readers increasingly become accustomed to the convenience of personal databases, search-engines, and electronic conferencing, mail, and publication, the printed books that now define the scholar's tools and end products that might possibly lose their primary role in humanistic scholarship.

A Digital World?

The contemporary French culture critic Jean Baudrillard attempts to erect a whole theory of contemporary culture upon digitization. With the self-dramatization and high emotional temperature that characterize pronouncements of structuralist and poststructuralist sages, he proclaims, "The true generating formula, that which englobes all the others, and which is somehow the stabilized form of the code, is that of binarity, of digitality" (145). According to Baudrillard, the primary fact about digitality is its connection to "Cybernetic control . . . the new *operational* configuration," since "digitalization is its metaphysical principle (the God of Leibnitz), and DNA its prophet" (103). Unfortunately Baudrillard, who does not seem to know much about computing, text-based or not, in true structuralist fashion assumes that digitality involves binary opposition—and only binary opposition: "Digitality is with us. It is that which haunts all the messages, all the signs of our societies. The most concrete form you see it in is that of the test, of the question/answer, of the stimulus/response" (115).

Baudrillard misconceives the primary nature and effects of electronic information regimes. Unlike Jacques Derrida, who has long concerned himself with the effects of information technology upon Western literature and philosophy, he pays no attention at all to verbal textuality that disproves many of his points about supposedly inevitable effects of digital computing. "True, at the most basic level of machine code and at the far higher one of program languages, digitization, which constitutes a fundamental of electronic computing, does involve binarity. But from this fact one cannot so naively extrapolate, as Baudrillard does, a complete thought-world or episteme" (Landow, *Hypertext* 20).

Baudrillard completely ignores digitized verbal text and jumps immediately from the fact of digital encoding of information to his stimulus/response—either/or—model. He also concerns himself almost entirely with nonalphanumeric media, such as photography, radio, and television. In fact, when Baudrillard argues for the role of digitality in contemporary culture, all his examples come from analogue, rather than digital, media. Instead of the serial, linear processing that analogue recording of sound and images enforces, digital technology permits one to go directly to a particular bit of information. Wanting to hear a particular passage in a speech or musical performance recorded in a common form of analogue technology, the tape cassette, one must scan through the cassette sequentially. When the speech or musical performance is digitally recorded, one does not find oneself so rigidly confined to sequence. The listener can quickly locate a desired passage, note it for future reference, and manipulate it in ways impossible with analogue technologies. For example, with the proper equipment one can "sample" any particular segment—that is, one can record it, duplicate it, and manipulate it, and in other ways intervene in the sound "text." With a compact disc player, one can instantly replay passages without having to scroll back through them by rewinding a tape, and one can program one's CD player to play only one's favorite passages on a particular disc. These examples suggest that even the most basic kinds of digitized information permit and encourage the reader, listener, or viewer to engage that information in a newly active, potentially aggressive and intrusive manner.

The way digitization invites the reader to approach text differently prompts one to inquire what will happen to texts that do not move from the currently dominant information technology, print, to the electronic one. Jean-François Lyotard predicts that "anything in the constituted body of knowledge that is not translatable in this way will be abandoned and that the direction of new research will be dictated by the possibility of its eventual results being translatable into computer language" (4). Antonio Zampolli similarly warns: "Languages which have not been involved with printing, have become dialects or have disappeared. The same could happen to languages that have not been 'informatized'—transferred to the world of electronic text storage, manipulation, and retrieval" (47). Texts and even entire languages that do not transfer to a newly dominant information medium become marginalized, unimportant, virtually invisible.

Electronic Text in an Electronic Age

Before the era of telecommunications and the computer, any distribution of a text— beyond the thirty- or forty-meter range of the human voice—required the text to be bound to an object. To send a copy to someone else also required sending them a physical letter, manuscript, or book. Printing made those objects relatively cheap and plentiful; and once they had been printed and sold, they came under the absolute control of their owners with profound consequences for literacy, individualism, intellectual freedom, and pluralist democracy. Nonetheless, the cost and the physical embodiment of texts means that any large collection of them has to be housed in a library, to which would-be readers must travel. Libraries are also needed because most books and almost all newspapers and journals will be, at any given moment, unavailable for purchase because they are out of print. Truly comprehensive collections of printed texts can only be found, therefore, in major repositories, ranging from university libraries to monuments like the new British Library and the Bibliothèque de France, where just the housing for texts costs over a billion dollars.

Print-based literacy has evolved over more than five hundred years, striking deep roots into every kind of social practice and taking a larger and larger share of economic activity (Bormuth). The computer systems that support virtual or digital literacy became widely used no more than about ten years ago, with the general adoption of word processing on personal computers and electronic mail in universities and corporations. Anything we say today about digital literacy therefore must be provisional, and sensibly we can do no more than sketch the outlines of some possible future information worlds. When it comes to predicting the effects of the new media on politics and everyday life in the next century, there can be no true authorities—which is why so many people turn for guidance or entertainment to the cyberpunk writers of near-future science fiction, such as William Gibson, Bruce Sterling, Vernor Vinge, John Shirley, and Pat Cadigan (Stivale). Without claiming to foresee all the future, then, we can at least indicate some of the fundamental features of text-based computing that will shape the emergent world of digitized and networked information.

Dematerialization

Because the electronic text exists only as a piece of code, it can be transmitted in a different medium and reconstituted at its point of arrival. Virtual copies—whether displayed on a screen or printed out—can be produced not only at the same reading site (the stand-alone personal computer) but also at any other reading site electronically linked to the first one. High-speed networks transmit in seconds the electronic codes that produce text from computer to computer and hence from user to user; magnetic media like floppy disks and CDs move large chunks of text at once, but more slowly. With print technology the text exists as a physical object complete in itself, capturing a fixed textual state, and readable everywhere, from a subway car to the beach. Electronic texts need a computer system to be readable; that system costs far more than an individual printed book, remains vulnerable to breakdowns and sabotage, has limited portability, and may allow those who control networks to monitor or censor the activities of users. On the other hand, the new medium offers speed, low cost for individual texts, continuous availability of texts that are materially out of print, and the ability to search through many texts rapidly and to display them in different forms. Such fundamental differences between printed and electronic text more or less guarantee that the two technologies will continue to exist side by side and to complement each other in many ways.

Manipulability

The ease of manipulating alphanumeric symbols first produces simple word processing. This word processing in turn makes vastly easier old-fashioned, traditional scholarly editing—the creation of reliable, supposedly authoritative texts from manuscripts or published books—ironically, at a time when the very notion of such single, unitary, univocal texts may be changing or disappearing.

Then, this same ease of cutting, copying, and otherwise manipulating texts permits different forms of scholarly composition, in which the researcher's notes and original data exist experientially closer to the scholarly text than ever before. According to Michael Heim, as electronic textuality frees writing from the constraints of paper-print technology, "vast amounts of information, including further texts, will be accessible immediately below the electronic surface of a piece of writing. . . . By connecting a small computer to a phone, a profession will be able to read 'books' whose footnotes can be expanded into further 'books' which in turn open out onto a vast sea of data bases systematizing all of human cognition" (10-11). The manipulability of the scholarly text, which derives from the ability of computers to search databases with enormous speed, also permits full-text searches, printed and dynamic concordances, and other kinds of processing that allow scholars in the humanities to ask new kinds of questions. Moreover, as in the process of writing, "The text in progress becomes interconnected and linked with the entire world of information" (161).

Virtuality also adds an entire new element to the digital word and digital text—electronic linking that reconfigures textuality. Our previous volume (Delany, *Hypermedia*) discusses the results of the way electronic linking creates hypertext, a form of textuality composed of blocks and links that permits multilinear reading paths. Since this present volume does not discuss hypertext except in passing (**DeRose, Landow, Stigleman,** and **Virbel**), we should point out that forms of dynamically generated electronic linking exist in other kinds of text retrieval not usually considered under the rubric *hypertext* or *hypermedia*. Heim has argued that word processing inevitably produces a new form of interlinked textuality:

> The distinctive features of formulating thought in the psychic framework of word processing combine with the automation of information handling and produce an unprecedented linkage of text. By linkage I mean not some loose physical connection like discrete books sharing a common physical space in the library. Text derives originally from the Latin word for weaving and for interwoven material, and it come to have extraordinary accuracy of meaning in the case of word processing. (160-61)

In the print world, individual texts remain stable, discrete and isolated, except insofar as the minds of individual readers perceive connections, references, allusions, and analogies, that obtain among various texts. The digital text, in contrast, permits one to use the resources of computing to *process* texts created within oral, manuscript, and print cultures, to do things otherwise difficult or even impossible with the texts in their original form. Such text-based computing, which comprises all forms of text searches, editing, comparison, and analysis, markedly shifts the balance of power from text to reader, because the scholar can now probe the text in ways formerly difficult or impossible. One result is that the scholar can intrude upon the text—probe it, search it, manipulate it, and interrogate it in ways never before possible without great personal expenditures of time, energy, and money. In the nineteenth and the earlier part of the twentieth centuries, scholars who wished to create systems of information retrieval for specific authors, say, for the Bible or for the works of Shakespeare and Coleridge, would labor endlessly to create an index and concordance of a single author's works. When word processing based on mainframe computing developed, such projects became far more feasible, so much so that projects that might have taken the entire careers of a team of scholars now took a year or less.

With the personal computer, as Heim has shown, scholars find themselves in an entirely different relation to the text. They no longer have laboriously to create information-retrieval devices to be published and consulted in a print form. Instead of producing any fixed concordance or reference tool, they only have to query a text base for the particular information useful to them for reading and understanding a text or set of texts. Another way of expressing this change appears in the fact that undergraduates, beginners in a particular field, can now carry out investigation of the text formerly impossible for expert scholars. As Gregory Crane and the Perseus team have reported, undergraduates—in fact, even first-year undergraduates who do not read Greek—can carry out detailed investigations of the way a particular word, phrase, or grammatical construction appears throughout an individual work or even throughout an individual author's career. Using parallel English and Greek texts, beginning students of Aeschylus and Homer, like lay readers of the Gospels, can probe the text (299).

Open Admission and New Discourses

The print system has established a remarkably stable, two-level hierarchy for written texts. Because of the substantial costs of printing and publishing, authors have to pass a strict gatekeeping test before their works can be circulated; but once that test has been passed, the printed text enters the cultural archive in a fixed and prestigious form. At the lower level, there exists a vast sector of unpublished texts, such as undergraduate essays, lecture notes, and the like, that by convention do not count as part of a discipline.

Networked text distribution is intrinsically cheaper, faster, more open, and less hierarchical than print. Once a text exists in digital form, the only significant cost in distributing it is a copyright fee—assuming that one is due and can be collected. The present low cost of electronic storage—less than a dollar for a standard novel—in a few years will become negligible. Space is already negligible: a hard drive the size of a book can store the texts of thousands of books. As a result, it is much easier both to "publish" and to "collect" digitized texts.

An important consequence for the humanities is a potential speedup in the circulation of ideas (**McKenzie**). It is not unusual, for example, for two years to pass between the submission of an article to a scholarly journal and its appearance in print. When it is at last published, more months or years pass before responses and citations in bibliographies appear. Electronic circulation short-circuits this lumbering process.[6] The article by Mark Olsen that we refer to below has been circulated and discussed on the networks—and now discussed in this book—months before its first appearance in print. In fact, a vast informal sector of academic discourse has emerged in conference groups and electronic bulletin boards.[7] Before the development of networked computing, scholarly communication generally relied upon physical rather than virtual textuality—the transportation of material objects with marks on them. As **Landow** argues, "Networked electronic communication so radically reduces the time scale of moving textual information that it produces new forms of textuality. Just as transforming print text to electronic coding radically changed the temporal scale involved in *manipulating* texts, so too has it changed the temporal scale of *communication*. Networked electronic communication has both dramatically speeded up scholarly communication and created new forms of it." True, as **Renear and Bilder** point out, most of this publication is vulgar or ephemeral, but it is widely available and easily stored in permanent form. The problem in networked communications has become not how to acquire texts but how to sift out the ones we value from the deafening babble of global electronic traffic.

Dispersal of the Text

The material requirements of printing and publishing created "containers" for text with a standard size and format, such as the journal article or book. Digitized and networked texts smash the containers. A traditional-size text may be broken down into smaller units or scaled up to merge with a docuverse of related texts (**Delany**). Instead of acquiring a complete Xerox copy of one scholarly article, we may now use a text manager or search engine to obtain from many articles just the paragraphs or footnotes relevant to our own project. Conventional ideas of the book and the author were called into question in the sixties by such poststructuralist concepts as intertextuality and the dissolution of the subject. Those conventions are now challenged in a much more literal way by the computer's capacity to manipulate, to disperse, and to recombine the elements of digital texts (Landow, *Hypertext*). New textual forms, such as hypertexts or phrasal graphs (**Lancashire**), are emerging. New kinds of careers and disciplinary influences will also emerge in the universe of networked discourse: seminal figures like Nelson (the godfather of hypertext) may become eminent without the benefit of so-called authoritative publications in major presses or journals.

Digital Texts and the Law

The same virtuality that permits all these new forms of scholarly activity also produces a cluster of new problems involving ownership, authorial control, responsibility, reader access, and transience of information. As Pamela Samuelson explains in "Digital Media and the Changing Face of Intellectual Property Law":

> What distinguishes digital media are six characteristics that will make it difficult for existing categories of intellectual property law to adjust to the protection of works in digital form. They are: (1) the ease with which works in digital form can be replicated, (2) the ease with which they can be transmitted, (3) the ease with which they can be modified and manipulated, (4) the equivalence of works in digital form, (5) the compactness of works in digital form, and (6) the capacity they have for creating new methods of searching digital space and linking works together. (324)

Samuelson's categories will seem familiar to anyone who has read thus far in these pages since they represent the very categories that make text-based computing in the humanities appealing to the scholar. In fact, every unique characteristic of the digital word itself leads to legal difficulties within a society whose intellectual foundations depend so importantly on print—so much so that our law, like our attitudes toward authorship, has taken certain attitudes and assumptions of the Gutenberg world as if they obviously applied everywhere, as if they were, in other words, facts of nature.

In fact, everything about the digital word that seems a source of enormous convenience can also be seen as a source of major problems. For example, the compactness of electronic texts, which makes them so valuable for the scholar, raises a host of potential difficulties. Samuelson, like Bolter, points out that "works stored in digital form are essentially an invisible string of stored electrical voltages" (334) that take up extraordinarily little physical space. Citing an announcement by IBM engineers that they had managed to store a gigabyte of information in a single square inch of magnetic material, she comments, "Had this same billion bits of data been typed in double-spaced format, the stack of paper would be three stories tall" (335). This is the kind of point in which everyone making plans for the scholar's workstation of the future and giant text bases finds great delight in making, but she adds the kind of observation humanists do not often wish to consider: "There is simply no comparison in the ease with which a square inch disk can be misappropriated and the ease of stealing a three story pile of paper. This is yet another reason why distributors of intellectual property will have more interest in controlling access to and uses of protected works in digital form than to traditional works. . . . Another consequence of compactness is that this very quality of digital works makes it increasingly difficult to get anything more than a small glimpse at the contents of these works at any one time" (335). We can draw the obvious conclusion that until our society finds equitable means of both sharing and protecting information, many of those giant text bases will never come into existence.

Many of the issues involving the legal implications of electronic technology do not obviously bear upon the digital word. Nonetheless, it takes little imagination to see that issues apparently far distant from electronic textuality might affect matters that scholars in humanities, like poets and novelists, find important. For example, at the moment the so-called look-and-feel lawsuits would seem to apply directly only to major proprietary matters of computer interfaces (Samuelson, "Interface Specifications," and Samuelson et al.), and yet one could see how such issues could affect artists producing electronic fiction and critics who write about them, particularly since a recent case involving patenting algorithms might have a chilling effect. According to Samuelson, "Traditionally it has not been an infringement of a patent to draw a patented machine or to write an article about it, for one could not thereby make or use the machine, whereas with mental processes like addition, one can use the invention by writing about it. Computer program innovations, if and when patented, mark the first time it can infringe a patent to embody the innovation in a copyrighted written text" ("Should" 27).

Another area of potential difficulty arises in computer-generated text, which might range from poetry, fiction, and research partially or even entirely generated by a computer program to scholarship based on computers, software, text bases, or all three that belong to someone other than the researcher. (See Samuelson, "Allocating Ownership" and "Creating," for some relevant background.) Traditionally, colleges and universities have rarely claimed that the results of research by their faculty or staff falls under the for-hire doctrine (which holds that work produced while one is being paid to work belongs to the employer). Institutions have rarely made such claims, in part because few publications in the humanities pay enough to make them worth consideration. Nonetheless, recent claims by universities on computer programs created with university-owned resources suggests that educational institutions have the legal right to assert ownership of all materials produced with their computing equipment and work in the humanities will not necessarily be excluded from such claims or control.

On a more positive note, progress is finally being made on comprehensive agreements covering fees for photocopying, and these agreements might provide a model for electronic copying. CANCOPY, a nonprofit coalition of Canadian authors, visual artists and publishers, has joined in a reciprocal series of agreements among ten countries—including, for the United States, the Copyright Clearance Center. This agreement will allow copiers in one country to use materials originating in any of the others. Negotiations are in progress with large-scale copiers, such as school boards and universities, on a formula for compensation. In Britain, where such an agreement already exists, the copyright collective distributed £386,304 to authors in the first half of 1989.

The Dissemination of the Digital Word

All these characteristics of digital texts contribute to a new intellectual environment and sociology of knowledge. A crucial consequence of the virtuality of coded text is that texts on an individual user's computer can merge instantly with the unimaginably complex universe of networked information. There now exists a collective mental space, with distinct kinds of dialogue and memory, sustained by the more than a million computers connected to global networks. Speculations about that universe have coalesced around the concept of cyberspace, coined by William Gibson in 1984 and now an emergent intellectual discipline in its own right (Benedikt). In this volume, we do not aim to soar into the wild blue yonder of cyberspace, exciting as such speculations may be. Rather we limit ourselves and our authors to the immediate future of networked textuality and to subjects closely relevant to humanistic scholarship. But even such modest inquiries can tell us much about the changes that the computer will bring to long-established disciplinary conventions. We shall survey these changes under three headings: the sources of digital texts, their distribution, and text management at the workstation. Present differences between North American and European practice suggest that the evolution of text-based computing need not follow a single path.

Text Sources

Contemplating text-based computing in Europe and North America, one encounters two opposing models—the individualistic, even anarchic mode that seems homologous with both much traditional humanities scholarship and the personal computer and, in contrast, the centralized mode associated first with mainframe computing and now with networks to which access is controlled by institutions or governments. The decentralized, anarchic mode of text-based computing appears embodied in a mass of texts that are being digitized by individual keyboarding or scanning; this work, which goes on without any central direction, appears in a great variety of unstructured formats. One can get digital versions of canonical texts by putting out a call for them on the Humanist conference, but texts thus informally acquired come with no guarantees of authority, accuracy, or completeness (Sperberg-McQueen). For example, one might get a digital Shakespeare from the network with no warning that it had come from someone who had tampered with the text to support the theory that Bacon wrote Shakespeare!

In contrast to the anarchic mode stand three examples of centralized control— the Text Encoding Initiative (TEI), the British National Corpus, and the Bibliothèque de France. The TEI, which is supported by public and private agencies in Europe and North America, is developing criteria for SGML that will make the formatting in electronic texts hardware and software independent (**Coombs**). In Britain, the British National Corpus, a project with joint public and private funding, will aid the continuing development of the Oxford English Dictionary and linguistic research in general (**Clear**). In France, the digitization program of the Bibliothèque de France is both centralized and government-funded (**Virbel**). This program assumes that the government should subsidize access to digitized texts just as it has traditionally done for printed ones. The French consider cheap information, in various media, to be an essential part of the nation's "knowledge infrastructure."[8] The roughly twenty thousand works digitized under this program already make up the world's largest general-purpose digital archive.[9] We should note, also, that the Bibliothèque de France program is only one element in a comprehensive, long-term strategy for investing in knowledge infrastructure, dating back to the Nora and Minc report of 1978, *L'Informatisation de la Societé*. It is too early to say which model will prove more effective for text-based computing: the decentralized, private-enterprise approach or the centrally directed and subsidized one, best embodied in the French program (of course, it is not just in the field of digital texts that national competition takes place according to different philosophies!).

Text Distribution

In North America the distribution of digitized texts has been conducted informally, for the most part, without expectation of profit. There have been some commercial ventures recently: the *Library of the Future* CD contains the text of several hundred novels; Chadwyck-Healey has announced the publication of *English Poetry 900-1900* on CD; and Apple has made an agreement with Random House to publish the Modern Library in electronic form. CD-ROM is a useful media for providing large blocks (up to 650MB) of structured text. The cost may be high for each disk, but by attaching a CD drive to a workstation, docuverse-sized textual resources can be loaded all at once. Such CDs provide packages of information that might be difficult to assemble from network sources or are otherwise unavailable because of copyright or proprietary restrictions (**Delany**).

In past years electronic texts usually traveled by surface mail using a magnetic or an optical disk or tape-storage medium; however, users are now shifting to network transmission, under the listserver utility for BITNET or file transfer protocol (FTP) for Internet. The Internet is likely to make BITNET obsolete; it transmits data faster—currently up to forty-five megabits per second—and allows computers to link up easily with one another. Traffic on the Internet is increasing by twenty to twenty-five percent per month. It seems clear that the Internet—and its proposed successor, the National Research and Education Network (NREN)—will form the backbone of the North American knowledge infrastructure in the course of the nineties (Hall, Peters, Weingarten, Kehoe). The pervasiveness in universities and high-tech businesses of the Internet, which connects more than three-quarters of a million powerful computers, makes available a standard utility for circulating public text files. However, relatively few of these texts, until now, have been literary or scholarly.[10]

High-speed access to the Internet currently requires that the user be connected at a university or corporation. But from late 1992 onward in North America, Integrated Services Digital Network (ISDN) telephone service will start to become available in private homes at moderate cost; ISDN will support fast (64Kbits/sec) connection from the home to the nearest Internet node, without the use of a modem (Garfinkel). Scholars who have ISDN service will have twenty-four-hour access to the Internet information world.[11]

Front ends to Internet textual resources have just begun to come into general use. Archie (archie.ans.net) is an Internet-wide directory, based at McGill University, that indexes over two million public files and programs. Any scholar can now place his or her article as a public file on a server and thus make it available via Archie to anyone who looks for it. Wide Area Information Servers (WAIS) and Gopher are programs that make it easier to search for and download information and thus add value to large docuverses of unstructured files. Moreover, WAIS is designed to support a "market sector," in which information providers will receive payment for the use made of their resources (Kahle, Lincoln, Stein). The search engine for WAIS is based on relevance feedback, which compares the contents of a file with the contents of the user's query:

> Documents are retrieved by starting with a question in English. A single line, or headline, would describe possible documents that are appropriate. These documents can be viewed, or used to further direct the search by

asking for "more documents like that one." Each document on the disk (or some other source) is then scored on how well it answers the question and the top scoring documents are listed for the user. . . . For text documents a useful and powerful measure is to count the number of words in common between the question and the text. (Kahle)

Not only are WAIS interfaces available for PCs, Macintoshes, NeXTs, and Suns but one intriguing feature of WAIS is that the Thinking Machines server is one of the world's most powerful computers, a pioneering example of the application of leading-edge supercomputing to a textual rather than a numerical or graphic task. WAIS and Gopher operate on different principles and have different strengths and weakness, as **Tomer** explains in detail. Whether WAIS, Gopher, or some other front end becomes a standard, Internet-wide information servers (IWIS) will surely play a key role in the evolution of text-based computing.

Text Management

Effective text management of large docuverses requires a suitably equipped workstation connected to a high-speed network. The current approximate standard for such a machine requires a 15MIPS processor, 16MB RAM, 17-inch monitor, 660MB hard disk, and CD-ROM drive. Whether one calls it a high-end personal computer or a workstation, the question is academic, since standards for each type of computer have begun to converge. What really counts is that such machines are now within the means of an individual humanities scholar. The next generation— RISC workstations with greater processing power and storage—will make feasible multimedia applications that require very large sound, graphics, and video resources. The hand-held digital reader, the logical successor to the book, has yet to appear in a practical and standard format, but we can look forward to monitors with more than two million pixels that will make on-screen reading more agreeable.

Software approaches to text management again differ in philosophy between North America and France. North American users divide up between PC, Macintosh, and workstation sects. The NeXT computer has made a start at comprehensive text management with its Digital Librarian facility, but this program remains undeveloped in several areas and is not fully integrated with word processors, mail, and other utilities. Each group of users encounters a wide choice of word processors, search engines, and every other kind of text-management program (**Stigleman**). Just as almost every computer is configured differently, so is there also a great range of skills from one humanist to another, varying from computer illiteracy to sophisticated programming ability. Nothing indicates that this disorderly (though also creative) scene will change rapidly or radically; as in other fields, humanistic computing in North America displays a kind of Darwinian churning, with some areas advancing rapidly and others stagnating. One North American advantage persists, however: because computing power at all levels costs much less than anywhere else in the world, more people can try their hands at every kind of project.

The Bibliothèque de France reading station, in contrast, attempts to create a single, advanced model for scholars' interaction with the massive digital text base being created for their use. The details may be read in **Virbel**; here we shall only touch on one practical and one philosophical point arising from the French initiative. The practical one is that the reading station will require a high level of skill and formal training to be used at the level intended by its designers. Instead of the gradient of skills found in a typical North American humanities department, users will have to sign up for the reading station, serve an apprenticeship, and be initiated into a coherent and exclusive work group. This approach represents an important shift in the sociology of humanities computing. Those who have qualified to use the reading station may find themselves at the strategic center of their disciplines instead of at the margin, as many humanist practitioners of computing tend to be today (see our discussion of Olsen below).

The philosophical point has to do with the opposition between central planning and decentralized spontaneity. The French reading-station project may turn out to impose prematurely a single quasi-official way of managing texts at a time when the whole field of text-based computing—on the evidence of the present volume—is still at such an early stage of development. The handling of texts at the level of the individual workstation will probably change radically over the next ten years, and the reading station may suffer from putting too many eggs, too early, into one basket. Nonetheless, such investment in an ambitious and integrated system of digital text handling could achieve a significant comparative advantage for France in the knowledge society of the future—just as, for example, Amsterdam gained many collateral advantages from its seventeenth-century pre-eminence in the equivalent information technologies of that time, printing and publishing (Murray).

Conclusion: Working with Texts

Mark Olsen has recently argued that three decades of literary computing have failed to have any substantial impact on the mainstream of literary criticism and scholarship. The results of computer-aided research, Olsen says, have been reported only in specialized journals; they fail to influence other critics and are rarely cited outside the computing community. This marginality can in part be explained by the traditional preference among literary critics for organic rather than mechanical modes of thought. Nonetheless, Olsen believes that computer critics have failed to convince their colleagues of the claim that their work can achieve "the systematic discovery of how a text achieves its literary effect."

Olsen does not argue, however, that computer analysis is doomed to remain a perpetual backwater of literary studies. Rather he thinks that its focus should change—from the individual text to the larger corpus or docuverse. Small, narrowly defined projects—an analysis of the imagery in *Hamlet,* say—have produced only trivial results because the meaning or implied authorial intention of *Hamlet* is too complex and indeterminate to be captured by quantifying single elements of the work. Olsen proposes a shift to a more impersonal and collective field of inquiry. "Authors," he argues, "function within symbolic universes of which they can only be partially conscious." Scholars should therefore take massive text bases as their unit of analysis and pass by local meanings to undertake "the systematic investigation of the development and transformations of 'meaning systems.'" Such systems, it is assumed, can be defined by computer analysis whereas authorial intentions and local effects can not.

We agree in part with Olsen but believe that both his critique and his prescription are too narrow. **Robinson**'s essay, and **Kaplan and Moulthrop**'s in another area, suggest that on the side of *producing* texts the computer will become even more central and that it will support new kinds of textual work that were impossible with the old informal methods. On the *analysis* of literary texts, **Lancashire** and **Miall** suggest ways of refining traditional computer analysis instead of simply abandoning it. Lancashire proposes that the computer is uniquely capable of testing certain critical claims about a literary work. He challenges impressionistic critics by showing how the computer may pass a cold-eyed judgment on their inventive interpretations. Miall suggests that at the very least the computer can raise the evidence for a particular reading to a higher standard of discrimination and completeness. He also argues that, in the future, artificial intelligence techniques should be able to operate on texts in a less blindered way than the searching and counting procedures of current programs.

In one respect, though, Olsen's thesis is congruent with much of the work reported in this volume. Early computer studies in the humanities did often target a manageable object of analysis—typically, an individual literary work—which was then subjected to a narrowly positivist and quantitative description. Such methods could easily be dismissed as reductive (Fish) in a critical climate that emphasized interpretive pluralism and the ability of any text to be affiliated with a myriad others. Now we see a reversal: computing humanists are likely to take the multitudinousness of the text for granted. They see the computer as helping them to confront a boundless universe of text and to draw from it the elements needed for a given project. In the terms of this volume, text-based computing implies openness to massive amounts of text and a recognition that we require new procedures to keep from ineffectual wanderings in the labyrinth.

We take for granted the value of older tools like indexes and library catalogs, because we know that our natural endowment cannot keep in order the contents of everything we have read. Text-based computing, with its ability to reconfigure at will the virtual space of digital texts, promises to deliver a higher level of control over that which passes through our memory and to give us access to realms that otherwise remain beyond our reach. Humanists have always revered those scholars, from Richard Bentley to Leo Spitzer or Lucien Febvre, who seemed to command a superhuman range of knowledge. The computer will grant to scholars of more modest gifts an equivalent power of retrieval from the cultural archive, and we can only hope that they will make wise use of their new-found wealth.

Notes

1. As late as World War II, major efforts to create Babbage's kind of mechanical analogue computers to solve complex differential equations continued. Ironically, Vannevar Bush, who is credited with inventing the notion of hypertext, worked on one of the last such major differential-analyzer projects at MIT (Owens).

2. Important elements of this environment are the emergent disciplines of hypertext and hypermedia; however, we do not consider these in detail here because they are covered by our previous collection, *Hypermedia and Literary Studies.*

3. Using a front end to file-transfer protocol called Fetch, for which we give heartfelt thanks to programmers at Dartmouth College. The NeXTMail facility on the NeXT computer goes a step further, by allowing users simply to drop a formatted file or program into an e-mail message.

4. Layout programs like Pagemaker use this metaphor, and increases in processing power and monitor size may lead to its general adoption.

5. This suggestion was made by Jody Gilbert.

6. There is a striking contrast between two events of major disciplinary importance: the discovery of the Dead Sea Scrolls in the late 1940s and the Cold Fusion controversy of the late 1980s. The scrolls still have not been printed in their entirety, and speculation about their content and significance persists. Cold Fusion generated such intensive debate and reporting of results over the networks that the basic issues were settled in less than a year.

---

7. For example, the one hundred thousand contributions a week "published" on Usenet, each of them removed from the system after three weeks.

8. It should be noted, though, that public and university libraries have been relatively undeveloped in France until recently; the French digitization program is part of a deliberate and expensive plan to modernize a backward sector, like the rapid advance in telecommunications over the past twenty years.

9. There is a parallel program under way for a multimedia archive of sound, video, graphics, and the like (**Virbel**); but this expansion is beyond our present scope.

10. Project Gutenberg, directed by Michael Hart at Illinois Benedictine University, distributes some noncopyright literary texts over the network.

11. ISDN is already available everywhere in France and has about one hundred and fifty thousand subscribers.

Works Cited

Baudrillard, Jean. *Simulations*. Trans. Paul Foss, Paul Patton, and Philip Beitchman. New York: Semiotext(e), 1983.

Benedikt, Michael, ed. *Cyberspace: First Steps*. Cambridge: MIT P, 1991.

Bolter, J. David. *Writing Space: The Computer in the History of Literacy*. Hillsdale: Lawrence Erlbaum, 1990.

Bormuth, John R. "Value and Volume of Literacy." *Visible Language* 12.2 (1978): 118-61.

Brennan, Elaine. "Using the Computer to Right the Canon: The Brown Women Writers Project." *Brown Online: A Journal of Computing in Academic Settings* 2 (1989): 7-13.

Bush, Vannevar. "As We May Think." *Atlantic Monthly* 176 (July 1945): 101-08.

Cadigan, Pat. *Synners*. New York: Bantam, 1991.

Chartier, Roger. *The Cultural Uses of Print in Early Modern France*. Trans. Lydia G. Cochrane. Princeton: Princeton UP, 1987.

Crane, Gregory. "Composing Culture: The Authority of an Electronic Text." *Current Anthropology* 32 (1991): 293-311.

Delany, Paul, and George P. Landow, eds. *Hypermedia and Literary Studies*. Cambridge: MIT P, 1991.

DeRose, Stephen J., David G. Durand, Elli Mylonas, and Allen H. Renear. "What Is Text, Really?" *Journal of Computing in Higher Education* 1 (1990): 3-26.

Eisenstein, Elizabeth. *The Printing Press as an Agent of Change*. Cambridge: Cambridge UP, 1979.

Fish, Stanley. "What Is Stylistics and Why Are They Saying Such Terrible Things about It?" *Approaches to Poetics*. Ed. Seymour Chatman. New York: Columbia UP, 1973.

Garfinkel, Simson L. "ISDN Comes of Age." *NeXTWORLD* Summer 1992: 42-45.

Gibson, William. *Neuromancer*. New York: Ace Books, 1984.

Hall, Stephen C. "The Four Stages of National Research and Education Network Growth." *Educom Review* 26.1 (1991): 18-25.

Heim, Michael. *Electric Language: A Philosophical Study of Word Processing*. New Haven: Yale UP, 1987.

Ivins, William M. *Prints and Visual Communication*. New York: DaCapo, 1969.

Kahle, Brewster. "Wide Area Information Servers Concepts." Thinking Machines technical report TMC-202, November 1989. Available on WAIS server wais-docs.src.

Kehoe, Brendan P. *Zen and the Art of the Internet: A Beginner's Guide to the Internet*. Revision 1.0, February 1992. Distributed by the author: guide-request@cs.widener.edu.

Landow, George P. *Hypertext: The Convergence of Contemporary Critical Theory and Technology*. Baltimore: Johns Hopkins UP, 1992.

Lincoln, Barbara. "WAIS Bibliography." Available on WAIS server: wais-discussion-archive.src.

Lyotard, Jean-François. *The Postmodern Condition: A Report on Knowledge*. Trans. Geoff Bennington and Brian Massumi. Minneapolis: U of Minnesota P, 1984.

McArthur, Tom. *Worlds of Reference: Lexicography, Learning, and Language from the Clay Tablet to the Computer*. Cambridge: Cambridge UP, 1986.

McLuhan, Marshall. *The Gutenberg Galaxy: The Making of Typographic Man*. Toronto: U of Toronto P, 1962.

Murray, John J. *Amsterdam in the Age of Rembrandt*. Norman: U of Oklahoma P, 1967.

Nelson, Theodor H. *Computer Lib/Dream Machines*. 1974. Seattle: Microsoft P, 1987.

Nora, Simon, and Alain Minc. *The Computerization of Society: A Report to the President of France*. Cambridge: MIT P, 1980. (Translation of *L'Informatisation de la Societé*, 1978.)

Olsen, Mark. "Signs, Symbols and Discourses: A New Direction for Computer-Aided Literature Studies." With responses. *Computers and the Humanities*. Forthcoming.

Owens, Larry. "Vannevar Bush and the Differential Analyzer: The Text and Context of an Early Computer." *From Memex to Hypertext: Vannevar Bush and the Mind's Machine*. Ed. James M. Nyce and Paul Kahn. Boston: Academic P, 1991. 3-38.

Peters, Paul E. "Coalition for Networked Information Sets Second-Year Priorities." *Educom Review* 27.1 (1992): 14-16.

Samuelson, Pamela. "Allocating Ownership Rights in Computer-Generated Works." *University of Pittsburgh Law Review* 47 (1986): 1185-228.

_____. "Creating a New Kind of Intellectual Property: Applying the Lessons of the Chip Law to Computer Programs." *Minnesota Law Review* 70 (1985): 471-531.

_____. "Digital Media and the Changing Face of Intellectual Property Law." *Rutgers Computer and Technology Law Journal* 16 (1990): 323-40.

_____. "Interface Specifications, Compatibility, and Intellectual Property Law." *Communications of the ACM* 33 (February 1990): 111-14.

_____. "Should Program Algorithms Be Patented?" *Communications of the ACM* 34 (August 1990): 23-27.

Samuelson, Pamela, and Robert Glushko. "Survey on the Look and Feel Lawsuits." *Communications of the ACM* 33 (May 1990): 483-87.

Shirley, John. *Eclipse.* New York: Popular Library, 1985.

_____ . *Eclipse Corona.* New York: Popular Library, 1990.

_____ . *Eclipse Penumbra.* New York: Popular Library, 1988.

Shurkin, Joel. *Engines of the Mind: A History of the Computer.* New York: Norton, 1984.

Sperberg-McQueen, C. Michael. Posting to Project Gutenberg E-mail List, 20 May 1992.

Stein, Richard. "Browsing through Terabytes." *Byte* May 1991: 157-64.

Sterling, Bruce, ed. *Mirrorshades: The Cyberpunk Anthology.* New York: Ace, 1988.

Stivale, Charles J. "Mille/Punks/Cyber/Plateaus: Science Fiction and Deleuzo-Guattarian 'Becomings.'" *Substance* 66 (1991): 66-83.

Vallée, Jacques. *The Network Revolution: Confessions of a Computer Scientist.* Berkeley: And/Or P, 1982.

Vinge, Vernor. *Across Realtime.* Riverdale: Baen, 1991.

Weingarten, Fred. "Five Steps to NREN Enlightenment." *Educom Review* 26.1 (1991): 26-30.

Williams, Michael R. *A History of Computing Technology.* Englewood Cliffs: Prentice-Hall, 1985.

Zampolli, Antonio. "Technology and Linguistics Research." *Scholarship and Technology in the Humanities.* Ed. May Katzen. London: British Library Research/Bowker Saur, 1991. 21-51. (Proceedings of conference held at Elvetham Hall, Hampshire, UK, 9-12 May 1990.)

Part II

Text Management

Reading and Managing Texts on the Bibliothèque de France Station

Jacques Virbel
Université Paul Sabatier

Overview

This chapter describes the current status of a reading station for the future Bibliothèque de France. The reading station is part of a more comprehensive program that includes creating a vast resource of digitized works and linking it to servers providing textual or bibliographical information. The project is based on the analysis of the emergent needs of specialized professional readers and on the integration of very diverse functions of textual access, analysis, and management as well as on the administration and archiving of individual databases. Those working on the definition of this reading station include researchers in computing science, computational linguistics, information systems, and ergonomics as well as corporate suppliers and professional readers.

The Digitization Program of the Bibliothèque de France

The Bibliothèque de France is a national library project that will take over some of the functions of the present Bibliothèque Nationale; it is expected to open in 1995 on a site near the Gare d'Austerlitz in Paris (Jamet).[1] The construction budget is estimated at 7 billion francs ($1.35 billion) and the annual operating budget at 1.5 billion ($290 million). The Bibliothèque de France, which will incorporate current computer and telecommunications technology, will have a completely computerized catalog and vast digital resources: sounds, still and animated images, and texts.[2] Accessible from a distance, it will provide connections to other libraries and servers.

The digitization and electronic support of works will guarantee the preservation of printed reference copies, provide for the archiving and conservation of the national heritage in a new technical context, and make the archive accessible at a distance over high-capacity networks. Electronic management will also allow synchronizing access to works with the research process, overcoming the classic problems of availability and of the regrouping and dividing-up of physical volumes. Finally, information systems will open up the potential of computer-assisted reading.

The available digitized texts will come from different sources. The Bibliothèque de France itself plans to digitize about 350,000 works in bitmap or alphanumeric mode; but users will also have access to other resources, either locally (for example, CD-ROM editions from various publishers) or from worldwide servers over the network.[3] These digitized texts, which will cover most disciplines, will include basic texts and reference works. They will also include tools for the reading environment such as dictionaries and encyclopedias. More than 20,000 works have already been digitized.[4]

Even taking into account the relative familiarity of a growing number of professional readers with computerized reading—thanks to the spread of PCs and word processing, of electronic editions of literary and other corpuses, and of dictionaries—it is undeniable that the very extensive program of the Bibliothèque de France, and its national and international networking, creates a new context.

This program also includes developing a specialized reading station for accessing and manipulating documents and for linking the user to the whole collection of resources (materials, software, and databases).[5] The station will encourage the incorporation of information tools into scholarly and professional reading, particularly for researchers in the human or social sciences but also for those in other disciplines and for students, journalists, archivists, writers, translators, and terminologists. The station will allow researchers

1. To make use of an information tool consisting of a personal computer linked to the information system of the Bibliothèque de France.

2. To access on-line catalogs and from there browse and select texts from the electronic textbase.

3. To download to the station the relevant works; the stations will have very large mass storage, with read-write capacity and portability (for example, optical disks).

4. To supplement the central corpus with the researcher's own digitized resources, entered locally either by keyboarding or by scanning.[6]

5. To support such operations as reading, annotating, commenting, and building personal databases, not to mention comparing, structuring, analyzing, managing, and publishing texts.

Basic Contextual Functions

These reading stations must provide a battery of functions, one group of which consists of capturing, entering, and retrieving texts and managing peripherals and communications. First of all, the station will permit each reader *to build a personal corpus.* Building a personal corpus involves three issues—access, acquisition, and archiving in mass storage. Access requires identification, skimming, browsing, selection, and control of documents; and this function extends the categories of traditional catalogs (tables of contents, summaries, lists of illustrations, digests, and indexes). Capture and acquisition of materials for the personal corpus requires downloading the works identified to the workstation, incorporating personal text bases, numbering paper-based documents (printed or manuscript), and converting formats. Archiving in mass storage logically extends the preceding two functions.

Second, the personal reading station must assist *readability.* It must therefore offer choice of screens adapted to the reader (size, resolution, color); type, speed, and general control of scrolling; creation of and logical and physical handling of screen windows plus provision for parallel scrolling windows; and ergonomic tools for textual navigation and annotation.

Third, the reading station must enable *editing and publishing.* It must, in other words, permit sophisticated text management, including software for Computer-Assisted Publication; preparation of reports, conferences, and courses (transparencies, slides, small database software, idea processors, and the like); and printing, transfer, and exchange.

Fourth, the reading station must furnish a rich *reading environment,* and this requirement involves providing mono- and multilingual dictionaries of language, translation, synonyms, and etymology as well as encyclopedias, language manuals and grammars; specialized thesauruses (for example, the *Getty Art and Architecture Thesaurus*); and bibliographical databases.

Fifth, the reading station must permit *communications* among different users (forums, electronic bulletin boards, programs supporting co-operative work, and so on), between users and library administration, and among the library and other libraries and information servers.

The Central Functions: Computer-Assisted Reading

A second major group of functions that implement computer-assisted reading and editing represents the heart of the system. Defining these central functions rests on a detailed analysis of reading for research in order to make these reading activities an integral part of the information system. Although such reading involves browsing and capturing, it differs fundamentally, despite some surface similarities, from the traditional consultation of a textual database.

This kind of reading has a *long-term horizon*. It has, in other words, a rhythm suited to research—to advances, halts, ranges of possibility explored more or less thoroughly, to fluctuations and crystallizations—a rhythm of rereadings and shifting perspectives. The preservation and management of the traces of this continuing process are essential to the whole regime of individual research.

This reading, moreover, takes an *individualized path:* the researcher deepens a theme, becomes conscious of the network of related themes that connect with it, enriches it with the ensemble of his or her culture, memory, and knowledge, and inscribes it within the whole of his or her research and reading programs. The reader's experience is embodied in the construction of personal lexicons, thesauruses, and dictionaries and in the assembly of files organized, indexed, and classified in accordance with the themes and objectives of the research. This work exists in symbiosis with the dynamic of the research and with the conceptual and physical restructurings that accompany and represent it. The ability to manage properly such tools and dossiers is an essential condition for research efficiency.

This reading is an *attentive reading, of inspection and assessment,* of contents, structures, forms, and vocabulary: a reading that not only continually activates similarities, comparisons, reminders, echoes, parallels, connections, and comparison of texts but also segments, regroups, redivides, schematizes, and synthesizes. Many textual-analysis programs (linguistic, statistical) already provide aids to the systematic observation of texts, and these programs will be integrated into the planned workstation. It will also include tools for managing the work of interpretation arising from the output of these textual analysis programs.

This reading is also, at the same time, an *exploratory reading:* for example, to the researcher who knows his field of research well and is pursuing explicit objectives, a good question is sometimes one that is novel and unexpected, even unforeseeable, one that arises during browsing or drifting or during unprogrammed exploration—indeed from the cultivation of chance. Consequently, to "overfly," "read askance," "flip pages," or "rummage" plays a significant part in such reading, and these practices need to be specified in the digital context.

This reading generates, finally, an intense *editorial activity* that ranges from primary discursive or graphic annotation to the recopying of passages judged useful for one purpose or another, from the assembly of notes, index cards, summaries, and commentaries to the composition, from such materials, of documents, courses, articles, and books. This editorial activity requires different principles of organization and structure for textual objects of varying status, for different stages of development, for primary materials and various kinds of derivative products, and in different states of composition and evolution.

Four groups of functions are planned for the handling of specific aspects of this kind of reading:

Structuring of personal corpuses, which involves organizing texts stored in bulk, unstructured databases, full-text searches, keyword descriptions, and automatic and/or manual indexing, as well as the conceptual, logical, or linguistic searches of units, fragments, and passages.

Analysis and management of texts, which involves not only operations of search (Boolean, statistical) and description (lexical occurrences, keywords, and concepts) but also visualization of structures (diagrams, histograms, tables, and graphs).

Dynamic annotation, which involves reformatting in accordance with emergent features or with structures decided in advance; annotations, that is, addition in or around the text of personal graphic symbols and of brief annotations or commentaries (responses, glosses, instructions for [re]reading); commentaries associated with particular passages; creation of links between passages (for example, between translations or among different versions), and typing and commenting on such links; and management (classifying, indexing) both of passages with annotations, commentaries, and links and of annotations and commentaries generated by reading.

Classification and archiving, which involves building structured dossiers that organize collections of documents and information derived from reading; creation of personal thesauruses; creation and management of personal text bases; and general interfaces between the station and the user, showing the status of their interaction.

Two points are worth making about this collection of functions, one having to do with the generalist nature of the station's tools, the other with interactivity and the relations between users and their personal databases of textual information. During the past thirty years or so, a considerable number of programs for analyzing and modeling texts have been developed in almost all social-science and humanities disciplines: psychology, sociology, literary history and criticism, history of the language, philosophy, patristics, anthropology and ethnology, and economics. The target texts cover a considerable range of genres (short novels, stories, descriptions, reports, all types of literary works, newspaper articles, [auto]biographies, correspondence, and all kinds of archives). The programs, which are based on very varied methods (linguistic, logical-conceptual, statistical, or combinatorial), engage the most diverse aspects of texts (lexicological, syntactic, semantic, stylistic, and rhetorical). Although most are just experimental, some have been commercialized, and their development has been visibly advanced by the coming of personal microcomputing. The development of these computer programs is being actively pursued.

This process is entirely legitimate, but it would not be realistic to integrate all these tools into the reading station, for reasons having to do with their extent and their diversity (making it difficult to achieve exhaustiveness), and with their specialized nature or instability (the difficulty of providing a rationale for the variety and opposition of schools of thought, premises, and technical or ideological points of view).

The station will therefore have, at least in its first version, a collection of very general utilities, useful for different levels or stages of any kind of research. Such utilities include lexicographic, lexicometric, syntactic, and stylometric analyzers and also tools for managing semantic relations (for example, synonymy) and research tools like keyword-in-context (KWIC) (see **Lancashire** and **Zimmerman**). This choice also follows from the need to ensure the openness of the station (file formats, compatibility with external software). This decision is analogous, also, to the one to make it possible for researchers to supplement the Bibliothèque de France text base with texts from other sources.

This relative generality does not mean simplicity. Work in lexicology has been revitalized by contemporary linguistic research that shows that, for a given language, there will be a deep complicity between lexical and grammatical properties. This research also suggests that the ideas of the *word* and the *expression* become surprisingly complex when one takes into account such phenomena as set phrases, discontinuity, and factorizing. Finally, developments in lexical semantics also show that mastery of lexical relations (synonymy, hyponomy, taxonomy, hierarchy, meronymy, opposition, and so on) is necessarily based on a very deep understanding (Cruse; Gross, "Les Limites," "Importance," and "Une Classification").

It is obvious that reading for study and research, and the intellectual work associated with it, involves practices and methods that are centuries, even millennia, old. Some seem easily reproducible in a digital context, others less so. Most seem to need a more or less profound redefinition. Finally, the computer opens up some entirely new reading practices. To take just a simple example: a radically new access to certain aspects of a text is provided by the systematic and exhaustive examination, at the level of a corpus, of a given linguistic form—in a specified context, having such and such frequency or co-occurrence with other forms (which can themselves be characterized in various ways). In traditional reading, this kind of reading would be hard to carry out, even hard to imagine. This is indeed a new kind of reading, experimental in nature. At the very least, the traditional author/reader relation is of a different kind. The systematic and exhaustive analysis of a work, when used to ensure the coherence of translation choices, leads to very similar reading practices. This kind of access to texts will be made standard and taken for granted in the Bibliothèque de France reading station.

In addition to the interest of such means of analyzing texts, another very important question has become evident in preliminary trials conducted by the Bibliothèque de France that involves defining a wide range of tools for *dynamic annotation*, that is, for tools possessing not only great flexibility but also the ability to affect directly the organization, management, and understanding of text bases. In its widest sense, this question concerns *personalized assistance* for the access and handling of documents by different kinds of users. In the context of the Bibliothèque de France, an innovative solution must be found in the design of tools for the appropriation and restructuring of documents—tools directly inspired by the traditional practices of active reading and annotation by specialized readers.

Dynamic Annotation

The reading station therefore retains, from the technical apparatus of traditional reading, an *annotation language* (in the broad sense of the term) that permits a reader or user of a document to make a personalized adaptation of it, along with the automatic management of the corresponding *acts of reading*, to incorporate them into the particular structures of the individual database.

Such an annotation language allows the user to express, in a partially coded form, a very large range of responses to reading. As far as we know, few studies have been devoted to annotation techniques (Nielsen; Virbel, *Etude*). In spite of its familiar nature, annotation seems a complex activity involving multiple functions. It is mainly an elementary technique of memorizing and storing the results of reading but not only that; it can also be used to note entirely perlocutory reactions or, in the opposite case, quasi-instructions for rereadings or other extratextual tasks. In the perspective of a collective and cooperative work—where annotations can be exchanged, modified, themselves annotated—they can also signify other kinds of information (for example, proposals for modification, correction, or restructuring).

One therefore finds a very great number of types of annotations. The most standard ones include (1) noting reactions (exclamations, value-judgments, or questions), (2) modifying the text (corrections, suppressions, insertions, or transpositions), (3) ranking passages (in terms of interest, importance, and representativeness), (4) differentiating passages according to their logico-linguistic type (for example, "definition," "example," "illustration," and "counterexample"), (5) marking characteristic terms (keywords, terminology, and diction peculiar to the author), (6) indexing passages, (7) creating commentaries, glosses, and translations of terms or citations, and definitions or explanations of terms, associated with phrases or passages, (8) using markers to make explicit logical-conceptual structures or implicit constructions in the text: enumerations, alternatives, stages of arguments, or segmentations into parts and subparts, (9) establishing cross-references, and more general connections between passages, and making comments on these relations, and (10) indicating operations to be done later ("to reread," "to see again," "to translate," "citation to be verified," or "to recopy").

The modalities of annotation, whether they concern markers used to classify annotations or the relevant passages or fragments themselves, are very varied: underlining, overlining, coloring of character-strings or backgrounds, and graphic marks (asterisks, exclamation or question marks, ellipses, braces, brackets, enclosures); insertion of terms, formulas, keywords, and numbers; and addition of commentaries (structurally independent or grafted into the text) or pseudo-footnotes.

There is a fundamental advance in one's having at least a partially automated management of the effects of annotation on a text, for one of the limitations of traditional paper-based methods is the difficulty of memorizing and retrieving the record of annotations across different works. These effects can then be represented in different ways:

1. *Visualization:* annotation marks, along with the relevant passages or fragments, can be individually shown, hidden, or merged with the text.

2. *Editing:* passages with a particular kind of annotation can be selected, combined, examined individually or in terms of the new combination, and formatted according to particular style sheets; a text can be scanned solely according to one or another annotation type.

3. *Analysis:* the collection of analysis tools applicable to a text could be implemented only for passages marked with a particular kind of annotation, within a single text or a group of texts annotated along similar lines—thus making possible extended comparisons.

4. *Text bases:* annotations have repercussions on the organization, display, and accessing of text bases. They support various kinds of management (for example, links between fragments, the search for annotations of the same type, the search by keywords, and the recopying of passages or fragments of a given kind from different files).

Personalizing Documents

This approach to dynamic annotation functions is clearly related to the means of personalizing documents that one commonly finds in electronic document management and in systems for producing and manipulating documents. At least seven basic approaches have relevance to personalizing documents: systems for computer-supported cooperative work, computer-aided writing, individualized archiving, on-line aids, hypertext, the electronic book, and computer-assisted reading.

Computer-supported cooperative work systems are undergoing intensive development. Theoretical approaches have shown how the control of message exchange needs to rely on high-level theories of dialogue and conversation (Winograd et al., Malone); several systems have been implemented using this approach (Winograd), particularly in hypertext environments such as TEXTNET (Trigg) and gIBIS (Conklin). The interest of these researches is that they show the importance of precise definition of the links between the text blocks that make up a dialogue, such as "is a reply to," "is an illustration of," "is an example of," or "replaces." A family of annotation tools has also been developed in this context, such as Internote (Catlin) and Quilt (Fish, Leland). These handle annotation in the narrow sense (association of commentaries with hypertext blocks).

Computer-aided writing systems, which are also under intensive development, began as extensions of environments for programming and managing texts (for example, the Writer's Workbench system), but they now tend toward autonomous systems using as models editorial activities (Writer's Assistant; Sharples), toward formalization of argument (Smolensky), or toward textual structures (Wright). This work shows the need for tools to define and manage the editorial activities themselves, including especially those used in the process of elaboration: document production or idea processing. These editorial activities seem also largely analogous to with those of analytic reading.

In regard to *individual archiving,* the critique of all-purpose document systems (Karlgren) suggests the possible development of personalized indexing tools, directly dependent on the particular concerns of a given user (Jones). An ambitious implementation of this approach proposes to have personalized indexing reflect the actual archiving systems used for documents thus indexed (Sedes).

Another perspective on the individualization and personalization of user-system relations emerges from current research on *on-line aids*, whether these relate to databases, operating systems, or software. In general there is more confidence in cognitive modeling of the user (Katzeff, Grice) than in using the traces of his or her activity (Rubens, Kelt).

Hypertexts use two concepts that are directly relevant to our purpose—the definition of systems in terms of links between blocks and the semantics of browsing and the formalization of hypertexts. One of the premises (often implicit) of the hypertext model is that a documentary resource can be consulted like an electronic encyclopedia, with the two aspects of direct access and navigation within nonlinear structures. This kind of analogy, which does not hold for dictionaries in the strict sense (Raymond), often seems rather arbitrary for documents conceived from the start in traditional form, that is, linear (Charney). Hence the need for defining strongly motivated typologies of links between blocks (Trigg), as well as efficient methods for visualizing links.

The navigation of a hypertext by a user soon needs to be guided and controlled. A semantics of browsing therefore seems necessary, and various mechanisms for searches and user commentaries have already been proposed (Stotts, Hofmann). More generally, a hypertext can be seen as a nontraditional database (without a structure known in advance, of whatever kind) or as a directed graph, where it is desirable to display the traces of user navigation (paths). Various attempts are currently being made to formalize hypertexts and to evaluate and define navigations.

The first approach tries to enrich the primitive hypertext model, which is judged to be too general and unconstrained, and to bring it closer either to more standard database models or to appropriate logico-mathematical models that are better developed: first-order logic (Garg), hypergraphs (Tompa), Petri networks (Stotts), object-oriented languages (Heather, Pasquier-Boltuck), and algebraic (Richard). The second approach, on the other hand, accepts this lack of restraints as an interesting or inevitable characteristic of hypertext but tries to model the paths taken by a user in probabilistic or topological terms (Canter; Aigrain, "Evaluation")

The *electronic book* is a type of hypertext application specially pertinent to our approach: a book or manual is seen as a specific database, equipped with different procedures for navigation or appropriation by a reader/user (Lewis, Marchionini, Pasquier-Boltuck, Savoy, Weyer, Yankelovich). The proliferation of editions in optical-disk format suggests that this area will become particularly active in the near future.

The cognitive activity of reading is the subject of research into theories and models (Spiro) but is only reflected in a few systems already implemented (such as ACTE, see Daoust). Nonetheless, new programs are being developed in the area of *computer-assisted reading* (Stiegler, "Machines"; Virbel, "Outils"). These projects approach in various ways the problem of defining the methods and tools for particularizing documents that were directed to a general or undifferentiated audience, in order to support a use that takes into account the background and purposes of the user. This task is the essence of the project described in this essay.

In the final analysis, this problematic is only a special case of the central question for human factors in interactive human/machine systems (theories and models of human/machine communication and interaction; interface types; individual differentiation and personalization of software), when the basis of such systems is a text base (Baecker). From this point of view, the approach taken to the Bibliothèque de France reading station is not an a priori cognitive modeling of the user but rather the self-modeling by the user through the production of traces of activities, insofar as they are accessible (representable, manipulable) and able to be activated (in this respect, similar to Parkes).

Implementation

The Computer-Assisted Reading Station project fits in naturally with the overall information system of the Bibliothèque de France. The expected timetable is as follows:

September 1990 - May 1991: formation of the specialized work group for the Computer-Assisted Reading Station (see note 5); preliminary study, survey of existing hardware and software, and definition of experimental use by a group of professional readers representative of future users of the station.

This experimental use relied on commercial hardware and software, with the aim of defining the basic functions to be supported in hardware and integrated and unified at the software level. The hardware of these provisional workstations comprised a Macintosh IIci, 8MB RAM, 80MB HD, two-page monitor, Apple scanner, 44MB removable Bernoulli drive, printer, modem, and CD reader. The experimental software included Word 4.0, MacDraw, Phrasea, Mark-up, Marco-Polo, HyperCard, and Candide. A collection of works (about 20,000 pages in alphanumeric mode and 2,800 in bitmap) was digitized to allow the readers to perform their work and evaluation in an entirely digital environment.

June 1991 - May 1992: call for tenders on experimental models integrating the desired functions into a software package. Two models are currently being developed by different companies. One is on a NeXT with twenty-one-inch monitor, NeXT laser printer and scanner, integrating WordPerfect and Sybase; the other is on a Sun Sparcstation 2, nineteen-inch monitor, 32MB RAM, 660MB HD, integrating PAT, Lector, and Island Write.

May 1992 - December 1992: testing of models and setting specifications for prototypes.

January 1993 - 1995: launching and testing of a series of prototypes; integration of the station with the overall Bibliothèque de France information system developed elsewhere; final choice of hardware; and launch of the final configuration.

In parallel with this project, a specialized multimedia station will be developed (see note 1). Copyright problems will be dealt with by negotiation between the relevant institutions and publishers.

When the Bibliothèque de France opens in 1995, three hundred stations will be available. These will be linked to the digital resources of the Bibliothèque and, via its information network, to other resources and libraries. Stations will also be installed in other libraries, providing equivalent access.

Conclusion and Reflections

The appearance of writing systems, then books (whether in codex or paper form), then typography and printing, and finally personal computers and text processing are events that invite speculation on the impact of these changes in media on the very concepts of the text, reading, and editing. Similar questions arise from the parallel history of tools supporting the management and memorization of reading, such as tables of contents, summaries, divisions into paragraphs and chapters, cross-references, indexes, synoptic and analytic contents, titles, subtitles, and rubrications.

Finally, the assembly of vast textual resources aiming at exhaustiveness (the ancient Library of Alexandria, the Treasury of the Greek Language), and universalized access to them, creates new uses and also new questions that can now be formulated and tackled—even, in due course, a new class of readers. The development program of the Bibliothèque de France aims first to satisfy in the contemporary cultural and technological context the needs and expectations of the users of a great library. But the massive digitization of works, international networking, and the definition of specialized reading stations obviously occurs in the context of shifts in the three areas listed above: textual media, reading tools, and textual resources. In consequence, new phases of bibliography and textology may emerge in the future. The old debate may also be reopened on the autonomy, or even incommensurability, of methods specific to each discipline—and also, between empirical and hermeneutical approaches to textual interpretation.[7]

Acknowledgments

I am indebted to Philippe Aigrain (Ministry of Culture and Institute for Research in Information Science of Toulouse) for a careful reading and for valuable and shrewd comments. His contribution is gratefully acknowledged here.

Translated by Paul Delany

Notes

1. Familiarly known as La TGB (Très Grande Bibliothèque).

2. For the ways the reading station thus supports multimedia, see the bibliography for various articles by Aigrain. However, the present article only deals with textual information (bitmapped or alphanumeric).

3. See the recent initiatives of the Oxford Text Archive and of the Georgetown Center for Text and Technology, which produces an annual list of electronic archive projects covering 312 entries for twenty-seven countries. It is notable that the domain of electronic archiving and reading is becoming organized on a world scale, as is also shown by the Text Encoding Initiative (Sperberg-McQueen).

4. The Bibliothèque de France digitization program is separate from the Frantext digital archive, though the two projects are collaborating to avoid duplication of effort.

---

5. Although there are several projects based on one or the other pole—reading station or digitization of archives—the *co-ordinated* development of these two aspects is, as far as we know, an original feature of the Bibliothèque de France project. It distinguishes it, for example—in spite of important points in common—from Project ATHENA (Stewart).

Work on desirable attributes for a reading station at the Bibliothèque de France began in September 1990 in a work group "Computer-Assisted Reading Station" created by A. Giffard, head of the Department of New Technologies, with the assistance of P. Bouf and D. Maillet of the same department. The work group, chaired by B. Stiegler (Technological University of Compiègne), includes researchers in the human sciences, in documentation, and in computer science.

The mission of this work group was

1. To make a detailed definition of the work of reading for study and research and to list the functions that a reading station should provide in this context.

2. To analyze the available hardware and software, and the trend of developments in electronic document-handling, with a view to evaluating the feasibility of the current approach and conducting trials.

3. To develop a progressive method of achieving final products, through a competition using a Call for Tenders, and trials conducted by professional readers representing the future users of the Bibliothèque de France.

(See the following Bibliothèque de France reports and documents: Bibliothèque de France; Cahart; Giffard; Stiegler, *Rapport;* Virbel, "Outils." Also Chouchan, Bertrand.)

The main results of my own participation in the work group, along with more personal commentary based on my research in a cognitive approach to the analysis, representation, and manipulation of textual structures, can be found in Virbel, "Représentation" and "Contribution."

6. The ease of use of current-generation scanners suggests that this function could be integrated into the hardware of the Reading Station. Optical Character Recognition still has limitations and requires careful checking by the user; however, rapid progress is being made in OCR and Document Analysis and Recognition (see AFCET).

7. This conclusion raises issues of a fundamental and hard-to-define nature, for which a very large literature exists. I can only indicate the scope of these questions by giving some key references: Detienne; Eisenstein, *Press* and *Revolution;* Gadamer; Goodman; Goody; Heim; Hirsch; Jonassen; Labarre; Laufer, "L'Alinea" and *Le Texte;* Martin; Nelson; Ong; Rouse; Steiner; Stiegler, "Machines"; Vezin; Virbel, "Langage"; and Yates.

Bibliography

L'Association Française de Cybernétique et Technique (AFCET). *International Conference on Document Analysis and Recognition*. Berlin: Springer-Verlag, 1991. (Proceedings of conference at Saint-Malo, 30 September to 2 October 1991.)

Aigrain, Philippe. *La Consultation des Archives Multimédias aux Etats-Unis*. Rapport interne, Institut de Recherche en Informatique de Toulouse, September 1991.

_____. *Lire en Image: Une Maquette pour la Bibliothèque de France*. Notice d'utilisation, July 1991.

_____. *Sketches on the Future Bibliothèque de France Multimedia Workstation*. Rapport interne, Institut de Recherche en Informatique de Toulouse, April 1991.

Aigrain, Philippe, and V. Longueville. "Evaluation of Navigational Links between Images." *Information Processing and Management*, forthcoming.

Baecker, R., and W. Buxton. *Readings in Human-Computer Interaction. A Multidisciplinary Approach*. San Mateo: Morgan Kaufmann, 1987.

Balpe, J-P. and Roger Laufer, eds. *Instruments de Communication Evolués, Hypertextes, Hypermédia*. Paris: Groupe Paragraphe, U de Paris VIII, 1990. (Proceedings of the Communication Interactive '90 Conference, Paris, 17 May 1990.)

Bertrand, R. "Naviguer à Travers les Hyperespaces du Savoir." *Micro-ordinateur et Traitement de l'Information*. Ed. R. Bertrand. Paris: Editions à Jour, 1991. 201-16.

Bibliothèque de France: Le Projet: Les Rapports des Groupes de Travail. Paris: Etablissement Public de la Bibliothèque de France, 1990.

Cahart, P., and M. Melot. *Propositions pour une Grande Bibliothèque: Rapport au Premier Ministre*. La Documentation Française, 1989.

Canter, D., R. Rivers, and G. Storrs. "Characterizing User Navigation through Complex Data Structures." *Behavior and Information Technology* 4 (1985): 93-102.

Catlin, Timothy, Paulette Bush, and Nicole Yankelovich. "InterNote: Extending a Hypermedia Framework to Support Annotative Collaboration." *Hypertext '89 Proceedings*. New York: ACM, 1989. 365-78.

Charney, Davida. "Comprehending Non-Linear Text: The Role of Discourse Cues and Reading Strategies." *Hypertext '87 Papers*. New York: ACM, 1987. 109-20.

Chouchan, D. "Du Livre à l'Ordinateur." *La Recherche* 288 (1990): 96-98.

Conklin, Jeff, and Michael L. Begeman. "gIBIS: A Hypertext Tool for Exploratory Policy Discussion." *Proceedings of the Conference on Computer-Supported Cooperative Work CSCW '88*. New York: ACM, 1988. 140-52.

Cordes, Ralf, Martin Hofmann, and Martin Langendörfer. "Layered Object-Oriented Techniques Supporting Hypermedia and Multimedia Applications." *Woodman '89, Bigre* 63-64 (1989): 286-96. (Workshop on Object-Oriented Document Manipulation at Rennes, 29-31 May 1989.)

Cruse, D. A. *Lexical Semantics*. Cambridge: Cambridge UP, 1986.

Daoust Francois, Luc Dupuy, and Louis-Claude Paquin. "ACTE: L'Ingénierie Textuelle et Cognitive pour L'Indexation Hypertextuelle." Balpe 83-100.

Delany, Paul, and George P. Landow, eds. *Hypermedia and Literary Studies*. Cambridge: MIT P, 1991.

Detienne, Marcel, ed. *Les Savoirs de l'Ecriture en Grèce Ancienne*. Lille: P U de Lille, 1988.

Eisenstein, Elizabeth. *The Printing Press as an Agent of Change*. Cambridge: Cambridge UP, 1979.

_____. *The Printing Revolution in Early Modern Europe*. Cambridge: Cambridge UP, 1983.

Fish, Robert S., Robert E. Kraut, and Mary Leland. "Quilt: A Collaborative Tool for Cooperative Writing." *SIGOIS*. New York: ACM, 1988. 30-37. (Conference in Palo Alto, 23-25 March 1988).

Frisse, Mark E. "Searching Information in a Hypertext Medical Handbook." *Hypertext '87 Papers*. New York: ACM, 1987. 57-66.

Gadamer, Hans Georg. *Truth and Method*. Trans. Garret Barden and John Cumming. New York: Seabury P, 1975.

Garg, Pankaj K. "Abstraction Mechanisms in Hypertext." *Hypertext '87 Papers*. 375-95.

Garg, Pankaj K., and Walt Scacchi. "On Designing Intelligent Hypertext Systems for Information Management in Software Engineering." *Hypertext '87 Papers*. 409-32.

Giffard, A. "Les Projets de la Bibliothèque de France en Matière de Mémoires Optiques." *SIGED 1990*. CNIT-Paris la Défense, 1-3 Octobre 1990.

Goodman, Nelson. *Languages of Art: An Approach to a Theory of Symbols*. 2nd ed. Indianapolis: Hackett, 1976.

Goody, Jack. *The Domestication of the Savage Mind*. Cambridge: Cambridge UP, 1977.

Grice, Roger A. "Online Information: What Do People Want? What Do People Need?" *The Society of Text: Hypertext, Hypermedia, and the Social Construction of Information*. Ed. Edward Barrett. Cambridge: MIT P, 1985. 22-44.

Gross, M. "Les Limites de la Phrase Figée." *Langages* 90 (1988): 7-22.

_____. "On the Importance of the Lexicon-Grammar for Discourse Analysis." *Colloque Informatique et Langue Naturelle*, Nantes, 12-13 October 1988. 261-87.

_____. "Une Classification des Phrases Figées du Français." *Revue Québecoise de Linguistique* 11 (1982): 151-85.

Heather, M., and Rossiter B. "Theoretical Structures for Object-Based Text." *Woodman '89, Bigre* 63-64 (1989): 286-96. (Workshop on Object-Oriented Document Manipulation at Rennes, 29-31 May 1989.)

Heim, Michael. *Electric Language. A Philosophical Study of Word Processing*. New Haven: Yale UP, 1987.

Hirsch, E. D. *Validity in Interpretation*. New Haven: Yale UP, 1967.

Hofmann, Martin, and Horst Langendorfer. "Browsing as Incremental Access of Information in the Hypertext System Concorde." In Balpe, 17-36.

Jamet, D. *Bibliothèque de France 1988-1991: De l'Utopie au Chantier*. Paris: Bibliothèque de France, 1991.

Jonassen, David, ed. *The Technology of Text*. 2 vols. Englewood Cliffs: Educational Technology, 1982.

Jones, W. "'As We May Think'? Psychological Considerations in the Design of a Personal Filing System." *Cognitive Science and Its Applications for Human Computer Interaction*. Ed. R. Guindon. Hillsdale: Lawrence Erlbaum, 1988. 235-88.

Karlgren, Hans, and Donald E. Walker. "The Polytext System—A New Design for a Text Retrieval System." *Questions and Answers*. Ed. Ferenc Kiefer. Dordrecht: D. Reidel, 1983. 273-94.

Katzeff, C. "System Demands on Mental Models for a Fulltext Database." *International Journal of Man-Machine Studies* 32 (1990): 483-509.

Kelt, S. "Wayfinding in an Electronic Database: The Relative Dependence of Navigational Cues *vs.* Mental Models." *Information Processing and Management* 26 (1990): 511-23.

Labarre, A. "Les Incunables: La Présentation du Livre." *Histoire de l'Edition Française*. Ed. Henri Jean Martin and Roger Chartier. Paris: Promodis, 1982. 1: 195-215.

Laufer, Roger, ed. "L'Alinea Typographique du XVI° au XVIII° siècle." *La Notion de Paragraphe*. Paris: Editions du CNRS, 1985. 53-64.

_____. *Le Texte en Mouvement*. Paris: PU de Vincennes, 1987.

Leland, M., R. Fish, and R. Fraut. "Collaborative Document Production Using Quilt." *Proceedings of the Conference on Computer-Supported Cooperative Work CSCW '88*. New York: ACM, 1988. 206-15.

Lewis, Brian T, and Jeffrey D. Hodges. "Shared Books: Collaborative Publication Management for an Office Information System." *SIGOIS*. New York: ACM, 1988. 197-204. (Conference in Palo Alto, 23-25 March 1988.)

Malone, Thomas, K. Grant, K-Y. Lai, R. Rao, and D. Rosenblitt. "Semistructured Messages Are Surprisingly Useful for Computer-Supported Coordination." *Computer Supported Cooperative Work: A Book of Readings*. Ed. Irene Greif. San Mateo: Morgan Kaufman, 1988. 311-34.

Marchionini, Gary. "Making the Transition from Print to Electronic Encyclopaedias: Adaptation of Mental Models." *International Journal of Man-Machine Studies* 30 (1989): 591-618.

Martin, Henri Jean. "Pour une Histoire de la Lecture." *Revue Française d'Histoire du Livre* 46 (1977): 583-608.

Moescher, J. *Modélisation du Dialogue*. Paris: Hermes, 1989.

Nelson, Theodor H. *Literary Machines*. P.O. Box 128, Swarthmore, PA 19091: Theodor Holm Nelson, Mindfull Press, 1990.

Nielsen, Jakob. "Online Documentation and Reader Annotation." *International Conference on Work with Display Units*, Stockholm, 12-15 May 1986.

Ong, Walter J. *Orality and Literacy: The Technologizing of the Word*. London: Methuen, 1982.

Parkes, A. Manipulable Inter-Medium Encoding for Information Retrieval. *RIAO '91 Conference Procedings*, Barcelona, 2-5 April 1991. 300-19.

Pasquier-Boltuck, Jacques, Gerald Collaud, and Jacques Monnar. "Conception et Programmation par Objets d'un Système Interactif de Création et de Consultation de Livres Electroniques." *Woodman '89, Bigre* 63-64 (1989): 7-17. (Workshop on Object-Oriented Document Manipulation at Rennes, 29-31 May 1989.)

Raymond, Darrell R., and Frank W. Tompa. "Hypertext and the New Oxford English Dictionary." *Hypertext '87 Papers*. New York: ACM, 1987. 143-54.

Richard, Gilles, and Antoine Rizk. "Quelques Idées pour une Modélisation des Systèmes Hypertextes." Balpe 1-16.

Rouse, M., and A. Rouse. "La Naissance des Index." *Histoire de l'Edition Française*. Ed. Henri Jean Martin and Roger Chartier. Paris: Promodis, 1982. 1: 77-86.

Rubens, Philip, and Robert Krull. "Designing Online Information." *Text, Context, and Hypertext: Writing With and For the Computer*. Ed. Edward Barrett. Cambridge: MIT P, 1988. 291-309.

Savoy, J. "The Electronic Book Ebook3." *International Journal of Man-Machine Studies* 30 (1989): 505-23.

Sedes, Florence. "Information Retrieval System Manipulation and a Posteriori Structuring." *RIAO '88 Conference on User-Oriented Content-Based Text and Image Handling*, MIT, 21-24 March 1988. 953-70.

Sharples, M., J. Goodlett, L. Pemberton. "Developing a Writer's Assistant." *Computers and Writing: Models and Tools.* Ed. N. Williams and P. Holt. Blackwell Scientific Publications, 1989. 22-37.

Smolensky, Paul, B. Fox, Roger King, and Clayton Lewis. "Computer Aided Reasoned Discourse; or, How to Argue with a Computer." *Cognitive Science and Its Applications for Human-Computer Interaction.* Ed. Raymonde Guindon. Hillsdale: Lawrence Erlbaum, 1988. 109-62.

Sperberg-McQueen, Michael C., and Lou Burnard. *Guidelines for the Encoding and Interchange of Machine-Readable Texts.* Chicago: Text Encoding Initiative, 1989.

Spiro, Rand J., Bertram C. Bruce, and William F. Brewer. *Theoretical Issues in Reading Comprehension: Perspectives from Cognitive Psychology, Linguistics, Artificial Intelligence, and Education.* Hillsdale: Lawrence Erlbaum, 1980.

Steiner, George. "Après le Livre?" *Le Débat* 22 (1982): 127-45.

Stewart, Jacqueline A. "How to Manage Educational Computing Initiatives— Lessons from the First Five Years of Project Athena at MIT." *The Society of Text.* Ed. Edward Barrett. Cambridge: MIT P, 1986. 284-304.

Stiegler, B. "Lecture et Ecriture Critiques Assistées par Ordinateur pour l'Edition Electronique." *Sciences Humaines*, forthcoming.

_____. "Machines à Lire." *Autrement* 121 (April 1991).

_____. *Rapport du Groupe de Travail "Postes de Lecture Assistée par Ordinateur."* Paris: Bibliothèque de France, January 1990.

Stotts, P. David, and Richard K. Furuta. "Petri-Net-Based Hypertext: Document Structure with Browsing Semantics." *ACM Transactions on Information Systems* 7 (1989): 3-29.

Tompa, Frank W. "A Data Model for Flexible Hypertext Database Systems." *ACM Transactions on Information Systems* 7 (1989): 85-100.

Trigg, Randall H., and M. Weiser. "TEXTNET: A Network-Based Approach to Text Handling." *ACM Transactions on Office Information Systems* 4 (1986): 1-23.

Vezin, J. "La Division en Paragraphes dans les Manuscrits de la Basse Antiquité et du Haut Moyen Age." *La Notion de Paragraphe*. Ed. Roger Laufer. Paris: Editions du CNRS, 1985. 41-52.

Virbel, Jacques. "The Contribution of Linguistic Knowledge to the Interpretation of Text Structures." *Structured Documents*. Ed. J. André, V. Quint, and Richard K. Furuta. Cambridge: Cambridge UP, 1989, 161-81.

_____. *Etude Technique d'Assistance à l'Elaboration de la Station de Travail de la Bibliothèque de France*. Bibliothèque de France, June 1991.

_____. "Langage et Métalangage dans le Texte du Point de Vue de l'Edition en Informatique Textuelle." *Cahiers de Grammaire* 10 (1985): 5-72.

_____. "Représentation et Utilisation de Connaissances Textuelles." *Cognitiva*, Paris, 4-7 June 1985. 879-883.

_____. *A Taxonomy of Annotating Acts in a Reader-Oriented Text Management System*. Note, Institute de Recherche en Informatique de Toulouse, 1991.

Virbel, Jacques., F. Evrard, and E. Pascual. *Outils Personnalisés de Modélisation de l'Utilisateur dans la Gestion Electronique de Documents*. Note, Institute de Recherche en Informatique de Toulouse, September 1990.

Weyer, S. "The Design of a Dynamic Book for Information Search." *International Journal of Man-Machine Studies* 17 (1982): 87-107.

Winograd, Terry. "A Language / Action Perspective on the Design of Cooperative Work." *Computer-Supported Cooperative Work: A Book of Readings*. Ed. Irene Grief. San Mateo: Morgan Kaufman, 1988. 623-53.

Winograd, Terry, and Fernando Flores. *Understanding Computers and Cognition: A New Foundation for Design*. Norwood: Ablex, 1986.

Wright, Patricia, and Ann Lickorish. "The Influence of Discourse Structure on Display and Navigation in Hypertext." *Computers and Writing: Models and Tools*. Ed. N. Williams and P. Holt. Oxford: Blackwell Scientific, 1989. 90-124.

Yankelovich, Nicole, Norman Meyrowitz, and Andries van Dam. "Reading and Writing the Electronic Book." *IEEE Computer* 18 (October1985): 15-30.

Yates, Frances. *The Art of Memory*. London: Routledge, 1966.

The FreeText Project:
Large-Scale Personal Information Retrieval

Mark Zimmermann
PARA Group

This essay describes the FreeText project: software for real-time, high-band-width, large-scale, free-text information retrieval (IR) on personal computers and workstations. The discussion consists of two parts: an analysis of key IR interface features and a report on specific FreeText project implementations of those features.

Four FreeText user-interface features have proved extremely valuable for efficient IR:

1. Fast indexed word lists

2. Fuzzy-proximity-neighborhood subsets

3. Browsing-oriented context views

4. Flexible retrieved-text displays

These concepts are widely applicable to diverse information-handling systems. After reviewing them, I describe in more detail the software I have written to implement and experiment with these (and other) IR interface concepts. All my FreeText project software is free, available with full source code for anyone who wishes to work further on these ideas. Versions of FreeText have been used by linguists, psychologists, lawyers, students, and diverse other people.[1]

Background

A key mission for a modern IR system is to provide real-time high-band-width responses to the simplest, most common user interactions with a large-scale free-text database. By "real-time" I mean that single-term retrieval requests should be answered in less than a second. (Complex Boolean proximity searches can take longer to set up and execute, but speed is still important.) By "high-band-width" I mean that the human has to get information back from the computer in a useful form that can be evaluated quickly—it is not good enough to return a list of documents or files, each of which must then be paged through in order to find a few relevant items. By "large-scale" I mean that the system must handle an information collection of tens of megabytes or more—too big (as of the early 1990s) to fit into commonly available fast computer memory—and apply simple sequential scanning and pattern-matching algorithms. By "free-text" I mean that the database cannot be assumed to include any consistent structure beyond words separated by delimiters (spaces, punctuation, and so on). The human user does not have time to put in tags or field markers, and the information itself may come from a variety of sources and be inhomogeneous, repetitive, multilingual, and noisy (for example, include typographical errors).

I developed the FreeText project software to help solve diverse problems. Lawyers have applied my programs to thousands of pages of depositions and testimony. Linguists have indexed text collections in multiple languages in order to build concordances and discover grammatical patterns. Environmental engineers have created and used huge databases of asbestos-removal regulations and guidelines. Students have integrated literary works and personal notes. Journalists and other researchers have poured megabytes of raw wire-service feed and scanned texts into custom databases, to make their research more efficient.

FreeText software complements other search and retrieval systems. Conventional database-management systems (for example, Ingres, Oracle, Sybase) handle large, shared collections of structured information and provide transaction-oriented security features. Network servers (for example, WAIS, Gopher) unify multiple, geographically distributed data sources. FreeText programs, in turn, give personal, interactive access to locally held textual subsets that may be downloaded from servers or extracted from structured databases.

Tools like FreeText are needed particularly in the earliest stages of research, when a person must be able to browse and free-associate without even knowing what are the right questions to ask. Users may have to access a database without intimate knowledge of the details of what is in it. A big database in a particular area may need to be a "corporate memory" for groups of scholars who are working on related topics. A new person has to come in and do research without extensive training, yet an experienced user must find the system transparent, so that it becomes a memory extension, not a barrier to getting at the data and thinking with it. Free-text IR tools must thus coexist with other types of tools, such as structured databases that are appropriate for answering well-formulated queries in later phases of the research effort.

There are four fundamental operations that I contend a good real-time high-band-width large-scale free-text IR system must support. A user must be able

1. *To view* lists of words that occur in a database.

2. *To select* subsets of a big database to work within.

3. *To browse* through candidate items efficiently.

4. *To read* and take notes on retrieved information.

I shall explain and discuss each of these four tasks below.

Word Lists

Viewing lists of words that occur in a database is exceedingly useful, for many reasons. An alphabetized word list makes it easy to spot many misspellings and variant suffixes for search terms. Word lists are also handy in working with mixed-language databases, particularly in spotting cognates and words that begin similarly to related native-language terms. The ability to view a word list, along with numerical information about occurrence rates in the whole database and in subsets, is valuable in formulating better queries that maximize good data retrieval. Perhaps most importantly, just being able to scroll around in a list of terms is a superb *aide-memoire* in thinking of words worth looking for in a database. Visible word lists are much better than blind searching, even when wild cards are permitted. It is precisely analogous to the recognize-*vs.*-remember dichotomy between menu-driven and command-line user interfaces.

Word lists are technically easy for a computer program to generate, provided that the IR software has built a complete inverted index to the database that is being browsed. For example, a segment of a word list might look like this:

```
       1      9511
    6774      A
       2      AA13961
       1      AA29900
      34      ABLE
     291      ABOUT
      29      ABOVE
```

Each word is preceded by the number of times it occurs in the database as a whole. Note the presence of numbers and document identifiers as well as common words. In my FreeText IR programs, word lists are a central part of the retrieval mechanism. A user can scroll around in a list of words in a given database and click with the mouse on any word to call up instances of that word in context in the database (see **Browsing** section below for details).

For many purposes, it is best to index every word in the database, even such common words as *a* and *the*. Many free-text IR systems call such terms stop words and omit them. The result is typically a saving of perhaps 20 to 40 percent in final index file size, depending on how long the stop-word list is. The cost, however, in many cases is too great—it becomes impossible to search for common terms in proximity to one another or as components of names, part numbers, dates, and so forth. A user can never find "To be, or not to be . . . " in the works of Shakespeare, since every word in that phrase is a common stop word! It also becomes impossible to look for "A. I. Smith" in a long name list or to find many short but significant Chinese or Japanese words at all.

Another common but sometimes dangerous feature of some free-text IR systems is stemming or truncation. Many systems attempt to remove suffixes so that they can index various forms of a word under a single entry; for instance, *compute, computer, computers, computational,* and *computing* might all be merged into a single `comput` entry. This saves a small amount of space, but at the expense of simplicity and control for the user. (At times, someone may really need to retrieve *computers* but not *computer*.) Many stemming systems also get confused easily and garble words (particularly proper nouns)—occasionally with disastrous results when a truncated term lands on the stop-word list and is left out of the index entirely! Foreign terms and Asian names are particularly vulnerable to butchery by such systems.

A central problem with both stemming and stop words in an IR system is that users cannot easily predict the behavior of the software. New or naïve users are the most likely to be confused, but if the stemming algorithm is complex enough, or if the stop-word list is long enough, even a sophisticated user can get into trouble. When a human cannot quickly know, to a high precision, where to look to find a desired word, then overall retrieval will suffer, sometimes disastrously. Users will fail to find needed information, and in many cases they will not even be aware that they are missing something. They will assume that the database does not contain the information that they seek, not that it has been filed elsewhere, under another name, or that it has been left out of the index to save storage space. A complex stemming algorithm or an extensive stop-word list is thus, in many cases, more dangerous than none at all.

Fuzzy-Proximity Searching

Researchers need to be able to select subsets of a big database to work within. As information collections get very large, there will still be unique or nearly unique terms that people will want to retrieve quickly—the last occurrence of a particular name, a bizarre word or document identifier that only occurs once, and the like. But increasingly often, an important word will occur too many times for convenient browsing (but see the **Browsing** section below for methods to delay that point). It thus becomes necessary to filter the input stream in a fast and flexible way, so that a human-usable volume of information is left to study.

Proximity search is a common free-text IR approach to data filtering. The usual proximity criteria, however, tend to be narrow, inflexible, and extremely hazardous to retrieval when applied to real-world databases (particularly by naïve users). A conventional form of proximity search is to enter a Boolean query such as `FREE(w2)TEXT AND (INFORMATION OR RETRIEV*)` which translates into "give me any document with FREE occurring within two words before TEXT, and which also contains INFORMATION or any word beginning with RETRIEV." Of course, this example cannot work at all if the database is not already divided into document units. Even if the query appears to work, the user will fail to see an unknowable number of near-miss items that contain some of but not all the specified words, which barely fail to meet the proximity criteria or which use alternative spellings (including typographical errors).

The user interface for conventional Boolean proximity search is terrible. It does not provide enough feedback to let the user avoid subtle (or obvious) mistakes, it requires too much human memory and creative energy in query formulation, and it gets in the way of seeing the data. Often, an apparently innocuous term deep inside a parenthesized Boolean search statement actually distorts the entire meaning of the query and eliminates all the useful information that was to be retrieved. Expert searchers can overcome some of the barriers that a command-line interface for proximity search imposes, but it is never easy.

In my IR programs, I have experimented with a different approach. Users define a neighborhood of interest in a free-text collection based on loose or fuzzy proximity to words chosen interactively from the full database word list (see **Word Lists** above). Figure 1 shows an example of how to perform a simple fuzzy-proximity search in FreeText.

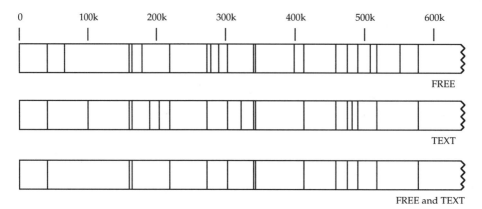

0   100k   200k   300k   400k   500k   600k

FREE

TEXT

FREE and TEXT

Figure 1: Sample fuzzy-proximity search in FreeText.

A searcher could ask a fuzzy equivalent of the Boolean query FREE and TEXT by starting out with an empty working subset of a database. The first step is to add the neighborhood around the word *free* to the region of interest. In the Macintosh version of the FreeText software, this is done by clicking on the word *free* as it is displayed in an Index View window—a perfect opportunity to see nearby alternative search terms.

The result is shown graphically as the first of the three spectrumlike bands above. Each occurrence of *free* in the database corresponds to a thin spectral line. At this point, an excerpt from the database subset's word list looks like this:

```
5/34         ABLE
49/291       ABOUT
0/29         ABOVE
0/5          ABSTRACTS
9/41         ACCESS
```

The term *able* occurs thirty-four times in the database as a whole, of which five instances are in the proximity neighborhood of *free*.

Next, after making a similar selection of the fuzzy neighborhood around the word *text* (see the second spectrum above), the user can narrow down the subset of interest to the intersection of the *free* and *text* subsets. This equivalent of the Boolean

AND operation is again done with a mouse click in the Macintosh version of this software.

The third spectrum shows the result. Now the database subset's word list looks like this:

```
2/34        ABLE
11/291      ABOUT
0/29        ABOVE
0/5         ABSTRACTS
1/41        ACCESS
```

That is, fewer instances of each word are meeting the more-restrictive definition of the subset of interest to the user—only those words near both *free* and *text* simultaneously.

My experience, and that of many users, is that neighborhood searching is far better than classical Boolean retrieval for finding the information that one really wants. It is faster, safer, and far more æsthetic to use as well. The mental model that the user has is simple and powerful: neighborhoods of influence that radiate out from interesting words and the possible overlap of those neighborhoods. The FreeText proximity-search interface, after a few minutes of use, becomes transparent and does not get in the way of thinking with the data.

In order to handle rare and complex proximity-search requests, most conventional free-text IR systems keep lists of sentence and paragraph and document delimiters. I have never found it necessary (or desirable) to pay much attention to rigidly defined boundaries such as sentences or paragraphs in actually performing proximity searches. Fuzzy-proximity-neighborhood search is, in actual experience, much safer and more likely to find the important data items that are being sought. A user will never lose a good piece of information because of an unfortunate sentence division or paragraphing choice by an author or an incorrectly identified sentence or document boundary. As a secondary benefit, there is no need to preprocess items flowing into the database in order to insert paragraph, section, or document boundary markers before indexing.

Browsing

The key to effective use of a free-text database is the ability to browse rapidly through many items in order to find the few that are of greatest interest. A good free-

---

text IR system has to provide lists of indexed words (see **Word Lists** above) and it has to fetch the full text of documents rapidly upon demand (see **Reading** below). But a truly useful free-text IR system should also provide facilities to bridge the gap between word lists and full-text retrieval. Part of the solution can be provided by an old concept, the keyword-in-context display, implemented in a dynamic and interactive new way. I call this interface feature a Context View.

A keyword-in-context listing, sometimes called a KWIC or a concordance, is made up of lines extracted from a database which show the instances of a word's occurrence, each with some context on either side. The keyword is lined up in a column down the middle of the page. Static, printed KWIC indexes have been around for many years and are better than no index at all, but they do not provide fast, transparent access to data. A user still has to track down the actual reference in order to get back to the full text of the item and still has no way to limit a search to a subset of the original database.

Context Views are KWIC displays that are generated on the fly, in real time, in response to user requests. They look like a common KWIC—for example, a Context View of five occurrences of *Macintosh* in a database might reveal:

```
rogram, without the Macintosh user interface features.
her features of the Macintosh Browser:  - easy access
megabytes/hour on a Macintosh Plus, and over 60 megabyt
[75066,2044].   The Macintosh Browser program is availa
O-MAC> and the MAUG Macintosh Hypertext Forum on CompuS
```

Tabs, carriage returns, line feeds, and the like, are all suppressed in a Context View, to let the user see the maximum amount of information on each line.

A user can scroll around in a dynamic Context View in a window on the computer's screen and can quickly eliminate many of the uninteresting instances of a word. When an item looks promising, a mouse click (in the Macintosh version of the FreeText software) immediately calls up the text from the original document for reading and possible further use (see **Reading** below). When working in a proximity subset of the whole database, the Context View only shows the lines surrounding word occurrences in the subset of interest.

My experience indicates that a user can comfortably browse through hundreds of lines in a Context View in order to locate a few good ones to retrieve. It is at least an order of magnitude easier (and more pleasant) than wading through full-text documents as they are conventionally retrieved by IR systems.

Reading

The bottom line for a free-text IR system is to get a desired document (or key excerpt) in front of the user quickly so that it can be read and worked with. It goes without saying that a good IR system must make it easy to scroll around in a database, copy out selections, and paste them into working papers, other programs, or any place else that the user desires. If the original document in the database has some structure (and thus is not purely free text) it may be valuable to reflect that structure in the retrieved data. Chapter or section titles can be displayed, for instance; or if there are graphics or font style changes, they can be shown properly. The ultimate goal is to have the original document (or a high-resolution image of it) appear in front of the user, open to the right page, with a highlight to draw attention to the key part. That is unfortunately not easy to do today; the Digital Librarian software on the NeXT workstation perhaps comes closest to the ideal form of document display.

Beyond mere retrieval, an advanced free-text IR system should make it easy to annotate retrieved information, add valuable comments, and leave a trail behind so that other explorers (or the same explorer, at a later date) could profit from previous experience. Hypertextual links between documents should be simple to create (as one type of annotation, perhaps) and should be easy to see and follow. Those links would then provide another set of paths through the data space. Hypermedia systems are under active research and development today, and perhaps within a few years robust, transportable systems to do such jobs will be widely available.

FreeText Project Implementations

FreeText software evolved out of my frustration with conventional IR systems. I began extensive work on inverted-index-building programs and on interfaces to word lists and context displays in 1984. My earliest FreeText code was written in the Forth programming language on the Apple Macintosh; it was named Browser and got wide distribution among hobbyists. In 1987 I redesigned and rewrote all the FreeText software in the C language. Generic command-line-driven FreeText programs thus run on many workstations under the UNIX or VMS operating systems. These C programs are available under the names qndxr.c (for the index-building part) and brwsr.c (for the browsing/retrieval part). A (command-line interface) version for MS-DOS systems is also available.

In late 1987, when HyperCard was released by Apple Computer, I seized upon it as a user-interface shell. I adapted my C routines to run as external functions behind a HyperCard façade and began giving away programs called Texas and Tex.

They evolved during the years 1988 to 1992 into the current (as of this writing) version 1.03 of FreeText. The FreeText Macintosh screens (shown in Figures 2 to 4) are good illustrations of one practical implementation of word lists, proximity subsets, context displays, and final text retrieval. I estimate that several thousand people are current users of FreeText on the Macintosh.

As shown in Figure 2, the task of indexing has been reduced to a single button-press: Build Index. Other aspects of the user documentation and background information (including an early version of this essay, "Free Text IR Philosophy") are also easy to access from this Help/Services control panel.

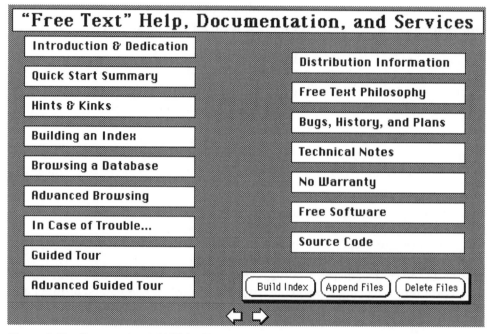

Figure 2: FreeText version 1.02 Help, Documentation, and Services introductory screen.

Most of a FreeText user's time is spent not on indexing, however, but on retrieval, working with databases. Figure 3 shows a typical view of a FreeText Browser window into a index of the 4.5 megabyte (MB) King James translation of the Bible, a commonly available public-domain text file. At the top of the window, two independently scrollable fields show lists of all the words in the database and their occurrence rates. Thus, *A* appears 8,277 times, the name *AARON* is used on 335 occasions, and so on. The scroll bars on the edges of each Index View work in the usual fashion, with a special option to jump quickly (via the ^z buttons) to an arbitrary point in the index.

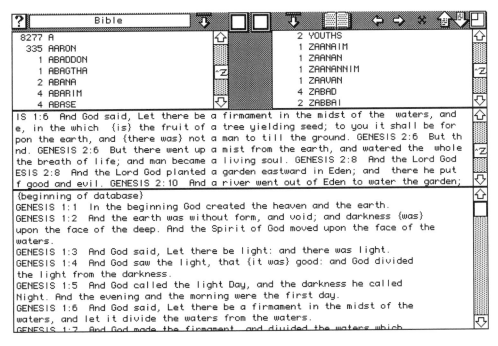

Figure 3: FreeText version 1.02 Browser screen, showing Index, Context, and Text View fields for a database containing the public-domain King James translation of the Bible.

The wide field in the middle of the Figure 3 window is a Context View (in this case showing the first seven instances of the word *A* in the database). A mouse click on any word in an index window causes the Context View to display the occurrences of that word, with half a line of context on each side. Carriage returns, tabs, line feeds, and other control characters are all suppressed in the Context View, to let each line provide the maximum amount of information. The Context View itself can be scrolled in the standard way. Finally, the bottom half of the FreeText Browser window is devoted to a Text View panel, where excerpts retrieved from the database are displayed. The Text View is scrollable and provides the user an opportunity to copy/paste notes from the information as it is displayed.

Figure 4 shows a graphically annotated quick-reference summary of some other FreeText Browser features—buttons to build proximity-based subsets of the data-base (using *and/or/not* intersections of retrieval neighborhoods), and other controls to speed common operations such as jumping an Index View to a selected word, moving from one database to another, taking notes, and so forth. The on-line FreeText documentation explains the details of all these features, and provides a guided tour illustrating how they can be used to speed the job of information retrieval.

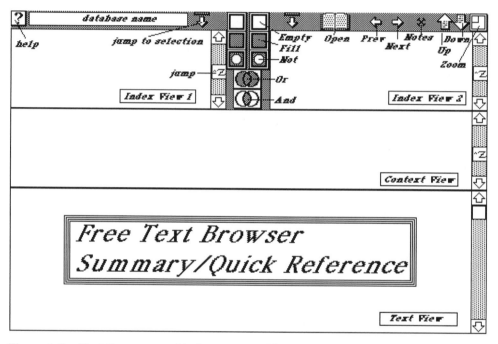

Figure 4: FreeText Browser graphical summary of features.

The FreeText system runs on any Macintosh that supports HyperCard. It is, naturally enough, more responsive on machines with faster processors, but I currently use it happily on an old Mac Plus with 2.5 MB of memory under System 7 and HyperCard 2.1. Enough disk space is needed to hold the text database file and the associated index files. Indexes typically occupy 80 to 100 percent of the size of the text. Thus, for a 10 MB text collection, one needs a total of 18 to 20 MB of storage. During index building, additional space on disk of about the size of the input text is needed for temporary files; that space is released when the indexes are completed. An index can be held on a remote file server and browsed via LocalTalk or Ethernet connections, even by multiple simultaneous users.

In addition to FreeText on the Macintosh, an excellent GNU Emacs interface to my generic browser program was developed by Todd Kaufmann of Carnegie-Mellon University in 1990. (GNU Emacs is the advanced, customizable, extensible editor created by Richard Stallman and the Free Software Foundation; it runs under the UNIX or VMS operating systems.) The Electric Browser mode of GNU Emacs is written in Lisp and provides good access to word lists, context displays, and full text upon demand. Rodney Peck II of the Rensselaer Polytechnic Institute also extended a UNIX-based version of the FreeText browser to operate as a server available for remote telnet use via the Internet, with a command-line interface or through GNU Emacs.

FreeText User Experience

I have corresponded personally with about five hundred diverse users of FreeText software. Many of them have been happy simply to apply fast, interactive IR tools to their personal data sets. But some researchers with special needs have modified or extended the standard FreeText system in unique ways, which may be of general interest.

CD-ROM

Compact disks can store hundreds of megabytes of text, but they suffer from slow access times. FreeText, with its efficient inverted indexes, is an ideal way for a CD-ROM to hold and organize information for quick response. I have experimented with CD-ROM simulators and with data on actual CD-ROMs and have found FreeText to be fully compatible with the medium. Several users have taken the FreeText indexer and browser and adapted them to make their own CD-ROMs, to work with voluminous legal or engineering data. As the cost of mastering and reproducing CD-ROMs continues to fall and as CD-ROM readers become more widespread, I expect this use of FreeText to become increasingly common.

Linguistics

Many researchers working on issues in language and psychology have found FreeText valuable in building concordances (exported from the standard FreeText Context View) and in compiling statistical data on word frequencies and usage patterns. With straightforward postprocessing of the FreeText index files, a user can edit out uninteresting or undesirable word occurrences, making it easy to clean up large data sets and to organize meaningful subsets for further analysis. The Macintosh version of FreeText also can display arbitrary fonts, making it possible to work with non-Latin alphabets on the screen and in printed output. One user has reported to me an innovative use of proximity search in a multilingual database: selecting text by proximity to *the, and,* and the like, predominantly gives English; proximity to *el, y,* and the like, gives Spanish; proximity to *der, und,* and the like, selects for German, and so forth. This kind of search has proved extremely useful in filtering retrieved information for diverse users from a common multilanguage database.

Hypermedia

Modifications of FreeText can add visible, easy-to-follow links between and among items of retrieved information. I have corresponded with people who have used FreeText to organize technical manuals, literary and legislative collections, and other compilations of structured information. A simple extension of the Macintosh FreeText retrieval interface also allows fast mouse-driven access to material in its original display format, in addition to unformatted text-only versions.

Reference

In collaboration with Apple Computer's Library, an experimental version of FreeText has been used to index and provide easy retrieval from a large collection of frequently asked questions accumulated by state libraries in several parts of the United States. Other modifications of FreeText systems have been used to build reference systems for work groups of a few to a few dozen researchers.

In short, the FreeText interfaces to indexed textual information have proved surprisingly extensible, particularly for the Macintosh versions that hide behind a HyperCard dashboard. Straightforward customizations can be done with relatively modest investments of time and expertise, which makes personalized databases possible to meet special needs.

Conclusion

People need to work with ever-larger collections of disorganized free-text information. They need to find out what is available in their databases to answer their questions—a task that can be greatly helped by quick and easy access to lists of words and to KWIC displays. People need to cut down their search spaces without losing important data—a task that fuzzy-proximity-neighborhood retrieval can assist. And once the right information has been located, people need to get it quickly where they can read and use it. Computer technology now exists to meet these needs for individual scholars.[2]

Notes

1. The best way to get a copy of the FreeText software described in this paper is from a colleague or via a computer network or bulletin-board service. Please check the major on-line archives on the Internet or on CompuServe, for example, or contact a computer-user group. For the Macintosh version of FreeText, the Boston Computer Society's Macintosh Group and the Berkeley Macintosh User Group are excellent sources. On CompuServe, you should check the data libraries associated with the Macintosh Hypertext Forum.

If you cannot find FreeText elsewhere, you can get a physical disk with the latest Macintosh versions and full source code from me by sending $25 (US) to P.O. Box 598, Kensington, MD 20895-0598, USA. If you want a copy of the MS-DOS or UNIX versions of the FreeText C programs, you may send $25 to the above address but be sure to describe what you need specifically if it is not the Macintosh master disk. The software is free; fees are used to cover distribution costs.

To contact me, good electronic addresses are zimm@alumni.caltech.edu on the Internet or [75066,2044] on CompuServe. Paper correspondence to me at the above post office box will be read, but a timely answer is much more likely if you include a stamped, self-addressed return envelope (or an electronic return address).

FreeText is copyright ©1987-1992 by Mark Zimmermann and is free software, under the terms of the GNU General Public License. In brief, you may modify, copy, and redistribute FreeText programs, provided you do not take away anybody else's right to do the same. GNU Emacs is a trademark of the Free Software Foundation. For additional information about the free software philosophy, please contact the FSF at 675 Massachusetts Avenue, Cambridge, MA 02139.

The Macintosh version of FreeText was developed in part with the kind support of the Library at Apple Computer Inc. I gratefully acknowledge that assistance and in particular the encouragement of Steve Cisler and Monica Ertel in the Apple Advanced Technology Group. I also wish to thank Todd Kaufmann, Robert Chassell, Rodney Peck II, Eric Roskos, and numerous other correspondents and FreeText users who have helped me immeasurably in my software-development and experimentation efforts. And, of course, I must give credit to my wife, Paulette Dickerson, and to my children, Merle, Gray, and Robin, for their support and tolerance.

2 . If the issues of free-text information retrieval analyzed in this paper are of interest to you, you may want to participate in the PARA discussion group on the Internet. To sign up, send a message addressed to para-request@cs.cmu.edu. The PARA archives are currently available for browsing at ipl.rpi.edu or katmandu.cs.cmu.edu, and those archives are good places to find the GNU Emacs interface to FreeText. In addition to free-text information retrieval, PARA discussions have focused on GNU Emacs implementations of hypertext-authoring tools and related issues.

Text-Management Software:
A Taxonomy

Sue Stigleman
University of North Carolina, Asheville

Electronic Text: The "Problem"

Electronic text is everywhere.[1] It flows out of word processors in a steady stream of articles, books, letters, memos, and notes. It lives in the dozens of primary humanities texts now available in electronic form. It travels from hundreds of databases through phone lines and computer networks to desktop computers. The sheer volume of this accumulating text can overwhelm the humanist's ability to manage it effectively.

A rapidly growing collection of software is now available to help manage this electronic text: to search it, organize it, code it, concordance it, sort it, and count it (Alperson, Lancashire, Lancashire et al., Perez, Tenopir, Tenopir et al.). Text-management software helps answer such questions as, How many times does the King James Bible mention dancing and in what context? Which letters and diaries in an archive collection illustrate childbirth practices on the American frontier? Were Shakespeare's sonnets all written by the same person? What are the themes in a series of interviews with traditional potters in North Carolina? What articles do I have on how the tango changed in France in the early 1900s? And, less profound but very useful, Where on my hard disk is that article I wrote five years ago on images of death in Mozart operas?

Unfortunately for the humanist just venturing into text-based computing, text-management programs are as diverse as the uses to which they can be put. Each program tackles one small area within the entire range of text management. To help humanists navigate through this confusing world, this essay presents a practical road map—a taxonomy of five types of text-management software. These five categories are text retrieval, text-database management, bibliography formatting, hypertext, and text analysis. Each has its own specific skill in handling text. Understanding the differences among these five types is important for choosing the most appropriate software program for a task. Each category is described along with some sample uses. Because the names of the categories are not standardized in scholarly journals, computer magazines, or software advertisements, additional names and a few representative software programs are given for each category. The software programs mentioned are intended as illustrations rather than specific product recommendations.

The general topic of text-management software is independent of any specific computer architecture, although of course specific software programs run on specific kinds of computers. Text-management programs are available for all major hardware and operating-system platforms. A typical individual program will run on one or possibly two. The text files themselves can be transferred from one computer system to another, provided they are pure text (containing only letters, numbers, and punctuation characters—no special control codes whose definitions are machine dependent).

Why Text-Management Software?

Text-management software is designed to accommodate the unique characteristics of text. Statistical programs, spreadsheets, and other numerical computing tools are designed to crunch numbers, not words. Spreadsheet programs and traditional database-management programs like dBASE will store text but prefer it in small and distinct pieces, like a customer name or an address, rather than a novel, a letter, or a diary.[2] Why has text prompted the development of specialized text-management software?

Text files can be large. Text as it is normally written or spoken is far from compact, resulting in files that would burst a program like dBASE at the seams. Text managers typically have large size limits and are beginning to add support for CD-ROMs and other large-volume storage media.

Text comes in variable lengths. One oral-history transcript may be ten pages, another, one hundred. One journal title may be short (*Art*), another long (*Journal of the American Institute for Conservation of Historic and Artistic Works*). Most non-text-oriented programs typically use fixed-length storage, forcing a user to choose between truncating long pieces of text and wasting disk space on short ones. Text-management software typically uses variable length storage.

Text often has repeating values. A typical citation has multiple authors and multiple keywords. Each research note may have several keywords. An interview transcript usually discusses a number of subjects. Generally these authors or subjects should be treated equally in searching. Most text-management software supports repeating values.

Text, especially in the humanities, may be in a variety of languages. Some text managers provide extensive support for a variety of foreign language alphabets.

Text has an intricacy and complexity that places great demands on software. Text is filled with synonyms and variations in capitalization, spelling, and word forms. The searching features in text-management software are more suited to this intricacy than those found in other types of software. In fact, searching is the heart of most text-management software. Searching is so important that I shall digress a moment into a list of those features required for carrying out efficient searches of a text base.

1. *For entering and combining search terms,* the user needs a means by which to search for a word or exact phrase; to look for different suffixes and prefixes (also called truncation and wild-card searching); to ignore upper and lower case, either routinely or selectively; to specify how close the search words should be to one another (proximity searching); to specify which fields to search when the text is divided into fields (field specification); to use the Boolean operators (AND, OR, and NOT) to combine search terms in various ways; to and to use parentheses to combine Boolean operators (nesting).

2. *For saving time,* the user needs a means by which to build and manipulate multiple search statements, to save a search strategy to use again later, and to store several search words in a group and then use all of them at once by entering the name of the group (thesaurus, synonym list, hedge, or macro).

3. *For increasing consistency,* the user needs a means by which to use an authority list for data entry, editing, and searching; to validate data as it is entered; and to enter abbreviations and have them automatically expanded.

These searching features are familiar to users of the bibliographic databases commonly used in libraries. However, underlying these searching features are certain assumptions:

1. The user knows what words are used in the text.

2. The user knows how to spell those words.

3. The words were spelled correctly in the text.

4. The user typed them without error during the search.

In text searching, these assumptions are often not true. Although some searches may be for a known citation, note, or paragraph, more searches will be for an idea that appears in the text in a variety of different words and word forms. To help users find the text they want, some programs are adding innovative searching techniques that go beyond simply matching a specific set of characters. Some examples include spelling checkers to check the spelling of search terms, automatic searching for plural forms of search terms, finding words that sound alike, searching for similar words or phrases (fuzzy searching), and assigning weights to each search term to indicate its relative importance in the search (weighted searching). Other examples involve displaying search results in order of computed relevancy rather than alphabetical or the common last-in-first-out order, displaying a profile of the most common words in a document the user selects from those found using other searching techniques—thereby suggesting additional search terms to consider, being able to say that "this record/document is what I want so go find others like it" (similarity searching), and looking for items that contain at least a certain number of the search terms (quorum searching).

Although no single software program in any of the five basic categories offers all these searching features, most commercially available text-management programs have several of them. A major criterion for selecting a text-management program will be its searching features.

Text-Retrieval Software

Searching in its purest form is illustrated in the category of text-retrieval software. Using a variety of search techniques, text-retrieval software searches through computer files to find ones that match a search request (Marshall, McCarty, Rupley). For example, a text-retrieval program could search through a thousand folk tales stored on a folklorist's hard disk and identify all the ones that include possums. Most text-retrieval programs could then display those files for the folklorist to look at, with the terms used in the search request highlighted. If several segments of these files are chosen for an article on possum images in Appalachian folk tales, many text-retrieval programs could copy those segments into the text of the article. (This feature led Burton L. Alperson to call text-retrieval software "search and squirt" software—it searches through existing files and squirts pieces of them into a new file.)

Text-retrieval programs come in two types: those that create indexes and those that do not. An index, most simply, is an alphabetical list of words with special pointers back to the original text. Indexing takes time and uses disk space, but because only the index is searched and not each of the files, the searching in indexing programs is much faster. Nonindexing programs must "read" each file in every search and so search more slowly, but no time or disk space has to be devoted to the indexes.

Yet another way of classifying text-retrieval programs is by the text structure they "understand." Some see the text simply as an unformatted stream of characters. Some can automatically recognize such divisions as line, sentence, paragraph, and page, or verse, chapter, book, and testament. The most important structure for humanities texts is Standard Generalized Markup Language (SGML), an evolving international standard for representing text structure. With SGML, texts can be shared without having to be recoded for each project or software program.

Another way of looking at text-retrieval software is by the format of the files that can be searched. The least powerful programs can search only through pure ASCII text. Somewhat more powerful programs can search text files in common word-processor formats. The most powerful programs can search through text found in database records, spreadsheet files, and other kinds of files. Some of the newest text-retrieval programs not only search through files but also can call up the application that created the file. If the program found the text the user was looking for in a Quattro Pro worksheet, it could start Quattro Pro and load that worksheet automatically.

The classic use of text-retrieval software is finding lost files. When one first starts using a computer, it is easy to remember every file. As time goes on, the files proliferate, filling up disk after disk, hiding behind ambiguous names only partially remembered. One article on text-retrieval software has a picture of a dog fetching a newspaper, an apt illustration: text-retrieval software is a computerized Fido, finding files and bringing them onto the screen.

As useful as finding lost files can be, the major use of text-retrieval software in the humanities is searching primary texts. An American literature scholar can search the complete works of Hemingway, pinpointing exactly where certain words or phrases were used. A theologian can compare several electronic versions of the Bible. With text-retrieval software, primary texts, no matter how large or numerous, can be explored swiftly and spontaneously to support research, writing, and teaching.

Text-retrieval software is also known as disk-hunting software, full-text search and retrieval software, full-text retrieval software, indexing software, indexing and retrieval software, search software, search and squirt software, textual information management systems (TIMS), and text-search software. Document-management software usually contains text-retrieval capabilities. Some examples of text-retrieval programs include Gofer, Isys, Magellan, and ZyIndex.

Text-Database Managers

Text-database managers are designed for creating and searching databases of textual material. The database may be created from the keyboard, using the data-entry features of the text-database manager, or by importing text created in other programs or downloaded from national databases. Searches are performed on records in the database, typically on one database at a time. Most text-database managers can display the records retrieved by a search, highlighting the terms in the search request.

Text-database managers are quite similar to text-retrieval programs in some respects. Both search through text and can usually display the retrieved text for browsing. However, text-retrieval software searches files that were created by other programs, usually word processors, while text-database managers search through text that has been stored in a text database. Text-retrievers typically have no data-entry module—they are searching machines. Text-database managers, on the other hand, have data entry and editing modules for creating and maintaining the text database.

For many applications, either a text-retrieval program or a text-database manager could be used. If the individual text items are very small, like bibliographic citations, using a text-database manager to combine them into a text database makes more sense than cluttering up a disk with hundreds of tiny files holding one citation each. Novels and other large texts would call for a text-retrieval program. A text-retrieval program would also be preferred when one wants to maintain specific print formatting for the files.

Text-database managers come in a variety of sizes. At the small end are the note programs, a kind of computerized Post-it note. The note variety of text-database manager holds small pieces of text and is often memory resident, allowing the program to be popped up whenever there is a sudden need to read or write a note. At the other end of the spectrum are the industrial-strength text-database managers, which can handle very large databases and are not usually memory resident (Matzkin).

Text-database managers can be subdivided into freeform text-database managers, which place no restrictions on the structure of the text, and programs that require text to be structured in a certain way. Some programs support a mix of structured and unstructured text. The freeform programs are useful for text that has no regular predictable structure, the structured text-database managers for text that divides naturally into segments.

The uses of text-database managers are infinite: research notes, citations, case studies, reminders, catalogues for any sort of collection—photographs, costumes, art works, or ham radio cards. A text-database can be created from letters, interview transcripts, legal notes and transcripts, laboratory notes, diaries, and folk songs. The database can be used to organize notes for writing, for faster retrieval of desired texts, or for studying and analyzing the text itself.

Text-database-manager software can be called archivers, full-text-retrieval software, indexing software, information storage and retrieval software, information-management software, lexical database management software, note managers, text-retrieval software, text-oriented file management software, text-based database managers, text-based management systems (TBMS), and text-oriented database managers. Some examples of programs for managing text databases are Agenda, askSam, Cardbox, ideaList, IZE, Nota Bene (the text-base portion), Notebook II, Nutshell, and TxT/SEARCH.

Bibliography-Formatting Software

Bibliography-formatting software lets one take a record that looks like this:

    AU   Myrsiades, Kostas//Myrsiades, Linda Suny
    TI   Using information management systems to study modern Greek folklore
    JR   Computers and the Humanities
    YR   1989
    VO   23
    PG   365-373

and turns it into a citation that looks like this:

Myrsiades, Kostas, and Linda Suny Myrsiades. "Using Information Management Systems to Study Modern Greek Folklore." *Computers and the Humanities* 23 (1989): 365-73.

---

and then easily turns it into a citation that looks like this:

1. Kostas Myrsiades and Linda Suny Myrsiades, "Using Information Management Systems to Study Modern Greek Folklore," *Computers and the Humanities* 23 (1989): 365-73.

Information from a citation can be entered once and then formatted and reformatted into a variety of citation styles. The software takes care of numerous details like how many authors to include, whether to spell out first names or use initials, where to put the date, and whether to capitalize all words in titles or just first word and proper nouns. If the citation information is correct, it stays correct in bibliography after bibliography. Volume numbers do not vanish, page numbers are not transposed, and authors' names remain correctly spelled, a result that will please readers and reference librarians for years into the future.

To make assembling a bibliography even easier, many bibliography-formatting programs can "read" a manuscript, find reference markers in the text, use the markers to find the cited references, and assemble and format those references into a bibliography. The author can concentrate on the content of the article. The computer can do the work of gathering the citations and assembling them into a correctly formatted bibliography. This process greatly speeds up the task of finishing a manuscript, particularly when using sequential reference numbers. If two sections of a paper are switched at the last minute, the bibliography-formatting software will renumber the references.

The obvious use for bibliography-formatting software is preparing bibliographies for articles, books, reports, and grant applications. It can also be used to prepare stand-alone bibliographies for publication or class use. However, the usefulness of bibliography-formatting software does not stop with preparing printed bibliographies.

Bibliography-formatting software is a natural home for citations downloaded from on-line or CD-ROM databases like the MLA Bibliography (Mead). Importing references from a database is faster than typing the references manually, and the imported references may already have abstracts or keywords. Users can enhance the references for their own use by adding their own notes or keywords, tracking their efforts to acquire the publications, or showing the items' locations in their homes or offices.[3]

The accumulated citation information becomes a citation database. If the citations represent the books and journal articles in a scholar's office, the scholar has created an on-line catalogue of the office. That scholar can search for items about a particular subject, written by a particular author, or published in a particular journal or during a particular year. A system of keywords will help to find articles on a subject without having to rely on the words in the titles. Each citation can be enhanced with summaries and notes about quality, points to pursue, relationship with other publications, the physical location of the publication, or notes about efforts to acquire the item. With some of the more flexible bibliography formatters, instead of an index to the papers in a professor's filing cabinet, the software can create a catalogue of traditional pottery, dance costumes, or film clips. This database power is why bibliography formatters are included in this essay as text-management software. If all a bibliography formatter did was format citations, it would be considered more properly a word-processing accessory.

Other names for bibliography-formatting software are bibliographic-file management software, bibliographic software, bibliography generators, citation managers, filing software, indexing software, literature-retrieval systems, and reprint software. Examples of bibliography-formatting software include BibTeX, Bookends, BiB/SEARCH, EndNote, Library Master, Papyrus, n.b.Ibid, Pro-Cite, and Reference Manager.

Hypertext and Hypermedia Software

Hypertext software stores text in pieces called nodes, chunks, or blocks, which are connected by links. The links allow users to move from one node to another. For example, a segment of text about North Carolina potters might mention that a potter was famous for his face jugs. If a definition of face jugs was stored in another node, a reader unfamiliar with face jugs could switch to the definition and then back to the text and continue reading. Hypertext in its simplest form can be regarded as computerized footnotes.

In a more involved example, if links in the text about North Carolina potters connected all the potters who did face jugs, the reader could skip through the text, reading about face jugs rather than read linearly about each potter in turn. In this sense, hypertext can be regarded as a computerized back-of-the-book index incorporated dynamically into the text.

When some of or all the nodes contain pictures, sound, or video, the result is hypermedia. To our text about potters, we could add film clips of potters at work, photographs of face jugs, and recordings of potters talking about their work, creating an animated, illustrated book.

These simple explanations do not capture the power of hypertext (Landow, Potter). The works of Shakespeare can be stored with historical annotations, stage directions, or thematic notes. A collection of early American literature can be enhanced with links showing relationships or similarities between and among authors, definitions of words that are now obsolete or have changed substantially in meaning, or connections to biblical images or themes. Hypertext and its potential in the humanities are explored at greater length in Paul Delany and George P. Landow's *Hypermedia and Literary Studies*.

The node/link structure of hypertext makes it an ideal platform for developing instructional software (Apple Computer). A popular example is *The Would-Be Gentleman*, a simulation of the France of Louis XIV. The user of the instructional program can travel through the program, following links rather than be forced to follow a single path from beginning to end. Instructional software, which is not text management in the sense used in this chapter, has been the most rapidly growing area of hypertext use.

Some examples of hypertext and hypermedia software include Guide, Hyper-Card, Hyperpad, Hyperties, Intermedia, KnowledgePro, PC-Hypertext, Storyspace, Textpro, and Toolbook.

Text-Analysis Software

Text-analysis software is a loose collection of programs for analyzing text (Conklin, Nielsen). In some ways, it is a catchall for the text-management programs that do not fit into the other categories. An examination of these programs shows that they perform one or more of the following operations: concordancing, coding, or statistical analysis. For example, WordCruncher is sometimes described as a text-database manager, but its concordancing and numerical-analysis features set it aside from the pure text-database managers like askSam or ideaList.

Concordance software generates lists of the words in a text, usually accompanied by the location of each word and often by some surrounding text.[4] A concordance program offers more flexibility than a printed concordance: users can choose what should be "concorded" (for example, all words, all nouns, all prefixes), specify how much context to include with the words, and choose the order of the concordance: by alphabetical order, by word frequency, by length of word, by reversed alphabetical order (from end of word). More sophisticated concordancing programs allow accompanying translations or annotations. Some examples of this type of interlinear text are foreign language translations, phonetic transcriptions of the text, grammatical categories, and indications of intonation and rhythm in song or speech (Simons).

Coding is the assignment of codes to specific sections of the text, allowing very specific retrieval of those sections of text. Coding is similar to assigning keywords, but each coded segment has a specific beginning and ending point. Codes can be overlapped and even nested within another coded segment. A search on *marriage* might retrieve a two-paragraph segment in an oral-history transcript whereas a search for *children* would retrieve only the two sentences within those paragraphs that were coded for *children* (Giordano).

Some text-analysis programs can count characteristics of text, such as the number of unique words, the number of times words appear, or the distribution of words in parts of the text. In an analysis of characters in a play, the number of words each speaks and the number of turns each takes may give insight into the relative importance of each character. Some programs will plot these items in bar graphs, density plots, and other visual forms.

Text-analysis software can be used to examine themes in an author's works (Potter), to determine authorship of texts of unknown origin, or to analyze the grammatical structure of a language. Researchers in history, anthropology, sociology, psychology, nursing, education, and journalism use text analysis to discover themes in interview transcripts, a process called qualitative or content analysis. Concordance programs are useful for preparing printed concordances. They are also useful for thematic or content analysis of literary works, preparation of glossaries and commentaries, study of a language, examination of folk tales or songs, or analyzing the vocabulary taught in foreign language lessons.

Text-analysis software can be called concordance software, content-analysis software, keyword-in-context (KWIC) programs, keyword-out-of-context (KWOC) programs, and qualitative-analysis software. Some examples of text-analysis software programs include the Ethnograph, Gator, Micro-OCP, MTAS, Oxford Concordance Program, Pat, TEXTPACK, and WordCruncher.

Conclusion

Printed text has long been a cornerstone of the humanities. Electronic text is taking on a similar importance. The various types of text-management software are designed for handling text, and each type has a specific strength. Text-retrieval software is useful for searching through large text segments stored in separate files.

Text-database managers are used to build and to search databases of text, ranging from small notes to collections of novels, letters, or folk songs. Bibliography formatters manage databases of citations and format citations into various styles. Building links among pieces of text is the strength of hypertext software. Text-analysis software generates on-line concordances, does coding of documents, or performs statistical analysis of text.

It is obvious that more and more text will be available in computerized form. It is also obvious that computer disks and other storage media are becoming larger and cheaper, making it possible to store increasingly larger quantities of text for local study. The future of text-management software is not so predictable, although one can anticipate a few trends.

In reviewing ZyINDEX, Willard McCarty observes that "this conceptually simple, generally useful tool, applicable in a variety of circumstances, is what a technical savant would call a 'utility.' One wonders, however, whether, as with some other utilities, its function will soon become a part of word processing." Most word processors already offer primitive searching features, although none yet match the power of a text-retrieval powerhouse like ZyINDEX. Powerful text-retrieval engines may show up in computer operating systems and windowing environments. Simple text-retrieval utilities have already appeared (for example, the grep command in UNIX, the File Manager in Windows 3.0). This approach offers the greatest flexibility—text-retrieval built into the user interface, always available, and able to work on any application's files.

A different scenario is emerging in the text-database arena. Non-text-database management programs are slowly becoming more friendly to text, which may eventually reduce the need for specialized software for managing text databases. At the same time, text-database managers are adding programming languages, security measures, and other features found in the more numeric database managers. The line between the text- and non-text-database managers may eventually disappear. Efforts like SGML to standardize electronic text structuring will increase the number of programs that can be used with the texts.

A link also seems to be growing between bibliography formatters and text-database managers. Bibliography formatters, after all, are just a specialized kind of text-database manager. When a text-database manager is used for a database of citations, the burden has been on the user to design the record structures and citation formats. Some text-database managers now come with bibliographic features (for example, Notebook II, ideaList). There also are third-party bibliography add-ons for some text-database managers (for example, n.b.Ibid for Nota Bene).

An interesting phenomenon has been the addition of hypertext to other kinds of software programs, such as text-retrieval or text-database managers. (Some examples are askSam, ideaList, Isys, FolioViews, Search Express.) Hypertext may become a searching feature in other types of software rather than a category of its own.

Concordancing programs serve a unique function and will probably continue to exist, particularly the ones designed for interlinear text manipulation. The future of coding and statistical-analysis software is less certain. Coding programs, although providing retrieval of precisely defined segments of text, are often primitive in other respects. One popular coding program, for example, does not permit editing of the codes. To change one code, the entire text must be coded again. For this reason, text-database management and text-retrieval software is sometimes used instead, even though keywords cannot be assigned as precisely. If text-database managers or text-retrieval software added more sophisticated coding, especially overlapped and nested coding, the rather primitive coding programs might disappear. Similarly, the addition of statistical-analysis features to text-database managers and text-retrieval software would lessen the need for separate programs to do this analysis.

There will probably continue to be no clear-cut connection between a specific task and a particular type of text-management software. One scholar studying William Butler Yeats's poetry might use a text-retrieval program to search through the file of poems, finding lines about candles and collecting them in a new file for study. Another might use a concordancing program to generate a custom-designed printed concordance for further study. Yet another might put each poem into a hypertext node and begin creating links from one poem to another or to other nodes containing information about Yeats's life, Irish politics of the time, or other writers' commentary and analysis. The choice of a program will depend on, and should enhance, the way an individual humanist works and thinks.

Notes

1. It would be impossible to count the amount of electronic text in the world. Some representative numbers may serve as an illustration. The Oxford Text Archive, one of several large text archives, contains over one thousand text files in twenty-six languages. The Cuadra and Associates 1992 *Directory of Online Databases* lists over five thousand databases available on line and on CD-ROM. WordPerfect Corporation, whose major product is the WordPerfect word processor, had sales of $532.5 million in 1991.

2. This is not to say that nontext programs cannot be used creatively for studying text. The article by Louis Janus and Gregg Shadduck describes their use of Lotus 1-2-3 and dBASE for linguistic analysis.

---

3. If one downloads information from a database and reuses it in a personal database, the user is responsible for abiding by the database producer's policies on downloading. Downloading may be forbidden, allowed with payment of a fee, or allowed within the copyright guidelines of fair use. Contact specific database producers for their policies.

4. T. H. Howard-Hill in *Literary Concordances* distinguishes concordances from two similar forms, verbal indexes and lexicons. In this essay, *concordance* is used, in the absence of a better word, as the general term for alphabetical listings of words in texts. Concordancing software can produce a variety of output, which may or may not match the technical definition of a concordance.

Bibliography

Alperson, Burton L. "Order out of Chaos: The RIPS Are Here." *Andrew Seybold's OUTLOOK on Professional Computing* 6 (28 March 1988): 1, 3-9.

Apple Computer. *Macintoshed Libraries*. Cupertino: Apple Library Users Group, 1988, 1989, 1990.

Conklin, Jeff. "Hypertext: An Introduction and Survey." *IEEE Computer* 20 (September 1987): 17-41.

Delany, Paul, and George P. Landow, eds. *Hypermedia and Literary Studies*. Cambridge: MIT P, 1991.

Giordano, Richard, Jonathan Cole, and Harriet Zuckerman. "Text Retrieval on a Microcomputer." *Perspectives in Computing* 8 (Spring 1988): 52-60.

Howard-Hill, T. H. *Literary Concordances: A Guide to the Preparation of Manual and Computer Concordances*. Oxford: Pergamon, 1979.

Janus, Louis, and Gregg Shadduck. "Beyond the Concordance: Lotus and dBASE as Text Analysis Tools." *Computers and the Humanities* 23 (1989): 375-83.

Lancashire, Ian. *The Humanities Computing Yearbook 1989-90: A Comprehensive Guide to Software and Other Resources*. Oxford: Clarendon P, 1991.

Lancashire, Ian, and Willard McCarty. *Humanities Computing Yearbook 1988*. Oxford: Clarendon P, 1988.

Landow, George P. "Hypertext in Literary Education, Criticism, and Scholarship." *Computers and the Humanities* 23(1989): 173-98.

Lundeen, Gerald. "Bibliographic Software Update." *Database* 14 (December 1991): 57-67.

_____. "Software for Managing Personal Files." *Database* 12 (June 1989): 36-48.

Marshall, Patrick, Rod Chapin, and Patrick Lyons. "Combing the Stacks." *InfoWorld* 12 (24/31 December 1990): 31-43.

Matzkin, Jonathan, and Catherine D. Miller. "Scratch Pads and Annotators: TSR Notes to Yourself." *PC Magazine* 6 (22 December 1987): 185-98.

McCarty, Willard. "ZyINDEX: A Package for Location and Retrieval of Textual Files." *Computers and the Humanities* 21(1987): 121-26.

Mead, Thomas. "Making the Link: Importing Downloaded Bibliographic References to Pro-Cite and EndNote on the Macintosh." *Database* 14 (February 1991): 35-41.

Nielsen, Jakob. *HyperText and HyperMedia.* New York: Academic P, 1990.

Perez, Ernest. "Managing Text." *Data Base Advisor* 8 (June 1990): 83-92.

Potter, Roseanne G., ed. *Literary Computing and Literary Criticism: Theoretical and Practical Essays on Theme and Rhetoric.* Philadelphia: U of Pennsylvania P, 1989.

Rupley, Sebastian, Tracey Capen, and John Richey. "Quiet Please, Text Search in Progress." *InfoWorld* 11 (30 October 1989): 55-72.

Simons, Gary F. "Multidimensional Text Glossing and Annotation." *Notes on Linguistics* 39 (July 1987): 53-60.

Stigleman, Sue. *Bibliography Formatting Software.* Chapel Hill: U of North Carolina at Chapel Hill, Institute for Academic Technology, 1991.

_____. "Bibliography Formatting Software: A Buying Guide." *Database* 15 (February 1992): 15-27.

Tenopir, Carol. "Software Options for In-House Bibliographic Databases." *Library Journal* 112 (15 May 1987): 54-55.

Tenopir, Carol, and Gerald W. Lundeen. "Software Choices for In-house Databases." *Database* 11 (June 1988): 34-42.

Markup Systems and the Future of Scholarly Text Processing[1]

James H. Coombs
Brown University

Allen H. Renear
Brown University

Steven J. DeRose
Electronic Book Technologies

In the last few years, scholarly text processing has entered a reactionary stage. Previously, developers were working toward systems that would support scholars in their roles as researchers and authors. Building on the ideas of Vannevar Bush, people such as Theodor H. Nelson and Andries van Dam (Drucker, van Dam, Yankelovitch) prototyped systems designed to parallel the associative thought processes of researching scholars. Similarly, Douglas C. Engelbart sought to augment human intellect by providing concept-manipulation aids (Engelbart and English, Engelbart et al.). Brian K. Reid developed Scribe, freeing authors from formatting concerns and providing them with integrated tools for bibliography and citation management. Although only a small percentage of scholars were exposed to these ideas, the movement was toward developing new strategies for research and composition.

Since the introduction of inexpensive and powerful personal computers, we have seen a change in focus away from developing such new strategies toward finding ways to do the old things faster. This transition manifests itself in part through a change in models. Previously, developers worked with the model of scholar as researching and composing author. Recently, however, the dominant model construes the author as typist or, even worse, as typesetter.[2] Instead of enabling scholars to perform tasks that were not possible before, today's systems emulate typewriters. Granted, these electronic typewriters have built-in search and cut/paste facilities, but for the knowledgeable user, such systems offer only minor improvements and may be less powerful overall than some of the systems available ten and fifteen years ago.

There are a number of reasons for this trend. Probably most important, the transition from centralized computing to distributed computing began in business and industry, which remains the most compelling market for developers. Traditionally, such installations hire secretaries to type documents that are already substantially complete. The only tools required in such an environment are typewriter, scissors, and paste—or now, their electronic equivalent.

Even in academia there is reduced impetus for more intelligent systems. Universities have their own business and administrative offices that make good use of business-oriented systems. Moreover, scholars often prefer these systems over the alternatives. Those who have access to more powerful systems rarely have the time to learn to exploit them fully, and many find them too complicated to use at all. This is quite understandable, since most text formatters on minicomputers and mainframes were developed under a model that is even more inappropriate than author-as-typist. Written by and for programmers, these systems often require quasi-programming skills, treating authors as programmer-typists. Most scholars experienced in computing are only too happy to escape such rough and poorly adapted systems for simple, handy little programs that help them get text onto paper quickly. Lacking the concepts necessary to recognize major recent improvements and unaware of the possibilities for new strategies for research and composition, they hail this movement backward as a major advance in scholarly computing. Because this response comes even from the most experienced scholars, it carries weight with potential systems developers as well as with those who are just beginning to use computers. More and more scholars call for computing facilities that simply enhance their capacity to type; they exert pressure pulling the industry away from significant development. The consequence is an industry that is clinging to the past; scholars seek to do what they have always done, only a little faster.[3]

This shift in dominant models creates three major problems: first, the incentive for significant research and development in computing systems is disappearing, and a major portion of resources has been diverted into the enhancement of a minor portion of the document development process. Lacking the time to train themselves in other disciplines, many of the scholars who are setting the trends in text processing do not understand or value the possibilities. Moreover, the resources required for the development of sophisticated systems have been severely underestimated throughout the industry, and people have become impatient with the lack of immediately useful products. Thus, we see far more attention paid to keyboards, printers, fonts, displays, graphics, colors, and similar features than to the retrieval and structuring of information or even to the verification of spelling and grammar.[4]

The development of tools providing new capacities has been replaced by safe and obvious enhancements of comfortable procedures. Second, developers and authors have lost sight of the fact that there are two products in the electronic development of a document: the printout and the "source" file. Currently everything is directed toward producing the printout; the source is a mere by-product, wasting valuable disk space, useful for little more than producing another printout of the same document. Proprietary formats and the lack of semantic and pragmatic coding make these files useless for sharing with colleagues or processing by intelligent systems. Finally, scholars' time and energy are diverted from researching and composing to formatting for final presentation. The authors of this article pay considerable attention to the quality of submissions and have typeset several books, but current systems tend to focus authors' attention on appearance all the time, not just when the document is ready for submission.

Although there is no simple solution to all these problems, major improvements in each can be made by converting to *descriptive* markup, which is already widely available. Briefly, the value of descriptive markup has gone unrecognized because authors and theorists believe the new document-development systems—the supertypewriters—do not require any markup. Goldfarb, one of the primary developers of Generalized Markup Language (GML), made clear the advantages of descriptive markup over the usual *procedural* markup, but because no one has analyzed markup systems fully, users believe that no markup is even better than descriptive markup. As our analysis of markup systems makes clear, however, there is no such thing as "no markup." All writing involves markup. "No markup" really consists of a combination of *presentational* and *punctuational* markup. Moreover, of the competing types of markup, descriptive markup is actually easiest to learn, simplest to use, and best adapted to the process of composition. Finally, descriptive markup encodes the information necessary to develop fully the two products in the document-development process: source files as well as printouts. Since the source files contain semantic and pragmatic coding instead of coding for formatting, they may easily be shared with colleagues, submitted directly to publishers, and processed by intelligent applications as they become available.[5]

In the first part of this article, we summarize the theory of markup systems and clarify the concepts necessary to evaluate the alternatives properly. We shall now present the main arguments for the superiority of descriptive markup over other forms of markup.

Markup Theory

Whenever an author writes anything, he or she "marks it up."[6] For example, spaces between words indicate word boundaries, commas indicate phrase boundaries, and periods indicate sentence boundaries. This fact is widely ignored; indeed, markup is usually treated as an unfortunate requirement of using electronic text-processing systems, that is, as something to be avoided. A careful analysis, however, reveals that authors regularly use two types of markup in their manuscripts: *punctuational*, for example, placing periods at ends of sentences; and *presentational*, for example, numbering pages. Thus, markup cannot be escaped because our writing systems require it.

These traditional, scribal types of markup clarify the written expressions. The markup is not part of the text or content of the expression but tells us something about it. When we "translate" writing into speech (that is, when we read aloud), we do not normally read the markup directly; instead, we interpret the markup and use various paralinguistic gestures to convey the appropriate information. A question mark, for example, might become a raising of the voice or the eyebrows.

With the advent of text-processing systems came new types of markup and new types of processing. When prepared for reading, either on screen or on paper, documents are marked up scribally. But when stored in electronic files, documents may be marked up scribally or with special *electronic* types of markup designed for processing by computer applications. One uses *procedural* markup to indicate the procedures that a particular application should follow (for example, `.sk` to skip a line), *descriptive* markup to identify the entity type of the current token (for example, `<p>` for paragraphs), *referential* markup to refer to entities external to the document (for example, `&mdash;` for an em dash), and *metamarkup* to define or control the processing of other forms of markup (for example, `<!ENTITY acm "Association for Computing Machinery">` to define the referential markup `&acm;`).[7]

Types of Markup

Punctuational. Punctuational markup consists of the use of a closed set of marks to provide primarily syntactic information about written utterances. Punctuation has been under study for hundreds of years and is considered part of our writing system. Because punctuation is relatively stable, generally familiar to authors, and very frequent in documents, the usual expectation is that authors will punctuate their document files just as if they were typing.

Unfortunately, punctuational markup suffers from several deficiencies: the system is relatively complicated and subject to considerable stylistic variation. The authors of this article, for example, do not agree about the use of commas after sentence-initial adverbial phrases; in fact, composition instructors regularly disagree on such details. In addition to variations in usage, punctuation marks vary in appearance. For example, some people insist dashes should be separated from surrounding words by spaces; others claim there should be no such space.[8] Even when authors agree about appearance, there is variation across printing devices. Some devices provide the ability to distinguish open- and close-quotation marks, and some devices distinguish hyphens, en dashes, and em dashes. Finally, the punctuational markup system is highly ambiguous. For example, the period is used to indicate abbreviations as well as sentence boundaries. This ambiguity creates problems for text formatters, which often improperly treat abbreviations as sentence boundaries and add extra spaces. Authorial aids such as spelling and grammar correctors must perform considerable extra processing to disambiguate punctuation marks and often have to settle for the most likely alternative.

Recognizing the problems with punctuational markup, authors regularly use referential markup instead. For example, the source files for this article contain — instead of "—" or " — " so the authors will be free to focus on the content and postpone stylistic negotiations until the end. Similarly, descriptive markup may be used to replace punctuation where the markup identifies a logical element. Short quotations, for example, are delimited by <q> and </q> instead of quotation marks, enabling text formatters to output open and close marks or neutral marks, depending on the capacities of the display and printing devices. In addition, applications can quickly locate the quotations, for whatever purpose the author desires.

Thus punctuation is not simply part of our writing system; it is a type of document markup that may vary and be replaced by other types of markup. Because the system is subject to stylistic variation, dependent on available printing devices, and highly ambiguous, we expect to see more and more punctuation replaced by referential and descriptive markup. On the other hand, we see little motivation for the complete replacement of punctuational markup. Not much is to be gained, for example, by replacing such standard punctuation as commas with referential markup. Publishers, or even text formatters, could use descriptive markup to determine whether a clause should be punctuated with a comma or a semicolon, but very few authors have sufficient training in syntax to mark up phrases and clauses descriptively. Consequently, punctuational markup will continue to be appropriate and need not be considered further in this article.

Presentational. In addition to marking up lower-level elements with punctuation, authors mark up the higher-level entities in a variety of ways to make the presentation clearer. Such markup—presentational markup—includes horizontal and vertical spacing, folios, page breaks, enumeration of lists and notes, and a host of ad hoc symbols and devices. For example, an author marks the beginning of a paragraph by leaving some vertical space and perhaps horizontal space as well. Occasionally, authors even number their paragraphs. Similarly, chapters often begin on new pages, may be enumerated in a variety of styles, and may even be explicitly labeled "Chapter."

Although authors have long performed presentational markup in their manuscripts and typescripts, most now prefer to have text formatters generate the most repetitive and error-prone markup. Pagination, for example, is usually automatic even in the most typewriter-oriented systems. "Local" presentational markup, however, such as centering lines, is still commonly performed by the author, often with the assistance of editing commands. In WordStar, for example, one strikes the key sequence `Ctrl-OC` to center the current line.

Procedural. In many text-processing systems, presentational markup is replaced by procedural markup, which consists of commands indicating how text should be formatted. For example, one might mark up a long quotation as in Figure 1. The initial markup directs the text formatter to do the following (roughly):

1. Skip three lines—the equivalent of double-spacing twice.
2. Indent ten columns from the left and ten columns from the right.
3. Change to single-spacing.
4. Start a new page if fewer than two lines remain on the current page.

Obviously, this markup is specific to a particular text formatter and style sheet. Moreover, it is device dependent; the skip, for example, might well be changed to a value such as eighteen points for a high-resolution printer.

Procedural markup is characteristically associated with batch text formatters, such as nroff/troff and TEX. Word processors like WordStar, however, supplement their presentational editing commands with "dot commands." For example, they use editing commands to center lines (`Ctrl-OC`), but include markup in the files for user-specified page breaks (`.pa`).

Descriptive. Under the descriptive system of markup, authors identify the element types of text tokens. In Figure 1 the tag `<lq>` identifies the following text as a long quotation, and the tag `</lq>` identifies the end of the quotation.

Authors who are accustomed to procedural markup often think of descriptive markup as if it were procedural and may even use tags procedurally. The primary difference is that procedural markup indicates what a particular text formatter should do; descriptive markup indicates what a text element is or, in different terms, declares that a portion of a text stream is a member of a particular class. When a text

NO MARKUP

(This example may look artificial, but ancient writing was often in such *scriptio continua,* with virtually no interword spaces and little punctuation.)

miltonexpressesthisideamostclearlylaterinthetracticannotpraiseafugitiveandcloisteredvi
rtueunexercisedandunbreathedthatneversalliesoutandseesheradversarybutslinksoutoftheracewhere
thatimmortalgarlandistoberunfornotwithoutdustandheatsimilarlywordsworth

PRESENTATIONAL

```
Milton expresses this idea most clearly later in the tract:

    I cannot praise a fugitive and cloistered virtue,
    unexercised and unbreathed, that never sallies oput and
    sees her adversary, but slinks out of the race where that
    immortal garland is to be run for, not without dust and
    heat.

Similarly, Wordsworth . . . .
```

PROCEDURAL

```
Milton expresses this idea most clearly later in the tract:
.sk 3 a;.in +10 -10;.ls 0;.cp 2
I cannot praise a fugitive and cloistered virtue, unexercised
and unbreathed, that never sallies out and sees her adversary,
but slinks out of the race where that immortal garland is to be
run for, not without dust and heat.
.sk 3 a;.in -10 +10;.cp 2;.ls 1
Similarly, Wordsworth . . . .
```

DESCRIPTIVE

```
Milton expresses this idea most clearly later in the tract:
(lq)
I cannot praise a fugitive and cloistered virtue, unexercised
and unbreathed, that never sallies out and sees her adversary,
but slinks out of the race where that immortal garland is to be
run for, not without dust and heat.
(/lq)
Similarly, Wordsworth . . . .
```

Figure 1: Forms of markup.

formatter generates a presentational copy of a descriptively marked-up document, it first reads in a set of rules, written in a procedural markup system, that establish what it should do for each occurrence of each element type. By adjusting this set of rules, the author (or support person) establishes a presentational markup design that will be executed automatically and consistently. Moreover, should there be reason to modify the design, only the rules will require editing; the document files remain intact. Not only will the author be relieved of painful and monotonous hours of mechanical editing, the text will not be exposed to corruption.

Most procedurally based systems provide macro facilities, which users have long exploited for descriptive markup (for example, the `-ms` facility for troff), and even some of the primitives of such systems may be descriptive (for example, the `.pp` "control word" for paragraphs in Waterloo SCRIPT). Generalized Markup Language (GML) provided a sound expression of the conceptual foundation for the systematic use of descriptive markup (Goldfarb). Unlike ad hoc macro packages, GML is a descriptive language generally implemented on top of a clearly distinct, user-accessible procedural language. In addition, GML contributed "attributes" to descriptive markup languages, providing markup support for such essential functions as cross-references (which are automatically resolved by applications). Another influential system, Scribe, enforces the use of descriptive markup by eliminating procedural markup from the author's normal access to the system. Instead of tuning procedural markup to control the processing of descriptive markup, authors select "document format definitions" for various types of documents.

The Scribe approach has been widely emulated recently, but with moderate success at best. LATEX, for example, provides a high-level interface with TEX, which is designed to provide a low-level typesetting control. Unfortunately, even the beginning LATEX user must think in terms of low-level markup. For example, contiguous quotation marks are to be separated by "/,", which is a "typesetting command that causes TEX to insert a small amount of space" (Lamport 13-14). Similarly, a number of word processors (Microsoft Word, XyWrite, Nota Bene) have recently adopted Scribe's document-format definitions under the metaphor of electronic "style sheets." Nota Bene, for example, includes such editing commands as `use style block` for long quotations and has the ability to reformat all blocks when the style sheet is changed. Unfortunately, the style-sheet metaphor orients authors toward the presentation instead of toward the role of entities in the document. Thus, the block style might seem appropriate for any of a number of entity types, and nothing motivates the author to make distinctions that may be important later. Furthermore, style sheets tend to be an optional feature instead of a standard interface.

Referential. Referential markup refers to entities external to the document and is replaced by those entities during processing. We have already noted the use of referential markup for device-dependent punctuation (for example, `&mdash;` for an em dash). Another characteristic use is for abbreviations, such as `&acm;` for "Association for Computing Machinery." Referential markup might also refer to entities stored in a separate file or even on a different computing system.

Most text formatters that support procedural markup offer referential functionality through user-defined "variables" and file `imbed` or `include` commands. For the most part, however, referential markup is associated with descriptive markup systems, primarily Standard Generalized Markup Language (ANSI).

Metamarkup. Finally, metamarkup provides authors and support personnel with a facility for controlling the interpretation of markup and for extending the vocabulary of descriptive markup languages. Procedural and descriptive systems provide ways to define markup delimiter characters. In addition, procedural systems include such instructions as `define macro`, which are typically used to create descriptive markup representing a series of processing instructions. The procedural markup in Figure 1, for example, would typically be included in macros with names such as `quo` and `quoend`. Applications that process GML, such as Waterloo SCRIPT, also provide markup to define tags, to specify valid and default attributes, and to indicate what instructions should be executed when the tag is encountered. Finally, in SGML, metamarkup appears in the form of "markup declarations," of which there are thirteen kinds.

All nontrivial systems support metamarkup, but most do not provide a suitable interface for nonprogrammers. One notable exception is the menu-oriented group descending from Xerox Bravo and Star; InterLeaf, for example, allows authors to create new tags simply by typing hitherto unknown identifiers in a dialogue box. Others have attempted to eliminate the need for metamarkup by providing complete referential and descriptive vocabularies, but such efforts are contrary to the spirit of human creativity.

Markup Handling

Briefly, markup is selected, performed, stored, and processed. Familiarity with particular systems often complicates the task of distinguishing the various types of markup. Authors perform markup in a variety of ways. They may type the markup almost as if it were text. They may strike function keys or select items from menus. In fact, the methods of markup performance are limited only by the ingenuity of applications developers in using input and display devices. Although at any time there may be a tendency to associate a particular type of performance with a particular type of markup, the relationship is merely historical and provides no basis for characterizing or evaluating the types of markup.

Markup must be stored someplace, but there are no relevant limits on how it is stored. Moreover, nothing prevents a system from eliciting one type of markup and storing another. XyWrite, for example, elicits presentational markup, but stores procedural markup. When the author, who has access to editor commands but not the the the markup language, specifies that text should be centered, XyWrite records the appropriate procedural markup around the text in the file and centers the line in the editing display. In a similar situation, WordStar simply centers the line; the surrounding blanks are not differentiated from the text either on screen or in the file. Thus, when evaluating their markup systems, authors must examine what is stored as well as what they see.

There are currently three major categories of markup processing:

1. Reading (by humans)
2. Formatting
3. Open-ended (including formatting).

Presentational markup is designed for reading. Procedural markup is designed for formatting, but usually only by a single program. Descriptive markup is moderately well suited for reading but is primarily designed to support an open class of applications (for example, information retrieval).

Exposed, Disguised, Concealed, and Displayed Markup

In "traditional" text-processing systems, authors type in electronic markup, and documents are formatted by separate applications. Recently formatters have been integrated with editors, and we need another set of distinctions in order to characterize markup fully in editing interfaces.

Markup is *exposed* when the system shows the markup as it occurs in the source file, that is, without performing any special formatting. Exposed markup is typical in systems that consist of separate editors and formatters. Many of the so-called WYSIWYG (What You See Is What You Get) programs do not so much format for editing as expose the scribal markup they elicit and store. Such systems typically expose any electronic markup they elicit as well. WordStar, a sophisticated example of this category, exposes the "new page" command .pa, but also displays a line of hyphens to represent the page break.

More sophisticated systems often process electronic markup and then *disguise* it behind a special character. XyWrite and Nota Bene, for example, display a "delta" so that authors can locate and edit markup. Such systems usually have the capacity to expose the markup as well. Other systems, such as Xerox Bravo and Star, MacWrite, *conceal* electronic markup entirely. One system, Janus, exposes descriptive markup on one monitor and conceals it on the other (Chamberlin).

Finally, systems have recently begun to *display* electronic markup; that is, an especially formatted representation of the markup in the source file is displayed along with the text. Etude and Interleaf, for example, format text for editing but display descriptive markup in a margin at the left of the editing window.

Because scribal markup is not well differentiated from text, currently systems simply expose it. In fact, no other approach makes sense. It can be profitable to view electronic markup in any of the four modes, however. Datalogics's WriterStation, for example, supports all four modes and allows authors to control the formatting of displayed markup.

To summarize, there are six types of document markup, but only three are in full competition: presentational, procedural, and descriptive. Presentational markup clarifies the presentation of a document and makes it suitable for reading. Procedural markup instructs a text formatter to "do X," for example, skip three lines, in order to create presentational markup. Finally, descriptive markup tells text formatters, "this is an X," for example, a long quotation. Normally, text formatters treat presentational markup in source files as if it were text; that is, no special processing is performed. Procedural markup, however, is processed according to the rules specified in the documentation for the system; and descriptive markup is usually mapped onto procedural markup. In addition, descriptive markup is well suited for processing by an open set of applications.

Development systems should provide maximum flexibility and support all four modes of markup viewing. The author-as-typist systems that we have seen embraced recently tend to elicit presentational markup and store presentational and procedural markup; consequently, they bind documents to particular devices and applications. Some integrated editor/formatters, however, support descriptive markup, which, as we shall argue, best supports the process of document development and publication.

Maintainability

As we point out in our initial characterization, descriptive markup eliminates maintenance concerns. The development of a scholarly article may take several months; a book may take several years. In this time, an author who is not using descriptive markup may have to modify the markup of document files for any of several reasons:

1. The author learns new techniques or finds that current techniques cause problems.
2. The computing environment changes.
3. The style specifications change.

In the development of *A Pre-Raphaelite Friendship* (Coombs et al.), for example, the editors initially used backslashes (\) to control highlighting. Their text editor, however, had the unfortunate habit of throwing away backslashes, and their early printouts suffered from random underscoring. They learned to avoid this problem by using the underscore character (_) to control underscoring, but they also had to edit all the text that had already been entered. When the book was typeset, they discovered the underscore character was also used as an en dash by their system (but only when typesetting). Consequently, when in the scope of an underscore command, en dashes were taken as underscore controls; instead of 1982-1986, the text formatter produced 1982*86*. Thus, the editors again had to edit all their files and change the underscore characters to pound signs (#) and hope that no further conflicts would occur and that they would not introduce errors into the text during the process of making the changes. Had they used descriptive markup for highlighted phrases, these maintenance problems would not have occurred.

Similar problems arise whenever the author or the installation changes the computing environment. When FRESS (File Retrieval and Editing System) users at Brown University learned FRESS would no longer be supported, authors either spent hours converting their files to the new format (Waterloo SCRIPT) or accepted the possibility of "losing" their data.[9] Even updates in the current text formatter often require modifications in files. Changing to a new printer may require modifications. In fact, almost any change in the computing environment poses a threat to one's files if they contain procedural or presentational markup.

Finally, formatting specifications may change during the process of document development. For example, the Modern Language Association (MLA) recently published a new style sheet. To give a sense of the consequences, we need consider only one change. The previous *MLA Handbook for Writers of Research Papers* specified that block quotations be "set off from the text by triple-spacing, indented ten spaces from the left margin, and typed with double-spacing (single-spacing for dissertations) but without quotation marks" (23). Accordingly, many manuscripts include the procedural markup shown in Figure 1. The 1984 edition of the *MLA Handbook* specifies that block quotations be "set off from your text by beginning a new line, indenting ten spaces from the left margin, and typing it double-spaced, without adding quotation marks" (49). This modification immediately renders much of the markup obsolete, and now authors must locate all long quotations and delete `.sk 3 a`. Because the markup encodes formatting procedures instead of element categories, however, the occurrence of `.sk 3 a` cannot be taken as an unambiguous indication that an element is indeed a long quotation. Thus, authors cannot take advantage of global change facilities, but must inspect every occurrence of `.sk 3 a` and determine whether the current element is a long quotation. The conversion process will be tedious at best, and there is always the risk of corrupting the text. In addition, there is no guarantee MLA will not change its style sheet again, requiring further markup maintenance.

Such maintenance problems would not be reduced by using presentational markup. In fact, updating might be even more difficult. With procedural markup, one has specific character strings, such as `.sk 3 a`, that may be located with normal editing facilities. Presentational markup, however, may not be be directly locatable. Some editors require a series of relatively advanced commands or the use of regular expression grammars to locate blank lines, for example. Moreover, simple editing facilities cannot distinguish, for example, a series of five blank spaces (for a paragraph indent) from a series of five blank spaces contained within a series of ten blank spaces (for each line of a quotation). Thus, locating presentational markup accurately often requires the services of a powerful macro language as well as the ability to program.

With descriptive markup, properly tagged source files never require modification, and there is no such thing as markup maintenance. A long quotation, for example, remains a long quotation, despite changes in presentation style or even changes in processing systems. To modify the action taken for long quotations by a text formatter, one need edit only the program's "rule" base. This localization of maintenance can serve numerous hours of editing, protects files from corruption, and makes it practical to have a single local expert perform necessary updating of a shared copy of the rule base. [10]

Document Portability

The ability to "port" or send one's documents to other scholars and to publishers has always been a major concern of scholars. When typewriters ruled the industry, we ported our documents in the form of typescripts and photocopies. Since there were no alternatives, people were generally satisfied with this procedure.

In the last five years, however, more and more authors have shelved their typewriters and converted to electronic document development. Now we can send documents from our homes across the continent and around the world, often receiving acknowledgment of receipt within a few hours. Our colleagues, with our source files on their own machines, can use programs to search for keywords and can integrate our contributions into collaborative documents, free of the normal retyping or cutting and pasting. Moreover, publishers can use our files as a source for typesetting, eliminating the need for rekeying documents; and once the rekeying process is eliminated, so is the danger of textual corruption as well as the need to read proofs.[11]

Unfortunately, current text-markup practices make this exchange a rarity. Although we have the technology for electronic transfer, we lack the markup standard necessary to guarantee that each recipient can process the documents prepared by any author. In fact, the compatibility problem is so severe that publishers often choose to rekey documents that have been submitted in electronic form, and sometimes do so without notifying the authors, who are left with a false sense of security about the integrity of their texts. As several publishers have pointed out to us, keying in documents is a simple, well-understood task requiring the services of people who are paid minimum wages. File manipulation, however, requires the services of personnel with programming skills, paid appropriately, and does not appear to offer sufficient gains to outweigh the risks of converting to a new process.

Descriptive markup provides an immediate solution to document incompatibility. Any document with accurate and rigorous descriptive markup can be ported from one system to another. This is true because descriptive markup guarantees a one-to-one mapping between logical elements and markup. Thus, element identifiers may be changed simply by performing global changes in an editor. For example, one might convert the markup for a prose quotation from `.quo` to `<lq>` and `.quoend` to `</lq>`. In the worst case, syntax differences may be resolved by trivial programs.

Recognizing this fact, representatives of publishers and of organizations with large publishing costs have joined in an effort to establish an industrywide standard based on descriptive markup. In its *Electronic Manuscript Project*, the Association of American Publishers (AAP) found that descriptive markup "is the most effective means of establishing a consistent method for preparing electronic manuscripts which can feed the publishing process" (7). The AAP has endorsed the ANSI-ISO SGML and developed its first application. Standard Generalized Markup Language (SGML), which is actually a metalanguage for generating descriptive markup languages, allows for considerable flexibility and customization. Authors who have been using descriptive markup will be able to turn their documents into SGML documents with little or no modification. Documents that have been prepared with presentational or procedural markup, however, will require extensive editing to conform with the new standard.

Advantages

Since people are generally reluctant to give up a technology they have learned, it is crucial that everyone be aware of what the industry has to gain by conversion to descriptive markup and, ultimately, to SGML. Consider this partial list of benefits:

1. Authors will be able to share documents and collaborate with colleagues without the current concerns about incompatibility between text formatters and printing devices.

2. Publishers will no longer have to rekey documents, eliminating an expensive and error-prone task.

3. In many cases, the proofing process may be eliminated from the production cycle, saving considerable administrative costs for publishers and reducing the time required to get a document into print. Moreover, publishers will no longer have to negotiate with authors who want to make changes after the galleys have been set. For their part, authors will be relieved of the burden of proofreading documents that were correct at the time of submission.

4. Subsequent editions, revisions, or collections may be generated from the source files for a document; rekeying will no longer be necessary.

5. Bibliographic information may be generated directly from the source files. This process will reduce errors and make citations available almost

immediately to users of on-line bibliographic databases. The time from submission of a text to entry in the literature of a field will be cut dramatically.

6. Documents may be included directly in on-line databases for electronic publishing and full-text retrieval, which is another way of introducing them into the literature almost instantaneously.

Publishers and authors have already begun to demand these improvements in the publishing process. With the expenses of scholarly publishing rising continually, cost containment will become more and more important, and authors will find properly marked electronic manuscripts more marketable than other electronic manuscripts and typescripts.

Alternatives to Portability

Four alternatives to document portability have been proposed, but they provide partial solutions at best. The alternatives include

1. Authors typesetting their own work and providing camera-ready copy

2. Authors submitting device-independent page-description files, in PostScript, for example

3. Authors submitting printouts and publishers using Optical Character Readers (OCRs) to convert them to electronic form

4. Authors sending source files without descriptive markup and publishers converting the markup with a special utility.

The first alternative involves authors excessively in the presentation process and distracts them from their role as authors. This procedure suffers from a number of severe problems: first, it should be clear that typesetting is a skilled task requiring special training in such concepts as typefaces, styles, and sizes—not to mention leading, weighting, kerning, widows, rectos, versos, letter-spacing, loose lines, and all the apparatus of professional designers. Moreover, most typesetting programs require either programming skills or extensive intervention. The nontechnical problems may be even more significant. Publisher's typesetting specifications usually suffer from a number of inadequacies that are customarily resolved through long-term relationships with local professionals. Thus, authors can expect to expend considerable time and energy clarifying specifications and resetting type. Moreover, like professional typesetters, author-typesetters may be held financially accountable for anything that is not set according to the publisher's specifications as well as any costs over the publisher's estimate. Finally, author-typesetters become subject to the tight deadlines of production cycles, which can interfere with their plans for teaching, scholarship, and administration.

The second alternative to document portability—providing page description files—still subjects authors to most of the problems of typesetting. In order to prepare page-description files, authors must have the full typesetting specifications and ensure that their files accord with those specifications.

The next alternative—submitting printouts to be read in by OCRs—relieves authors of typesetting problems but does not significantly improve the production process. Although OCRs are becoming faster and more accurate, they are still expensive and error prone. Because of the need for operator intervention, there is little chance that proofreading could be eliminated from the production cycle. Moreover, OCRs have limited capacity to generate marked-up files from printouts. Current systems can generate some procedural markup, but none can distinguish a theorem from an axiom, for example, or even a section from a subsection. Thus, OCR-generated files still require the intervention of personnel trained to recognize and code textual elements. (Note also that even the operators will not be trained to make sophisticated distinctions, for example, to distinguish an axiom from a theorem.) As character-recognition problems are solved, we might expect OCR manufacturers to concentrate on element recognition. Without explicit coding, however, automated element recognition will always be a haphazard task, and nothing could be more wasteful than to develop systems to recover knowledge that was thrown away when it could easily have been recorded in the source files.

Finally, there is a popular belief that publishers can convert authors' source files to their own formats by using special equipment. For example, according to *The Seybold Report on Publishing Systems*, "The Shaffstall communications/conversion system has gradually become known as a sophisticated tool capable of handling nearly anything that came along in the interfacing field" ("Interfaces" 37-38). In their test of the Shaffstall 5000 XT, however, the reporters tried files from MacWrite 2, MacWrite 2, PageMaker, readySetGo, and Microsoft Word. They found the system processed the MacWrite 4.2 file "nicely" but failed with the others because "those programs handle the data differently." Obviously, the utility of such a system is jeopardized by every new version of every program. Moreover, such systems do not provide necessary element recognition; they simply generate source files with rudimentary procedural markup. Trained personnel are still required to identify each element type and mark it up appropriately. Lastly, files are once again subjected to corruption. [12]

SGML has recently been criticized even by supporters of descriptive markup.[13] Above all, critics consider SGML too complicated for both authors and implementors. With its WriterStation, however, Datalogics has already demonstrated that sophisticated SGML tools can be developed and SGML document creation can be an intuitive process. Similarly, SoftQuad has produced an AAP text processor for the Macintosh. Sobemap has an SGML parser running under both Microsoft Windows and UNIX Version V.

This list of products is representative, not exhaustive, and development is actually just getting started. The Department of Defense is investing approximately $200 million per year in its SGML-based Computer-aided Acquisition and Logistics Support (CALS) initiative. Various other large government agencies, such as the Internal Revenue Service, are investing in SGML, and private organizations, such as McGraw-Hill, are planning to convert their systems fully in the near future. Some developers resent this pressure, especially from the government ("Integration" 25). The early successes mentioned above, however, will lead the way, and we can expect resistance to transform into serious development efforts.

Finally, SGML has been criticized for its lack of support for mathematics, graphics, and tabular material. SGML has metalinguistic properties, however, and AAP has already demonstrated that SGML applications can support mathematics and tabular material. We have no reason to believe the standard cannot support graphics through descriptive markup as well as through referential markup.

Portability Not Dependent on a Standard

We do not advocate waiting for SGML to become dominant. As we have illustrated, descriptive markup is vastly superior to both presentational and procedural markup. The superiority of descriptive markup is not dependent on its becoming a standard; instead, descriptive markup is the basis of the standard because of its inherent superiority over other forms of markup.[14]

Those of us who have converted to descriptive markup are already enjoying some of these outlined benefits. We have sent the source files for articles published in newsletters at Brown University to the University of Barcelona, which processed them without modification. Journals produced at Brown, such as *NOVEL: A Forum on Fiction* and *Philosophy and Phenomenological Research*, use descriptive tagging in the typesetting process and are preparing to accept submissions electronically. We can expect more and more journals and publishers to convert to this process when they realize the tremendous savings in administration and preparation costs. Ultimately the industrywide standard will accelerate this conversion to descriptive markup.[15]

Document portability promises significant reductions in costs and labor. The alternatives to document portability fail to address the need to share documents with colleagues and do not adequately address the problems of the production process. As AAP has recognized, descriptive markup provides the most complete and effective solution to the problem of establishing document portability. Many of the advantages may be enjoyed immediately, and those documents that have been descriptively coded can be updated easily if necessary as SGML becomes the industrywide standard.

Minimization of Cognitive Demands

Basic Theory

All document markup takes place in three steps:

1. *Element recognition.* One recognizes the current element is a token of a particular type—paragraph, prose quotation, footnote, and the like.

2. *Markup selection.* One determines the markup that applies to the element type recognized in (1).

3. *Markup performance.* One marks the element.[16]

The best markup techniques require the least cognitive processing (ceteris paribus). We believe that steps (1) and (3) can be ignored. The first step, element recognition, is the same for all forms of markup: we have no pretheoretical motivation for positing that an author recognizes an entity is a footnote, for example, in one way when using descriptive markup and in another way when using other forms of markup. The third step, markup performance, has received the most attention, resulting in various forms of "keystroke minimization" and alternative interfaces (such as pull-down menus). Again, however, we have no pretheoretical motivation for believing that one form of markup is more susceptible of performance optimization than another.[17] A brief look at markup selection demonstrates that descriptive markup requires less cognition than either presentational or procedural markup. The differences have been represented visually in Figure 2.

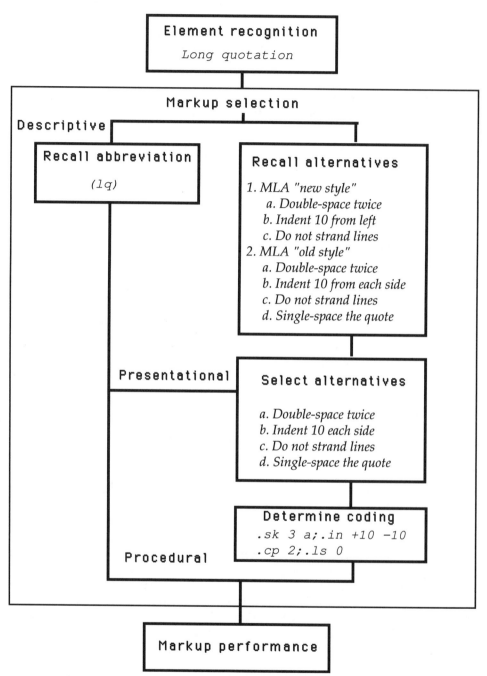

Figure 2: Markup selection for a long quotation (roughly).

Presentational Markup

Under presentational-markup schemes, markup selection requires an author to identify the set of typographical conventions for the current element type and then select the proper alternative.[18] This process is complicated by the fact that the relationship between typographical convention and text element is arbitrary and unstable. We have already discussed the maintenance problems that occur because of the instability of presentational markup conventions. When MLA changes its specifications for long quotations, for example, authors not only must update their files, they also must relearn the markup and are bound to go through a short period of confusion.

Even more important, the arbitrariness of presentational markup provides no support for recall and creates situations where there are an indefinite number of alternatives. High-frequency elements such as paragraphs may not present major recall problems, but infrequent elements such as citations require trips to style manuals. Similarly, elements with few alternatives such as paragraphs often do not require considerable reflection (although one may waver over whether a document is a personal letter or a business letter and, consequently, whether paragraphs should be marked up by skipping lines or by indenting). The number of alternatives for higher level elements such as chapters, however, increases quickly with the flexibility of text formatters and printing devices. Publishers, who are at the extreme of flexibility, hire professional designers to select presentational markup. Authors, however, must decide for themselves how to mark up such elements and may spend numerous hours adjusting and readjusting fonts and skips.

One would naturally expect considerable simplification of the process after the initial selection of markup for a text element. Authors report, however, that their memory fails and they often have to look back in a document to see how they have been formatting an element type. Moreover, they may well change their minds about the markup in the middle of the development of a document and interrupt the process of composition to reformat previously entered elements.

Procedural Markup

Markup selection is considerably more complicated for procedural-markup schemes. First, the author has to perform the same markup selection that is required for presentational markup. Then the author has to determine the procedural markup required by the target text formatter to create the selected presentational markup. Authors using procedural markup keep program documentation at their workplaces alongside style manuals.

Descriptive Markup

Descriptive markup reduced the process of markup selection to a single step falling naturally out of element recognition. Once the author had identified the element type, the proper markup may be determined simply by selecting the identifier that abbreviates the natural-language name for the current element type. In fact, the natural-language name may be used for the identifier and often is for infrequent elements such as "address." Such abbreviations as pq for "poetry quotation" simply provide for keystroke minimization.

Moreover, the markup selection for the termination of an element type (where necessary) is short-circuited by the convention of using a standard affix for the markup that was just selected to initiate the element. For example, once an author has selected <pq> as the appropriate markup to initiate a poetry quotation, markup for the end of the quotation is automatically </pq>, which may be arrived at through applying a standard and unchanging rule of affixation. Thus, descriptive markup is well suited for selection optimization.[19]

Descriptive markup minimizes cognitive demands by requiring little more than the normal linguistic processing already necessary to perform element recognition. Although the relationship between a text element and its natural-language name may be arbitrary, the relationship between the name and the descriptive markup is nonarbitrary. The tag for a paragraph might be p or para, for example, but it would not be sk or address. Moreover, the relationship between element name and descriptive markup is stable. The MLA could modify its style sheet every day, but the descriptive markup for long quotations would remain <lq>. Not only do authors not have to revise their markup but they also do not have to learn new markup for every style variation. Thus, the composition process need not be interrupted by trips to style sheets, and authors do not have to look back into their files to see how they have been formatting a particular element type. In fact, they are freed from formatting concerns altogether.

Although authors generally believe that integrated editor-formatters simplify document development by eliminating the need for markup, our analysis reveals not only that such applications require markup but also that the markup currently required by most popular systems is considerably more demanding than descriptive markup. Whether or not our analysis of the required processing is accurate in detail, it should be clear that (1) procedural markup selection requires previous presentational markup selection and (2) because of the stable and nonarbitrary relationship between tag and element name, descriptive markup selection requires less cognition than other forms of markup. Finally, the additional cognitive processing required by presentational markup wastes energy that could be applied to the content of the document and may even cause a lengthy suspension of the composition process.

Content Orientation

One of the more subtle advantages of descriptive markup is it supports authors in focusing on the structure and content of documents. Both presentational and procedural markup tend to focus authors' attention on physical presentation.[20]

When one marks up text descriptively, one makes the logical structure of the text explicit. For example, the standard tag sets include "heading-level" tags, such as `<h1>`, `<h2>`, `<h3>`, and so on. Such markup clarifies both hierarchical and sequential relationships. In fact, some of us regularly begin our documents as skeletal outlines composed of these tags. As our documents expand, this markup of the structure helps us stay aware of the planned focus for each section. Moreover, as we shall detail, we are able to use special applications to zoom in and out on the structure.

Unlike descriptive markup, presentational and procedural markup fail to support the writer in developing the structure; even worse, they distract from the content. As we have already discussed, the first step of marking up a document, element recognition, is the same for all forms of markup. The next step, markup selection, always involves some additional effort, but descriptive markup keeps this effort focused on the element and its role in the document. Presentational markup turns the author's attention toward typographic conventions and style sheets; and procedural markup leads even further away from the document toward the special markup required to make a particular text formatter produce the selected presentational markup.

There are a number of subtleties that we cannot address in detail here. The reader should bear in mind, however, that our argument addresses itself primarily to the process of markup selection. We have already noted it may be possible to perform complicated presentational or procedural markup as easily as it is to perform descriptive markup. In other words, any form of markup can be reduced to a single edit action. Conversely, a bad interface could make the performance of descriptive markup difficult and distracting.

In addition, we have raised, somewhat obliquely, issues of what authors view. We have suggested briefly that interfaces that expose or display descriptive markup will help authors focus on content and stay aware of structure. This is clearly an oversimplification. First, not all markup provides significant structural information or, better, information that is important to the author at the moment. Second, even descriptive markup can become so dense as to obscure the text. Furthermore, it might be in the author's best interests at any particular time to see, for example, the enumeration of items in a list instead of the descriptive markup. Ultimately, we have to conclude there is no simple relationship between viewing format and content orientation. An ideal system would provide authors with the ability to select among a number of different views of a file, and it should be possible to display the markup for some textual elements and to conceal the markup for others.

Composition Assistance and Special Processing

Using descriptive markup to identify the logical elements of a document not only simplifies composition, maintenance, collaboration, and publication but also enables authors to apply a wide range of tools for composition assistance. This feature must be exploited if text processing is going to fulfill its original promise significantly to assist scholarly composition and become more than just improved typing.

Without the structural identifications provided by descriptive markup, the text is simply a "character string that has no form other than that which can be deduced from the analysis of the document's meaning" (Goldfarb 68)—and this is a deduction for which computers are entirely unsuited. The addition of content-descriptive markup changes this formless character string into a structured database of text elements, enabling the scholar to address those elements selectively and systematically. Two composition-assistance functions that exploit the ability to address text elements selectively through their markup are *alternative views* and *structure-oriented editing*.

Alternative Views of a Document

If a document is prepared with descriptive markup, then the text elements that are to be displayed in the editor can be globally specified by referring to the markup that identifies those elements. For instance, one could specify that all block quotations be concealed from view. Where once a lengthy quotation intervened between two sentences, there might now be only a flag indicating the number of lines concealed, or, if the user prefers, no flag at all: the sentences appear adjacent to one another. Similarly, all footnotes could be concealed or all annotations or all annotations of a certain class—say, all annotations about translation or by annotators other than the author. In this way the sections of the text that are of current interest are distinguished for attention whereas those not of interest are hidden. Of course, at any point in the editing process, concealed text can be immediately and selectively disclosed for viewing.

Also useful are more specialized views, ones that are not just efficient for general composing and editing but finely adjusted to assist the scholar in *thinking* about the particular subject matter or topic at hand. Consider a specific example: one of the authors of this article writes papers on epistemic logic. His papers contain text-element tags such as *primitive* (to mark up text that explicitly introduces a term that is primitive within the axiomatic system being proposed), *definition* (for definitions of the system), *axiom* (for axioms of the system), and *theorem* (for these that follow from the axioms). An editing utility that exploits this markup maintains a current list of every axiomatic element in the document. This list can be quickly consulted while editing—it is sometimes displayed in a concurrent editing window—and can be automatically updated and included as an appendix whenever the file is printed. Optionally, the listed axiomatic elements may be sorted and reviewed by *kind*—primitive terms, axioms, definitions, theorems—regardless of their order in the paper. As well as simply providing a quick reference to the current status of the axiomatic elements in the developing system, this utility is used to compare systems (sorted summaries of their axiomatic elements are put in adjacent windows) and to explore ideas about the relationships among elements. Similar techniques can be applied in other disciplines.

One source of the effectiveness of these viewing strategies is the simple juxtaposition of related sections of text for comparison. Another is the directed rearrangement of these regions—this is because frequently the chosen rhetorical structure of a document dictates a narrative order of text elements that is not the best sequence for the author's own thinking about the subject matter. In both cases the editing utilities described are using descriptive markup to overcome in the compositional environment the limitations imposed by the presentational requirements of the intended rhetorical form. This is exactly the sort of assistance a scholar should expect from the computer.

What is being accomplished here is something that cannot be performed effectively with conventional scholarly tools: scattered sections of text that have been specified by certain content-related properties are being quickly presented for comparison and editing. With a conventional writing medium, like paper, only a laborious searching out of passages and cutting and rearranging could accomplish the same thing and even then with a significant likelihood of error. The time and energy required by this traditional physical method limit the number of rearrangements the author can afford to attempt and make the more experimental rearrangements especially impractical. With the computer-assisted approach, every hunch can be immediately explored, and viewing strategies can be progressively refined in accordance with the results of each trial, all with a minimal cost in time and energy. All these techniques require the structural information provided by descriptive markup; without that, computing scholars are little better off than they were with pencil, paper, and scissors.

Although the value of alternative views of a file as an intellectual tool has been described by a number of authors, surprisingly few scholars are taking advantage of these features.[21] Part of the problem is that the ability to present for display and editing alternative views of files is represented as a *feature* of particular experimental text-processing systems rather than a general *strategy* for text processing. However, by simply using a descriptive markup scheme and a general-purpose programmable editor, any scholar can begin to take advantage of these tools immediately.[22]

Outlining and Structure-Oriented Editing

A special example of an alternative view is the *outline* (see Figure 3). Documents have a natural hierarchical structure: chapters have sections, sections have subsections, and so on, until one reaches sentences, words, and letters. If the sections of a document are marked up as such, then it is frequently a simple matter to command a general-purpose editor to display only the section titles, presenting the scholar with a working outline. Furthermore, as section markup is keyed to section level, the author can easily have the outliner display the outline to any desired depth of detail, the lowest level of detail being the full text or, perhaps, the text with annotations and alternative versions. The level-by-level concealing and revealing of successive levels of detail may be controlled by a "zoom" function. One may also employ editing utilities to move hierarchical components of the document, as displayed in an outline view, and have the overall document structure adjust accordingly. For instance, one might directly move a section, complete with all its nested subsections and text, to another chapter. Or one might raise a section from a third-level section to a second-level section and have all its nested subsection headings adjust their depth markup accordingly. Exploiting the natural hierarchical structural of text in this way has also been frequently recommended by text-processing theorists.[23] Although recently a number of powerful outlining applications have been marketed, again, these products are mostly specialized applications rather than general implementations of a strategy based on descriptive markup.

This kind of maneuver is an instance of a superior style of editing made possible by descriptive markup: *structure-oriented editing*. Descriptive markup allows the

```
(h0) Background and New Concepts
    (h1) Markup Theory
        (h2) Types of Markup
            (h3) Punctuational
            (h3) Presentational
            (h3) Procedural
            (h3) Descriptive
            (h3) Referential
            (h3) Metamarkup
        (h2) Markup Handling
        (h2) Concealed, Exposed, Disguised, and Displayed
        Markup
        (h2) Summary
(h0) Advantages of Descriptive Markup
    (h1) Maintainability
    (h1) Document Portability
        (h2) Background
        (h2) Advantages
        (h2) Alternatives to Portability
        (h2) Portability Not Dependent on a Standard
        (h2) Summary
    (h1) Minimization of Cognitive Demands
        (h2) Basic Theory
        (h2) Presentational Markup
        (h2) Procedural Markup
        (h2) Descriptive Markup
        (h2) Summary
    (h1) Content Orientation
    (h1) Composition Assistance and Special Processing
        (h2) Introduction
        (h2) Alternative Views of a Document
        (h2) Outlining and Structure-Oriented Editing
        (h2) Summary
    (h1) Conclusion
```

Figure 3: Outlining with descriptive markup.

targets of editing operations to be not only characters, words, and lines but also the actual text-element tokens, the regions of text that fall within the scope of a particular markup tag. For instance, one can execute operations such as "Delete this footnote" or "Move this quotation." Structure-oriented editing enables authors to address their documents at a level of abstraction appropriate to their authorial role; other forms of editing require the mediation of line displacements, line numbers, and marked regions. Thus, structure-oriented editing minimizes cognitive demands and helps authors focus on content.

Composition-assistance features such as alternative views of a document and structure-oriented editing promise immense improvements in the effectiveness and productivity of the scholarly composition environment. The realization of most of these features depends on descriptive markup. Text processing with any other kind of markup will ensure that the anachronistic strategies of discarded technologies will continue to dominate computer-assisted document preparation.

Conclusion

Descriptive markup solves many of the problems that scholars face in document development. First, the process of marking up the text is simplified because the author's attention is focused on the content instead of on controlling a computer program or on the typography of the presentation copy. Second, maintenance problems are reduced to a few easily identifiable locations external to document files; updating for style changes is easy, and documents are not exposed to corruption. Third, as has been recognized by AAP, descriptive markup provides the best means for establishing the industrywide standard that we need for full document portability. Document portability enables authors to share files with colleagues and significantly reduces both the cost of publication and the nonauthorial demands on authors. Finally, in descriptively marking up a document, an author provides the semantic and pragmatic information necessary for such aids as alternative views on documents and structure-oriented editing. Without descriptive markup, only special systems with incompatible formats will offer even a portion of the authorial support that scholars have a right to expect from their computers.

In the end, it should be clear that descriptive markup is not just the best approach of the competing markup systems; it is the best imaginable approach. Currently, acceptance of descriptive markup is being retarded by authors' desires to retain familiar technologies and practices and by developers' use of proprietary formats to lock users into their products. Equipped with the basic concepts from the general theory of markup systems, however, authors quickly recognized the superiority of descriptive markup. As this awareness spreads, we can expect significant improvements in the quality of scholarly computing.

Acknowledgments. We are indebted to Mary Elizabeth McClure for stimulating our thinking about descriptive markup and to Richard A. Damon, Elli Mylonas, and David Durand for many helpful discussions. We would also like to thank Robert J.

Scholes and Maurice Glicksman for their roles in acquiring the support necessary to research and develop this essay.

Further reading. For the seminal ideas on sophisticated authorial support systems, see Bush, Carmody, Engelbart and English, Engelbart et al., and Nelson, "Getting It" and *Literary Machines*. Some important recent discussions are presented in Corda, Trigg, and Yankelovitch. A number of good papers on document development and structure-oriented editing, including Goldfarb's important 1981 paper on GML, are contained in ACM. This volume also contains the useful "Annotated Bibliography of Background Material on Text Manipulation" compiled by Reid and Hanson. Meyrowitz is the standard survey of editing systems and provides considerable information about formatters as well. Finally, the AAP and SGML standards are documented in ANSI and in the AAP's *Standard for Electronic Manuscript Preparation and Markup*.

Notes

1. This work, which first appeared in *Communications of the ACM* 30 (November 1987): 933-47, was supported in part by the Mellon Foundation. Although the issues addressed in this essay bear on all electronic document development, we have chosen to focus on the domain that we know best: scholarly text processing.

2. Although there remain some important exceptions (for example, Corda, Trigg, Yankelovich), this older, limited model of machine-scholar interaction has become dominant.

3. See Drucker for a discussion of the costs of this tendency as well as of the failure to take calculated risks.

4. At last count only four research groups in the country were attempting to develop sophisticated grammar-checking programs (see Alexander). Spelling correctors and thesaurus programs have begun to appear in increasing quantities, but they tend to be uneven in quality and are hardly the subject of intense scrutiny.

5. This last point should not be underestimated; if we are to correct the current imbalance in allocation of resources, we must make it possible for newly developed products to process files created by all text-processing systems. Currently, not only do most files contain only paper-directed coding but they also occur in very incompatible formats. Even for a relatively trivial program, such as a spelling verifier, it can now cost a developer several months and thousands of dollars to develop the auxiliary programs required to process source files. Moreover, those who do not use the most common text processors are cut out of the market and do not have access to the new systems. The extra costs and the reduced market created by incompatible and nondescriptive coding constitute a considerable disincentive to the development of sophisticated systems.

---

6. The following discussion is based on work by Coombs. This section owes major debts to Goldfarb and to the recent ANSI Standard Generalized Markup Language. All descriptive markup examples are presented in SGML notation.

7. Strictly speaking, some of our "electronic" markup occurs on manuscripts and typescripts in the form of proofreader's marks and typesetting directions, but such markup did not become prominent in the document development process until the advent of electronic systems. Goldfarb and SGML consider our electronic markup "explicit" and our scribal markup "implicit." Actually, Goldfarb ignores presentational markup (70); SGML distinguishes "natural language notation" (punctuational markup) from "formatted text notations" (presentational markup) (ANSI 90-91). Both types of scribal markup, however, have physical instantiation and, thus, are not really implicit. Moreover, both are part of a writing system and, thus, are part of a medium for conveying natural language expressions instead of part of the languages themselves.

8. We have observed, for example, that Cambridge University Press favors the first style of dash; Oxford University Press, the second.

9. FRESS was directly based on the prototype system HES (Hypertext Editing System) (see Prusky, Carmody).

10. Rigorously used, electronic style sheets may provide the same solution to maintenance problems. Since style sheets are presentation oriented, however, we expect that authors will not make all the necessary distinctions. The "block style," for example, might temporarily provide appropriate formatting for many different entities such as prose quotation, poetry quotations, theorems, definitions, and examples. Later, it may be necessary to distinguish the elements, and the markup will need revision.

11. Although most of the literature seems to assume the authorial reading of galley and page proofs will remain part of the publishing process, we have eliminated that tiresome task from the production of books that we typeset ourselves. We see no reason for not retaining these advantages once publishers are able to typeset directly from authors' source files.

12. For more sophisticated translation efforts, see Mamrak. Note, however, that they seek to support translation into and out of standards, not from one arbitrary format to another. Moreover, they choose a descriptive markup system for their prototyping: SGML.

13. See "Integration" 21-25 for a report of criticisms. Most of the information in this section on SGML activity has been derived from reports in *(TAG)*.

14. The opposite is true of another proposed standard—IBM's Document Content Architecture (DCA). Instead of declaring the logical status of textual entities, Revisable-Form-Text DCA declares formatting aspects and is presentation oriented. Thus, DCA would not enable a publisher, for example, to switch from endnotes to footnotes or even to change to smaller fonts for block quotations without revising the source files.

15. Our current incompatibility problems are not limited to document files. Every database management system, for example, has its own format, making it difficult to share information or even to switch from one system to another. With his Information Management System for Scholars (IMSS), Coombs has established that descriptive markup provides an appropriate and effective format for database portability. Not only can IMSS data files be ported to other database systems, scholars can now create bibliography and note files on a variety of machines and import them to IMSS to take advantage of its advanced functions. As they become aware of the possibilities, authors will consider such flexibility a requirement instead of a feature.

16. This analysis generalizes on the three steps of procedural markup Goldfarb discusses (68).

17. On the surface, it would seem that descriptive markup would provide for optimal markup performance. Whatever the interface, it should be possible to reduce the act of describing an element to a single edit action, but the process of identifying formatting procedures may well require multiple edit actions. Many editors, however, provide facilities for reducing a complicated series of editorial functions to a single keystroke. If the user thinks, for example, "by striking function key 1, I will double space twice, indent ten from the left, start a new page if necessary, and switch to single spacing," then the user has performed relatively complicated presentational markup with as little effort as would be required to perform descriptive markup. The process of deciding how to mark up the element, however, will have been much more complicated, and we allow our argument to rest on that point.

18. There is a whole range of possibilities for recall and selection that cannot be discussed here. This section should be considered suggestive instead of exhaustive.

19. For the sake of markup minimization, SGML introduced an "empty end tag" </>. Since this tag can only be used in certain contexts, this feature may complicate mark selection rather than optimize it.

20. Recognizing this fact, Brian K. Reid took presentational and procedural markup out of the hands of authors altogether. Only the Scribe Database Administrator has access to procedural markup and format definitions.

21. Important early discussions of alternative views of text are Nelson ("Getting It" 193-95), Engelbart and English, and Carmody (288-300). But over a decade later, Meyrowitz and van Dam describe "the principle of multiple views" as "one that has been sorely underutilized in the hundreds of editors that have been created" (405).

22. Most of the functions described in this section have been implemented by the authors to meet some immediately perceived compositional need—they used only IBM's standard VM applications Xedit and Rexx.

23. For an early discussion of outlining and structure-oriented editing, see Engelbart and English. For a selection of later work on structure-oriented editing and related topics see the papers in *Proceedings of the ACM SIGPLAN SIGOA Symposium on Text Manipulation.*

Bibliography

Alexander, Gary B. "Computer Aids for Authors and Editors: A Natural Extension of Word Processing and Typesetting?" *Seybold Report on Publication Systems* 13 (13 February 1984): 3-21.

American National Standards Institute (ANSI). *Information Processing —Text and Office Systems—Standard Generalized Markup Language (SGML)*. ISO 8879-1986(E). New York: ANSI, 1986.

Association for Computing Machinery (ACM). *Proceedings of the ACM SIGPLAN—SIGOA Symposium on Text Manipulation*. New York: ACM, 1981.

Association of American Publishers. *Author's Guide to Electronic Manuscript Preparation and Markup*. Electronic Manuscript Series. Washington, DC: AAP, May 1986.

_____. *Electronic Manuscript Project: Task 1 Report*. Rockville, MD: Aspen Systems, 1984.

_____. *Standard for Electronic Manuscript Preparation and Markup*. Electronic Manuscript Series. Washington, DC: AAP, February 1986.

Beach, Richard, and Maureen Stone. "Graphical Style—Towards High Quality Illustrations." *SIGGRAPH '83 Conference Proceedings*. New York: ACM, 1983. 127-35.

Bush, Vannevar. "As We May Think." *Atlantic Monthly* 176 (July 1945): 101-08.

Carmody, Steven, Walter Gross, Theodor H. Nelson, David Rice, and Andries van Dam. "A Hypertext Editing System for the /360." *Pertinent Concepts in Computer Graphics*. Ed. M. Faiman and J. Nievergelt. Urbana: U of Illinois P, 1969. 291-330.

Chamberlin, Donald D. "JANUS: An Interactive System for Document Composition." *Proceedings of the ACM SIGPLAN SIGOA Symposium on Text Manipulation*. New York: ACM, 1981. 82-91.

Coombs, James H. "Information Management System for Scholars." Technical Memorandum TM 69-2. Providence: Brown U Computer Center, December 1986.

Coombs, James H., Anne M. Scott, George P. Landow, and Arnold A. Sanders, eds. A *Pre-Raphaelite Friendship: The Correspondence of William Holman Hunt and John Lucas Tupper*. Ann Arbor: UMI, 1986.

Corda, U., and G. Facchetti. "Concept Browser: A System for Interactive Creation of Dynamic Documentation." *Text Processing and Document Manipulation*. Ed. J. C. van Vliet. Cambridge: Cambridge UP, 1986. 233-45.

Drucker, Peter F. *Management: Tasks, Responsibilities, Practices*. New York: Harper, 1973.

Engelbart, Douglas C., and William K. English. "A Research Center for Augmenting Human Intellect." 1968. *Computer-Supported Cooperative Work: A Book of Readings*. Ed. Irene Greif. San Mateo: Morgan Kaufmann, 1988. 81-105.

Engelbart, Douglas C., Richard W. Watson, and James C. Norton. "The Augmented Knowledge Workshop." *Proceedings of the AFIPS Fall Joint Computer Conference*. Reston: AFIPS, 1973. 9-21.

Goldfarb, C. F. "A Generalized Approach to Document Markup." *Proceedings of the ACM SIGPLAN SIGOA Symposium on Text Manipulation*. New York: ACM, 1981. 68-73. (Adapted as "Annex A. Introduction to Generalized Markup" in ISO 8879.)

"Integration and Pagination: Long Documents, Proposals, Books." *Seybold Report on Publishing Systems* 16 (27 April 1987): 21-27.

"Interfaces, Media Converters and OCR Devices." *Seybold Report on Publishing Systems* 15 (2 June 1986): 34-39.

Lamport, Leslie. *LATEX User's Guide and Reference Manual*. Reading: Addison-Wesley, 1986.

Mamrak, S. A., M. J. Kaelbling, C. K. Nicholas, and M. Share. "A Software Architecture for Supporting the Exchange of Electronic Manuscripts." *Communications of the ACM* 30 (May 1987): 408-14.

Meyrowitz, Norman, and Andries van Dam. "Interactive Editing Systems: Parts I and II." *ACM Computing Surveys* 14 (September 1982): 321-415.

Modern Language Association. *MLA Handbook for Writers of Research Papers*. New York: MLA, 1977.

_____. *MLA Handbook for Writers of Research Papers*. 2nd ed. New York: MLA, 1984.

Nelson, Theodor H. "Getting It out of Our System." *Information Retrieval: A Critical Review*. Ed. G. Schecter. Washington, DC: Thompson, 1967. 191-210.

_____. *Literary Machines*. Nashville: Self-published, 1981.

Prusky, John. *FRESS Resource Manual*. Providence: Brown U Department of Computer Science, 1978.

Nievergelt, J., G. Coray, J. D. Nicoud, and A. C. Shaw, eds. *Document Preparation Systems*. Amsterdam: North-Holland, 1982.

Reid, Brian K. "A High-Level Approach to Computer Document Formatting." *Proceedings of the 7th Annual ACM Symposium on Programming Languages*. New York: ACM, 1980. 24-30.

(TAG) The SGML Newsletter. Alexandria: Graphic Communications Association.

Trigg, Randall H., and Mark Weiser. "TEXTNET: A Network-Based Approach to Text Handling." *ACM Transactions on Office Information Systems* 4 (January 1986): 1-23.

van Dam, Andries, and David E. Rice. "On-line Text Editing: A Survey." *ACM Computing Surveys* 3 (September 1971): 93-114.

Yankelovich, Nicole, Norman Meyrowitz, and Andries van Dam. "Reading and Writing the Electronic Book." *IEEE Computer* 18 (October 1985): 15-30.

Markup Systems in the Present

Steven J. DeRose

Electronic Book Technologies

Introduction

In our 1987 article "Markup Systems and the Future of Scholarly Text Processing," reprinted elsewhere in this volume, James H. Coombs, Allen H. Renear, and I presented a theoretical framework for understanding systems for marking up documents. We defined *presentational, procedural,* and *descriptive* markup methodologies and argued for the superiority of descriptive markup. Our arguments were based on perspicuity and consequent portability; minimization of cognitive demands for the user; flexibility of interpretation, application, and processing; and a variety of benefits of standardization per se.

Now, five years later, a number of historical developments have affected the movement toward the future we described. In this article I shall survey progress and major trends in markup systems and discuss likely future directions and issues.

Descriptive markup is the practice of categorizing and labeling portions of documents in terms of their functional roles, rather than in terms of their intended processing. For example, a section title would be marked up as such, rather than as "Helvetica 18-point bold." Obviously the first characterization is useful for a wider range of purposes than the second; it captures an essential quality that the second neglects, and (perhaps most importantly) it is directly related to the author's model of a document, rather than a typesetter's.

In 1987 we described three major problems arising from the historical shift of emphasis in text-system design from modeling the user as an author to modeling the user as typist, typesetter, or programmer-typist. Those problems were

1. Decreased awareness of the significance of the document's electronic form in its own right

2. Decreased incentive for research in advanced document-creation systems for authors

3. Distraction of authors from their primary tasks of research and composition toward managing typesetting and page-layout details.

In general, the first problem has been largely overcome, and this success is gradually leading to resolution of the second. The third, however, remains.

State of the Art

It has now become possible to handle structured electronic documents with much more facility than in the past. Portability of raw data has been nearly, though not fully, achieved. Tools for composition are more available, if still not advanced. However, software only incompletely supports the life cycle of electronic documents because electronic submission to publishers and electronic document delivery are not yet simple or widespread.

Portability

The need for portability of documents has been continually increasing. Paper documents' strongest advantages over electronic ones center on portability and compatibility. Many causes have contributed to an increased consciousness of the need for comparable portability of electronic documents and manuscripts and thence to consciousness of the advantages of descriptive, structure-centered markup. These causes include

1. Drastic increases in the cost of paper

2. Increased access to wide-area networks such as the Internet

3. Increasing internationalization of the network community

4. Increasing availability of major on-line text collections of interest to researchers, particularly in the humanities.

Such factors have led to growing awareness that having a different proprietary format for each person's favorite word processor—or each person's favorite printer, fonts, and paper size—is maladaptive. Users have begun to value the ability to pass electronic documents around transparently, as they have been doing for centuries with paper documents.

Strategies for achieving portability have been myriad. At the lowest level, networked users must still employ special strategies just to move bytes without loss, since nodes on the Internet currently disagree about how and whether to forward both eight-bit characters and some seven-bit characters such as braces and brackets, backslashes, and exclamation points.[1]

At the next level, software vendors still build multiple Save As Format X options for their most popular competitors' formats. These features, now as then, break with each new software version. A subtler problem is that even when the input document encodes some structural information (say, by style sheets), such information seldom survives the transfer: conversion is usually limited to producing a similar page layout. Many users give up and mail page images instead of documents, either via PostScript or bitmaps, or discard all but the most rudimentary presentational markup, calling the result "plain ASCII." Such representations neither represent nor even encourage the recovery of structural information. Similarly, no consensus on graphics formats seems to be present, and there is not even an analog to "plain ASCII" as a fallback.

For network communications, a variety of presentational markup methods are typically used, such as blank lines, indentation, and conventional meanings for strings such as > (quotation), * (emphatic), and even ;) (joke). Unfortunately, these methods are neither rigorous nor unambiguous and have limited capacity for expressing document structure.

In communities with large document communication needs, or with many levels of co-authors working together, the problems of interchange are felt especially acutely. Particularly in such environments, Standard Generalized Markup Language (SGML) has become the medium of choice for document interchange, and therefore, tools to convert into and out of it as an "interlingua" have proliferated. Such tools are only beginning to be accessible to most users.

Writing Tools

Tools that cater to writers' needs as opposed to typesetters' and graphic designers' needs are still rare. Page-layout tools are much more sophisticated, but the lamented regression from cognitively appropriate markup has not been entirely reversed. Useful structural tools such as outline processors also continue to improve but remain in isolation from other tools. It remains difficult to treat the same document as a source for publication and for outline processing, presentation management, information retrieval, on-line delivery, and other uses.

Three trends, however, give hope that writer-oriented tools employing document models analogous to document structures will grow in availability and use. First, style sheets are now an expected feature of serious word processors of all kinds. Style sheets encourage at least a rudimentary level of descriptive markup, although such markup is not rigorous (for example, software that makes it easy to create new styles when needed tends also to make it easy to create redundant or ill-conceived styles when such are not needed).

Second, recent emphasis on object-oriented design has encouraged software designers to think of data structures in terms of classes, subclasses, and instances. This approach contributes to acceptance of analogous structured document models such as SGML, and research in object-oriented design provides enabling methodologies for building effective structured document systems. Briefly put, a kind of document element such as a chapter, bibliography entry, or emphatic phrase is comparable to a class. An instance of such an element must have internal structure conforming to the class definition, and SGML-element instances may have attribute lists, comparable to instance variables. The analogy, though useful, is not perfect: although class hierarchies typically represent relations of type and subtype, for documents the more salient hierarchy is one of containment. Tools that directly manipulate these hierarchical structures have now become available to authors.

Third, a number of products have begun to add processing capabilities to documents via "scripting languages" that provide for interaction between the user and document portions. Although such systems as yet lack an advanced model of document structure, they open the door to processing a single document in various ways for various purposes.

Much as with the advent of structured programming, those managing very large projects feel most acutely the need for a rigorous and abstract approach. Hence, two groups have been particularly quick to adopt descriptive markup and create major documents and collections using it: high-tech industries, which have enormous manuals, and humanities scholars, who work closely with large collections of literary texts.

Electronic Submission

Publishers were early supporters of descriptive markup, presumably because of the potential economic advantage gained if authors submit usable manuscripts in electronic form. The Association of American Publishers (AAP) developed one of the first industry-standard applications of SGML, and it has now become an

---

American National Standards Institute (ANSI) standard. However, few publishers yet permit electronic submissions, and rekeying of manuscripts is still the norm except for authors willing to assume the entire responsibility for producing camera-ready final copy.

The ubiquity of Internet access makes authors increasingly reluctant to accept delivery delays and postal costs for manuscripts. An interim solution adopted by many publishers has been to accept manuscripts in one or two word-processor formats, or "plain ASCII," the definition of which varies. The latter option saves rekeying text but foregoes representation not only of document structure but even of formatting. It also fails to represent basic nonlinearities such as footnotes and cross-references, as well as document portions with complex structures such as tables, graphics, and equations.

Electronic Delivery

Electronic document delivery has not yet arrived, although a few systems do exist. Sony has produced the Data DiscMan, a hand-held device that can display documents from an optical disk several lines at a time. Microsoft has published many documents on line in its Bookshelf series. Owners of large data and statistics collections frequently sell them in electronic form.

The present situation, however, is that these products provide only minimal functionality. In almost all cases the data can be read, searched, and printed—but only by proprietary software sold with it, and only on specific hardware and operating system versions. Such specific software cannot anticipate all legitimate uses for the data, and so users with novel applications are left out. In addition, the formatting capabilities of such systems seem primitive even when compared to low-end word processors.

A few large projects in academia and industry are moving toward delivering extremely large documents on line, again because such documents present the need most acutely. The US Department of Defense has continued with the CALS initiative, and is working toward an Interactive Electronic Technical Manual system much like those prototyped in the seventies (Feiner). Scholars have also moved in this direction, as the primary literatures of many fields are being encoded and distributed, and text archives around the world gradually convert to common formats.

Theodor H. Nelson's vision has yet to be achieved: "We must leave paper behind at last if we are to move to the new worlds of tomorrow. And that includes leaving behind such last-ditch anachronisms as 'Wizzywig' and 'modelessness.' These all have their eye on the past. . . . Today's 'computer literacy' and styles of operation will seem to us then like poking the cat's-whisker on the crystal in the radio set of 1920. 'It's what we had to do then,' we'll say" (24).

Factors Slowing Adoption of Descriptive Markup

Working against these encouraging developments there remain two major technical issues and one major economic one, all of which have yet to be resolved before all the benefits of descriptive markup can be realized. First, there remains a concern (sometimes legitimate and sometimes fatuous) for "page fidelity": keeping line breaks, page breaks, and text geometry constant across transmission. It is still widely thought that a page-description method such as PostScript will address this issue, but such solutions are limited because (1) the text content and structure are not well represented, making any processing other than printing difficult, and (2) even printing another's PostScript or similar document is incompletely reliable because of incompatibilities of fonts, printer resolution, and so on.

In the realm of legal publishing, and for certain other very particular applications, exact page fidelity may be needed. However, the usefulness even of current legal databases that do essentially no formatting is great, so this concern is clearly limited. Also, even highly format-oriented software often fails to produce *exactly* the same layout and appearance, owing to factors such as round-off error in calculating page placements and character widths and a proliferation of program options that cannot be automatically synchronized when a file is transferred.

The second technological factor slowing adoption of structured and portable documents is the ubiquity of the facsimile machine. Despite poor image quality and the fact that not even the individual characters of a document can be easily recovered from a facsimile's bitmap result, fax machines are so convenient and so standardized that they decrease the perceived need for processable representations.

Economically, issues of copyright plague electronic texts as they do many other areas of computer science.

New Capabilities

As the number of electronic texts grows, so does the need for tools with which to process and present them. The areas most under development now include structured search, custom-tailored display and rendering, and interactive documents, commonly treated under the heading "hypermedia."

As we described the situation in 1987, structured representation encourages processing document portions by class. For example, a logician may require special handling of axioms, expressions, and proofs, whether for formatting, indexing, or even validation by expert systems. Research in the particular problems of search in structured documents is only beginning.

The central theoretical problem is the notion of containment. When it was sufficient to model documents as unitary objects with minimal internal structure, retrieval methods employed criteria such as how many times a document contained a word, contained two words near each other, and so on. Most systems provided a single level of granularity, typically either "document" or "paragraph," but not both, and certainly not an unlimited number of named levels with user-defined significance.

As large documents with complex structure have come into use, programmers often use two strategies to recycle available retrieval methods: first, documents are restructured to fit the available methods, fragmented into topical portions that become "documents" in their own right. This strategy is problematic for two reasons: pre-existing documents must be changed, and new documents must be written in a new staccato style so that information prerequisite to a fragment is duplicated in the fragment or referred to. Such style has some advantages and imposes a perhaps desirable discipline on authors; however, it is prescriptive and precludes presentation in a flow or sequence of greater size when the topic or the author's rhetorical style justifies it.

The second strategy is to choose a small number of the more tractable document elements and index them specially. This approach almost always builds upon a relational database model and may even refer to document elements as fields. As a consequence of the relational model, the indexers choose elements that tend not to repeat within a document: author, publication date, and similar front matter. Such models fail to describe the structure of real documents, in which very few fields occur only once or have no significant internal structure (of the 210-plus element types defined in the AAP tag set, only 15 can have only a limited number of subelements).

Relational implementations for searching hierarchical documents are possible; indeed many exist. However, by definition a relational element ("record") cannot provide for a variable number of subelements ("fields"); thus, such an implementation must force-fit document structure into an inappropriate model, which is ineffective for large documents or document collections. An adequate system must associate text content with multiple containers, not just one: a word occurs not only in its paragraph but in every higher containing element, up to the book itself. Only a handful of systems treats this problem seriously.

Recent efforts such as those of Forbes J. Burkowski at the University of Waterloo in developing text algebras for predication of containment and precedence relations, and treatments of similar structures developed by theoretical linguists, promise to lead to more sophisticated tools in this area.

Dynamic Display

If a markup system expresses in documents information only about document layout and formatting, then it naturally will express only one such layout. However, descriptive markup's separation of formatting from structural information opens the possibility of associating any number of layouts with a single document. Similarly, if the paper page is definitive, only one form makes sense; but if a changeable medium such as a screen is the document's destination, an unlimited number of specialized layouts should be possible. Tools that format documents on the fly have occasionally been developed in the past, and most current word processors can do this vertically for small documents (although few permit even so simple a horizontal operation as rebreaking text to fit the window).

The capabilities of early systems such as FRESS (Carmody, Catano, Prusky) to hide structural document elements selectively, and to change display styles at the user's whim, have only now begun to reappear. Excessive focus on page layout has led virtually all presentation systems to implement serial formatting algorithms, which are in principle not capable of adjusting rapidly to user actions that globally affect large documents.

Structure-aware tools permit readers to customize documents to their needs, such as by hiding information required only for experts or novices, or showing only the chapters of a document that contain certain content or have certain attributes. Database viewers support all these operations but still have display quality too impoverished for dealing with documents.

Hypertext/Hypermedia

Many of the topics already discussed impinge on hypertext and hypermedia, topics that have grown since the first major conference (Hypertext '87) to become required

---

Markup Systems in the Present

check-box items for new software and which have in the process lost some of their meaning.[2] Hypertext-related software provides a means to journey from here to there at the click of a button. However, the natures of "here" and "there" themselves are commonly neglected, and documents are often constrained by a model even less revealing than those of format-oriented word processors: the card.

The earliest hypertext systems were closely related to the earliest descriptive markup systems and consequently treated documents under much more sophisticated models. Augment (Engelbart) provided a work environment where substantial documents as well as day-to-day electronic mail were created, edited, and linked. Brown University's FRESS provided for intermixing hierarchical and nonhierarchical structures, associating keywords with document elements and preserving links to all these across editing while supporting documents as diverse as poetry, textbooks, and faculty-salary databases. Nelson, who contributed to the development of FRESS, calls it "the first visual word processor" (15), and it was also the first hypertext system used in teaching. Scribe, perhaps the earliest pure descriptive markup system, grew to become HyperScribe (see Reid).

However, at the same time that the popularization of WYSIWYG word processing was accompanied by proliferation of inadequate document models based upon the typewriter, the popularization of linking was accompanied by proliferation of inadequate hyperdocument models based upon the Rolodex card-index. Indeed, some popular authors have suggested that the essence of hypertext is the division of text into "chunks," a claim at odds with the ideals of Vannevar Bush, Douglas C. Engelbart, Nelson, Andries van Dam (see Carmody), and other hypertext pioneers. These researchers instead emphasized the support of full-sized documents, with all the complexities of authorial structure.

Even broad-based and influential essays on hypertext such as Jeff Conklin's "Hypertext" have often been read as supporting limited document models. An earlier version ("Survey") completely neglected intra- as opposed to inter-document links, which are crucial in any document of nontrivial size; it also ruled out links to locations within documents in general. Limitations that remained in the later article include requiring a one-to-one correspondence between windows and documents (which precludes some effective interface structures) and Conklin's devoting much discussion to methods for force-fitting documents into chunks while giving little motivation for such fitting except that many software systems impose it (35). Perhaps most unfortunate is that although Conklin states that the essence of hypertext is linking, not chunking, later references to his work have quoted primarily the parts that describe linking of directed graphs; at least when taken out of context these seem to imply that nodes in such graphs have no significant internal structure.

As with typewriter-model word processors, Rolodex-model hypertext systems have been warmly welcomed as a vast step forward, when in many ways they are more primitive than earlier systems. Indeed they provide many useful benefits and permit authors to create simple hypertexts easily and quickly; unfortunately, their too-concrete model leads to a fragmented computing environment of noncommunicating "hyper-islands" (Meyrowitz, "Cholesterol"). As the sophistication of document processing increases, so will perception of the limitations imposed by overly simplistic document models.

Standards

Syntax: SGML and ODA

Two major ISO standards exist for representing documents: SGML is in fact a meta-language, in which a set of document-element classes, additional notations, and containment rules is declared, and a program can then parse and validate documents conforming to the declaration. SGML strongly encourages that the element classes constitute descriptive rather than procedural markup, though this is impossible to enforce fully. The Office Document Architecture (ODA) is more specific and provides a fixed set of descriptive-element classes and notations along with a representation of formatting. The standards' names reveal not only their designs but also their histories: SGML has been adopted for markup in a wide range of contexts because it easily describes a wide range of structures; ODA has been adopted for use in business contexts because its direct provision of formatting features is important there while the diversity and structural complexity of documents is lower.

The rapid spread of SGML exceeds anything we anticipated in 1987 and does not appear to be slowing. It is far from a perfect markup system, but it has been very effective in focusing attention on document structure rather than transient formatting and in facilitating document interchange.

Text Encoding: TEI

Perhaps the most hopeful sign of all in the last five years has been that major text-encoding projects have committed themselves to a single, descriptive standard for marking up and interchanging the many documents they encode. As the Internet has made it convenient to pass around large documents, change them, enhance them, and send them back, it has also revealed the dangers of proprietary formats and permitted scholars to avoid them.

The Text Encoding Initiative (TEI) is a major international effort to provide guidelines for the encoding of machine-readable texts, particularly documents of interest to scholars. It is funded by the National Endowment for the Humanities, the European Economic Community, and the Mellon Foundation and has the support of many academic and professional societies. The efforts of many scholars during the first four years of the TEI's work have produced a volume of tagging guidelines that includes methods for marking up the detailed structure of literary prose and poetry, drama, multilingual texts, linguistic corpora, textual commentary and criticism of texts, links and temporal structures, and much more, including methods for creating extensions (see Sperberg-McQueen).

Several "affiliated projects" are preparing large bodies of text in accordance with the TEI guidelines. For example, the Women Writers' Project at Brown University is collecting, keying, and marking up all available works by female authors of English from 1350 to 1900. The encoding is particularly ambitious in that goals include producing a paper edition closely approximating the layout of the originals as well as a useful electronic edition. Other projects are encoding the works of philosophers such as Wittgenstein, Pierce, and Nietzsche.

The Perseus Project at Harvard University has encoded much of Classical Greek literature, plus a variety of secondary sources and thousands of linked images, again using SGML as the basis (see Mylonas). The database and the search and navigation tools for this database will be available before publication of this volume.

The computational linguistics community has found that electronic lexica continually diverge as various researchers restructure and annotate them, making it difficult to combine the enhancements made by different groups. This discovery led to the founding of the Dictionary Encoding Initiative, which is developing an SGML-based interchange format for natural language processing lexica and closely cooperates with TEI.

The entire Oxford English Dictionary has been encoded descriptively and is available on optical media with structure-aware search tools that support retrieval on the basis of etymologies, pronunciations, citations, dates, and many other features of the text (Tompa, **Clear**).

Hypermedia Syntax: HyTime

Although hypertext and hypermedia have not been so amenable to standardization as has text per se, common threads in the several standardization efforts have been markup of structure as opposed to layout and frequently the use of SGML. Descriptive markup appears in a different guise for hypertext but, in short, involves marking up the fact and nature of the connection between linked objects, as opposed to the placement, form, or procedure for navigating among them.

A draft ISO standard called HyTime is now under consideration, which would provide methods for encoding links not only to text but to media, time-based phenomena, and anything else that can be modeled as a co-ordinate space (ISO). HyTime uses SGML as its syntactic basis, and many independent hypertext encoding efforts have chosen similar descriptive markup over previous proprietary forms.

Barriers to the Future

It seems then that the trend is strongly toward the kinds of markup we advocated in 1987: descriptive markup of document structure, rather than procedural or presentational markup of ink structure. However, several issues remain, and these must be addressed by descriptive models as time goes on. A few of those issues are presented in this section.

Tables, Equations, and Semi-textual Media

For both tables and equations, some have rejected descriptive markup on the spurious ground that it imposes a silly interface, such as typing pointy-brackets directly:

```
<sum><from>i=0</from><to>n</to><of>i</of></sum>
```

In fact neither descriptive markup in general nor SGML in particular requires silly interfaces; at the same time, neither procedural nor presentational markup is immune to them. Precisely the same internal or interchange representation can be generated from any style of interface the user desires. The equation could be assembled graphically, via menus, or even via a natural language interface and displayed in whatever form is most convenient at any given moment:

```
The sum of i, taken from i=0 to n.
```

We defined descriptive markup in terms of what kinds of labels are associated with text portions: ones that describe the meaning or function of those portions, as opposed to ones that describe the appearance or particular processing. If we apply this same definition, descriptive markup for equations means marking them up for the meaning or function of each component as opposed to the layout. This is precisely the approach mathematicians seem to prefer, given the widespread use of AMS-TEX, which uses essentially this model (American Mathematical Society). Procedural, nondescriptive markup for the same sum shown above would be more as shown below, an interface that seems far less appealing than even the least attractive descriptive alternative:

```
stack(8pt times 'n'; 24pt greek 'S';
    8pt times 'i=0') i
```

Effective representations for tables and equations still need work. Although the hierarchical model used by SGML is superior to the flat "series of paragraphs" model that preceded it, tables and equations can only be treated as hierarchies at the cost of some naturalness. Nevertheless, descriptive markup itself, whatever its syntactic form, retains the advantages originally claimed.

Name Spaces

The capability to transfer and archive large collections of documents immediately raises the issue of how they can be named, so that the same document can be retrieved by the same name tomorrow or next year. This problem reaches beyond the question of how individual documents are encoded, into technological issues of file system and network topology and social and political issues of information access, publication, and copyright. It interacts closely with one issue raised first by Nelson in relation to hypertext: what happens when documents change?

Version Management

Historically, the act of print publication created a fixed form, which could not be changed although, of course, a new edition could be published in addition. The high cost of production, particularly when new printing plates were required, also made new editions major events. These realities have kept the number of editions of most works very small and therefore made the management of versions tractable.

Now that authors can change documents cheaply and easily and can redistribute the result, nothing guarantees fixed form. Electronic documents change without notice for reasons ranging from the author's correction of errors to a reader's desire to print with a particular device. The old standby of citing the date or number of an edition no longer suffices to distinguish the actual version to which reference is being made.

As documents change, possibly along divergent paths, unique and temporally persistent names for each version must be assigned and managed if references to them (hypertextual or not) are to remain valid. None of the current cataloging and identification schemes is prepared for this contingency. Library-catalog-numbering schemes do record version information but provide no means for verifying that a version is what it claims to be or has not changed subtly without the cataloguer's knowledge. Publisher's systems such as the ISBN, or international identifier registration mechanisms such as ISO Formal Public Identifiers, could be used to assign a unique name to each version, but they impose no principled way of determining that two objects with different names are versions of each other. Much work is needed in this area, developing reliable means for cataloging, naming, distinguishing, and validating the variant forms of electronic documents.

Legal Vagueness

The problem of versions is compounded by a lack of legal clarity over issues of copyright and intellectual property. At a time when the durability of document value is decreasing, new laws have extended the duration of copyright. Further, recent decisions appear to have extended the scope of copyright in ways the academic community (and much of the legal community) has found objectionable.

The vagueness in what constitutes copyrightable creative effort has led to great multiplication of text-encoding effort. Several firms sell expensive electronic copies of the King James Bible, dating from 1611, obviously a questionable practice. I count no fewer than five projects that have independently annotated the Greek New Testament with similar part-of-speech tags, plus one more that was narrowly averted by last-minute license concessions from another.

Many academic efforts have been compelled to encode older, less reliable texts of major authors because of inability to come to terms with those holding copyright over newer editions. Sometimes publishers put so high a price on electronic editions that scholars recreate their own from scratch, which decreases sales and sometimes leads to a vicious cycle. In one recent incident scholars who were displeased with colleagues for failing to organize and release certain ancient texts quickly enough were moved to use computers to assemble the texts piece by piece from a concordance or inverted index and distribute that, to the dismay of some and delight of others (see Shanks).

The issues of copyright law are complex, bewilderingly so when their objects are in electronic form. However, it is of the utmost necessity to resolve them equitably, for the present waste of time, money, and effort is great indeed.

Conclusions

A variety of factors—technological, economic, social, and legal—have affected the acceptance and actual use of advanced models of document structure in preference to relatively primitive ink-and-paper-oriented models. As scholars attempt more and more to pass their documents around, to co-author across networks, and to use their documents for multiple applications rather than only printing, they will demand increased portability, standardization, and flexibility of representation.

Just as in 1987, descriptive markup continues to offer a clear path to many of these goals. These few years have seen great advances in the availability, sophistication, and interface quality of systems. The problems that keep us from fully realizing these goals are increasingly economic and social rather than technological or theoretical in nature.

The seemingly inexorable move toward on-line literature raises profound questions about the nature of intellectual property, authorial control over not only the content but also novel applications of their documents, and publishers' and readers' roles. It is to be hoped that the next few years will bring serious consideration of such issues and perhaps some effective resolutions.

Notes

1. The International Organisation for Standardisation (ISO) and a variety of industries are working together on a "universal character coding" standard, ISO 10646, which many hope will lead to a consistent solution to portability of data at this level.

2. See Meyrowitz, "Cholesterol," for a discussion of this proliferation.

Bibliography

American Mathematical Society. *AMS-TEX Version 2.1: User's Guide.* Providence: AMS, 1991.

Burkowski, Forbes J. "An Algebra for Hierarchically Organized Text-Dominated Databases." Manuscript. Department of Computer Science, U of Waterloo, 1991. (Portions previously appeared in "Intelligent Text and Image Handling," paper presented in Barcelona, Spain, April 1991 at RIAO '91.)

Bush, Vannevar. "As We May Think." Atlan*tic Monthly* 176 (July 1945): 101-08.

Carmody, Steven, Walter Gross, Theodor H. Nelson, David Rice, and Andries van Dam. "A Hypertext Editing System for the /360." *Pertinent Concepts in Computer Graphics.* Ed. M. Faiman and J. Nievergelt. Urbana: U of Illinois P, 1969. 291-330.

Catano, James. "Poetry and Computers: Experimenting with the Communal Text." *Computing and the Humanities* 13 (1979): 269-75.

Conklin, Jeff. "A Survey of Hypertext." MCC Technical Report Number STP-356-86, Rev. 1. Austin: Microelectronics and Computer Technology Corporation, 1986.

_____. "Hypertext: An Introduction and Survey." *IEEE Computer* 20 (1987): 17-41.

DeRose, Steven J., David G. Durand, Elli Mylonas, and Allen H. Renear. "What Is Text, Really?" *Journal of Computing in Higher Education* 1(1990): 3-26.

Engelbart, Douglas C., and William K. English. "A Research Center for Augmenting Human Intellect." 1968. *Computer-Supported Cooperative Work: A Book of Readings.* Ed. Irene Greif. San Mateo: Morgan Kaufmann, 1988. 81-105.

Feiner, Steven, S. Nagy, and Andries van Dam. "An Integrated System for Creating and Presenting Complex Computer-Based Documents." *Computer Graphics* 15 (August 1981): 181-89.

International Organisation for Standardisation. ISO 8879. *Information Processing—Text and Office Systems—Standard Generalized Markup Language (SGML).* 1st ed.—1986-10-15. Ref. No. ISO 8879-1986.

_____. "ISO/IEC DIS 10744: Hypermedia/Time-based Structuring Language: HyTime." Draft. 1991.

Killough, Ronnie Lynn. "Hypertext Interchange with the Dexter Model: Intermedia to KMS." Master's Project. Department of Computer Science, Texas A and M U, August 1990.

Meyrowitz, Norman. Closing address at Hypertext '87. Chapel Hill, 13-15 November 1987.

_____. "Hypertext—Does It Reduce Cholesterol, Too?" Keynote address at Hypertext '89. Pittsburgh, 6 November 1989. (Reprinted in *From Memex to Hypertext: Vannevar Bush and the Mind's Machine*. Ed. James M. Nyce and Paul Kahn. Boston: Academic P, 1992. 287-318.)

Mylonas, Elli, Gregory Crane, Kenneth Morrell, and D. Neel Smith. "The Perseus Project: Data in the Electronic Age." *Computing and the Classics*. Ed. J. Solomon and T. Worthen. Tempe: U of Arizona P, forthcoming.

Nelson, Theodor H. *Computer Lib/Dream Machines*. 1974. Seattle: Microsoft P, 1987.

Prusky, John. *FRESS Resource Manual*. Providence: Brown U Department of Computer Science, 1978.

Reid, Brian K. *Scribe: A Document Specification Language and Its Compiler*. Dissertation. Pittsburgh: Carnegie-Mellon U, 1980. (Available as Technical Report CMU-CS-81-100.)

Shanks, Hershel. "Why Transcripts of the Dead Sea Scrolls Had to Be Released." *Chronicle of Higher Education* 38 (2 October 1991): B1-B2.

Sperberg-McQueen, C. Michael, and Lou Burnard. *Guidelines for the Encoding of Machine-Readable Texts*. Chicago: Text Encoding Initiative, 1989.

Tompa, Frank W. "What Is (Tagged) Text?" *Dictionaries in the Electronic Age: Proceedings of the Fifth Annual Conference of the UW Centre for the New Oxford English Dictionary*. 1989. 81-93.

Part III

Textual Resources and Communication

Emerging Electronic Library Services and the Idea of Location Independence

Christinger Tomer
University of Pittsburgh

In the last decade, many academic libraries have installed on-line public access catalogs (OPACs). Recently many of them have also begun to provide users with dial-up access and access across various networks, including the Internet. As these connections have multiplied, the combination of electronic library services and connections across high-speed telecommunications networks have begun to transform both the use of library resources and the way in which users and librarians perceive the library. This chapter focuses on means and issues associated with the development of what Mark Kibbey and Nancy H. Evans have termed "location independence" (16), and it suggests how remote access to library resources may prove of special benefit to scholars in the humanities and other areas of scholarship highly reliant on library services.

Today electronic access to catalogs and other library resources provides users with Kibbey and Evans's location independence to the extent that access to certain basic library services is no longer necessarily a function of physical proximity.[1] In fact, researchers at the Massachusetts Institute of Technology can search the BARTON, MIT's electronic library catalog, or ALEX, the campuswide information service. Or they can use Harvard's campuswide information service, which includes an electronic gateway to HOLLIS, the catalog for the Harvard library system, or the catalogs of the members of the Boston Library Consortium. Or they can use MELVYL, the catalog of the University of California system, or the catalog at the Australian National University or INFOTRAX, the library information system at Rensselaer Polytechnic Institute in Troy, New York. (For an example of one established gateway, see Figure 1.) Perhaps more important, the array of options facing these hypothetical students at MIT seems to grow larger with each passing month.[2]

The Internet, the wide-area network that provides the transport for such services, is widely viewed as the province of the chemist, the physicist, and the engineer since so much attention and money has been concentrated on the use of computers and networks to enhance communications in areas such as science, technology, and biomedical research.[3] For this reason many tend to see scientists and engineers as the principal beneficiaries of the information services that the Internet can support. If, however, libraries have been and continue to be the laboratories for research in the humanities (and to a lesser degree, in the social sciences), then the availability of library catalogs and other library resources over the Internet (and other wide-area networks) may be as much as, if not more of, a boon for the linguist as for the physicist, because the linguist studying at an institution like the University of Pittsburgh now has access to several hundred OPACs that have been linked to the Internet and to an increasing number of literary resources offered in concert with Internet-accessible OPACs or via other services.

INFORMATION GATEWAY

```
NOTES: Instructions for beginning and ending each system will be provided
when you select a system. Please make a note of them. Each catalog will have
its own set of search commands. Follow the searching instructions given in
each system. There is a 20 minute limit on Information Gateway connections.

   1. Case Western Reserve University - "EUCLID" - the Library Catalog
   2. Cleveland Free-Net - Community Computer System
   3. Cleveland State University - "SCHOLAR" - the Library Catalog
   4. Cuyahoga County Public Library - "EASY-ACCESS" Catalog
   5. Kent State University - "CATALYST" - the Library Catalog
   6. Oberlin College - "OBIS"- the Library Catalog

   Enter Line # for Database        QUIT to Exit

   Enter choice:
```

Figure 1: Gateway service offered by the Cleveland Public Library.

In the short term, however, many crucial issues remain unresolved. Among them is the issue of how network-accessible library and information services may be made more useful for scholars in the humanities, who seem a technologically disaffected group. According to David Farrell, "Humanists have unreasonable expectations of the machine [i.e., the computer] and yet are ignorant of what it truly can do for them [whereas the] librarian knows better than anyone else the incredible power of the online catalog and the array of new resources in digitized format that serve the humanities" (69).

Scholars in the humanities face other problems as well. The language of the electronic environment is rife with obscure jargon and inside jokes; the electronic document is a comparatively complex thing whose successful presentation depends as much on the proper functioning of hardware and software as it does on the ideas it proposes to convey; and according to Stephen Lehmann and Patricia E. Renfro,

> The most fundamental distinction between researchers [in the humanities] and librarians is perhaps the emphasis on content by the one and on access by the other. Generally, the concerns of librarians—information organization, control, and access—hold the same kind of interest for scholars as a car does for family vacationers: it's what gets you there. The separation of process (technique, technology) from content accounts largely for librarians' failure to excite teaching faculty about library instruction and also explains, at least in part, their lack of interest in on-line searching. Librarians marvel at the retrieval power of on-line search systems, Boolean capabilities, keyword searching, and the rest of it, but the humanist scholar, after checking for his or her own publications, looks for that seminal work published in Belgium in 1937 and wonders what the use is of a system that does not include it. (410)

Geraldene Walker and Steven D. Atkinson suggest that if end-users in the humanities are to be included in the new computing capabilities available through integrated academic information environments, system and database designers must explicitly take them into account when creating the user interface—Walker and Atkinson advocate a mouse-activated, object-oriented command interface—and when selecting databases (31-32). What are the necessary conditions for getting scholars in the humanities to make regular, extensive use of OPACs and other electronically delivered library resources? According to Farrell, Lehmann and Renfro, and Walker and Atkinson, effective, uncomplicated navigational tools and simple-to-use but powerful search instruments are minimal requirements. Beyond that, one must have access to relevant databases and, since abstracting in the humanities tends to be more indicative and less directly informative than in the sciences, to full-text resources as well.

What sorts of navigational tools are available today? How easy is it to locate library catalogs and information services mounted on Internet-connected machines? To what extent are full-text services available at this point? This essay will assess the current situation and address those questions from the perspective of the end-user, with special reference to the existing resources that make location independence feasible for scholars in nontechnical areas such as the humanities. Within that context, the essay pursues three more specific aims. First, it examines some of the most basic, most popular approaches to navigating the Internet, focusing on how a user with access to the Internet can use the library resources and other information resources currently available across the network by means of the so-called software solutions. Here this essay emphasizes software solutions aimed mainly at end-users, in other words, client applications and front ends and shell scripts designed to support users who employ local and wide-area networks as means to other ends. The second objective is to consider the extent to which client-server implementations satisfy the general needs of users, focusing on trends likely to contribute in the long term to greater location independence for library users, particularly those in the humanities. Such trends include the development of an infrastructure for the creation and distribution of electronic texts and of a client-server model capable of providing an integrated approach to the identification, location, and use of network-based resources. The third objective is to assess, albeit briefly, the extent to which electronic access to library services is changing libraries and their relationships with clients.

Operational Basis for Location Independence

Connections and information serve as the crucial means of tapping the Internet's library resources. In terms of connections, the key is Telnet, the terminal emulation built on the TCP/IP (Transmission Control Protocol/Internet Protocol) suite. Telnet supports remote log-in, enabling local users to connect to a remote machine over the Internet, with the local machine emulating a terminal of the remote computer. (The file-transfer protocol [FTP], the other principal application built on the TCP/IP suite, allows users to transfer files in various formats from machine to machine on the Internet. Using FTP, one can transfer text [ASCII] files, software programs, graphic images, and other files that are not ASCII text, including files that have been reduced through use of a data compression utility.) Telnet requires a command specification, that specification being the address of the remote machine to which the user wants to connect. For example, a user with an account on a UNIX system with Internet access might enter the following command at the $ prompt: `telnet pittcat.cis.pitt.edu <Enter>`. Assuming that the remote service—in this case, PITTCAT, the OPAC of the University of Pittsburgh's libraries—is available, the local user obtains direct access to that service. In other instances, access to remote library resources may require the use of a logname; for example, to use HOLLIS, Harvard's electronic catalog, the user might enter the logname "hollis" when prompted by the system's gateway menu. In such circumstances Telnet acts as both client and terminal emulator while the remote machine acts as the server.

The problem with Telnet lies in the availability of the information needed to take advantage its capabilities. At the time of writing, the documentation concerning network resources of various types is wholly inadequate, and the addition of new information resources and services is growing at a rate that only exacerbates the problem of keeping abreast of these changes. At present three guides to libraries are available across the Internet, each of them informative and useful, none altogether adequate. The first guide is published by Art St. George of the University of New Mexico. The second, which first appeared during 1990, is prepared by Billy Barron of the University of North Texas. The third guide entitled *Library Catalogs on the Internet: Strategies for Selection and Use,* which was prepared by the American Library Association's Committee on Direct Patron Access to Computer-Based Reference Systems, has recently been released in electronic formats with a printed version scheduled to follow as an occasional paper of the American Library Association's Reference and Adult Services Division (ALA/RASD). St. George and Barron update their guides every three months, posting new versions on machines at the Universities of New Mexico and North Texas, respectively, in ASCII and Postscript versions. Barron also posts a WordPerfect 5.1 version, and he has recently added source code for versions of the directory that can be compiled and run on UNIX or VMS systems; this program, discussed below, is called Libtel.

One obtains access to updated versions of the lists via anonymous FTP, whereby the user logs onto the remote machine under the logname "anonymous" and the password "guest," thus gaining limited access to files usually posted in the directory /pub and branching subdirectories. The major library-oriented listservers, such as PACS-L, LIBREF-L, and GOVDOC-L, provide notice of availability. Although copies are posted at other sites, the primary sites for two guides are host ariel.unm.edu and host vaxb.acs.unt.edu.

Like the St. George and the Barron guides, the ALA/RASD guide is directed toward users interested in exploring the library catalogs on the Internet. In contrast to them, *Library Catalogs on the Internet* provides an overview of how to use the Internet to reach remote systems, lists resources for determining which catalogs are available and for selecting among them, and offers tips on navigating the Internet and using unfamiliar systems. Basically nontechnical in its approach, this guide's greatest value in the near term may be that it consolidates information that previously has been widely scattered. (In electronic format the ALA/RASD may be obtained via anonymous FTP from host dla.ucop.edu, directory pub/internet, filename libcat-guide, or host vaxb.acs.unt.edu, directory library, filename libcat-guide. Printed copies of the guide will also be deposited in the LOEX Clearinghouse on Library Instruction, where it can be borrowed by members, and in the ERIC system.)

It is interesting to note that the appearance of the guide prepared by Barron aroused some controversy among the librarians who contribute to PACS-L and other library-oriented listservers. At least a few observers felt that Barron's guide was an unnecessary duplication of effort, and their comments suggested that they feared the possibility that its availability might cause confusion among users. Barron countered that his guide offers the reader more detailed information about the use of the OPACs than does the documentation prepared by St. George. However, there is no evidence that the availability of two lists of Internet-accessible libraries has caused confusion; in fact, it seems more likely that the periodic publication of two lists has tended to promote greater awareness and hence use of the library resources accessible via Internet. It may also tend to make librarians more aware of the issues underlying the development of documentation for users of electronic library services. The availability of Libtel is also important, although few of the users who download Barron's list appear to have installed this software on their systems.

Software Solutions

Software developers are producing tools based on one or more of these directories to facilitate access to library catalogs and related resources. Some of these applications search the machine-readable copies of the Barron or the St. George library directories mounted on the hard disk of a personal computer; others are essentially gateway programs that provide directory information and initiate connections to specified remote services via batch files and/or executable binaries.

Peter Scott, a librarian at the University of Saskatchewan, has used a user-supported utility in the MS-DOS environment called Hyperrez, as the basis for an application called Hytelnet. Hyperrez is a serial interpreter that links ASCII files to create hypertextlike effects. Hytelnet is designed to permit easy browsing of the library systems listed in the St. George and the Barron directories. Since Hyperrez is memory-resident, one can call Hytelnet, search the listing of library systems, and ascertain the Internet address and log-in procedures for a specific system. Hyperrez, at least as configured by Scott, does not initiate a connection but is easily customized, and that customization could include not only updated listings but also batch files written to initiate connections with specified machines. (The current version of Hytelnet, release 5.0, is available via FTP from several hosts including vaxb.acs.unt.edu, directory library, filename hyteln60.zip.) More recently, Earl Fogel of the University of Saskatchewan has ported a version of Hytelnet to UNIX and VMS, thus enabling systems administrators to make this software guide available on multiuser systems. An important difference between the MS-DOS and the UNIX versions of Hytelnet is that the UNIX version is capable of initiating connections to remote services, a capability more easily implemented in this instance because UNIX is a multi-processing system. (For more information about this implementation, see Figure 2, which reproduces a list of full-text services as presented by the UNIX version of Hytelnet.)

Another MS-DOS application, a hypertext version of the Barron directory called CATALIST, runs under Microsoft Windows 3.0 and supports string searching by geographic location or name. Since it can be run in conjunction with Windows-compatible telecommunications software, a user can search CATALIST in one window, run Telnet in a second, and take notes in a third, assuming, of course, that the microcomputer running Windows is connected by a local-area network to an Internet node. (CATALIST, which was developed by Richard H. Duggan of the University of Delaware, is available via FTP from host zebra.acs.udel.edu, directory pub/library or host vaxb.acs.unt.edu, directory library/catalist.)

For UNIX or VMS hosts, the aforementioned shell script, Libtel, presents users with a menu-driven approach to access that lists most of the entries in the St. George guide, includes other types of databases and bulletin boards, and reduces initiating a connection to selection of a menu item corresponding to a requested system. First written by Dan Mahoney of the University of New Mexico, the script has been modified a number of times in the last twelve months, the latest versions being available via FTP from host ftp.oit.unc.edu, directory pub/docs, filename libtel. The UNIX version and a VMS version are also located at host vaxb.acs.unt.edu, directory library, filename libtel—for the UNIX version—or libtel.com—for the VMS version.

Another approach, at once more complicated and more practical, involves using the scripting capabilities of a UNIX-based command interpreter, such as the C shell or the Korn shell. A command interpreter is basically a gateway to other programs; in the extract provided below, the script provides the instructions necessary for the C shell to establish a gateway via Telnet to other machine services, using a simple method known as command aliasing to record and repeat on command the desired scripts facilitating connection to remote services.

For example, the alias "weather" connects to an information service at the University of Michigan's College of Engineering that provides menu-driven access to short- and long-term forecasts for major metropolitan areas, hurricane advisories, reports on ski conditions, and the latest data on earthquakes occurring in the United States and Canada. The alias "words" connects to a machine-readable version of *Webster's Collegiate Dictionary* that has been mounted on a NeXTstation at the University of Oregon.[4] The dictionary may be searched in several modes, including a mode that retrieves all entries containing the term specified in the search. The aliases "pittcat" and "cmucat" connect to the OPACs of the University of Pittsburgh

Full-Text Databases and Bibliographies

```
<FUL034> Aesop's Fables
<FUL026> Alice in Wonderland (Lewis Carroll)
<FUL001> Bible (King James Version)
<FUL038> BLAISE-LINE (British Library's On-Line Service)
<FUL002> Book of Mormon
<FUL039> British Library Document Supply Centre
<FUL003> Choice Book Reviews
<FUL035> Concise Oxford Dictionary, 8th Ed.
<FUL004> CONSER database (journal/serial/periodical indexes)
<FUL005> Constitutional Documents (USA)
<FUL006> Court of Appeals of Ohio, Eighth District, County of Cuyahoga
<FUL007> Dartmouth Dante Project
<FUL008> Environmental Education Database
<FUL009> ERIC (Educational Resources Information Center Documents)
<FUL031> Federalist Papers
<FUL010> General Accounting Office Documents
<FUL011> Government Publications (USA)
<FUL024> Hacker's Dictionary
<FUL028> Hunting of the Snark (Lewis Carroll)
<FUL012> Koran
<FUL013> Library of Congress Cataloging (DRA)
<FUL014> Magazine Index
<FUL015> Martin Luther King Jr. Bibliography at Stanford University
<FUL030> Moby Dick (Herman Melville)
<FUL016> NPTN/USA Today Headline News
<FUL037> Oxford Dictionary of Familiar Quotations (and Modern Q.)
<FUL036> Oxford Thesaurus
<FUL017> ONLINE newsletter & ONLINE libraries and microcomputers
<FUL032> Paradise Lost (John Milton)
<FUL029> Peter Pan (J.M.Barrie)
<FUL018> Project Hermes (Supreme Court Decisions)
<FUL025> Roget's Thesaurus 1911 edition
<FUL019> Shakespeare's Plays and Sonnets
<FUL033> Song of Hiawatha (Longfellow)
<FUL020> State of Hawaii Data Book
<FUL027> Through the looking glass (Lewis Carroll)
<FUL021> UnCover (Periodicals information)
<FUL022> Webster's Dictionary
<FUL023> World Factbook
```

Figure 2: A list of full-text sources accessible via Hytelnet 6.0.

and Carnegie Mellon University, respectively. The alias "cpl" connects to the Cleveland Public Library system, the alias "carl" to the system maintained by the Colorado Alliance of Research Libraries, the alias "mss" to the FOLIO service at Princeton, which provides access to a machine-readable version of the *Monthly Catalog of United States Government Publications* as well as to Princeton's manuscript collections, and "wais" to the experimental server that has been established by the National Science Foundation to support the continuing development of the WAIS protocol. The alias "archie," run in conjunction with a command specification, loads a client application that queries a server at McGill University in Montreal and reports on the whereabouts of specified files or programs on Internet-accessible servers.[5] And so on.

Client-Server Models

Wide Area Information Servers

Efforts to implement various client-server relationships across wide-area networks expand upon similar themes. Perhaps most promising from the perspective of library service is the so-called Wide Area Information Server (WAIS) protocol, which is currently under development by Thinking Machines, Incorporated, of Cambridge, Massachusetts. The basic concept underlying the WAIS protocol is that in a client-server relationship, a client can formulate a search strategy on a local machine and then carry out the search in terms of a series of databases arrayed across a network.

The WAIS system attempts to automate what librarians call the "reference interview." Traditionally, a reader presents the reference librarian with a question, and the reference librarian then asks a few background questions, the answers to which enable the librarian to identify appropriate sources and to select a set of potentially relevant articles, reports, or references. The reader subsequently sorts through the selected materials to find the most pertinent documents, redefining relevance on the basis of the contents of the documents and revising the terms of the follow-up search, if one is necessary.

The WAIS system has three components. A client program provides the user interface. Servers index databases and retrieval documents, and a standard protocol transmits queries and responses. The client and the server are isolated from each other through the protocol. The WAIS protocol is open: any client capable of translating a user's request into the standard protocol may be used in the system; similarly, any server capable of responding to a request encoded in the protocol may be used. Since the WAIS system permits natural language queries, the client application translates a question into the WAIS protocol and transmits it over a network to a server. The server receives the transmission, translates the received packet into its own query language, and searches for documents satisfying the query. The list of relevant documents is then encoded in the protocol and transmitted back to the client. The client decodes the response and displays the results. The documents can then be retrieved from the server.

The WAIS scheme compensates for the attendant problems of natural-language queries by providing "relevance feedback," which enables users to mark select documents from a retrieved set as relevant and then rerun the search in order to identify documents with similar content. The prototype implementation defines "similarity" by the number of common words in the description of a file or its contents. (In the implementation devised by Thinking Machines, the protocol is compliant with ANSI Z39.50: *Information Retrieval Service Definition and Protocol Specification for Library Applications.* To promote the development of both clients and servers, the protocol specification is public, as is its initial implementation. Any client that is capable of translating a user's request into the standard protocol can be used in the system. Likewise, any server capable of answering a request encoded in the protocol may be used.)

The WAIS system, which was initially designed for use by accountants and corporate executives relatively untrained in on-line search techniques, has four important characteristics. First, it uses English-language queries rather than a special-purpose query language; second, it provides a standard interface so that clients need to familiarize themselves with only one front end; third, the WAIS system is capable of concurrently searching many sources and many different types of sources within the framework of the standard interface; and, fourth, the system augments queries with relevance feedback.

As the WAIS system or ones like it develop, accessible sources of information will proliferate, making it difficult for users to keep track of all servers that may be available at any one time. To help solve this problem, a directory of servers will be established; Thinking Machines already maintains such a directory of servers in a widely accessible location. The directory, which contains indexed textual descriptions of all known servers, may be queried like any other source. Instead of returning text documents, however, it returns source structures—specially formatted files which can be used as the basis for queries.

To provide an illustration of how the concept works in practice, Thinking Machines has established a series of demonstrations and trials across the Internet, including a link that allows users who have installed the beta or alpha version of the

WAIS software to employ their machines as clients and to search a network-accessible version of Barron's catalog of Internet library resources mounted on a server at the University of North Texas. (See Figure 3.)

```
SWAIS   Source Selection Sources: 18

#     Server                      Source                Cost
01:   [next2.oit.unc.edu]         NeXT.FAQ              Free
02:   [uncvx1.oit.unc.edu]        unc-jobs              Free
03:   [next2.oit.unc.edu]         ibm.pc.FAQ            Free
04:   [quake.think.com]           directory-of-servers  Free
05:   [hub.nnsc.nsf.net]          ietf-documents        Free
06:   [hub.nnsc.nsf.net]          internet-drafts       Free
07:   [quake.think.com]           internet-rfcs         Free
08:   [cmns.think.com]            info-mac              Free
09:   [quake.think.com]           US-Gov-Programs       Free
10:   [cossack.cosmic.uga.e]      cosmic-abstracts      Free
11:   [cossack.cosmic.uga.e]      cosmic-programs       Free
12:   [wais.eff.org]              eff-documents         Free
13:   [sol.acs.unt.edu]           online-libraries      Free
14:   [microworld.media.mit]      poetry                Free
15:   [cmns.think.com]            wall-street-journal   Free
16:   [cmns.think.com]            world-factbook        Free
17:   cmns.think.com]             usenet-cookbook       Free
18:   [cmns.think.com]            sun-mail              Free

Keywords: <space> selects, w for keywords, arrows move,
<return> searches, q quits, or ?
```

Figure 3: Opening screen of National Science Foundation's experimental WAIS. The term SWAIS signifies that Thinking Machines's prototype server for UNIX is in use.

Imagine that a client needs to know the current gross national product of Peru but has no idea where to find it. Access to a directory of servers will enable identifying likely sources of relevant information; for example, a search of the directory that Thinking Machines has mounted at hub.nnsc.nsf.net would identify several documents, including the *World Factbook*, an almanac maintained by the CIA and made available electronically by Project Gutenberg. This document could then serve as the source field of a question, and the query would rerun against the almanac. (Brewster Kahle, one of the principal architects of the WAIS system, has also noted that a directory of servers provides a means for information providers to advertise the availability of new data and services. When a new source becomes available or an existing source undergoes significant changes in content or structure, the developers can submit a textual description, along with the necessary information for contacting the server. This information is added to the directory, thus allowing users to revise prior and/or standing searches in view of newly available resources.)

The developers of the WAIS protocol realize how applications of this intellectual technology might affect publishing and libraries and readers. In an essay posted on 28 December 1991 to the Usenet newsgroup called alt.wais, Kahle wrote:

> When written material is distributed over wires, the difference between a public library and a bookstore becomes fuzzy, raising difficult problems for the venerable tradition of free access to information in the public library system. . . . Public libraries have served two clashing goals, to allow open access to published information and to archive written history for future scholars and posterity. This uneasy combination has been joined into a single institution—public libraries, both centralized and branch—due to the technology of distribution of information, paper. . . . As electronic distribution (so called, electronic publishing) becomes common for different segments of written material, access and archiving become quite different, since making a copy is easy and inexpensive, and delivering a copy can be done without requiring a person to come into the library. . . . The result of this technology [in] change can be an exciting one where the public library system can refine its charter and serve the public in a . . . way that was not possible with paper. The unique aspects of libraries—service oriented staff, lack of profit motive, prevalent locations, and the role in schools—can give them a more important role in the future than they ever had in the paper era.

Kahle envisions a future in which the public library is replaced by a network of "reading rooms" that stock popular reading materials and provide access to electronic archives of materials of various types. In Kahle's conception, a reading room would offer readers access to all published information in printed form or for screen display via network access to various library collections. The reading room would also furnish computers for browsing and reading of machine-readable files, a printer and binder for printing copies of such files for clients, and a librarian during regular hours. Interlibrary loan would be used when a particular volume is needed.

The main problem with the existing WAIS system lies in the searching mechanism, which is at once sophisticated and crude. The WAIS system has important desirable features, including its support for natural-language queries and its relevance-feedback mechanism, and its client interfaces, particularly those running on Macintosh and NeXT computers, are easy to master and manipulate. But the current implementation, admittedly experimental in nature, does not allow searches based on Boolean operators, nor does it allow searches limited to specified fields. (However, as an extension of Z39.50 and the prototype for projected commercial applications, it is reasonable to imagine that WAIS will be enhanced to support Boolean and limited field searches.) Furthermore, some evidence exists, albeit anecdotal and inconclusive, that suggests the relevance-feedback mechanism does not support end-user needs as effectively as expected. But that problem may be as much a product of the fact that all but one of the servers available under the NSFNet implementation of the WAIS system are noncommercial databases prepared to run under the WAIS protocol by volunteer labor and on serial machines. According to Craig Stanfill of Thinking Machines,

> For WAIS to succeed, it must be possible to build full text retrieval systems which can deliver quick responses (1-2 seconds is ideal) when searching databases having anywhere from a few megabytes of text, e.g, a personal database, to hundreds, thousands, or even tens of thousands of gigabytes. Some databases can be adequately served by serial machines, e.g., personal or departmental databases having a few megabytes to one gigabyte of data. Other databases—those which are either extremely large or accessed very heavily, e.g., an external database service—will require levels of performance which cannot be attained on serial machines. For these databases, parallel text servers are an appropriate technology.

Internet Gopher System

Another, similar approach to information sharing across the Internet is the so-called Internet Gopher system, which has been developed at the University of Minnesota. This system is a distributed document-delivery service that enables users to access various types of data residing on multiple hosts in what its designers refer to as "seamless fashion." The Internet Gopher system presents users with a hierarchical arrangement of documents by using a client-server communications model, with clients available for platforms running UNIX, VMS, MVS, CMS, Macintosh OS, MS-DOS, and the NeXT OS (and an experimental set for real-time radio).

The Gopher protocol consists of a client's connecting to a server and sending the server a selector (a line of text, which may be blank) via TCP/IP. The server responds with a block of text terminated with a period on a line by itself, after which it closes the connection. No state is retained by the server between transactions with a client.

The simplicity of the protocol is based on the common need at the campus-wide-network level to implement quickly and efficiently servers and clients for the slow, smaller desktop computers (for example, Macintosh and MS-DOS machines). In the Internet Gopher system, the clients basically function as navigational tools that enable users to move through servers and files on servers. The servers are interconnected; once the Gopher client has connected to a Gopher server, the user can browse through information on any additional Gopher servers about which the first server knows. The server presents and the client displays information in the form of lists of items; items can be files, directories containing other directories or files, or access to searching capabilities on index servers.

The Gopher protocol was designed to resemble a file system because file systems provide good models for locating documents and services. The Gopher client software presents users with a hierarchy of items and directories; in fact, the items are files and services mounted on machines arrayed across the network. From the perspective of the user, the Internet Gopher appears similar to MS-DOS 5.0's DOS shell for file management, since it transforms the complex business of navigating across a network and locating relevant material on a remote server into the simple task of activating the appropriate buttons.[6]

In addition to browsing through hierarchies of documents, Gopher users may submit queries to Gopher search servers. In most instances the search servers have full-text indexes for a set of documents; the response to a query is a list of documents that matched the search criteria. Internet Gopher servers accept simple queries sent over a TCP connection, to which they respond by sending the client a document or a list of documents. This distributed protocol permits the use of many servers and makes this network of servers both extensible and effectively fault-tolerant, although the current network's reliance on the server at the University of Minnesota, Minneapolis, tends to undermine operational stability.

Which approach is better, WAIS or the Internet Gopher? At this point the Internet Gopher system seems the more timely, if not the better, implementation, especially for unsophisticated or nontechnical users. WAIS is a potentially powerful retrieval tool, but the Internet Gopher system addresses the more immediate, more basic problem of enabling new or infrequent users of network-based services to navigate them easily and efficiently. For example, connecting to the weather-information service at the University of Michigan's College of Engineering within the framework of the Gopher system simply requires clicking on a series of so-called radio buttons. In fact, Gopher clients provide an interface to the weather-information service that enables users to employ radio buttons to select the type of report desired and to specify the location of interest. Similarly, Gopher clients enable users to select and connect to various library services by means of radio buttons, thus enabling a local user to locate and then engage the services of a remote machine without having to negotiate the Internet address or the terminal emulation.

Not surprisingly, the Internet Gopher system serves as the basis for the campuswide information system at the University of Minnesota and a couple of dozen other colleges and universities. Another practical advantage of the Gopher system is the availability of easy-to-install clients for microcomputers operating under MS-DOS and the Macintosh OS whereas the MS-DOS and Microsoft Windows clients for WAIS are considerably more difficult to install. However, at least two factors tend to favor WAIS in the long run; first, the WAIS protocol is expected to support increasingly sophisticated searching procedures in a development environment consistent with the ANSI Z39.50 standard for library technologies; and, second, the WAIS protocol is expected to realize its greatest potential with the widespread use of large-scale parallel processing by the information industry and other information providers. In contrast, the Internet Gopher system is clearly an intellectual technology whose greatest value lies in the short term—or until the physical technologies upon which it is based become obsolete.

Electronic Books

The growing trend toward electronic books and journals raises the question, How close are we to full-text libraries in electronic form? That is a difficult question to answer, but there are reasons to believe that the access to libraries of this sort will be available within the next decade or so. For example, the version of the High-Performance Computing Act of 1989 sponsored by Senator Albert Gore of Tennessee proposed the creation of a National Digital Library, which would have been developed at a projected expense of $820 million. The textual materials held by the Library of Congress, roughly 25 terabytes of data, provided the basis for the proposed library. Gore envisioned that users with access to the National Research and Education Network (NREN) could search the catalog of the Library of Congress and download copies of relevant books and journals via a file-transfer utility; in effect, scholars throughout the United States, and perhaps beyond, would have more or less direct access to the holdings of the Library of Congress. The 1989 version of the legislation failed, owing mainly to an inability to clarify the issues of funding and governance, and subsequent versions of the so-called NREN legislation have not included the proposal for a National Digital Library. But the seed has been planted, and it seems reasonable to imagine that at some point in this decade Congress will enact legislation authorizing the creation of a National Digital Library.

In the meantime, there are other projects aimed at establishing the basis for full-text, on-line libraries, most notably Project Gutenberg at Illinois Benedictine University, the Advantage Foundation's Paperless Library program, the Oxford Text Archive, the Georgetown Center for Text and Technology, the National Center for Machine-Readable Texts in the Humanities at Princeton University, and the Text Encoding Initiative (see also **Virbel**).[7] Project Gutenberg, which is directed by Michael Hart of the University of Illinois, began twenty years ago "as an attempt to explore the text-crunching applications of mainframe computers, and has evolved, with the advent of personal computers, into a more decentralized structure, stitched together by network communications." Project Gutenberg's goals for the 1990s are to place a collection of ten thousand of the "most used books" in electronic form and reduce "the effective costs to the user to the price of roughly one cent per book plus the cost of media and of shipping and handling." At the operational level, Hart's plan calls for contributions in the form of digitized text from individuals and organizations with access to scanning technologies and connections to networks such as BITNET or the Internet. Today, copies of several works by Lewis Carroll (including *Alice's Adventures in Wonderland*), *The Book of Mormon*, *The Song of Hiawatha*, *The Federalist Papers*, *The World Factbook*, and *Moby Dick* are available through Project Gutenberg. In the next twelve months or so, Hart expects to post copies of *Peter Pan*, *Paradise Lost*, the first edition of G. & C. Merriam's *International Unabridged Dictionary*, the *New English Dictionary on Historical Principles* (through the 1916 installment), the eleventh edition of the *Encyclopaedia Britannica*, and the *Century Dictionary*.

The PaperLess Library is an ongoing project of the Advantage Foundation, a nonprofit organization dedicated to preserving and distributing the great literature of the world in paperless form. Thus far, the Paperless Library includes *Common Sense* by Tom Paine; *The Adventures of Sherlock Holmes*, *The Sign of Four*, and *A Study in Scarlet* by Arthur Conan Doyle; *Around the World in Eighty Days* by Jules Verne; *The Adventures of Huckleberry Finn* and *The Adventures of Tom Sawyer* by Mark Twain; the United States Constitution; *The Time Machine* and *The War of the Worlds* by H.G. Wells; and *The Great Gatsby* by F. Scott Fitzgerald. These works may be downloaded free of charge from the Advantage Foundation's bulletin-board system (BBS) at Houston, Texas, or via CompuServe, where copies have been posted to the IBMNEW Forum. (Readers not familiar with CompuServe should note that for the basic service there is a charge of $12.50 per connect hour. It should also noted that access to the Foundation's BBS entails long-distance telephone charges outside the Houston area, so the notion that the books noted above are available cost free is an arguable one.)

The Oxford Text Archive is, according to Jack Kessler, "an ambitious national effort to establish a depository library for every full-text file produced in the UK—

along the lines of depository libraries everywhere and, more particularly, the British Lending Library at Boston Spa—and it appears to be succeeding" ("Summary"). More scholarly in its approach and more highly developed than Project Gutenberg, the Oxford Text Archive now has approximately one thousand texts on tapes, which they distribute at a cost of roughly £ 5 (UK) per text. Texts available through the Oxford Text Archive include selections from the *Anglo Saxon Chronicle*, the *Alliterative Morte Arthure*, and collections of early and modern Arabic prose. (The catalog list of the Oxford Text Archive may be obtained by e-mail from LISTSERV@BROWNVM.BITNET with the message `GET OTALIST FORMAT` for a formatted file, or `GET OTALIST SGML` for a tagged file. General e-mail inquiries about the Oxford Text Archive should go to ARCHIVE@VAX.OXFORD.AC.UK.)

Perhaps equally ambitious are the efforts of the Georgetown Center for Text and Technology, which is at present engaged in more than three hundred projects on a worldwide basis. Projects include a concordance to Carroll's *Alice* and *Looking Glass*, a compendium of medieval German lyric poetry, a corpus of English-Canadian writing, electronic versions of Browning and Tennyson, a Masoretic text of the Hebrew Bible, anthologies of Italian music and lyric poetry of the Renaissance, and a digital archive and thesaurus of Spanish texts.

The Text Encoding Initiative is a cooperative undertaking of the Association for Computers and the Humanities (ACH), the Association for Computational Linguistics (ACL), and the Association for Literary and Linguistic Computing (ALLC), to formulate and disseminate guidelines for the encoding and interchange of machine-readable texts. Its goal is to formulate and disseminate guidelines for the encoding and interchange of machine-readable texts intended for literary, linguistic, historical, or other textual research. The need for the program stems mainly from the chaotic diversity of the encoding schemes used for such texts, which make difficult moving texts from one software program to others; researchers who exchange texts with others also lose valuable time deciphering the texts and converting them into their local encoding scheme. The primary goal of the Text Encoding Initiative is to provide explicit guidelines that define a text format suitable for data interchange and data analysis, that is, to define a format for encoding texts in a linear data stream that is suitable for the interchange of textual material between researchers and to provide concrete recommendations, for those who can use them, about what features of texts should usually be encoded. A basic aim is to establish a standard for information interchange that is hardware- and software-independent, rigorous in its definition of textual objects, easy to use, and compatible with existing standards. The Standard Generalized Markup Language (SGML) serves as the basic notation for the encoding recommended by the guidelines. The other major intended use is as a guide for those encoding texts for general use.

Yet another interesting conjunction of resources appears in the increasing number of institutions that have established gateways that enable the users of their OPACs to utilize select full-text resources. For example, authorized users of the CARL system have access to Grolier's *Encyclopedia* and *CHOICE*. Users of Dartmouth's OPAC are offered access to Shakespeare's plays and sonnets. And at Carnegie Mellon, authorized users have access to twelve reference sources, including a dictionary, an encyclopedia, and a series of periodical databases; in effect, Carnegie Mellon's libraries have put a so-called ready-reference collection on line.

On the commercial front, publishers have begun to pursue the development of markets for electronic books and journals. A new electronic journal, The *Online Journal of Current Clinical Trials,* is scheduled to appear in April 1992.[8] In the event that *Current Clinical Trials* succeeds, it will almost certainly be followed by a flurry of interest in electronic formats among the publishers of professional and scholarly journals now offered as print-on-paper documents. The development of sufficiently large markets for electronic journals in subject areas such as medicine, business, and the basic sciences will enable publishers to maintain revenues at relatively high levels while they slash operating costs by as much as seventy-five to eighty percent by eliminating the costs of printing, binding, and postage.

The conventional wisdom is that commercial publication of electronic books may take somewhat longer. Yet there are reasons to believe otherwise. For example, it seems reasonable to assume that the vast majority of the books published in this country today have been written, edited, and/or prepared for printing in machine-readable formats and that, like the on-line database services that began a generation ago as by-products of computerized typesetting, the first generations of commercially produced electronic books will soon begin to appear as part of a tentative exploration of a new market. It is difficult to know what sort of a reception such publications will receive, but in view of the remarkable social and technological transformations that characterized the 1980s—and in view of the fact that book publishing is an industry whose profitability is severely limited by its antiquated approaches to production and distribution—it may be improvident to expect the growth of the electronic book's niche in library and literary markets will be anything short of remarkable.

Conclusion

"Location independence" may be an inelegant term, but the phenomenon it describes may prove to be the most important library-related development of this century, inasmuch as it will tend to level the informational plane on which resourceful students and scholars operate. As noted by Thomas Peters, in his *Online Catalog:*

A Critical Examination of Use, "remote access to online catalogs makes distance less important in the process of identifying, locating, and retrieving information." It is interesting that Peters writes that "the purpose of the library catalog is no longer clear.... The era of computerization has radically altered the old economies of scale, so the information profession should be thinking in terms of institutional, regional, national, or even international information storage and retrieval systems." It may also lead to forms of collaboration and collectivization that enable groups of libraries to pursue more fully the manifold missions of the institution—which is to say that distributed approaches to library service should enable libraries to collect, to preserve, and to deliver services on scales that approach the professional ideals of many generations of librarians. There is a politics of library technology, and therein resides the possibility that the intelligent, caring use of information technology may produce a reduction in elitism, since the connectivity born of these technologies allows users from many different strata of scholarship to gain access to the same information.

Many assume that scholars in the humanities are generally not interested in attaining the modest degree of technical competence that until recently navigating the Internet required. Many also assume that location independence is important to most scholars in the humanities only if it is supported by tools that render the tasks of locating and retrieving relevant data brutally simple. However, when offered access to resources like those described above, scholars in nontechnical disciplines will likely begin to explore the Internet and eventually begin to reinvent aspects of it for their own purposes.

Will the tools they require be retrieval oriented like WAIS or file oriented like Gopher? The answer is that, at least ideally, they will have the option of selecting from among an array of tools that differ in terms of their function and their performance.

The problems? First among them is certainly the issue of intellectual property rights. The plasticity of machine-readable data and the relative ease with which files may be moved across networks threaten the stability afforded by copyright law. Such problems are only exacerbated by software tools that simplify navigation and by the availability of transferable full-text sources. On the other hand, in the United States, where the primary beneficiary of the copyright statute is supposed to be the public interest, the controversies attending the growth and implementation of ideas like location independence may provide the impetus needed to reconcile the social consequences of technological progress with the more proprietary underpinnings of intellectual progress. Another problem, perhaps no less serious than the first, is that for all of the virtues of the Internet, location independence, WAIS, and electronic

---

books, none are likely to help stem the rising tide of largely useless data that threatens to overwhelm the libraries and information systems upon which we depend.

Notes

1. Why search library catalogs and other information resources across the Internet? At present it permits library users to collect and evaluate bibliographic data from other, remote collections. The remote OPAC system may have searching capabilities, such as keyword searching, Boolean operators, searching two or more fields, and the like, that a local OPAC lacks; for example, the OPACs based on the Innovative Interfaces system, such as the JANUS system at the University of Oregon, allow users to identify topically related materials by reproducing relevant portions of the shelf list and/or running searches based on related subject headings. Or users may wish to exploit the fact that an increasing number of libraries have established gateways to specialized indexes created at the local level, for example, the University of Michigan's Meeman Archive on environmental journalism, the full text of Shakespeare plays and sonnets at Dartmouth, or site-licensed commercial services, such as INFOTRAC database at the Cleveland Public Library or the *CHOICE* book reviews on Colorado's CARL system. (See Figure 1.) In the future, it seems likely that library users in one location will be able to identify the availability of and initiate requests for certain services at other locations through network access to OPACs.

2. In the longer term the next major phase in the development of information transfer will come about as libraries of electronic books and journals become available and as continuing efforts to automate basic aspects of the search-and-retrieval process reach the next significant plateau of development. Then users will have the means to locate textual information distributed across a network, the wherewithal to search library collections on a integrated basis, and the capability to configure access on the basis of a personalized scheme. Key factors in this scenario are the development of protocols and tools that will enable users to locate pertinent resources arrayed across a wide-area network and then search them as an integrated source. In this extension of the client-server model, software loaded on a desktop workstation will prompt the user for relevant search criteria, organize the data, and then query a remote directory of servers in order to identify potentially relevant sources. The user will then select a source server or set of source servers to be searched, at which point the search engine will attempt to match the specified search criteria against descriptions and/or the contents of entries in the targeted source server(s). In response, a list of documents will be presented to the user, and the items selected from that list will be displayed in full text on the client's screen display or written to a remote storage device at the instruction of the user. In this scenario the network will be the library, every source will be, at least potentially, a reference tool, and the desktop computer will be a gateway to libraries and books and newspapers and journals.

3. "The Internet is a network of networks. Each subsidiary net adheres to a minimal set of common protocols that allow data to pass transparently among computers attached to the

Internet, even though the various networks may use different data formats, transmission rates or low-level routing algorithms" (Cerf 79). The basis for connections and the exchange of data across the Internet is the TCP/IP protocol—Transmission Control Protocol/Internet Protocol. The backbone of the network has been upgraded to T-1 bandwidth (1.544Mbps), and there are ongoing experiments with T-3 bandwidth (44.736Mbps) capacity, which is expected to be the bandwidth at which the National Research and Education Network (NREN) operates initially. "This vast interconnection of computers provides an unparalleled infrastructure for resource sharing. An Internet user can connect to a computer on the other side of the world as quickly and easily as if it were in the next room. Mail messages can be delivered to any of thousands of individual mail boxes in dozens of countries. Large computer files can be transferred quickly with a few brief commands. These capabilities are bringing a vast array of resources to our desktops at little or no charge to users" (American Library Association).

4. Since this chapter was first drafted, systems administrators at the University of Oregon have blocked access from machines outside their domain, thus reserving this service for local clients. It is not clear whether this action was taken in order to comply with the terms of the agreement with the dictionary's publisher or as a tactic for dealing with excessive external demands on the relevant files. In any event an earlier version of *Webster's Collegiate Dictionary* is mounted on a machine at MIT and may be queried through an extension of GNU Emacs.

5. Until recently, locating files mounted on anonymous FTP servers was a haphazard affair. Jon Granrose's monthly list of anonymous FTP sites was helpful in general terms—the brief annotations might indicate, for example, that scripts written in PERL are posted at a particular site—but there was typically no indirect way of verifying that a specific application or version of an application had been posted to a site. However, the advent of the Archie system has gone a long way toward solving the problem. Archie is an Internet archive server listing service first established at McGill University. There are now Archie servers at several locations and on faster machines, in addition to the original server that continues operation at Montreal. The main feature of the Archie system is that it allows a user to query a database containing a list of software available via anonymous FTP on hosts connected to the Internet network and obtain a report locating the files in question by IP address, subdirectory, and filename(s). For hosts with more limited access, for example, services attached to BITNET, NetNorth, EARN, and so on, the software may be obtained by electronic mail through the Princeton bitftp service. The Archie system itself is designed to be accessed interactively or through e-mail. To use the interactive system, a user connects to the host system via Telnet, using the logname "archie." No password is required. Searching is based on the full name of the file sought, but it is also possible to conduct a search based on a more limited expression. There are client applications for the Archie system, which enable remote users to search the database without Telnet, and there is also an e-mail interface, which allows remote users to send and receive the results of queries via e-mail.

6. A major advantage of the Internet Gopher system is that the file-system metaphor is extensible. By giving a type attribute to items in the pseudo-file system, it is possible to accommodate both simple text documents and more complicated forms. As a result, complex

database services, such as OPACs, can be handled as a separate type of item. Moreover, a file-system metaphor does not preclude database-style queries for access to documents. To provide database-style queries for access to information, a database server type is defined in Gopher's pseudo-file system.

7. The level of activity in this area has reached a point great enough that Meckler has recently issued the *Directory to Fulltext Online Resources* edited by Kessler.

8. *Clinical Trials* is a cooperative venture involving the American Association for the Advancement of Science (AAAS) and OCLC (Online Computer Library Center). According to its founding editor, *Clinical Trials* "will be the first journal to make immediately available findings that could save or extend the lives of critically ill patients." The journal, which will be fully abstracted in *Biosis*, will provide hypertext links to abstracts of cited articles, thus enabling readers to scan any journal article's references within a pop-up window on screen without leaving the issue they are reading. Although there are a number of electronic journals already available via computer networks, *Clinical Trials* is most likely the first electronic journal to incorporate hypertext links from typeset text to charts and graphics.

Bibliography

American Library Association. *Library Resources on the Internet: Strategies for Selection and Use.* Chicago: American Library Association, 1991.

Atkinson, Steven D., Judith Hudson, and Geraldene Walker. "The User Interface for CD-ROM and OPAC Systems." *Interfaces for Information Retrieval and Online Systems.* Ed. Martin Dillon. Westport: Greenwood Press, 1990. 277-96.

Basch, Reva. "Books Online: Visions, Plans and Perspectives for Electronic Text." *ONLINE* 14 (July 1991): 13-23.

Cerf, Vinton G. "Networks." *Scientific American* 265 (September 1991): 42-51.

Davis, Franklin, Brewster Kahle, Harry Morris, Jim Salem, Tracy Shen, Rod Wang, John Sui, and Mark Grinhbaum. "WAIS Interface Protocol Prototype Functional Specification." Unpublished paper. Cambridge: Thinking Machines Corporations, 1990.

Farrell, David. "The Humanities in the 1990s: A Perspective for Research Libraries and Librarians." *Library Hi Tech* 9 (1991): 69-71.

Hart, Michael. "Information about Project Gutenberg." BITNET communication, 11 May 1990.

Humanist Discussion Group. Vol. 4, No. 0371, 7 August 1990.

Kessler, Jack. "Full-Text Online Summary." PACS-L communication, 7 July 1991.

_____, ed. *Directory to Fulltext Online Resources 1992*. Westport: Meckler, 1992.

Kibbey, Mark, and Nancy H. Evans. "The Network Is the Library." *EDUCOM Review* Fall 1989: 15-20.

Lehmann, Stephen, and Patricia E. Renfro. "Humanists and Electronic Information Services: Acceptance and Resistance." *College and Research Libraries* 52 (September 1991): 409-13.

Library Resources on the Internet: Strategies for Selection and Use. Ed. Laine Farley. An electronic publication of the American Library Association, Reference and Adult Services Division. Chicago, 1991.

Peters, Thomas. *The Online Catalog: A Critical Examination of Public Use*. Jefferson, NC: McFarland, 1991.

Stanfill, Craig. "Massively Parallel Information Retrieval for Wide Area Information Servers." Paper presented at the IEEE International Conference on Systems, Man, and Cybernetics, Charlottesville, VA, July 1991.

Stein, Richard Marlon. "Browsing through Terabytes." *BYTE* 16 (May 1991): 157-60, 162-64.

The British National Corpus

Jeremy H. Clear
Oxford University Press

Corpus-Based Lexicography

This paper discusses the uses of large English-language text corpora, with a particular emphasis on corpus-based lexicography, and on the tools and methods employed in exploiting a computerized corpus of modern English within the dictionary departments of the Oxford University Press (OUP).

By way of introduction, I shall place the discussion of the corpus and associated resources on which I am currently working within a very much simplified historical and theoretical frame. Throughout this paper I use the word *corpus* as shorthand for a computerized collection of authentic, naturally occurring language (either spoken, written, or both). My particular interest is in large corpora, and generally I mean by this that it is practical to observe and analyze the corpus with the aid of a computer. This emphasis on size is important, as I have become convinced that there are nontrivial features of natural language (or, at least, of my own native English) that become apparent only through computational analysis of very substantial quantities of primary data. By *primary data* I mean data about language obtained by direct observation of language in action, unfiltered by the processes of human analysis and interpretation. It follows then that two widely used sources of data, informant testing and introspection, cannot yield primary data, since the process of thinking about one's own language behavior entails analysis and interpretation. Typically, a person's *beliefs* about his or her language behavior can be shown to be inconsistent with his or her *actual* behavior.

Lexicography is a linguistic activity well placed to benefit from computational analysis of corpora since it is concerned with documenting the idiosyncracies of individual words. Inevitably, therefore, the observation of particulars in a corpus is more apposite for lexicography than it is for the grammarian or the theoretical linguist. From the earliest period of lexicography in Britain, most significantly in Samuel Johnson's *Dictionary* of 1755, dictionaries have been compiled on the basis of direct evidence of language use collected laboriously from authentic text sources. During the nineteenth century in Britain, the scientific community working in the area of philology and related disciplines became increasingly concerned with data gathering as a proper preliminary to serious scientific investigation. Compilation of the *Oxford English Dictionary* (*OED*), a monumental work of scholarship in lexicography, was based from the beginnings in the 1860s on the painstaking collection of citations from text. A fine balance was achieved by the *OED* and by many lexicographers throughout the twentieth century, between the demands of empirical research rooted in exhaustive fieldwork and the prescriptive, didactic tone felt to be appropriate to a language reference work.

In lexicography, as in all areas of linguistic study, prescriptivism became unfashionable during the second half of the twentieth century, and more recent dictionaries gradually shifted from their prescriptive stance. Curiously, however, they also moved away from presenting authentic citations as evidence of usage—perhaps to avoid seeming to hold up examples from the best, the greatest, most stylish and elegant writers, as models for instruction and guidance (rather than simply as attested instances of use).

Computer corpora began to be collected during the 1960s when the emerging technology made such a venture possible. The production of the Brown corpus (one million words of printed American English from 1961) (Francis) was a salient event in the history of corpus linguistics, and it and its sister corpus of British English from the same date (the Lancaster-Oslo-Bergen corpus, compiled during the late seventies) have been very valuable resources for many linguists. Corpus-based lexicography in English did not really begin, however, until the COBUILD project was set up at Birmingham University, with funding from Collins publishers, to build a large corpus and to compile a lexical database and dictionary for foreign learners of English based upon it (Sinclair; Clear, "Corpora"). COBUILD was, and continues to be, an enterprise committed to a very direct reliance on the evidence furnished by its extensive corpus resources. Concluding his introduction to the *Collins Cobuild English Grammar* (*CCEG*), John Sinclair stresses this point and, giving four corpus examples of the phrasal verb *break out*, writes:

> The independence of real examples is their strength. They are carefully selected instances of good usage. A set of real examples may show, collectively, aspects of the language that are not obvious individually. . . . Note that it is bad things that break out, not good ones. Any such points emerging from a set of constructed examples could not, of course, be trusted.

This point, almost a footnote to the *CCEG*, seems to me to be crucial to the new age of corpus-based language study. The existence of large corpora enables the testing of existing linguistic theories and the formulation of new ones in a way that had not hitherto been feasible. Introspection and intuition are not subject to brutal comparison with the facts of language performance. One should perhaps point out that the trust required from the user of a grammar book does not differ much from that demanded by all such reference works, whether compiled from corpus evidence or not. The user must have faith in the ability of the lexicographers or grammarians to analyze and evaluate their data rigorously and fairly. To put it bluntly, why should the user take these four selected examples (taken from a selection of authentic texts) as a true indicator of the behavior of the phrasal verb *break out*? Were there examples in the corpus of good things breaking out that the grammarian chose to ignore or explain away as "creative" or "humorous" uses? The user is being asked to trust the corpus and additionally to trust the analysts of the corpus and compilers of the grammar.

Of course, in many areas of scientific and social scientific study, information is disseminated to an audience of nonexperts on the assumption that the experts have done their best and are to be trusted—economic and financial statistics, weather reports, census data, exam results. In corpus linguistics the possibility and effects of experimental error are often overstated: indeed, good scientific estimation of the possibility and scale of experimental error is seldom carried out at all. As a simple check on the example given by Sinclair to support the claim for trustworthiness, I compared the occurrences of the phrasal verb *break out* in the thirty-million-word sample made up from newspapers, fiction and nonfiction books, magazines and ephemera (predominantly post-1985) currently held on line at OUP. Not surprisingly the evidence confirmed overwhelmingly what is noted by the *CCEG*: that only bad things break out (war, fighting, hostilities, plague, riots, and so on). There is one clear counterexample: "A great roar of applause broke out . . . ," and there are several instances of peace breaking out, though this might be considered to be a humorous or witty exploitation of the underlying principle. Observations such as this are often possible from a computer corpus but are not retrievable from intuition.

It may be, however, that the samples are biased in some way. Indeed it is an important theoretical consideration in corpus linguistics that a corpus inevitably has some sort of bias. There is always the possibility that both samples (the corpus in use at COBUILD and the OUP corpus) have either missed a whole category of English text in which *break out* occurs with good things as its subject or, owing to chance, have not captured any such examples. I judge this possibility to be low enough to be disregarded, and with every new text added to these corpora and with every new corpus created, this possibility diminishes.

This evaluation of the evidence has to be made continually. It is clearly dangerous to conclude from the absence of any instance of, for example, the word *suppletion* in the OUP corpus that this word is not part of the English language of the late 1980s. Instances of usage found in a corpus must be taken seriously and explained satisfactorily; the absence of evidence from the corpus on the other hand cannot be taken to be indicative of the state of the language—there is always the possibility that the corpus simply did not chance upon such instances. It is a major problem for the compilers of corpus-based language reference works to know when to trust the data and when to suspect it. Although increasing the size of the corpus will always improve the situation, one cannot say that the evidence will support strong claims about the nature of the language as a whole once the corpus reaches a particular size threshold. The vastness of the population of, say, the totality of spoken and written British English from 1980 to the present day ensures that any attempt to compensate for the difficulty of setting up a sampling frame by gathering ever-larger samples will not of itself advance our state of knowledge significantly—given current and foreseeable resources, it will always be possible to demonstrate that some feature of the population is not adequately represented in the sample. An attempt must be made to define the population to be sampled if data drawn from the corpus is to be used to make generalizations about language beyond the sample. If we suspect the corpus of bias, we can hypothesize about the nature of the bias and seek to correct it. In the example here, it may be that *suppletion* occurs only in particular technical discourses (so my intuition tells me) and that the corpus sample we have at present may not contain the sort of texts that might illustrate it. Conversely, the construction might occur rarely. The difficulty of drawing firm conclusions in this case underlines the need to question how the sample was obtained and to assess whether this is likely to have a bearing on the validity of the conclusions reached.

Gathering citations for dictionary compilation is quite unlike corpus study. The nature of the process of reading source material with the intention of recording particular sentences or passages that illustrate interesting features of a language clearly places the filter of intuitive knowledge and expectations about language at the point when the data are recorded. There is an important sense in which reading for citations is a matter of looking for examples of what the linguist knows or believes to be the case. Such a process will be unlikely to reveal much that was not known or anticipated, and few preconceptions about language will be placed in any danger. Computer corpora are being adopted more widely as additional tools for lexicography and other fields of language study, and such corpora provide a fascinating new perspective on linguistic analysis.

The British National Corpus

The British National Corpus

The OUP was already engaged in the collection of a large corpus as a research resource for the compilers and editors of dictionaries, grammars, thesauruses, usage guides, and other language reference works at the time the British government, through the joint-funding program of the Department of Trade and Industry (DTI) and Science and Engineering Research Council (SERC), invited research-project applications in the area of information technology. Research proposals were invited that were to be collaborative among commercial organizations and that should address the needs of information-technology research and development in the United Kingdom as presented in a number of documents arising from consultation with the so-called speech and language community. The interest in corpus-based computational linguistics had been growing rapidly toward the end of the eighties, and several corpus initiatives in the European Community, the United States, and Japan[1] were indicative of this focus on the value of a large computerized body of authentic running text. The British National Corpus (BNC) consortium was formed during 1989, and its initial membership was OUP, Longman, Oxford University Computing Services (OUCS), Lancaster University's Unit for Computer Research on the English Language (UCREL), and the British Library. We submitted a proposal to collect a corpus of at least one hundred million words, to add linguistic annotation (word-class tags to the whole corpus and skeleton parse trees to a much smaller "core" subset), and to make the resulting corpus available to the research community in industry and academia. The bid for public funding of the project was successful, and up to 50 percent of the £1.2 million estimated total cost is to be met by the DTI and SERC.[2] The remaining costs are borne by the nonacademic participants in the consortium.

Although it is apparent that the dictionary publishers in the consortium have the concerns of reference-book publishing at the center of their perspective on the BNC, the project is intended to be a significant advance for the benefit of all linguistic researchers who might find it useful to have such a corpus, with grammatical annotations, and who would not otherwise have the funds or the resources to gather such a body of data for their work. In the next sections I shall discuss briefly the major issues underlying the design and construction of the BNC.

Representativeness

The BNC aims to build a corpus that can be taken to be representative of modern British English. Other world varieties of English will not be included in the corpus (except incidentally as, for example, when a quotation that happens not to be in British English occurs within a text). *Representativeness* and *balance* are two words that are often used by lexicographers and corpus linguists, but at present these concepts are poorly defined. The central problem is to how to strengthen the claims that can be made after analysis and observation of linguistic features in a corpus. To use a hypothetical illustration, if I have a very large corpus (say, two hundred million words) taken from several years' issues of a national daily newspaper and I discover by observation that *airspace* is far more frequent than *air space* or *air-space*, does this tell me anything about British English? Can I use this information to prefer the solid form over the others in a dictionary? It might be, indeed it is, argued that any quantitative results obtained from such a corpus are seriously unreliable because the corpus itself is not "balanced." What is clear once these intuitive notions of balance and representativeness are investigated in detail is that even though objections concerning bias introduced by the corpus composition can always be raised, there is no defensible measure of representativeness of such an ill-defined population as, for example, "modern British English" (Clear, "Corpus"). The corpus may be representative of some population—and it is a matter for statistical-sampling theory to consider how sampling might best be carried out—and if the population is finite and clearly bounded for operational purposes (as, for example, the plays of Shakespeare) then representativeness is an achievable goal. For the purposes of lexicography, however, what is most frequently sought is empirical and perhaps quantitative data about the English language (or a substantial, central portion of it, at least).

This issue is closely bound up with the question of the optimum size of a corpus. Clearly, a corpus that is bigger than another has a better chance of capturing all the relevant phenomena of a language. But it is not clear, and little published research is available on this topic, whether a wider variety of sources (and correspondingly smaller samples from each source text) will yield data that is equally reliable as data drawn from a larger but more homogeneous corpus.

The BNC approaches this difficult problem by setting out to be both large and eclectic. The corpus will include texts from no earlier than 1960, and the majority will be post-1975. The written component (of ninety million words) will be composed of texts that are classified in terms of five major parameters: Informative/Imaginative, Subject Domains (eight macro categories), Level (highbrow, intermediate, popular), Date (1960 to 1975, post-1975), and Medium (published, unpublished, books, periodicals, written to be spoken, ephemera, and so forth). The spoken component (up to ten million words) is split primarily into two partitions: one collected to cover a scheme of text categories; the other collected by recording a demographic sample of native British English speakers across the UK over a period of several days. The design of the BNC is necessarily a compromise between conflicting demands from specialists who view the corpus and its value from different perspectives, and the lexicographic needs of the commercial participants will clearly take priority. Nevertheless, the aim is to establish a compositional profile for the BNC that will make it useful for a wide range of purposes (many of which cannot be prescribed at this stage) while justifying its cost in terms of its value for language reference publishing.

Availability

The BNC is intended to benefit not only the organizations that participate in its construction but also the wider research community in speech and language technology. One of the impediments to the development of natural language processing (NLP) systems is the current difficulty in obtaining a large enough corpus to permit work on, for example, statistical models of English grammar or wide-coverage NLP lexicons (those that might contain a large enough vocabulary to give reasonable coverage for general-purpose applications). The feeling of the UK research community, and it is clearly one that is shared by others in the US and Europe, is that corpus data should ideally be available as part of the research infrastructure. This would save the current duplication of effort by organizations that, in the absence of generally available data, are building their own corpora to suit local needs. The BNC is a step toward providing a common corpus sample that can be used in research by commercial as well as academic organizations.

The main obstacles to the free exchange of corpora are two: copyright protection and data-capture costs. If texts included in a corpus are modern, then it is quite likely that they will be protected in some way by copyright and may not be freely copied onto computer and distributed. The BNC is negotiating copyright permissions on every text that is included that will allow the complete corpus of one hundred million words to be distributed for research purposes. If we are successful here, we shall have achieved a significant advance because at present there is very little corpus material that is not tightly constrained by copyright. The situation is particularly difficult for commercial organizations such as publishing and software houses, computer manufacturers, or commercial research laboratories since the proprietary nature of most existing corpora precludes their wider use and such organizations do not benefit from the relaxing of copyright constraints that is often (and often erroneously) assumed within the universities. The DTI funding program that contributes to the BNC's costs set out as specific goals to promote the establishment of common infrastructure resources (corpora, computer lexicons, analytic tools) for the NLP research community.

If copyright were no problem, there would still remain the initial investment costs of compiling a large corpus. For some researchers a viable shortcut is to acquire large volumes of corpus data from some abundant renewable source—daily newspapers, for example. Such sources enable corpus-based work to proceed without involving high expenditure on data capture (the newspapers are already in machine-readable form) or copyright permission clearance (one agreement can be sufficient to obtain a large volume of data). For dictionary makers this is not a satisfactory solution since the homogeneity of a single newspaper source does not satisfy the lexicographers' demands for evidence of language use across a wide range of text types. The wider the range of text types to be included in the corpus, the more likely it is that the data capture will have to involve labor-intensive keyboarding, optical character reader (OCR) scanning, and postediting. The collection of one hundred million words made up from a broad range of text sources can therefore easily become very expensive.

Another aspect of the issue of availability is the encoding and documentation of the corpus. The BNC project is affiliated with the Text Encoding Initiative (TEI), and the text is being encoded in conformance with TEI guidelines. The use of standard generalized markup language (SGML) and its application within an international standard framework for the markup of text data provided by the TEI will certainly facilitate interchange of the data. The detailed, formal documentation of the corpus—the system for classification of text samples and their sources, encoding and transcription methods, copyright notices and acknowledgments, and so on—can also be incorporated into the electronic version of the BNC by means of TEI-conformant header blocks.

Linguistic Annotation

The BNC data will be tagged automatically with word-class labels using the CLAWS software developed by the Unit for Computer Research in the English Language (UCREL) at Lancaster University. A small but representative subset of the whole corpus (the "core" corpus) will be annotated with basic syntactic tree parses—by processing that Lancaster terms "skeleton parsing." Further linguistic annotation will be added as far as resources permit in order to produce a sample of a few million words that is linguistically annotated to a much greater degree of delicacy than is possible for the complete corpus. The annotation cannot be guaranteed to be 100 percent correct: partly because the state of the art of automatic word-class tagging and parsing does not permit it but also because a corpus of such a size and scope will constantly throw up details of analysis about which there is no clear consensus. (This issue is discussed more generally in the section Word-Class Tagging below.)

The word-class tags will be incorporated on line into the machine-readable corpus using a concise form of TEI-conformant encoding with the aim of minimizing the storage requirements.

Corpus Software Tools for Lexicographers

The essential benefit to be gained from a corpus for all language study is the access to *many* instances of words in their natural context. Consequently the essential methodology of corpus linguistics is to observe, to describe, and to make generalizations about language in use. For this approach the standard keyword-in-context (KWIC) concordance is an essential tool. When the focus of attention is the orthographic word, as it is for lexicographers, the KWIC concordance display is particularly informative.

At OUP I have written programs to index a large corpus and to provide interactive KWIC concordance displays. There are many software packages currently available that provide free-text retrieval (often using KWIC display as standard) from preindexed text files.[3] However, there is one overriding advantage in developing in-house programs to perform these operations if one has the resources: the opportunity to design the features of the software to suit exactly the applications that are intended for the corpus. In the case of the growing corpus at OUP, there were several key factors to be taken into account in the design of indexing and access software.

First, since the anticipated size of the corpus was over one hundred million words, it was essential to develop an indexing strategy that was highly efficient with respect to the size of data files and the amount of computer resources consumed in building the indexes. Since we design and write our own software, we can fully exploit the available computing hardware resources. There is always a tradeoff between the cost of writing code that will make the hardware work and the cost of extra hardware to cope with inefficiencies in the software. In the case of OUP's corpus-analysis software, we can control both sides of the equation, and that enables us to make most cost-effective use of resources. Second, it was clear that as the users of the corpus became more involved and proficient in corpus analysis, there would be a continuing need to revise the software—to add new functions, to streamline or to remove redundant features, to add modular postprocessing options, and so on. Within the organization I expected that there would be different groups of users with different requirements for corpus access and that the software could have a number of core elements that, with simple modification, could be configured into a number of versions each with different functionality and characteristics.

In the following pages I will describe the functions of the various corpus-access tools and illustrate how they are used within OUP.

Word Lists

It is not surprising that lexicographers should have some interest in lists of words. One of the most obvious processing operations to be carried out on a large corpus is the production of a complete word-frequency listing. At OUP this operation is carried out each time the growing corpus is enlarged and reindexed. A number of listings are held on line for access:

1. A simple alphabetical list of word forms and frequencies (the type list)

2. A lemmatized list, derived from the type list (the lemmatized list)

3. An alphabetical listing of words subdivided into the frequencies of their word-class assignment (the tagged list)

4. A lemmatized list of words and their word-class assignments (the lemmatized tagged list).

The process of lemmatization groups together the inflected forms of a verb or noun under one head word (lemma) in a word list. The two lemmatized lists are produced by quite different procedures (and yield different results). The lemmatized list is produced by a program that simply reads the type list as input, looks up each word form in a specialized dictionary of word forms – lemma pairings, and puts out the base form. If the input word form is not found in the dictionary, then a few very simple suffix-stripping rules are applied to generate a base form. This method produces a crudely lemmatized listing: crude, because forms such as *saw* cannot be disambiguated (since the lemmatization is done on the type list, not on the whole corpus, there is no context available on that to disambiguate) and *saw* is arbitrarily treated as a variant of *see*. The noun use is conflated within the frequency count for the lemma *SEE*. Nevertheless, the list collates very many regular verb inflections and plural nouns into satisfactory lemma groupings, which can have a dramatic effect on, for example, the listing of the most frequent words in the corpus. If the type list is ordered by descending frequency, none of the forms of the verb *to be* occurs in the top seven forms. If the lemmatized list is ordered by frequency, then the lemma *BE* occurs as the second most frequent word between *the* and *of*. The lemmatized list is also more easily matched against actual or potential dictionary head-word lists that, of course, are made up primarily of base forms, not inflected forms.

If one is able to add word-class labels to all the words of the corpus, then a fully lemmatized word list can be produced. The following is a very small sample from the current tagged lemmatized list. The indented lines are the inflected forms actually occurring in the corpus: these are subordinated in the list to the base lemma and the sum of the frequencies of the inflected forms is shown.

```
aspiration N 430
   NN aspiration 87
   NNS aspirations 341
   NP aspiration 1
   NP aspirations 1
aspirational JJ 7
aspirator N 1
   NN aspirator 1
aspire N 3
   NP aspire 3
aspire V 305
   VB aspire 79
   VBD aspired 32
   VBG aspiring 151
   VBN aspired 12
   VBZ aspires 31
aspirer N 2
   NN aspirer 1
   NNS aspirers 1
```

The lemmatization is carried out using an algorithm described by Roger Garside, Geoffrey Leech, and Geoffrey Sampson that removes inflexional suffixes from nouns and verbs. In the implementation used at OUP, a dictionary of irregular inflexions is first consulted and, if the form is found to be irregular, the root form is supplied by the dictionary. Otherwise regular *-s*, *-ed*, and *-ing* suffixes are removed in accordance with some straightforward pattern matching: most of the tricky cases involve the retention or removal of a final *e*, in cases where crude lopping of final characters would yield incorrect results, as with *interfering–interfere, bothering–bother*, or *blasted–blast, pasted–paste*. The program makes mistakes; and if these are noticed, enhancements are made to the dictionary list or the suffix rules, but overall the results are good enough to provide a very useful supplement to the basic type list. One area where the tagged lemmatized list is proving its worth is in the formulation of a lexicographic policy toward the placement of derived and inflected forms within the overall structure of the alphabetical list of main lemma entries. Even though the pressure is strong to adopt a universal, consistent rule regarding, for example, *-ing* forms of verbs used adjectivally (*amaze–amazing*), the lemmatized corpus list quickly shows up forms for which the so-called standard rule seems unsatisfactory. It is possible for the lexicographer to locate all adjectival *-ing* forms in the corpus that have a frequency significantly greater than their base forms that might merit special treatment, *boring* or *sweltering*, for example.

Further word lists can be produced on request or for specific investigations. A frequency list of bigrams from the corpus (all word pairs) is a preliminary step in investigating the collocational patterns of the corpus. The majority of new words in the language are not completely new single-word forms but are multiword lexemes such as *equity stub*, *couch potato*, or *new age traveler*. The bigram list can be searched on a keyword-by-keyword basis during dictionary compilation to check for any new, unusual, or idiomatic pairs.

Interactive KWIC Concordancing

The Show program uses pre-existing index files to a large corpus in order to provide an acceptably fast response to interactive requests for concordance display. Every word of the corpus itself has already been tagged automatically with word-class labels, using a tagging program written by Kenneth W. Church of AT&T Bell Laboratories. (The tagging of text corpora is discussed in more detail in the section Word-Class Tagging below.) The tagged corpus has also been previously indexed. The indexing algorithm is very simple but efficient and involves building an inverted file of all the word types in the corpus accompanied by pointers into the single large ASCII file that is the corpus file.

The user interface is not sophisticated in that it makes no use of windows, icons, mouse, or pointer. The software is designed to run on virtually any display device that is connected to the computer, and it requires only the most basic screen-manipulation functions. It does not exploit the technology of the emerging Graphical User Interface standards (X-Windows, NeWS, Microsoft Windows) but has the compensating advantage that it runs on almost any kind of terminal or terminal emulator, irrespective of the hardware and software of the terminal device. The corpus is currently set up on a UNIX (Sun Microsystems) workstation, and regular users access it from Apple Macintosh PCs, IBM PCs, and other workstations, connected via Ethernet. The user might be connected only via an RS232 serial connection and be using a dumb terminal or a terminal emulator on a PC—the software is functionally identical in all cases.

The program prompts for a simple word, for word combinations, or for a set of words. The frequency of the target word or words is displayed, and the user is prompted for several display options before the KWIC concordance is presented.

The concordance lines can be ordered by the context either to the left or to the right of the keyword and reordered and redisplayed on demand.

As the corpus grows in size, it becomes clear that many words are so frequent in the corpus that a simple display of every instance in KWIC format will be so lengthy that the lexicographer will not want or be able to view it as one massively long stream of concordance lines. The Show program therefore offers a number of features intended to help the lexicographer focus on more detailed aspects of the word or words they are working on or else to give them some summary information that helps to break down the mass of data into manageable subsets. First, the user has the option simply to view a sample of the concordances for a given word. The sample is taken by selecting every n^{th} instance for display—so if the word occurs ten thousand times in the corpus and the user asks to see a sample of only two hundred, then every fiftieth instance in sequence is displayed. It is important that the sampling presents an unbiased cross-section of all the corpus instances since the lexicographer may want to get an overall impression of the syntactic or semantic features of the word from the two-hundred-sample instances. If the two hundred were taken from only one or two text samples within the corpus, this could give a very distorted impression.

Another strategy for breaking down the analysis of a large set of instances of a word is to restrict the view to one of a number of subcorpora. The Show program allows the user to select a subcorpus and then to operate only within that subset. Subcorpora may be defined to isolate the spoken texts or the written texts only, for newspapers, imaginative texts, particular subject domains, and so on. The lexicographer can then view concordances within these subcorpora in turn if it seems appropriate.

The word-class tags provide another angle on the analysis of a large set of concordance lines. The program will display a breakdown of the frequencies of each word class to which the keyword has been assigned in the corpus. For a word like *top*, which in the current corpus of twenty-three million words has a frequency of around five thousand, the capability of the software to sift the verbal instances of *top* from the adjectival and nominal gives the user a very effective means of focusing on the meaning and the use of the word. In this case the verbal uses of *top* number only around a hundred, and concordances to these instances can therefore be analyzed conveniently. The program is very much oriented toward the keyword, the word type that is the focus of a concordance display, and a search based on word-class tags is carried out as a subsidiary operation to the basic KWIC concordance display. The design reflects the fact that the starting point for compiling a dictionary entry tends inevitably to be the head-word lemma, and word-class distinctions are dealt with as part of the analysis of the structures and meanings associated with each lemma. The program design encourages a fail-safe working method: rather than assume that we know which word classes are relevant for the keyword and specify these directly (for example, by having the user enter a "wordstring/TAG" pair as the primary search target), the program *shows* the user a breakdown of the tags associated with the keyword and invites the user to select from these. That way the user will be reminded (even, occasionally, discover) that the keyword can be, for example, a noun as well as a verb; and moreover, the relative frequencies of its occurrence in its various syntactic roles will be apparent.

Another reason why the word-class tagging is accessed in this rather passive way is that the tagset that is used in the automatic tagging has around forty different labels, based upon the major classes of noun, verb, adjective, adverb, pronoun, and preposition. It would be quite difficult for the user to be sure exactly how to specify which of the full set of word-class labels might be attached to the keyword. The current approach provides a menu of word-classes to select. So, for example, the user may ask for a display of the KWIC concordance for *hit*. This word is likely to have many citations in a large corpus, and after the first screenful of the concordance is displayed, the user may call up a frequency breakdown of word-class tags, which might look something like this:

VB	124
VBD	765
VBN	344
NN	98
NP	4

The user can then mark the three verb labels for selection, omitting the nominal instances. The stray four instances of *hit* labeled NP (proper noun) may be significant (and could, of course, be quickly checked) but are more likely to be noise caused by errors in the automatic tagging—or indeed a person or place named *Hit*. The use of ordinary words as proper nouns (or quasi-proper nouns) is often overlooked by the language theoretician. Many words are susceptible of deployment as proper nouns (*Mr. Clean* [a household cleaning product], *Your Honor*, *Mr. President*, *Level 42* [a rock/pop group], *Rupert Bear*), and lexical study of a large corpus of authentic modern texts provides many thousands of examples of such uses. This phenomenon is so pervasive that, as linguists, we tend to push it aside as of little consequence, but in corpus analysis it has to be taken into account.

Collocation

The Show program described in the preceding section provides some obvious basic facilities to search for or identify collocations. Here I am using the term *collocation* in a loose sense to mean simply the co-occurrence of two or more orthographic words. First, the ordering of concordance lines alphabetically by the word immediately to the left or the right of the keyword draws the eye of the user to recurrent word pairings:

```
Prince ther room which had an examination couch like a doctor's surgery in
Lantrn ilde had termed marriage bed 'the couch of lawful lust.' A young g
Smallh  tillage . Perennial weeds such as couch or coltsfoot are more diffic
RmTemp und in the cool depths of the blue couch or under the seat of the car
WaveMg the passive media consumer _ or 'couch potato' _ may be drawing to
Indept self-analysis, a psychiatrist's couch potato , but he also wanted
Nudist t to do is to share a place with a couch potato. You're getting a p
DogTod aining. It is no good you being a couch potato and having a Doberman
Indept airly squarely at the late-night, couch potato and pub spill-over cr
Guardn nments that reduce young people to couch potatoes, summer camp in Al
FaceMg hort, too good to woo American's couch potatoes . .PP As int the bo
RmTemp e, straddling the arm of the blue couch so as to twonk the buried ro
```

Second, the program performs the usual proximity search for word pairs: displaying concordance lines in which the keyword occurs to the left, the right, or either side of some other word or set of words. The proximity search locates pairings within a range defined by a maximum number of intervening words. In this way noncontiguous collocations can be studied in detail:

```
Treasr 00 square yards . .PP We were soon hard at work using small hand-rakes
Palest iew, at a time when Kissinger was hard at work with his piecemeal dip
Arctic ost unusually, was already up and hard at work with his camera when I
Guardn dents and lecturers work extremely hard because they have to justify t
Guardn construction sites not to work so hard because they showed the indige
NewSci , this work is made unnecessarily hard because most technical textboo
Indept s. Sukova made her work extremely hard before she was able to celebra
Ballet d. Different dancers have to work hard both technically and as indivi
Indept thing about the money. We work so hard but our Marks are worth nothin
LadyMd f, pleads with her not to work so hard but she never heeds them. The
Guardn y ordinary . .PP 'We Germans work hard but we also like to live well
Guardn ed to display their work only to a hard core of aficionados is measure
```

Both these features of Show have shortcomings, however. The ordering of concordance lines shows up only contiguous collocates and requires that the user sort both ways and scan the full set of concordance lines. If one is interested in discovering the collocates of a word as frequent as, for example, *music*, then such a procedure can be unacceptably time consuming. On the other hand, the proximity-search feature is very useful if one knows in advance what word pairings will be of interest, but it does not provide any information for the user about the collocates that occur that are in the corpus but may pass unnoticed.

A separate program, Collocate, takes as input a word or set of words and presents as output a list of "significant" collocates. The algorithm is very simple: every instance of the keyword is located, and a frequency list is made of the words occurring within a defined span (the default is to read two words left and two words right) of the keyword. This raw list of all the collocates of the keyword is then annotated with a "significance" statistic that is calculated from the frequency of the co-occurrence, the frequencies of the collocating word and the keyword, and the overall size of the corpus. The output is sorted into descending order of "significance." I use scare quotation marks for the word *significance* because the significance of the collocation is defined wholly in terms of the statistic deployed. Of course, the real significance of any collocation depends on the analyst, who might assign it significance because it is very frequent or because it is idiomatic or because it is a multiword unit previously unrecorded in any printed dictionary. The purpose of the collocation program is to get the computer to draw summary information about many hundreds or thousands of individual instances of a word in context and to present the user with an ordered list of collocates such that the ones that the computer deems to be "significant" are also interesting to the user. If the output from the software is judged to be of interest, then it can save the user a great deal of tedious scanning of concordances.

A number of different statistics can be used, but in all cases the statistic compares the *observed* frequency of co-occurrence in the corpus with some *expected* frequency (based on a simple nonlinguistic assumption about the probabilities of word co-occurrence). The Collocate program uses a t-score statistic (Church et al.) by default, but a command-line option causes the program to calculate Mutual Information (MI) as an alternative. The use of different statistics turns out to have some interesting effects on the ordering of collocates.

MI is a measure of the strength of association between words x and y. In a given corpus MI is calculated on the basis of the number of times the pair was observed together versus the number of times the pair was observed separately.

To illustrate, let us consider two (made-up) examples: first the pair *kith* and *kin*, when *kith* never appears without *kin*. In a large corpus one might observe the pair, say, three times. The frequency of *kith* itself will almost certainly be three also. So, statistically, the probability that one will see *kin* if one has seen *kith* is absolute certainty. Although it may not be true vice versa (there may be some instances of *kin* without *kith*), the frequency of *kin* overall in the corpus may not be much higher than three (perhaps six or seven). The MI will therefore be very high—these two words will be very strongly associated. Now consider the pair *falling prices*. Each of these two words is likely to have a medium to high frequency in a large general corpus. One might see the pair together perhaps forty times. Now the MI figure will not be particularly high because there will be plenty of evidence of *falling* occurring without *prices* and vice versa. Unlike *kith* and *kin* the frequency of co-occurrence will not dominate either of the individual frequencies, so statistically the strength of association (and the MI) between *falling* and *prices* is much less.

The t-score is a measure not of the strength of association but of *the confidence with which we can assert that there is an association*. It takes account of the *variance* of the co-occurrence figures and is weighted according to the actual number of observations of the pairing to assess whether we can be confident in claiming any association. So the t-score for *kith/kin* is likely to be lowish, or lower anyway than for *falling + prices*, because having seen forty instances of the latter, we can be more confident that there is some association (albeit a much weaker one) than we can in the former case.

Let us look at some real examples for the word *taste*. Below are the first fifteen items taken from the output of the collocation program being used by the lexicographers within OUP. The columns are, from left to right, the collocate, the overall frequency of the collocate in the corpus, the *expected* frequency of co-occurrence (that is, if words were distributed randomly), the *actual* frequency of co-occurrence, and finally the *significance* value. The first list shows collocates ordered by Mutual Information; the second, by t-score.

```
                        List 1

arbiters      20         0.008          5         9.26
ve            29         0.012          3         7.99
aroma         97         0.040          9         7.83
buds          109        0.044         10         7.81
decency       127        0.052         11         7.73
arbiter       59         0.024          5         7.70
salty         64         0.026          5         7.58
```

's	1411	0.575	99	7.43
sans	45	0.018	3	7.35
seasoning	165	0.067	10	7.22
lapses	70	0.029	4	7.13
savour	72	0.029	4	7.09
texture	382	0.156	19	6.93
pepper	465	0.190	20	6.72
salt	900	0.367	37	6.66
sour	248	0.101	9	6.48

List 2

's	1411	0.571	99	9.92
for	252486	102.121	256	9.64
and	720454	291.395	451	7.53
good	22178	8.970	71	7.39
bad	4484	1.814	56	7.28
salt	900	0.364	37	6.06
season	4216	1.705	31	5.31
first	37597	15.207	51	5.06
with	188775	76.352	134	5.01
pepper	465	0.188	20	4.49
popular	3628	1.468	22	4.43
acquired	1185	0.479	20	4.42
texture	382	0.155	19	4.38
my	37077	14.996	42	4.22
bitter	861	0.348	17	4.10
smell	895	0.362	17	4.10

What are the differences? The MI list has *arbiter(s)* figuring very prominently, along with *salty*, and *sans*. It is questionable whether such collocates as these deserve special attention in a dictionary. Would one expect to find *sans taste* (a snippet presumably of a quotation from *As You Like It*) in a dictionary? What about the cliché *arbiter of taste*? These collocates have high MI scores because they are not very frequent overall (*arbiters* occurs only twenty times in our corpus; *sans* only forty-five times), so to occur three times with *taste* is a remarkable event in terms of chance occurrence. *Sans* and *ve* are idiosyncrasies, and they get into the list because of some peculiarity of this corpus (a repetition of a Shakespearean phrase perhaps, and a spurious enclitic form of *have*—most probably caused by use of double quotation marks instead of apostrophes in *we"ve* or *they"ve*). MI is very good at highlighting such peculiarities. The word *buds* is not an oddity at all but a recognizable part of a compound, though not a very frequent one, that we would expect most dictionaries to include.

The t-score list on the other hand has *good, bad, popular,* and *acquired* showing up. These seem to me to be more interesting lexicographically: first these collocates are pointers to the semantic area of *taste* in the sense "socially acceptable aesthetic, moral or ethical attitudes," and second, these collocates are more *typical* of the collocational behavior of *taste* than *salty, sans,* or *arbiters.* Note too that *for* gets a high t-score (because of the locution "have/develop/acquire/get/etc a taste for sth"). This idiomatic usage should probably be dealt with in a bilingual or learners' dictionary. Indeed the *Collins Cobuild English Language Dictionary* includes as sense 5 "a taste for sth" and the *Oxford Advanced Learners Dictionary* (4th edition) also gives this phrase special treatment. Both references draw special attention to *in good/bad taste.* Both deal with *acquired taste* under the main entry for *acquire.* These collocates will not score high MI values because they are themselves frequent words in English and because it cannot be said that *taste* strongly predicts *good* or vice versa. *For* does appear further down the MI list—it is at rank 205 with an MI (MI=1.31) score that is below the statistical confidence level (MI=1.5) and is unlikely to have been picked up among the many chance co-occurrences. The collocate *buds* did not get into the very top of the t-scores because we only saw ten of them out of a corpus of thirty million words. But it ranked 27 in the t-score list, with a value (t = 3.23) well above significance (t=1.65). So the t-score seems to get more typical collocates *without* missing the important MI collocates.

Word-Class Tagging

Automatic word-class tagging has become a fairly standard text-processing operation in computational linguistics. The attitude of researchers toward word-class tagging has shifted over recent years, and the nature of the problem and its solutions are, I think, much better understood than they were when the first automatic corpus tagging program (TAGGIT) was applied to the Brown corpus. There are a number of word-class tagging algorithms that have been reported in the literature (for example, Church, Garside) and that have been used successfully in tagging significant quantities of natural corpus data. At OUP I have been developing a word-class tagging program that uses a combination of dictionary lookup, suffix clues, and a large set of context-frame rules to assign word-class labels to the raw input stream. OUP also has access to the PARTS program that, at the time of writing, was claiming the lowest error rate of any tagger operating on natural, unconstrained English text.[4]

The PARTS program uses a statistical Markov modeling technique to assign word-class labels based on the a priori probability of a word's belonging to a class and the probabilities of word-class trigrams or triples. The initial estimates of parameters to the Markov model are provided by statistics drawn from the tagged Brown corpus. Despite the facts that the Brown corpus is American English, dates from 1961, and is only one million words in size, the PARTS program does a remarkably good job of disambiguating word-class assignment for thirty million words of modern British English. Its weaknesses are typical of word-class taggers—my own program tends to fail in exactly the same circumstances—and they raise some interesting issues about word-class labeling. Two examples are the labeling of proper names and the treatment of *-ing* or *-ed* forms of verbs used in adjectival positions. First, the problem with proper names: should the automatic tagger label the word *states* in *The United States of America* as a proper noun or as a common noun? The most satisfactory solution seems to be to treat the complete phrase as one lexical unit, labeled as a proper noun. But then a large corpus shows many thousands of multiword units of this kind, and it is not at all clear how far this lumping process should or could be taken. Here, for example, is a sentence taken from a car magazine that lies on the desk in front of me: *"The combination of front wheel drive and an all independent suspension system make the Renault 21 Savanna an estate car that the driver and all passengers can feel relaxed in!"* A strong case could be made for treating *front wheel drive* and *estate car* as multiword lexical units. Or perhaps *front wheel* is a multiword adjective modifying *drive*. And would we consider *all independent* as another compound adjective? The combination of a large corpus and an automatic tagging program provides copious evidence of the slipperiness of English morphology and syntax. It quickly becomes apparent that to expect 100 percent accuracy in a program is somewhat naive. "Accuracy" here would presumably mean "yielding the same analysis as skilled linguist," yet it is clear that many skilled linguists do not agree on the analysis of a number of borderline and doubtful instances. The operation of the computer program has the merit of being consistent and subject to inspection.

The PARTS program achieves a success rate somewhere between 90 and 97 percent. Although this may sound shockingly hit-or-miss, it has proved to be extremely valuable as a corpus tool. Work is currently underway to carry out grammatical analyses using the tagged corpus, and software is being prepared to carry out more complex pattern matching for grammatical features than is available from the current Show program.

Corpus Linguistics over the Next Decade

Lexicography is just one discipline within the humanities that has been able to make direct use of text corpora in ways that have demonstrably advanced the state of the art. Because of its applied nature, lexicography has, for several decades in English-speaking countries at least, been seen by many linguists as lying on the periphery of the field of language study. This is partly perhaps because lexicography in the English language has suffered from its tongue-in-cheek characterization as "harmless drudgery" by the weary and self-deprecating Dr. Johnson. Partly too, lexicography is tainted with the stain of commercial goals: to carry out linguistic study that is to be published for popular consumption at competitive prices and perhaps for profit has been regarded by many as hack work. Lexicography has traditionally made extensive use of authentic text data, by means of the manual methods of citation collection. Through the period when the dominant movement in academic linguistics was concerned with formal models of grammar and semantics, when the lexicon was consigned to the footnotes and appendices of serious linguistic research, lexicography and its data-oriented, atheoretical methodology received little attention. Fashions have changed over the last decade, and now lexicography finds itself suddenly in the vanguard of a movement toward the development of very large and comprehensive lexicons, built upon the firm foundation of empirical investigation of massive text corpora.

This shift has been brought about by the growing importance of computational linguistics and the need in the information-technology age to develop computer systems that have much better natural language processing capabilities. There is now a growing consensus in computational linguistics that the elaboration of formal grammars (transformation-generative, systemic or systemic-functional, unification or attribute grammars, and so on) does not yield anything approaching a comprehensive model of a natural language and that the lexicon is at least as important as grammar as a knowledge base for language processing applications. In any real language processing application the size and complexity of a lexicon adequate to cover even a restricted subset of English becomes sufficiently great that it is not feasible to construct it from scratch by hand. Lexical knowledge derived from large text corpora is now being recognized by many nonlexicographers as more robust and reliable than that furnished by "blackboard" linguistics.

A large text corpus can be used to provide basic statistics about words and word classes: their independent probability of occurrence, the frequency of particular sequences and structures, collocations, and so on. Lists of frequently occurring proper names, organizations and companies, abbreviations and acronyms can be drawn from a corpus and used to supplement the lexicon. Such items as these are typically given scant coverage in dictionaries and grammars. In the specific area of speech recognition, it is now taken for granted that some sort of corpus-based data will be used in building a statistical model of the language that can then be used to guide the speech recognizer. Another application that has more widespread impact now is spelling- and grammar-checkers that are often built into word-processing packages. It is clear that crude lookup of each word of the text in a target dictionary list of correct forms is far from ideal as a spell-check strategy. Even some simple corpus-derived statistics about common word pairs might assist in identifying *Net Jersey* as a mistake (even though both words are valid English forms) and in suggesting *New Jersey* as a correction.

The economic, social, and political benefits of progress in NLP, and its application in such key areas as the translation of official documents, telecommunications, speech-driven computers, or information retrieval from large text databases, are great, and consequently it seems that there will be no shortage of funds to support work that is seen to promote advances in these areas. The need for sound statistics based on empirical data will lead to the construction of ever-larger corpora. It is an unfortunate fact that a corpus of thirty million words, composed of a wide variety of different text types and subject areas, yields examples of only about one third of the vocabulary items in a single-volume desk dictionary such as the *Concise Oxford Dictionary* and more than one-half of the total vocabulary of that corpus occurs with a frequency of 1 or 2. If we want statistics about word pairs, then simple arithmetic tells us that a restricted lexicon of twenty thousand words has the potential to form four hundred million pairs—in order to distinguish with some degree of confidence that a given pair is rare while another pair is common, we shall need corpora of orders of magnitude greater than twenty-five million.

Another trend, also caused by the need for better statistics, is toward the analysis of restricted sublanguages. Real-world language types (meteorological reports, road-traffic reports, airline bookings, and the like) that have limited lexicons and stereotyped grammatical patterning can be more tractable for NLP, and corpora of manageable size can be collected and processed in these domains. Specialized dictionaries of the vocabulary of particular subject areas are already a feature of printed reference-book publishing, and we can expect to see an increase in the range of such dictionaries as subject-specific corpora become available.

The impetus provided by the NLP and computational-linguistics communities has inevitably lead corpus development to focus upon corpora of modern English intended to meet the needs of linguists. Many lexicographers are involved in preparing historical dictionaries for which corpora such as the BNC are only of limited interest, and one might anticipate an extension of corpus-based efforts into the collection and analysis of large corpora covering earlier periods. The development of historical language corpora might be attractive to historians and social scientists as well as to literary scholars and linguists. To some extent historical corpora are already far more advanced than linguistic ones since it is taken for granted as part of the methodology of historians and students of literature that they collate and archive the texts fundamental to their work. The Oxford Text Archive, the Toronto corpus of Old English, the Trésor de la Langue Française, the Thesaurus Linguae Graecae are all long-established computerized text archives whose function is primarily to serve the community of humanities scholars. There is a distinction to be drawn between corpora composed of texts selected because they have particular literary merit or because, taken together, they form the whole of an author's œuvre and corpora intended to represent in some way the demotic or vernacular in its undifferentiated mass. The BNC is distinctly aimed at serving the latter purpose, and the major effort involved to collect up to ten million words of authentic natural speech as a component of that corpus underlines the distinction between a historical archive of documents and a corpus of modern language: the further back in time we move our investigation, the more restricted are the sources of data.

For the linguist, one exciting prospect arising from computational analysis of very large corpora is the potential to see entirely new patterns and features of language by means of statistical methods. The theoretical models with which linguists have worked throughout this century seem to be challenged by the mass of data that can be sifted and sorted on a machine. A language like English, having such a vast community of speakers worldwide and employed in so many social situations, seems to be of a scale that cannot be exhaustively and satisfactorily accounted for by grammars and dictionaries of the kind we presently have available. The new perspective opened up by computational analysis of corpora suggests that models and methods once considered to be the proper domain of information theory and mathematics might be increasingly valuable in the study of language. Such a shift (a paradigm shift, as some would call it) would take place not merely because of its novelty but also as an inevitable consequence of our being faced with increasing evidence of the inadequacies of existing linguistic models to represent and account for natural language.

Notes

1. The EC-funded Network of European Reference Corpora project, the ACL Data Collection Initiative, and the massive Japanese Electronic Dictionary Research (EDR) project.

---

2 . The project is number IED1/2184 of the Advanced Technology Programme administered by the Information Technology Division of the DTI.

3 . For example, PAT, Texas, WordCruncher, Micro-OCP, and TACT.

4 . I am grateful to Ken Church and to AT&T Bell Labs for making this software available for our research use.

Works Cited

Church, Kenneth W. "A Stochastic Parts Program and Noun Phrase Parser for Unrestricted Text." Second Conference on Applied Natural Language Processing, Austin, TX, 1988.

Church, Kenneth W., W. Gale, P. Hanks, and D. Hindle. "Using Statistics in Lexical Analysis." *Lexical Acquisition: Using On-Line Resources to Build a Lexicon.* Ed. Vri Zernik. Hillsdale: Lawrence Erlbaum, 1991.

Clear, Jeremy H. "Computers, Corpora, and Modern Lexicography: The COBUILD Experience." *Computers in Literary and Linguistic Research. Literary and Linguistic Computing.* Ed. Yacov Choueka. Paris: Champion-Slatkine, 1990. (Proceedings of the Fifteenth International Conference, Jerusalem, 5–9 June 1988.)

_____. "Corpus Sampling." *New Dimensions in Corpus Linguistics: Proceedings of the Eleventh ICAME Conference, Berlin, June 1990.* Ed. Gerhard Leitner. Berlin: de Gruyter, forthcoming.

Francis, W. Nelson, and Henry Kucera. *Manual of Information to Accompany a Standard Sample of Present-Day Edited American English, for Use with Digital Computers.* Providence: Department of Linguistics, Brown U, 1964.

Garside, Roger, Geoffrey Leech, and Geoffrey Sampson. *The Computational Analysis of English. A Corpus-Based Approach.* London: Longman, 1987.

Johansson, Stig, Geoffrey Leech, and Helen Goodluck. *Manual of Information to Accompany the Lancaster-Oslo/Bergen Corpus of British English, for Use with Digital Computers.* Oslo: Department of English, U of Oslo, 1978.

Sinclair, John M., ed. *Looking Up: An Account of the COBUILD Project in Lexical Computing.* London: Collins, 1987.

____. Introduction. *Collins Cobuild English Grammar.* London: Collins, 1990.

From the Scholar's Library to the Personal Docuverse

Paul Delany
Simon Fraser University

A *docuverse* can be defined as a large collection of electronically stored and linked documents, connected to a computer network.[1] The basis of a docuverse is digitization: texts previously stored in a fixed and substantial medium—normally ink on paper—now exist in the virtual medium of electronic coding. Paper may be used to move particular texts into and out of a docuverse; but inside the docuverse world texts are dematerialized—which means that they are freed from the constraints that accompany embodiment.[2] The traditional idea of an archive or library as a determinate textual resource gives way to a different model, the programmable text base, out of which an infinite variety of texts can be generated for display on a computer screen. These texts are "virtual" in two important senses. First, they are *temporary* structures, the product of a local reorganization of the text base. Second, they are *partial:* the user of the text base may have a mental model of the whole document he or she is working with, but only a page or two at a time can be displayed on screen. Scrolling or paging may allow users to see the whole thing in sequence, but if they want to see it simultaneously, they must leave the docuverse and have recourse to a printed copy.

In the docuverse world, we thus encounter great differences of scale from the old kind of scholarly reading. The amount of text that can be handled as a single unit is vastly larger: we could, for example, use a single command to find all occurrences of a particular phrase in Frantext, a digital archive of some two hundred million words of French texts. Also, the current or effective size of a docuverse can be constantly modified by creating subsets. The full Frantext search stands at one end of the scale; a search of just seventeenth-century texts within Frantext might be in the middle; at the smallest scale, we might isolate a single paragraph in order to perform some textual operation on it.

My main concern in this essay will be with what I call the personal docuverse, which is roughly equivalent to a scholar's private library but has radical differences in its mode of use. Most scholars in the humanities will have a personal library of between one and five thousand volumes, supplemented perhaps with a few filing-cabinet drawers of Xerox copies of articles. We distribute the books around our home and office in whatever way helps us to locate information, guided by vague memories of what is on a particular shelf or of a particular color or size of book. Such a library is typically the largest amount of paper-based textual information that is managed informally, without recourse to catalogs and call numbers. It is a collection molded to the interests of an individual mind and in some physical way corresponding to it: each of us moves back and forth between a mental model of our library and the actual books it holds.

What happens when a personal library is wholly or partly replaced by a personal docuverse? I shall take up this question in a specific context, the study of James Joyce. In scope, Joyce studies are second only to Shakespeare. It has been estimated that 10,000 books and articles have been published on Joyce; the exact number must remain uncertain, but the *James Joyce Quarterly* currently records about 500 new bibliographical entries each year. A selective guide to research from ten years ago (Rice) listed 65 books and 391 articles on *Ulysses* alone. Clearly, even a fairly large personal Joyce library can only contain a fraction of the existing criticism. The same would be true for the primary texts: every Joyce scholar will have at least one book edition of each work, but few will have all the successive published states (including periodical excerpts) of *Ulysses* and *Finnegans Wake*. Fewer still would have a substantial proportion of the books known to have been in Joyce's personal library.[3] For Joyce then—as for Shakespeare—no personal scholarly library can be comprehensive or able to keep up with the annual flood of new publications.

Could a Joyce docuverse do better? In terms of physical storage, undoubtedly yes. Everything ever published on Joyce—assuming 10,000 items—should fit on a 1.2 gigabyte hard drive, which currently costs under $1,800, is about the size of a paperback book, and saves its information on a single disk three and a half inches in diameter. To add appropriate sound and graphic resources might increase storage requirements by one or two orders of magnitude; but cost and hardware capacity present only manageable and steadily diminishing barriers. The real difficulties lie in the intellectual labor of assembling the texts and the cost of digitizing them. In addition, there is the legal obstacle posed by copyright. These difficulties can be tackled, though success would require effort, ingenuity, and a higher commitment to scholarly cooperation than has been usual in the humanities.

A Joyce docuverse could be compiled in two very different ways; each model has its own advantages and drawbacks, and both might, in fact, be pursued simultaneously. I shall call them the CD Model and the Network Model.

The CD Model for a Joycean Docuverse

The standard way of undertaking textbases in CD-ROM format is this: choose a large, clearly defined, and potentially useful group of texts; digitize and transfer them to CD; add software to index and search the texts; and sell to libraries enough copies to cover costs.[4] Typical examples are Chadwyck-Healey's *English Poetry Full-Text Database* and *Patrologia Latina*. The former includes 4,500 volumes of English poetry from 600 AD to 1900; the latter, 221 volumes of J. P. Migne's edition of the Latin Church Fathers. For the *Patrologia* copyright has expired; this is also true for almost all the *English Poetry*, but here Chadwyck-Healey cannot offer current and best editions because these include copyright editorial materials. Still, these CDs will allow a library to make a comprehensive acquisition in a single purchase and to search or copy from the entire corpus through the accompanying software.

Projects like this are extremely "lumpy": a great deal of time and money must be invested in advance, to produce something that arrives on the marketplace all at once.[5] The cost is typically far beyond the means of an individual scholar—$54,000 for the poetry CDs, $60,000 for the *Patrologia*. In order to be viable, a Joyce CD would probably have to be a nonprofit initiative, with much voluntary input by Joyce scholars. Two very successful CDs have been produced with a similar formula: the *MLA Bibliography* and the *Thesaurus Linguae Graecae* (which includes most Greek texts written before the sixth century AD).[6]

It is easy to see what a Joyce CD should include: the primary texts, an extensive selection of criticism, and useful reference works such as Thom's Dublin directory for 1904, Victor Bérard's *Les Phoeniciens et l'Odyssée*, and the like. Unfortunately, although the primary Joyce texts became free of copyright on 1 January 1992,[7] most of the critical literature is still in copyright. None of the CD projects discussed above face a significant copyright problem; but under present law, permissions and fees would have to be negotiated individually for every copyright book or article to be included in a Joyce CD. This requirement would constitute a daunting obstacle, perhaps sufficient to prevent the compilation of such a CD for years to come—in spite of the usefulness of such a centralized resource for Joyce studies.[8]

The Network Model

A Joyce CD would be a "domain docuverse," providing exhaustive coverage of a well-defined disciplinary field. Such a docuverse is intermediate in size between the "global docuverse"—which we can define as all digitized documents that are currently accessible—and the "personal docuverse," which will be a mixture of public and private files, controlled by a single person and largely resident on that person's hard disk. In the past decade, personal docuverses have mainly been assembled by individual users typing in one file after another. However, scanners are becoming a convenient way of digitizing texts (including the hand-held type, which can be taken into a library and rolled across the page); and more and more documents are becoming available on computer networks, from which they can easily be downloaded to personal storage.[9] To assemble a personal docuverse on Joyce from network sources would have distinct advantages in *feasibility* (by-passing problems of finance and copyright), *adaptability* (particular scholarly interests within the field could be accommodated), and *scalability* (the docuverse could grow from small beginnings, instead of requiring a single massive effort like the CD). Scholars could use the network to acquire documents in two ways, which I shall call the formal and the informal methods.

Formal Acquisition

The formal method would use central services that offer on-line searches of bibliographies and, for a fee, delivery of full-text documents over the network. In the United States, the two main providers of related services are Online Computer Library Center (OCLC) and CARL Systems of Denver, Colorado (Wilson, Whitaker). On-line bibliographical search services have been available for many years, but in September 1991 CARL made a giant step forward by starting to deliver full-text documents by fax. When an article is requested from CARL, permission is automatically cleared, either with the publisher directly or through the Copyright Clearance Center, Salem, Massachusetts.[10] Before placing an order, the user sees on screen the copyright fee (typically $2 or $3) and the total cost of delivering the article (typically $7 to $10 for fax delivery, sent within twenty-four hours).

CARL also announced in 1990 its intention to deliver full text over the network, as a digitized file. However, as of May 1992 on-line delivery had not yet begun, partly because of programming difficulties and partly because some copyright holders were reluctant to permit distribution by this means. If CARL goes to on-line delivery, costs of digitizing texts would be more widely shared. Only when a document is requested would it be digitized, and costs would be spread over thousands of users of the system instead of the few who can afford publications like the *English Poetry 600-1900* CD.[11] Both CARL and OCLC currently offer access to about ten thousand journals and a million articles published since 1988. These systems are mainly oriented toward resource-sharing by libraries: for most journals it is cheaper to order single articles on demand than for each library to have its own subscription. But an individual scholar may be reluctant to order, say, twenty articles to support research on his or her own article in progress—unless the purchase is subsidized by research grants or other institutional support. We can expect CARL and OCLC to become widely used information utilities, but there will still be scope for informal alternatives.

Informal Acquisition

To participate in informal systems of text sharing, scholars will need only a powerful microcomputer or workstation, a large-capacity hard disk, and a network connection. The other services needed will be free, as long as universities maintain their current policies of not charging for e-mail, file transfer, or remote log-ins. Many scholars already belong to e-mail conferences, which can support exchange of documents via Listserv and other means. But we are seeing rapid development in new ways of posting, finding, and acquiring texts over the network. These new systems promise the biggest advance in rapid and comprehensive circulation of information since the invention of printing.

The backbone of these systems is the Internet for North America and EARN for Europe. Any computer with an Internet connection is given its own address, which makes it a potential server or supplier of files to other computers. It is then a simple matter for any user to make files public—that is, accessible to any other users who want to transfer the files to their own machines. A central registry for more than two million public files is kept at the Archie archive (archie.mcgill.ca).

The flow of public files over the network can be defined, in theory, by an Internet Wide Information System (IWIS). Two pioneer implementations of such a service are Gopher, based at the University of Minnesota, and WAIS (Wide Area Information Servers), developed by Thinking Machines Corp (Caruso, **Tomer**).

WAIS's front end supports simple and uniform searches for public documents anywhere in the Internet world:

> If a server is registered on the WAIS system, all I have to do is type—in English—a few words about what I'm looking for in the WAIS text field labeled, Look for documents about.
> The client computer encodes my request in "WAIS-speak" and sends it out to the worldwide network of WAIS servers. The servers translate the query (I don't need to know how), find articles they think match my request, and send them back to me.
> I look at the "hits" and select those that look most applicable. Based on

that feedback, I can send the query out again until I've gotten the specific information I was looking for. (The method is called "relevance feedback," and it's proven to be a very efficient way to hone in on information.) (Caruso 5)

So, once relevant public files were mounted on a server, Joyce scholars could query, "Look for documents about *Dubliners*"; " . . . about metempsychosis"; and so forth. It should also be possible simply to search for the word *metempsychosis* across the network in the full text of any document.

At present (June 1992) WAIS information is free, though the system provides for a charged sector if information providers want to set a monetary value on their information. WAIS and similar systems have great potential for promoting scholarly exchange. Copyright materials might be distributed through the charged sector so that publishers—also, perhaps, scholarly sponsors—might recover some of their costs. Alternatively, WAIS may be able to circumvent copyright by posting, not an actual document, but a pointer that gives an address where the document can be found. Authors might want to have their articles widely read but be legally forbidden to distribute them because the materials have been copyrighted by the journals in which they appeared. WAIS would allow such authors to say, in effect, "The article is in room 123 and the door is unlocked."

With all such systems, effectiveness requires a critical mass of information providers and users. A public archive of ten articles on Joyce would not have much value, but a hundred articles would draw interest, and a thousand would be close to indispensable. At present, building such a mass in any one domain is hampered by the existence of many different ways to set up groups over the network and by the absence of any central information registry or directory of e-mail addresses. Many scholars do not see the value of electronic communication, just as the value of the telephone system was limited when only a few pioneers were connected. In the network world, however, Usenet has become a standard utility, looked at regularly by a high proportion of workstation users, and having over three hundred thousand active postings at any given time.[12] Most of these postings deal with computer issues, but there are active discussions on innumerable other topics (**Renear**).

Before too long, then, we can expect Joyce scholars (and other humanists) to use the network routinely as a resource for acquiring texts, which they will then merge with their personal Joyce docuverses. We can draw an analogy with the effects of xerography on scholarly practice over the past twenty years or so (Mort). The Xerox machine made it vastly easier to acquire and distribute texts, especially article-length ones. Virtually all scholars have made their own small archives of articles relevant to their work. But a drawerful of offprints has no retrieval facility, other than the scholar's thumbing through what is there in the hope of finding a reference or significant passage. Digitization gives us full control over such documents. Improvements in scanning technology should allow us, over the next few years, to capture documents digitally as easily as we now run them through the Xerox machine.[13] Alternatively, they can be acquired formally or informally over the network, as already described.

Personal Docuverse Management

The management of personal docuverses will vary widely, according to individual skills, interests, and ownership of hardware and software.[14] Everyone will want facilities for scholarly communication, for indexing files, and for conducting full-text searches of his or her docuverse. Many will want to be able to make hypermedia links among blocks of text, sound, and graphics. Beyond this interconnection, some will cobble together word processors, database programs, and the like; others will prefer an integrated and centrally planned text-handling system. **Stigleman, Zimmerman,** and **Virbel** indicate various approaches and resources for text management. When scholars develop a specialized text-handling module, it will be easily passed on to others who might benefit. Heyward Ehrlich, for example, has developed "The James Joyce Text Machine," which he describes as "a collection of machine readable primary texts, critical commentaries, and related indexes and concordances." Currently running on 386 PCs, this program will, among other functions, search for "any word pattern or patterns in one pass through the combined full texts of *Dubliners, Portrait of the Artist, Ulysses,* and *Finnegans Wake.*" A future workstation version will feature "multi-window displays, full graphics capability, and multimedia aspects."[15] Another program, by Miilumäki, collates variants among successive versions of *Finnegans Wake.* We can also expect the development of gateways or information brokers between one docuverse and another: someone interested in classical elements in *Ulysses* could pay a visit to *Perseus* (a massive hypermedia resource on classical studies), in order to explore parallels between the Ulysses of Eccles Street and the Odysseus of Ithaca (Crane).

How might these advances in text management affect the scholarly culture of the later part of the decade? Some effects may be of dubious value. It will be as easy to skim a hundred articles as it now is to skim ten; lists of works cited will become longer, but critical thinking may not necessarily benefit. Other changes could be more significant. The ability to search large docuverses and quantify the results will tend to devalue the traditional impressionistic and rhetorical skills of literary critics. There will be more emphasis on "para-scholarship": an informal zone of scholarly communication that is more topical, rapid, and flexible than publication in printed journals. There may also be a blurring of boundaries in our response to canonical texts. The Gabler edition of *Ulysses* and the continuing Cambridge edition of D. H. Lawrence inherit the New Critical concept of the literary text as a fixed, solid, and multifaceted aesthetic object. Computerized text management, along with other kinds of theoretical decenterings, will help disperse the highly finished canonical work into a more diffuse textual field. The integrated classical object is there broken down into different kinds and levels of text, with multiple links to other documents. A text like *Ulysses* ceases to be a fixed and bounded unit (a notion reinforced by the physical dimensions of a book) but rather becomes a textual resource from which a series of virtual versions of *Ulysses* can be generated, according to the scholarly or critical purpose to be served. Such versions might include

The **comparative** *Ulysses:* produced by Ehrlich's demonstration program that highlights variant readings between passages of the Random House and the Gabler editions.

The **intertextual** *Ulysses:* hypertext links connect the text of the novel with its sources and with the record of annotation and criticism. This *Ulysses* recognizes that Joyce made the novel a machine for generating interpretations of itself, as the text on the page incites dialogue with the whole corpus of Western writing.

The **literal** *Ulysses:* in a reversal of the previous perspective, *Ulysses* is seen as a culmination of the nineteenth-century tradition of documentary realism. Everything in the text can be hooked onto the particularities of life in Dublin in 1904. Through hypermedia links, *Ulysses* would be revealed as the product of a specific time and place—and also as being, itself, the highest form of documentation of that society.

The **oral/aural** *Ulysses:* one may view digitized text as the end point of a long process of abstraction. Originary cultures are exclusively oral and dependent on face-to-face contact; they fall under the domination of first writing and then print; finally, print yields to the disembodied medium of screens of text generated from electronic codes. Against this implicitly gloomy scenario—of communication becoming progressively less organic—we could argue that the new multimedia technologies, from the cinema on, promise to restore much of the sensuous immediacy of oral cultures. Ideally, *Ulysses* should be spoken and performed, not just read in silence (starting with Joyce's own reading from "Aeolus"). *Ulysses* is, furthermore, effectively a libretto: no other major novel has so much music running parallel to its text, and we shall not experience the work that Joyce imagined until that music is restored to its proper place.

9. On the present extent and future potential of computer networks see Quarterman, Hall, and Weingarten. For an overview of plans to distribute networked scholarly information, see Peters.

10. About half of the journals available through CARL deal with copyright directly; the others have delegated permissions to the Copyright Clearance Center.

11. CARL has installed an optical jukebox drive with 84 gigabytes of WORM (Write once, read many) storage, so that once an article has been digitized, it will remain available on line.

12. Postings to Usenet expire automatically after three weeks; if they did not, storage media would be filled with over five million messages a year.

13. At present, personal scanners may take up to two minutes per page, with about a 1 percent error rate (that is, roughly twenty errors per 350-word page).

14. I expect this to be true for North America; the more unified and centralized approach being taken in France is described by **Virbel**.

15. Electronic mail message from Ehrlich to Delany, 13 May 1992.

Works Cited

Caruso, Denise. "Where There's a Will, There's a WAIS." *Digital Media* 1 (17 February 1992): 5-6.

Crane, Gregory, and Elli Mylonas. "Ancient Materials, Modern Media: Shaping the Study of the Classics with Hypertext." Delany 205-20.

Delany, Paul, and George Landow, eds. *Hypermedia and Literary Studies.* Cambridge: MIT P, 1991.

Ehrlich, Heyward (ehrlich@andromeda.rutgers.edu). "The James Joyce Text Machine: A Scholar's Work Station." Demonstrated at *Joyce in Vancouver* conference, 15 June 91.

Ellmann, Richard. *The Consciousness of Joyce.* London: Faber, 1977.

Garreau, Joel. *Edge City: Life on the New Frontier.* New York: Doubleday, 1991.

Hall, Stephen C. "The Four Stages of National Research and Education Network Growth." *Educom Review* 26.1 (1991): 18-25.

Joyce's probing of the limits of the traditional literary text poses th
challenge to critical reading. Computers cannot blunt that challenge, in t
relieving readers of the task of interpretation. Nonetheless, the merge:
writings with docuverses and hypermedia resources will offer new kinds
to his fallible readers as they wrestle with the intricacies of his vision. In tl
sense, the personal docuverse is simply an archive that is more com]
more flexible, and more responsive than the books sitting inertly on ou
or the blank sheets to which we manually commit our thoughts. Ther
substitute for the aura that print culture has accumulated over the centu
usefulness to scholarship of computerized knowledge management ens
the century that awaits, these technologies are bound to prevail.

Notes

1. "Document" actually could mean a block of information in any media: pr
sound, or video. The computerized linking of such blocks is an emergent discipli:
(Delany).

2. A fax machine, for example, takes the coding and "discards" the paper; at
the receiving machine puts the paper back. Some of the broader social co1
dematerializing technologies are discussed in Garreau 132-34.

3. For a list of these books up to 1920, see Ellmann 96-134.

4. CD-ROM: Compact Disc, Read Only Memory. This format holds about 6
which cannot be changed or erased. A CD player to transfer informatior
computer currently costs less than $500.

5. The Chadwyck-Healey projects are to be completed in three stages, startin
of 1992.

6. The *MLA Bibliography* costs about $1,600 for four quarterly CDs. The *Thesauri*
o n a High Sierra CD ROM (compatible with Mac and PC), by the TLG Pr(
Brunner) University of California, Irvine CA 92717.

7. As originally published. Recent versions, like the Gabler edition of *Ulysse:*
copyright—though their exact status has yet to be tested in a court of law.

8. If a Joyce CD were issued, it would of course require periodic updates to acc
criticism.

Paul Delany

Miilumäki, Risto. "Computerized Joyce Studies." Paper given at *Joyce in Vancouver* conference, 15 June 1991.

Mort, Joseph. *The Anatomy of Xerography: Its Invention and Evolution.* Jefferson, NC: McFarland,1989.

Peters, Paul E. "Coalition for Networked Information Sets Second-Year Priorities." *Educom Review* 27:1 (1992): 14-16.

Quarterman, John. S. *The Matrix: Computer Networks and Conferencing Systems Worldwide.* Bedford: Digital P, 1990.

Rice, Thomas J. *James Joyce, A Guide to Research.* New York: Garland, 1982.

Weingarten, Fred. "Five Steps to NREN Enlightenment." *Educom Review* 26.1 (1991): 26-30.

Whittaker, M. "Uncovering the Future: Online Document Delivery through CARL Systems." *Colorado Libraries* December 1990: 38-40.

Wilson, David L. "Researchers Get Direct Access to Huge Data Base." *Chronicle of Higher Education* 9 October 1991: A24.

The Academic On Line

Alan T. McKenzie
Purdue University

Network. n.s. [net *and* work] *Any thing reticulated or decussated, at equal distances, with interstices between the intersections.*

—Samuel Johnson, *A Dictionary of the English Language*

Le soi *est peu, mais il n'est pas isolé, il est pris dans une texture de relations plus complexe et plus mobile que jamais. Il est toujours, jeune ou vieux, homme ou femme, riche ou pauvre, placé sur des <<noeuds>> de circuits de communication, seraient-ils infimes. Il est préférable de dire: placé à des postes par lesquels passent des messages de nature diverse. Et il n'est jamais, meme le plus défavorisé, dénué de pouvoir sur ces messages qui le traversent en le positionnant, que ce soit au poste de destinateur, ou de destinataire, ou de référent.*[1]

—Jean-François Lyotard, *La Condition Postmoderne: Rapport sur le Savoir*

If a humanist is someone who takes texts too seriously, then humanists ought to venture on line, where texts, serious texts, may be sent further and received faster, with less effort and expense, than even Dr. Faustus might have imagined. On-line researchers can identify and then rummage around in remote storehouses of information; they can also reach widely scattered humanists and *(mirabile dictu)* elicit prompt replies from them. Such possibilities ought to embolden everyone, even those academics who still pride themselves on their technological antipathies, to log on to some of the networks currently available. Word processors enable humanists' texts to accumulate accuracy and survive innumerable revisions; modems can help humanists enrich and distribute those texts quickly, with little cost to themselves, their institutions, or the environment.

Those readers whose eyes are gladdened by my second epigraph may need less encouragement. Electronic texts, having been rendered independent of ink, paper, agent, and human memory, are always already in a state of excitement. They weave their way along lines that are largely inexplicable and only partly determinate. Texts that arrive over a network have no margins to speak of; they present themselves to every gaze in a hierarchy yet to be established, and even then they are infinitely subject to revision. Anyone who takes time to develop the necessary technological and linguistic competence can enter an assortment of discourse communities that could well exhaust language itself.

This essay seeks to entice those readers with academic connections to reach out electronically, to learn what keys to strike and why. My instructions, however, include only as much technological detail as is unavoidable. The readers I have in mind have already succumbed to the siren call of the word processor, and they are now willing to exploit some of the other powers the computer can put in their hands. Even academics who do not wish to venture on line themselves may wish to know what the rest of us are up to.

Colleges, universities, federal agencies, and corporations have established computer connections that scientists, administrators, and hobbyists have been using for years. Any academic at a well-connected institution may participate.[2] All you need is a personal computer, a little know-how, and patience.[3] The ideal is to have the computer connected on campus directly to a high-speed network; but you can do quite well from home with some communications software, and a modem. The know-how, at least, can be acquired from friends, colleagues, on-line instructions and help screens, and, as a last resort, manuals.[4] Once connected, you can log into library catalogs and exchange messages and texts almost instantaneously with scholars all over the world. With a little more expertise, you will be able to receive everything from calls for conference papers to warnings about computer viruses and stolen rare books. Soon you will find yourself searching inexhaustible databases from your home or office computer, all for the price of a local phone call (except with some commercial databases).

The first step is to locate a mentor, someone who knows the setup of centralized, mainframe computers on your campus and the networks discussed below.[5] It helps considerably if this person also knows something about your computer and communications software. The protocols—the technological conventions that make communication between your computer and the mainframe possible—are complex, but once they have been set, you can forget about them. When you can skillfully execute the commands for your communications program, you are ready to access a mainframe and contend with its operating system and resident programs. After you have figured out the dozen or so basic commands for each of these programs, you are ready to embark on vast and only recently charted seas. In the course of your computer work, *never* give your mainframe password to anyone else, and *never* lend anyone the use of your account. Unscrupulous users can wreak havoc once they have gained access to the networks.

The mainframe operating system to which your modem and communications program connect you will very likely be either UNIX or VM, and, as with DOS, the operating system on the PC, you will want to get out of it and into an applications program as quickly as you can.[6] Glance at the manual, summon a few help screens, and get your mentor to write down the few essential commands you will need to start: those for saving, listing, and deleting files; summoning the text editor; interrupting the program; and logging off. You will also need to learn how to move the cursor, correct typos, and summon help screens not just in the mainframe operating system but in each of the programs you run. Unfortunately, but necessarily, the commands vary from level to level and program to program. On-line help is available at every turn, from help screens written into every program and from other users who, as I have said, respond patiently and lucidly to all sorts of queries. In this essay, I assume that you will be making your own step-by-step connections to information sources. However, new programs like Gopher and WAIS promise to cut out intermediate steps and make it very much easier for average users to find the information they want and download it to their own machines.

Having found your way into a mainframe, you can now connect to other mainframes all over the world. Your keystrokes will probably travel over either BITNET or the Internet, though you will not have much say in the matter, and it will not make much difference. An electronic address with periods in it (for example, vyc@mace.cc.purdue.edu) is on the Internet.[7] The letters and figures to the left of the @ are the user name, and the first group to the right is the node, the name of the computer that connects that user to the network. The remaining groups to the right are the subdomains and, finally, the domain that collectively govern the Internet's intricate structure. BITNET names have only a user name and a host (for example, MLAOD@cuvmb). (The upper-case letters in the BITNET user name are a convention; BITNET is not case-sensitive, nor is the Internet so far as user names are concerned.) Although numerous gateways exist between the two networks, users on the Internet who want to communicate with BITNET may have problems. Check with your mentor, or try adding `.bitnet` to the end of the address (for example, MLAOD@cuvmb.bitnet). Because the term *bitnet* is not actually a domain, this use is, technically, a solecism.

The Internet, an outgrowth of the Advanced Research Projects Agency (ARPA) of the Department of Defense, dates back to 1969 and now connects some 750,000 individual machines through a backbone funded by the National Science Foundation (NSF) and several dozen regional networks funded jointly by NSF and the participating institutions. Most machines on the Internet run the UNIX operating system and employ the sophisticated TCP/IP protocol, which supports remote logins and anonymous file-transfer protocol (FTP). Using FTP on its own to send or receive files over the network is a tricky task; but programs like Fetch for the Macintosh make it much simpler. DOS users can always read the manual. A word of warning: UNIX is case-sensitive for commands (for example, `telnet`, `mail`). If you put an upper-case letter to the right of the @ in a UNIX command, the mainframe may not know what to do with it.

BITNET, an alternative to the Internet, was founded in 1981 between CUNYVM and YALEVM (mainframes at CUNY and Yale running VM as an operating system); at present it links some 2,100 hosts in this country alone. (The term *host* refers to a computer of any size configured to communicate with other machines on the net and to store data received from them.) Employing a fairly simple (some would say primitive) store-and-forward protocol whereby messages are moved in blocks from one host to another, BITNET offers direct connections to Listserv—a program that stores files for the network and distributes them over it. But BITNET has no connections to Telnet, the Internet connection to library catalogs discussed in the next section.

Traffic on both networks is increasing rapidly, and something will have to be done about the Internet's funding and BITNET's technology. It is too soon to guess what will be done by whom or when, but many people on campus and on line are willing to do so anyway. The National Research and Education Network (NREN) is a gleam in the eye of EDUCOM, a consortium of academic institutions that supports information technology and develops resources for higher education (see Hall, Weingarten). Well-informed academics would do well to participate in this discussion.

Whichever network you use, you will have to learn, literally, to find yourself again and again when you are on line; you will have to remember or to ascertain precisely where you are and which program or machine is awaiting your command or refusing to take your latest instruction: sometimes it is your communications software asking you to turn the printer on, sometimes it is the electronic catalog of a library oceans away waiting stubbornly for you to "turn the page," sometimes it is the mainframe balking at a typo. Your communications software requires one command to print a file while UNIX or VM on the mainframe requires another, and the mail program within that mainframe expects still a third. Typing the UNIX command while you are in the mail program will baffle the computer, but it will not hurt it—you cannot do much damage to the hardware or the software. You can, however, mangle or lose texts or send them to the wrong people.

Learning to navigate within, between, and among programs is an exhilarating challenge. It used to be the humanist's texts that sometimes got mislaid, but now humanists can, temporarily, lose themselves. This frequent disorientation can be salutary, humbling, or infuriating, depending on your personality and mood and the sense of urgency with which you sat down at the keyboard. The prompt on your screen and the most recent commands you issued will be all you have to go by. Do not get lost. And when you do, do not panic. Summon a help screen, send a break—press `Ctrl-]` on most systems—or close the connection by exiting your communications program or hanging up the phone to which your modem is attached. Academics who have been drawn into the networks can survive and even thrive there. But I recommend that you begin with familiar territory and then venture forth gradually.

On-Line Library Catalogs

Take your first voyage into an on-line public access catalog (OPAC) at the nearest college or university library with which you are already familiar. Many libraries are now adding remote catalogs to the menu of choices on their home catalog; all you have to do is select the external catalog you want and you are led through the connection step by step. Failing this, the reference desk at your library should be able to supply the phone number, electronic address, and terminal settings. Someone at your computer center may have to help you establish the initial connection. If you are on the Internet, use Telnet, a protocol of that network. If you are on BITNET, leave the network and use your modem to call OPAC over phone lines. Either connection will help build facility and confidence as well as a repertoire of keystrokes and anecdotes and a numbing vocabulary.

Next, practice downloading some of your searches into either your allotted storage space on the mainframe or a disk on your own computer. The second is probably easier, as most mainframes have forbidding interfaces and restricted storage. Your communications package should have a `log` command that enables you to open a file on one of your disk drives and store everything that shows up on the screen. You can then call this file into your word processor to edit, rearrange, and print it. The communications software should also allow you to send everything from the screen directly to your printer or to print (dump) one screen at a time.

Once you can find your way into and then around a familiar library's on-line catalog, venture farther afield, to one of the OPACs that follow.[8] As soon as you gain access to a new library, find out how to exit—pressing `Ctrl-]` gets you out of most Telnet connections—how to summon a help screen, how to move to the next screen, and how to return to the main index. Print these screens or jot down the instructions and keep them at hand, because you can seldom remember or find them when you need them, and they differ for every library. Here are the addresses of three libraries

---

on which you can practice and the initial commands to get you started.[9] The Telnet address will work only if you are on the Internet. Otherwise, use your modem to call long distance. I have included the modem settings you may need to set in your communications program. Once you are connected, press the enter key several times to alert the system. VT100 usually works as a response to the query "terminal type." Work your way through the help screens, be patient, and start by looking for books you know will be there.

> Harvard University—HOLLIS (Harvard On-Line Library Information System).
> Address: telnet hollis.harvard.edu
> Phone access: (617) 495-9500 (settings: 7E 1 F)
> Press the enter key at the TS prompt. Type hollis at the next prompt. For help with the connection (not with the catalog), call (617) 495-9388.

> University of Illinois—ILLINET On Line.
> Address: telnet garcon.cso.uiuc.edu
> Type Ics at the login: prompt.
> Phone access: (217) 333-2494 (settings: 7N I H). For help with the connection or the catalog, call (217) 333-2290.

> University of California On-Line Catalog—MELVYL.
> Address: telnet melvyl.ucop.edu
> For help with the connection or for the nearest phone number to dial, call (415) 987-0555. MELVYL has many helpful screens for you to work your way through. Try lookup mode the first few times you search this catalog.

When you get very bold, try JANET, the Joint Academic Network of the United Kingdom (telnet sun.nsf.ac.uk). The gateway between JANET and the Internet is smooth, and the packet assembler disassembler (PAD) program to which you will be connected is uncommonly clear and helpful. At the log-in prompt, type janet; at the hostname prompt, type uk.ac. janet.news; and at the user prompt, type news. Read the Index and Help files there. If you want to go right to a library, try typing uk.ac.aberdeen.library for Aberdeen or uk.ac.cam.ul for Cambridge at the hostname prompt. The electronic addresses of other libraries are available in the Catalogs subfile of the Library file.

Discussion Lists

The instructions on connecting to British libraries came over one of the discussion lists to which I subscribe (c18-l@psuvm.psu.edu). The Telnet addresses for research libraries in the United States came over another one (humanist@brownvm.brown.edu). Dozens of other addresses are now available. Several hundred lists of interest to academic humanists already exist, and new ones are formed every month, with word of their creation arriving over the networks. Each list has many subscribers who receive all the files posted to it by others on the list. Scholars and others from all over the world are already exchanging news, information, knowledge, opinion, and queries of every description electronically. In the past few months the following items have found their way onto my screen from one or another of these sources:

1. Instructions for reaching electronic mail addresses in South Africa.
2. A comparison, from American University in Cairo, of the different forms taken by commentaries on recent editions of the Koran, medieval philosophy, and hypertext.
3. News of two rare-book short courses at the Lilly Library at Indiana University.
4. Description of the Jacobite literature holdings at the Harry Ransom Humanities Center at the University of Texas.
5. A list of machine-readable dictionaries available on line, including a Coptic-English dictionary, Liddell-Scott, *Lo Scaffale Elettronico*, and *Macquarie Dictionary*.

The day Northrop Frye died, a colleague of his at Victoria College posted an eloquent electronic tribute, the subject line of which read, "A Death in the Family." During Operation Desert Storm, scholars in Haifa and Jerusalem supplied nightly accounts of the personal lives of academics in and out of sealed rooms. Although postings like these (both came over Humanist) put a human face on the network, you will not, of course, want to read everything that appears on your screen. What does not interest you can be easily ignored and discarded without recycling.

The most interesting of all such lists, and the one to begin with, is Humanist. To subscribe to it, send a message to editors@brownvm.brown.edu asking to do so. Among the many other current lists likely to be of interest to readers in the humanities-related professions are those discussing Anglo-Saxon topics (ANSAX-L@wvnvm); Jane Austen (AUSTEN-L@mcgilll); bibliographic instruction (BI-L@bingvmb); comparative literature (lawall@complit.umass.edu); Jacques Derrida (DERRIDA@cfrvm); Ficino, a list about Renaissance and Reformation studies (editor@epas.utoronto.ca); film (CINEMA-L@auvm); rare books (exlibris@zodiac.rutgers.edu); Shakespeare (ksteele@epas.utoronto.ca); Thomas Pynchon (pynchon-l@sfu.ca); and rhetoric and composition (PURTOPOI@purccvm).

All these lists are stored in and distributed by the BITNET software Listserv, which resides in various hosts on that network. To subscribe, for example, to the Anglo-Saxon list over BITNET, type (in the mail utility on your mainframe) the message `tell Listserv@wvnvm subscribe ANSAX-L` and add a space and your full name. If you are on the Internet, send (mail) the one-line message `subscribe ANSAX-L` plus your full name to listserv@wvnvm.bitnet. To subscribe to the others, change the node (the part of the address immediately to the right of the @) and the title of the list accordingly. You may be asked (by return electronic mail) to supply a brief biography before your name is added to the list. Do *not* send your subscription request to the list itself (for example, do not type `mail PURTOPOI@purccvm`) because, unless the moderator intercepts it, the request will go to everyone who already subscribes, several hundred people or more, all over the world. They will not be glad to hear of your wish to subscribe.

If there is an editor's or a moderator's name to the left of the @ (as in Humanist, Ficino, and the Shakespeare Conference), send a message to that user name, indicating your interest in subscribing. Moderators sort and arrange postings to the list and keep track of contributors and readers. Their efforts are benign, very helpful, and enormously time consuming.

For a list of all 2,500 discussion lists currently available, send the message list global to any Listserv. If you are on BITNET, send it to your local Listserv. From the Internet, try, working westward, YALEVM, UGA, UICVM, or UCLAVMXA. Diane Kovacs (DKOVACS @kentvm on BITNET; dkovacs@kentvm.kent.edu on the Internet) maintains a list of lists of special interest to humanists. To retrieve it on BITNET, type (again in the mail utility on your mainframe) the message `tell LISTSERV@kentvm get ACADLIST FILE1` and then repeat the message but substitute `FILE2`. On the Internet, send listserv@kentvm.kent.edu the two-line message `get acadlist file1`, press enter key, then type `get acadlist file2`. If you want to try an FTP, the address is ksuvxa.kent.edu. Good luck!

Once you have been recognized as a subscriber, every message posted to that list will be distributed automatically to the electronic mailbox on your mainframe account. The mail program (or utility, as the programs running on mainframes are usually called) enables you to scan, read, forward, edit, save, and reply to each of these postings. Be especially careful with the reply function. In most mail programs if you type a lower-case *r*, everything you type thereafter will be distributed to everyone else who received that message. An *R* (that is, upper case), however, sends your reply only to the machine that sent you the message. As with other discourse communities, it is probably a good idea to listen for a while before barging in with postings of your own. When you do have something to say, send it over the network using either the reply function or the mail (or send) function in the mail utility.

Be advised that electronic mail from these discussion lists piles up, or at least the bytes accumulate somewhere. When you log on to the mainframe, you will be told, "You have new mail," and when you enter the mail program, you may well find a message like "37 messages, 31 new, 34 unread." Your electronic mailbox not only fills up but also nudges you to tend to it.

To post a message to all the subscribers of the discussion list Humanist, you send mail to humanist@brownvm.brown.edu. You can type the message directly within the mail utility on the mainframe or use one of the text editors running elsewhere on that mainframe. But the text editors I know, vi and emacs, are excruciatingly cumbersome. They seem to have been designed to discourage even the slightest change in a text. You will want to prepare most of the documents you send over the networks, whether notes, letters, inquiries, proposals, or articles, on the word processor you normally use. Save each text as an ASCII file (that is, one without such formatting features as underlining, justification, and font changes), then upload that file into your account on the mainframe using your communications software and, probably, the Kermit software running on the mainframe. Once you have stored the file in your mainframe account, you can send it to discussion lists, colleagues who are also on the network, or journal editors who have kept up with technology. A draft of this article, for instance, was submitted to the MLA (MLAOD@cuvmb) via electronic mail. The final draft traveled the same rapid route, followed, at a considerable distance, by a hard copy.

You can reverse the process with any postings, messages, or files that come in over the networks. Save them on your mainframe account, download them to your computer, and then call them up in your own word processor for editing, formatting, and rearranging. You will have crossed the network's *pons asinorum* when you accomplish your first transfer of a stored file from a remote node to your own account on the mainframe.[10] By the time you have managed this transaction, you will no doubt have encountered several mailer daemons, notices from the mainframe that mail you have tried to send has been returned, abruptly, because it was erroneously addressed.

Users already on the networks will initiate you into etiquette, conventions, and procedures that prevail there. The software will take care of your grammar, at least that of your commands and responses to the computer. You will become acutely attentive to punctuation and capitalization, as the instructions and cautions distributed throughout this article suggest. Soon too you will be familiar with the @ and ! signs and other signifiers in the domain-naming system that determines where texts go. Eventually you will become responsive to the different prompts (the indications on your screen that the system is awaiting an instruction or a reply) of different programs and utilities, fluent in abbreviations like BTW and RTFM, inured to flames (violent replies by readers opposed to the content, or dismayed at the naïveté, of previous messages), and alert to the subtleties of emoticons—faces constructed out of letters and punctuation marks like :-) and ;-) to indicate the mood of the writer. The first few times you see these figures, you will have to tip your head slightly to the left to get them. (Then you will probably shake it slightly.) After a while you may learn to ignore them altogether, but it is interesting to watch a new mode of communication develop extra-alphabetic signs.

Network users are still struggling to find ways to enhance electronic texts with italics, underlining, and diacritical marks, few of which can pass through the current gateways and protocols intact. The ownership and the privacy of electronic texts are also being debated, and such questions are not likely to be resolved before you join the discussion. A related problem is the documenting of material quoted from an evanescent, electronic source. Some kind of acknowledgment and attribution is certainly called for, but the date of origin of a posting may have little bearing on its composition or its present whereabouts. Electronic texts move very far, very fast, and their origins (and whereabouts) are difficult to keep track of, even after they have arrived at your computer. Copyright ownership of electronic texts is not yet established, and the possibilities for plagiarism loom large. At the moment, except for the authors of some software, the connected community seems more willing to share than to claim and to keep texts moving and improving. A spirit of generosity prevails on the networks, and whereas that attitude may encourage both haste and verbosity, no faster, more supple, cheaper, or more convenient mode of creating, enriching, and distributing texts is likely to come along soon.

Because electronic texts have few external clues and no established conventions, tone is even harder to control and convey electronically than in print. All computer screens look pretty much alike, and the transmissions that appear on them have little to indicate gender, age, class, rank, or level of expertise. Most humanists will welcome such uncontaminated texts, and some will want to take part in shaping the future of electronic discourse. That activity, of course, can only be pursued on line, where the discussion continues, implicitly and explicitly, by both precept and example.

Journals

Several journals already accept submissions, solicit reviews, and distribute texts over the networks. They store back issues on a machine that can be accessed by the alarmingly named procedures mentioned above (anonymous FTP; Listserv). One such publication is *EJournal* (EJOURNAL@albnyvms), which describes itself (over the networks) as "an all-electronic, Bitnet/Internet distributed, peer-reviewed, academic periodical. [It is] particularly interested in theory and praxis surrounding the creation, transmission, storage, interpretation, alteration, and replication of electronic text." *Postmodern Culture* (PMC@ncsuvm) also accepts submissions, sends them out for peer review, solicits book reviewers, and distributes its issues on line.

Electronic Mail

Electronic mail (e-mail) follows the same lines—electronic, social, and professional—as the discussion lists, except that you send it only to people whose addresses you know and designate, and you get it only from people who have designated you as a recipient. In addition to speed and economy, several features make e-mail a major improvement over its predecessor—referred to derisively on the networks as snailmail. Once a text is in the mainframe computer, you can send it to one or more recipients effortlessly, no matter how long or complex it is. Conversely, a text drawn off the network and into your computer, whether from a discussion list, a colleague, or a database (see below), will submit to all the ministrations of a word processor. Some students, I suspect, are beginning to realize the usefulness of e-mail for plagiarism. The day cannot be too far away when well-connected undergraduates (and perhaps not just undergraduates) will circulate, locate, or commission texts that satisfy assignments perfectly and that are conveniently reattributable.

On a happier note, replying to e-mail is virtually effortless and instantaneous. When you tell the mail utility that you want to reply to a message it has just shown you, it automatically makes the "from" line of that message the "to" line of a new one, so all you have to do is start typing your reply. Thus, you will hear from some correspondents who would not otherwise write, and you will hear much sooner from others who would heretofore have waited until they had time, inclination, writing paper, and stamps at hand simultaneously. But again, be careful not to fire off a personal letter to a half-dozen unintended recipients or to launch a hasty electronic text that you would have been well advised to let cool overnight.

Most mail programs let you designate groups of people as cohorts, mail aliases, or some similar term drawn from natural language into computer terminology. These groups may consist of colleagues from your department or from a committee, panel members from a national organization, or scholars from the worldwide academic community who share your interest in the poetry of Robert Ferguson. The mail system enables you to send the same document, of which you need type only a single copy, to everyone named as a cohort. Other procedures allow you to forward messages and save them in various folders. You will, of course, have to contend with the vagaries of whatever mail utility is already installed on your institution's mainframe. Ask your mentor about supplementary interfaces like Mail Handler (MH) or Elm, which can take a lot of the excitement out of your initial ventures on line.

The biggest problems with e-mail are finding the electronic addresses of people who are already on line and, perhaps more difficult, persuading others you would like to reach over the networks to acquire such addresses. The discussion lists you read are a good source of information, since authors' electronic addresses become part of their texts. The names and electronic addresses of old friends and former colleagues will undoubtedly show up on one list or another, and those connections will draw you deeper into the net.

You can retrieve addresses from remote sites by using the whois command in various on-line directories, called White Pages, and by using something called Knowbot Information System (telnet nri.reston.va.us 185), but the odds are against your success. One hopes that the MLA will soon include electronic addresses in the directory issue of *PMLA* and make them available on line as well. Incidentally, e-mail is bringing the business card into and out of academic pocketbooks and wallets, as electronic addresses are clots of utterly forgettable characters, every one of which must be exactly right.

Usenet

Usenet follows the same electronic lines as the discussion lists mentioned above, up to a point. Actually it follows lines laid out for UUCP, the UNIX network, and goes only as far as the host machine on your campus, dumping postings from all over the world into the storage capacity of a mainframe, where they wait for you to summon them. Usenet differs from the lists in its procedures, which are more passive, its members, who are more heterogeneous, and its contents, which are so various as to be virtually indescribable. Although Usenet probably has a half million users by now, using Usenet consists largely of discarding hundreds of articles, as postings to this service are called, that do not interest you. The various programs for reading Usenet, such as rn, or NewsGrazer for the NeXT, offer convenient options for discarding articles without even glancing at them. You can, for instance, instruct your mainframe not to show you articles from specific nodes.

Nearly a thousand different newsgroups operate on Usenet, on subjects from alt.rock-n-roll.metal to rec.humor.funny, rec.woodworking, sci.military, and soc.culture.african. A Usenet host holds articles posted to these groups until you enter the Usenet utility on your mainframe (for example, by typing rn) and ask to read them. As with other texts, you may save, edit, and reply to those you derive from Usenet. Do not entangle yourself in this network, however, unless you have many hours to spare, since it is both voluble and insidious. Whatever other groups you elect to have dumped into your account, ask for and read news.newusers.questions, a forum in which new users ask, and old users answer, all sorts of questions about procedures, protocols, and courtesies applicable everywhere on Usenet.

Databases

The networks will draw you into other sources of information and knowledge (but they will not help you tell the difference). Project Gutenberg, at the University of Illinois (hart@vmd.cso.uiuc.edu), plans to have ten thousand books available electronically by the year 2001. Recently, in honor of National Library Week, the project administrators encouraged terminal users everywhere to download electronic copies of *Alice in Wonderland* and *The Hunting of the Snark* and put them before the young and the curious. Project Gutenberg tries to post books suggested by users of the database. Their goal is "to provide the texts which will be used most, . . . to create a literate and computer literate environment for the benefit of all." The Center for Computer Analysis of Texts, at the University of Pennsylvania (kraft@penndrls.upenn.edu), is another valuable repository, especially of biblical materials. The Oxford Text Archive (archive@vax.oxford.ac.uk) is one more such resource available on line.

Before you download any files, be sure that you have storage space available, either in your mainframe account or on your own computer. Be careful, too, where you retrieve files from, since viruses, worms, and other electronic contaminants can make their way over the networks into both mainframes and personal computers. Other databases are available commercially, especially Knowledge Index, the poor scholar's (forgive the pleonasm) after-hours version of DIALOG (3460 Hillview Avenue, Palo Alto, CA 94304). This database allows you to search the *MLA International Bibliography*, *Magill's Survey of Cinema*, *Consumer Reports*, *Petersons College Database*, *Art Literature International*, the electronic files of nearly a dozen newspapers, and several hundred other databases for a moderate hourly or rather, minutely, charge.

The Research Library Information Network (RLIN) is also available to subscribers for a fee. It includes the *Eighteenth-Century Short-Title Catalogue* and other troves

I have yet to plunder. All these riches, and more, are out there, waiting to be summoned onto the computer screens, and then into the texts and minds, of academics.

Notes

1. "A *self* does not amount to much, but no self is an island; each exists in a fabric of relations that is now more complex and mobile than ever before. Young or old, man or woman, rich or poor, a person is always located at 'nodal points' of specific communication circuits, however tiny these may be. Or better: one is always located at a post through which various kinds of messages pass. No one, not even the least privileged among us, is ever entirely powerless over the messages that traverse and position him at the post of sender, addressee, or referent" (Lyotard 15).

2. Perhaps half of all colleges and universities are currently connected to the several networks, but the number appears to be growing steadily, and all major institutions will be on either BITNET or Internet. Check with your colleagues in the sciences or in the campus computer center to find out the present status and plans of your institution. Institutions connected to the networks do not usually pass on the charges for these connections to individual faculty members or students.

3. Virtually any computer will do, from relics like the CP/M or TRSDOS machines to the powerful NeXT and 486 computers now in the showrooms. Apples and IBMs and their compatibles work equally well—the communications software imposes (or feigns) compatibility. As for software, I like Procomm, a communications program bundled with some modems or available from Datastorm Technologies (Columbia, MO). I find it comparatively simple, logical, and helpful. Several other commercial, semicommercial, or public-domain programs are available, including Kermit. Your campus computer center can probably give you a free copy of Kermit, but you should know that its interface is unhelpful, indeed stubborn. Other machines and programs you reach out to around the world will offer you resistance enough, so you will not want to contend with a communications program that defies you.

4. Like all other computer tasks, operating on line is best learned at the keyboard, by trial and error. People already on the networks are wonderfully generous with their skills and knowledge; indeed, this willingness to share information, advice, and techniques is a strong indication that humanism can thrive on line. Much of the material in this article was derived from messages posted on the various sources discussed in it.

For those who insist on print, Brendan P. Kehoe's *Zen and the Art of the Internet* is a concise practical guide. John S. Quarterman's fascinating and authoritative work *The Matrix* is especially good on the domain-naming systems that control the syntax of network addresses; the gateways between various networks; and the history, scope, protocols, and conventions of the networks. Tracy L. LaQuey, *The Users Directory of Computer Networks*, offers 630 pages

---

of useful diagrams, electronic addresses, and phone numbers. *REACH* (Research and Educational Applications of Computers in the Humanities), the newsletter of the Humanities Computing Facility of the University of California, Santa Barbara (HCF1DAHL@ucsbuxa), comes out every two months, in both electronic and hard copies.

5. I am pleased to acknowledge specifically the expert and personal assistance of Tharon Howard, a graduate student in the Purdue English Department and moderator of Purtopoi; Eugene Spafford, assistant professor of computer science at Purdue and a manager of Usenet; and John Steele, director of the Purdue University Computing Center, and his staff.

6. Macintosh users are offered a graphical user interface (GUI) in place of the mysteries of DOS. Once they are connected to a network, though, they may well have to type most of their commands, just like everyone else.

7. Enter electronic addresses into the system exactly as they appear, but do not type the parentheses.

8. You can retrieve a frequently updated list of on-line libraries, including Telnet numbers, phone numbers, and instructions for getting into on-line catalogs. On the Internet, in the mail utility of your mainframe, send the message `get internet library` to LISTSERV@unmvm.bitnet, leaving the subject line blank. On BITNET, type `tell LISTSERV@ unmvm get internet library`. The scholars who maintain and distribute this list are among the many whose expertise and benevolence make the networks work.

9. Type the Telnet command and the address at the basic prompt of your mainframe. Get someone to show you how to build a Names file on VM or an Alias file on UNIX. These macros for the mainframe will allow you to send mail and to Telnet into libraries by retyping a manageable, and rememberable, nickname.

10. The first texts you retrieve ought to be the "Internet Resource Guide" (available from nnsc@nnsc.nsf.net); BITNET USERHELP (type `tell listserv@bitnet send bitnet userhelp`); and the "Humanist Guide" (on the Internet, mail to listserv@brownvm.brown.edu the one-line message `get humanist guide`; on BITNET, type `tell LISTSERV@brownvm send humanist guide`).

Works Cited

Hall, Stephen C. "The Four Stages of National Research and Education Network Growth." *Educom Review* 26.1 (1991): 18-25.

Johnson, Samuel. *A Dictionary of the English Language.* 2 vols. London, 1765.

Kehoe, Brendan P. *Zen and the Art of the Internet: A Beginner's Guide to the Internet.* Revision 1.0, February 1992. Distributed by the author: guide-request @cs.widener.edu.

LaQuey, Tracy L. *The Users Directory of Computer Networks.* Bedford: Digital, 1990.

Lyotard, Jean-Francois. *The Postmodern Condition: A Report on Knowledge.* Trans. Geoff Bennington and Brian Massumi. Minneapolis: U of Minnesota P, 1984. (Translation of *La Condition Postmoderne: Rapport sur le Savoir,* 1979.)

Quarterman, John S. *The Matrix: Computer Networks and Conferencing Systems Worldwide.* Bedford: Digital, 1990.

Weingarten, Fred. "Five Steps to NREN Enlightenment." *Educom Review* 26.1 (1991): 26-30.

Two Theses about the New Scholarly Communication

Allen H. Renear
Brown University

Geoffrey Bilder
Brown University

Introduction

Until now the greatest impact of computing on academic life and scholarly communication has appeared in text processing. In less than twenty years text processing
has gone from being practically nonexistent at universities to having become the
dominant means of preparing manuscripts and a very visible part of academic life.
This change has had myriad effects: computer-based text processing has simplified
the production of books and articles, created new forms for collaboration, and even,
some have argued, changed the nature of scholarly research, communication, and
thought. But as widespread and possibly profound as the influence of text processing
has been, we predict that in the current decade its effects will be easily surpassed by
another (though related) innovation in information technology: computer-mediated communication.

Although the reader is likely to be tired of new technical phrases and acronyms,
perhaps even suspecting that many hardly exist outside a single article or research
group, we strongly recommend using "computer-mediated communication." This
phrase, well established in the literature of networks, goes back at least to Starr
Roxanne Hiltz and Murray Turoff's classic study *The Network Nation: Human
Communication via Computer*, and it has been used regularly up to the present. John
S. Quarterman's definitive work on the current state of computer networks and
conferencing systems in fact categorizes network services as either (a) computer-
mediated communication or (b) resource sharing (which involves sharing storage
space, processing, software, data, and peripheral devices).

In this chapter we use the term *computer-mediated communication* (CMC) to refer
broadly to a wide variety of services that allow users of computing systems to

communicate with one another, using computers and telecommunication networks. The best-known example of such computer-mediated communication is electronic mail sent and received by individuals. Other examples that are likely to be familiar to academic users include bulletin-board systems, such as those on CompuServe, group-mailing lists like Listserv lists, and the Usenet conferencing facility NetNews.[1] In addition to electronic mail and bulletin boards, computer-mediated communication also includes a number of specialized systems in use in industry and government designed to support group decision-making and cooperative projects. Finally, computer-mediated communication includes a wide range of experimental applications that are implemented mostly in laboratory settings or that exist only in technical reports or the minds of researchers.

Like many others, we believe that electronic conferencing has already had an enormous impact on our intellectual lives, and we believe it will produce fundamental changes in our culture and intellectual life as radical as those effected by writing and print. But in this essay we do not argue for the importance or revolutionary nature of computer-mediated comunication (see McLuhan, Ong, Hiltz and Turoff, Bolter, Heim, and Landow). Instead, we focus on two very simple and very general, if often overlooked, theses that provide an essential background for sound theorizing about computer-mediated communication.

First, computer-mediated communication is a *general purpose* technology. The role of computer-mediated communication in the development of new forms for scholarly communication must be seen against the background of computer-mediated communication as a *general purpose* communication technology used extensively in areas entirely unrelated to academic research and scholarship.

Second, the significance of computer-mediated communication lies in its protean nature.[2] Computer-mediated communication promises to have a huge impact on academic culture, but that effect will not derive from any one single, specific feature of computing. Instead, it will come from its protean form, from its capacity to create astonishingly powerful, and yet astonishingly flexible, environments for human interaction.

These two theses have a common theme: variety. The first asserts that computer-mediated communication varies in *content;* the second, that it varies in *form*. And although much of this variation already exists and can be enjoyed today, the larger part of it is still to come. The possibilities for computer-mediated communication are as limitless as the possibilities of form and content for human interactions in general. And probably no one is better situated to appreciate these possibilities than are scholars and other thoughtful participants in this new medium. So if we seem at

Two Theses about the New Scholarly Communication

times to direct our arguments at the theorizing participant, we do so because we suspect that leadership and innovation are as likely to come from them as from social scientists, systems designers, and specialists in computer-supported cooperative work. Our imagined audience, in other words, consists not just of developers of computer-mediated communication systems but rather that broader group of scholars and other participants who have been unable to resist reflecting on the significance of this new medium for scholarly communication and who are frequently called upon to help to develop the policies and procedures that will assimilate it into academic life.

Thesis 1: Computer-Mediated Communication Is a General Purpose Technology

The Range of Conferences

The vast network of interconnected networks that Quarterman, following William Gibson, calls "The Matrix," already consists of nearly one million computers and ten million users and reaches every continent and almost every country. It is difficult to estimate the number of computer conferences on the net, given any reasonable definition of conference, but even restricting consideration to global, publicly accessible conferences, we would guess that the number is well over ten thousand.

Electronic conferencing, then, is as large as the world—its electromagnetic tendrils cover our planet and reach the most remote outposts of progress. Since the fact might not appear so obvious, we wish to emphasize that the intellectual range of computer conferencing equals its physical extent: just as computer networking covers the planet, so too the content of current computer conferencing also encompasses the entire world of human interests and action.

Nothing human seems alien to electronic conferencing. After all, there exist conferences on set theory, DNA chemistry, and Anglo-Saxon philology; conferences on medieval China, Derrida, and the care of laboratory primates; conferences on cancer therapy, Hellenistic Judaism, and agricultural economics. There are in fact many hundreds of public conferences such as these, and their existence comes quickly to mind if we are academic Internet or BITNET users sitting down to ruminate on the new scholarly communication. Yet before concentrating too quickly on scholarly communications, we might take a moment to remind ourselves that although hundreds of such conferences exist, they reside within a field of *thousands* of other public Internet conferences, many of which focus on concerns that have had a far wider and much more enduring place in human history than the academic—conferences on topics like cooking, beekeeping, brewing, dancing, sex, astrology, weaponry, politics, popular music, tattooing, and body piercing.

As we consider the new scholarly communication, we are likely to employ familiar models of scholarly interaction: is this conference like a seminar or a faculty lunchroom conversation? Is that one like a moderated journal or a page of letters to the editor? And is this other like a lecture or a symposium? Again, we should bear in mind that although many conferences are devoted to assisting the increase of knowledge or the enjoyment scholarship, most serve other purposes entirely. Their participants promote political causes, search for jobs, flirt, titillate and are titillated in return, resolve emotional problems, and even worship. If we look for models for these interactions, we shall again have to look beyond the traditional forms of academic conversation and scholarly communication to more enduring institutions and practices—parties, parks, taverns, theaters, and churches.

In fact when we look up from the conferences, public and private both, that academic networks make available, we must remind ourselves that the larger networked world uses computer-mediated communication to set about its usual business of entertainment, commerce, social life, and government. Contemporary computer-mediated communication is used to deliver X rays and movies, to invoice bank accounts, to adjust satellite orbits, and to guide bombing runs.

The Net Imitates Life

Computer-mediated communication per se connects no more intimately or exclusively to academic scholarship and research than does print or any other major communications medium. Although this morning's newspaper might include a book review or a report on new findings in science or medicine, it is likely dominated by sensationalistic news of fires, robbery, rapes, and moral turpitude. It devotes even more space to commercial advertisements, fashion commentary, weather forecasts, advice to the confused, sports, games, comics, stock prices, and classified ads. In our text-drenched environment, university presses and scholarly societies do print many scholarly monographs, but the printed page is more likely to appear in an invoice, tabloid newspaper, or mail-order catalogue than in an academic research report.

It should not come as a surprise, therefore, that today research and scholarly communication form only a small part of the conference traffic even on university-dominated research and academic networks. Moreover, even as the absolute quantity of scholarly and academic use increases over the next few years, its *share* of of the total quantity of computer-mediated communication will probably fall even further. Discussions of the significance of network communication that overlook these facts present a confused and misleading picture of the relationship between computer-mediated communication and scholarly communication.

This point can be made vividly by comparing the topics of the most popular Netnews conferences with the table of contents from any daily newspaper. Figure 1 shows a table estimating the relative popularity of the forty most popular NetNews groups.[3] Figure 2 is the table of contents from the 29 March 1992 issue of the *Providence Journal-Bulletin,* a prize-winning urban daily, far better than most; we took the index from the day we wrote this section of the essay. No comparable information is available for distribution list conferencing, but BITNET-based Listserv lists and Usenet distribution lists have a larger proportion of academic conferences. Public conferencing on the major commercial networks such as CompuServ and Prodigy is even more lowbrow.

A number of works of science fiction like Vernon Vigne's "True Names" and William Gibson's *Neuromancer* have described a future in which the data and services of the network appear to the user as a virtual reality of landscapes, creatures, machinery, buildings, and so on. These works assume that a user interface of this sort provides the most effective means of conveying and manipulating large amounts of information. Suppose one entered such a virtual world created from the set of networked conferences that currently exist on the Internet. One would find oneself, perhaps disappointingly, in a more or less typical United States city with its full range of entertainment, cultural, and commericial services and activities. The most prominent features would be public amusements: movies and plays, idle chatting, and opportunities for flirtations, insults, leering, and political haranguing. In short, the usual mix: a lot of low culture, a spot of high. And beyond the open public world, in vast buildings with doormen and security guards, the business of business, government, and education would steadily hum away.

Life on the nets, it seems, is just that—life. And so will life be on the proposed data highways of the future. Discussions of the proposed National Research and Education Network have used the metaphor of "data highways" to describe a proposed integration and enhancement of the current Internet, suggesting, correctly we think, that it would prove as valuable to the infrastructure of our country as has the national highway system. This metaphor makes our point as well. Our national highways are undoubtedly valuable infrastructure without which we could not so efficiently transport goods, provide services, or distribute labor. But a survey of the traffic on a stretch, say, of Interstate 95 near Providence, Rhode Island, will reveal that many, if not most, travelers have goals less directly utilitarian than distributing goods or labor. They are going to the movies, visiting their children, heading for Boston to watch the Red Sox play—or just out for a drive. Some may be off on idle amusements and unsavory errands. None of this should surprise us. The national highway system is a general-purpose transportation technology, just as computer-mediated communication is a general-purpose communication technology.

```
+— Estimated total number of people who read the group worldwide
|      +— Actual number of readers in sampled population
|      |      +— Propagation: how many sites receive this group at all
|      |      |      +— Recent traffic (messages per month)
|      |      |      |      +— Recent traffic (kilobytes per month)
|      |      |      |      |      +— Crossposting percentage
|      |      |      |      |      |      +— Share:percentage of news readers
|      |      |      |      |      |      |        who read this group
V      V      V      V      V      V      V
```

#	Est. total	Actual	Prop.	Msgs/mo	KB/mo	Cross	Share	Group
1	260000	5905	70%	2343	5883.7	16%	13.8%	alt.sex
2	210000	4653	84%	717	1340.7	17%	10.9%	misc.jobs.offered
3	180000	4126	83%	73	183.9	0%	9.7%	rec.humor.funny
4	180000	4065	89%	9	141.2	100%	9.5%	news.announce.newusers
5	170000	3871	84%	1603	1990.9	33%	9.1%	misc.forsale
6	160000	3669	82%	2439	4143.1	4%	8.6%	rec.humor
7	140000	3199	73%	6	42.8	0%	7.5%	rec.arts.erotica
8	120000	2786	90%	1415	2608.4	15%	6.5%	news.groups
9	110000	2572	86%	702	1101.1	13%	6.0%	comp.graphics
10	110000	2547	66%	1525	5016.3	1%	6.0%	alt.sex.bondage
11	110000	2471	91%	576	1434.3	22%	5.8%	news.admin
12	110000	2452	82%	2245	2642.6	20%	5.7%	misc.forsale.computers
13	100000	2359	82%	583	558.7	25%	5.5%	misc.wanted
14	100000	2324	87%	54	298.7	0%	5.4%	news.announce.conferences
15	100000	2306	83%	354	658.6	9%	5.4%	misc.jobs.misc
16	100000	2302	87%	888	1600.7	9%	5.4%	comp.lang.c
17	100000	2278	79%	154	3579.0	7%	5.3%	alt.sources
18	100000	2275	88%	778	1303.9	17%	5.3%	comp.unix.questions
19	100000	2268	51%	1118	56017.0	12%	5.3%	alt.binaries.pictures.erotica
20	100000	2267	80%	1463	3673.0	20%	5.3%	rec.arts.startrek
21	100000	2263	89%	80	622.9	100%	5.3%	news.announce.newgroups
22	100000	2256	84%	37	1522.8	0%	5.3%	comp.binaries.ibm.pc
23	99000	2253	87%	1132	2020.8	14%	5.3%	comp.windows.x
24	99000	2249	86%	73	3283.3	0%	5.3%	comp.sources.misc
25	98000	2226	76%	2531	5198.3	7%	5.2%	soc.culture.indian
26	95000	2149	86%	253	505.1	14%	5.0%	comp.misc
27	93000	2099	80%	968	1483.6	10%	4.9%	rec.travel
28	90000	2039	80%	5	80.6	60%	4.8%	news.answers
29	88000	1984	84%	248	622.2	19%	4.6%	comp.ai
30	86000	1954	89%	399	581.7	6%	4.6%	news.newusers.questions
31	85000	1933	86%	1016	2195.9	11%	4.5%	comp.lang.c++
32	85000	1927	86%	1	5.2	0%	4.5%	news.announce.important
33	85000	1927	83%	1127	1751.2	11%	4.5%	sci.electronics
34	84000	1910	80%	2586	5639.8	4%	4.5%	rec.arts.movies
35	83000	1879	86%	36	2075.7	0%	4.4%	comp.sources.unix
36	82000	1862	81%	2371	3867.0	13%	4.4%	rec.music.misc
37	82000	1859	81%	1288	2324.7	12%	4.3%	misc.consumers
38	81000	1839	73%	2275	5782.5	46%	4.3%	talk.politics.misc
39	81000	1832	82%	514	2446.5	5%	4.3%	misc.jobs.resumes
40	80000	1822	69%	519	1679.8	42%	4.3%	alt.activism

Figure 1: Usage statistics for "Top 40" Netnews news groups, ranked by popularity for two weeks in the spring of 1992.

Two Theses about the New Scholarly Communication

INSIDE
TODAY'S JOURNAL

FOUR SECTIONS / 40 PAGES

LOCAL
Climb every mountain—in
Pawtucket   **A-3**

Televised RISDIC hearings resume
this evening   **A-3**

NATION
An AIDS-infected Philadelphia
businessman, charged with paying
boys and young men for sex is
being held on $20 million dollar bail.   **A-4**

WEATHER
Rain developing late today,
continuing tonight and tomorrow   **B-8**

INDEX

Ann Landers	**D-6**	Editiorial	**A-10**
Bridge	**D-6**	Legal ads	**A-8**
Business	**A-6**	Lifebeat	**D-1**
Classified	**C-5**	People	**D-2**
Comics	**D-7**	Sports	**B-1**
Crossword	**D-6**	Television	**D-5**
Death Notices	**C-4**	What's Happening	**D-6**

Figure 2: Index from the *Providence Journal-Bulletin*, 29 March 1992.

Differing Views

Our first thesis might appear obvious, but many discussions of the significance of computer-mediated communication for scholarly communication imply quite a different view. For instance, in a deservedly well-known article, Stevan Harnad,

---

founding editor of both the prestigious print journal *Brain and Behavioral Sciences* and the electronic journal PSYCOLOQUY, which is sponsored by the American Psychological Association, argues:

> The current low intellectual level of the net is purely the result of incidental initial conditions. The medium was created by engineers and computer scientists, and they (along with students, reared on video games, with little knowledge and a lot of time on their hands) are the ones who have been setting people's expectations and standards so far, giving the impression that the net is just a global graffiti board for trivial pursuit. But this initial condition—which is rather as if Gutenberg and a legion of linotype operators, instead of Shakespeare and Newton, had determined what the printed page was to be used for—is surely destined to rectify itself as the net's demography changes and the serious demonstrations of its scholarly potential start to appear. (342-43)

This, we have argued, is simply not true. To begin with, one cannot suggest without gross exaggeration that playwrights and scientists have "determined what the printed page would be used for." The printed page *has* been used and *continues* to be used, as we have said, for an astonishing range of things, including legal documents, mail order catalogues, and sensationalistic magazines. Shakespeare and Newton had only a small hand in that development. And if the development of printing in the sixteenth century involved the production of Bibles and catechisms, the nascent publishing industry soon found that the production of astrological almanacs and other popular commodities ensured commercial success.[4] In a similar fashion, the natural range of human interests and projects, not the specialist enthusiasms of an intellectual elite, determine the character of contemporary network traffic.

Of course, the opportunities for access and the limitations of software also influence the nature of contemporary network traffic, but as access broadens beyond universities and modem-connected users of commercial services to reach every suburban home with a cable-TV connection, we have little reason to expect a *rise* in the intellectual level of the net. Harnad is right that the current situation will change as the net's demography changes, but that change will not have the effect he expects. Conferencing on public services such as Prodigy and CompuServe does suggest that the broadening of access changes the tone and subject matter of communications, but it does not promise to elevate them.

Consequences for Theorizing

The new forms of scholarly communication arise and grow only from within the larger world of human interest and action. They will always form a small part of this larger world, and to the extent that they distinguish themselves from it, that will only be through the evolution—or design—of structures and norms that constitute forms for interaction. Today those structures and norms are largely lacking, at least in the conferencing with which most humanists are familiar. And this absence of structures and norms provides much of the excitement and stimulation we feel in our conferences today: the wonderful vitality of life itself seems constantly to break through in surprising contributions, wide-ranging connections, flip remarks, angry words, and insane mutterings. Whether "All cough in ink / all think the thoughts that others think" ever fairly characterized any scholarly community, it could never plausibly caricature current electronic conferencing.

But if on some days our conversations seem lifted by the vitality of the net, on other days they seem burdened by its obtuseness. We are reminded then not of life's rich novelty, insights, and skill but of its repetition, ignorance, and incompetence. On those days we long for editors, referees, and other bars to entry—or at least for a protective apparatus of directories and indexes. Again, it is only from within the real world of human interests and action, and human strengths and weakness, that the new forms of scholarly communication will be created. Scholarly communication is *in* the world and *of* the world. The riot of disorder and tedium that we see around us and the riot of disorder and tedium that seems constantly to erupt from within our earnest electronic conferencing are in fact the same.

Does computer-mediated communication have the resources to construct these new forms? Can it create forms that will not only provide the benefits of the old institutions of scholarly communication and remedy the defects of the old forms but then go on to deliver, as promised, a new and liberating world of the mind? Those questions lead us to our second observation.

Thesis 2: The Significance of Computer-Mediated Communication Lies in Its Protean Nature

What Is Distinctive about Computer-Mediated Communication?

In *The Network Nation* Hiltz and Turoff offer "communication system morphology" (32) that draws attention to the salient features of computer-mediated communication. They point out that computer-mediated communication

---

— does not require geographical coordination of participants
— does not require temporal coordination of participants
— can involve very large groups of interacting participants
— allows fast transmission
— allows fast (reading speed) reception
— has an integrated memory with sophisticated retrieval capability
— can easily transform its content into other forms (for example, print)
— has a dynamic and adaptable structure.

A comparison with other forms of communication—such as face-to-face conversation, paper mail, print, telephone, video, and unenhanced person-to-person electronic mail—makes the distinctiveness and power of computer-mediated communication apparent. Moreover, computer-mediated communication leverages the dominant means of writing in the Western world—text processing—for in addition to presenting text, it can also incorporate interactive multimedia structures of still and moving images, sound, and data. All these features lead scholars like Harnad and organizations like the Coalition for Networked Information to follow earlier visionaries, such as J. C. R. Licklider, Douglas C. Engelbart, Theodor H. Nelson, Hiltz, and Turoff, in predicting a revolution in scholarly communication.

Lee Sproull and Sara Kiesler have recently reviewed the evidence that computer-mediated communication produces not only expected "first-level efficiency effects" but also equally valuable "second-level social effects" (20-32). For instance, current systems seem to encourage more equal participation, to focus more on the merits of a position than on the status of its proponents, and to support a wider range of extensively developed positions. Nearly twenty years of fascinating empirical studies reveal that the social effects of computer-mediated communication have unique advantages beyond expected efficiencies.

However, the many discussions of computer-mediated communication, whether empirical studies or impressionistic speculation, tend to focus on features that are particular to some implementation or class of implementations. They might point out, for instance, that some particular conferencing system allows anonymity or egalitarian access, changes the dynamic of discourse features such as turn taking, or integrates electronic tools for information management. But overgeneralizing from such studies obscures the fact that the fundamental power and significance of computer-mediated communication derive not from some *particular* feature but rather from its ability to control with astonishing ease and precision almost *every* salient feature of communicational settings. If anonymity, egalitarian access, variant turn-taking protocols, and special topic-threading and annotation tools are desired, then a system can be designed to ensure these things—but if these characteristics are deprecated, then, alternatively, a system can implement the desired restrictions. As Hiltz and Turoff emphasize, "the fragrance of the future of computerized conferencing emanates from its ability to provide structure to enhance the human communication process" (27).

Information Overload

Discussions of the phenomenon of information overload offer a very simple, but clear and familiar, example of the distortions resulting from neglecting the protean nature of computer-mediated conferencing. All conference readers have encountered the perennial complaint that there are too many postings in a conference, that too many of these are off-topic, or that contributions are too long; "list etiquette," the violators are admonished, requires keeping contributions short and to the point.

But to some conference participants this sounds odd. After all, no one complains petulantly that a university library is too large, has too many books that do not interest him or her, or has books that are too long. So why should anyone care if electronic conferences are busy or have have lengthy contributions?

Part of the problem, of course, is that conference participants are frequently in vastly different technological circumstances. Those that feel burdened by conference traffic generally participate in conferences by receiving all contributions as electronic mail and trying to read each one in their general-purpose mail reader.

On the other hand those indifferent to heavy traffic usually use specialized software to manage many conferences and hundreds of received contributions each day. This software allows them to glance quickly over new contributions for items of interest that thay can then easily read, save, or mark for future reference. Many tools can be used to manage conference participation: text-searching software can scan recent transcripts for items of interest, perhaps exploiting keywords or subject lines; topical threads can be followed exclusively, or the reader can examine other topics in the same conference; repetitions of postings or cross-postings that have already been seen can be automatically concealed from all subsequent browsing; and kill-file filters eliminate the appearance of topics or authors that have been specifically identified as not of interest.

To get a sense of what this variation means for the experience of electronic literacy, we take a brief look at a number of existing software applications for reading conferences. As varied as reading circumstances are now, the range of software applications will increase even further in the near future.

Mail Management. Electronic mail provides the foundation for most conferencing over the Internet. The simplest procedure requires participants to send their contributions to a server that then forwards a copy, also by electronic mail, to every person on the list of participants. The recipients then view this mail, using their general-purpose mail-reading software.

In Figure 3 we see one of the best mainframe mail-management systems, Rice Mail, developed at Rice University. The reader can see at a glance who sent each piece of mail, when it was sent, and its subject. Rice Mail, which permits automatic sorting of mail by sender, date, or subject, allows it to be easily deleted, forwarded, replied to, or archived in a topical notebook. While reading a piece of mail, all the viewing, editing, and finding resources of the system editor remain available. Unfortunately many mail-reading systems do not so nicely facilitate such viewing, browsing, and sorting.

But even Rice Mail is ultimately unsuitable for users who wish to track many conferences. Note that the user must still deal with each piece of mail individually, even if only reading the subject line before deleting. Users must manage archiving on their own storage media. Finally, the system has no special tools for following subject threads, for eliminating cross-postings, or for retrieving back transcripts by keywords, text searches, and so on.

News Readers. Terminal-based news readers can provide an improved environment for conference participation. The one shown in Figure 4, which was developed at Brown University, derived from the IBM Grand conferencing system. It has the immediate advantage over the Rice Mail system shown in Figure 3 of segregating all conference groups from the user's private mail. A single copy of each conference contribution is received at the site (in this case a university) and is then centrally maintained for viewing. The bulletin board also organizes all the conferences into one hierarchy, grouping contributions to the same conference together in chronological order. The system notes which contributions have already been read by the user and only shows the "new" ones. Readers can easily scan the subject lines of the new postings, read any that look interesting, or mark the list as "read." A lengthy archive of postings is kept for each conference and can be scanned with the fast text-searching software that is integrated into the bulletin board.

Still, even with these improvements this system produces a daunting list whenever one has not read one's conferences for a while or if one regularly follows a large number of them. In addition, the system provides no way to personalize the

```
┌──────────────────────── Brownvm ───────────────────────────┐
│ >>> MAILBOOK 90.01.01 <<< Reviewing CURRENT NOTEBOOK G0      Line 1 of 19 │
│ ====>                                                                     │
│ From:              To:                 Date:   Subject:                   │
│ LINKLTR@MERIT      ALLEN@BROWNVM        4/30/91 Merit Networking Seminar   │
│ Marina Karelina    ALLEN@brownvm.brown 12/11/91 Answer from Moscow        │
│ ROLAND HALL        Allen Renear, CIS,  1/03/92 Lucian and the 79 quiet people │
│ Steve DeRose       uunet!brownvm.brown 1/03/92 No Subject                 │
│ Bob.K.Meyer@arp.anu relevant-logic@exet 2/23/92 Tennant on Good People    │
│ GBKeene@exua.exeter relevant-logic@exet 2/28/92 No Subject                │
│ CAROLE@BROWNVM     lob@BROWNVM         3/05/92 appts/w/dcw                 │
│ GBKeene@exua.exeter relevant-logic@exet 3/17/92 Teaching Preferences      │
│ Stevan Harnad      Allen Renear        3/19/92 Abstract: What Scholars Want a │
│ Bruno@             LISTS.HUMANIST.5630 3/19/92 5.0765 CFP: Probabilistic Appr │
│ Bruno@             LISTS.HUMANIST.5631 3/19/92 5.0766 CFP: Knowledge Represen │
│ Bill Drew -- Serial Allen Renear       3/23/92*SGML for Electronic Journals │
│ christian kloesel  Allen Renear        3/24/92 Oxford B&B                  │
│ Marek Wesolowski   Allen Renear        3/27/92*a msg frm Moscow           │
│ Mary Jo Lynch      visions%library@sds 3/28/92*VISIONS meeting at ACRL     │
│ David Owen         ALLEN@BROWNVM       3/28/92 ACH Exec meeting, Oxford    │
│ Stevan Harnad      Allen Renear        3/29/92 Talks on "Scholarly Skywriting │
│ George P. Landow, P Allen Renear       3/29/92 two more days              │
│ WALTER H RENEAR    Allen (AHR)         3/30/92 COMMUNICATIONS             │
│ PF1=Help     PF2=Read      PF3=Quit  PF4 =Print  PF5 =Reply   PF6 =Forward │
│ PF7=ScrollUp PF8=ScrollDown PF9=Discard PF10=SortUp PF11=SortDown PF12=Select │
└───────────────────────────────────────────────────────────────────────────┘
                                          04/42  Mon 30 Mar 09:18
```

Figure 3: The Rice Mailer's presentation of personal and conference mail.

hierarchy or to collapse and expand it selectively; it does not permit grouping articles by threads or topics; and it has no mechanism to suppress already-read cross-postings or authors and topics in permanent disfavor.

NetNews. The Usenet conferencing system NetNews is mail based, but like the bulletin board system above, it does not send mail to individual users. Instead it stages large sets of conference contributions on local computers. Readers then access these servers over the network, using client software on their local workstations, and browse through the desired conferences. Like the terminal-based systems described above, this software usually filters the available conferences by maintaining personal "subscriptions" and keeping track of which postings in subscribed conferences have already been read.

Figure 5 shows a NetNews reader called NewsWatcher, a Macintosh client. Note that upon opening the list of NetNews conferences on a server, one seems to have landed on the "other side of town" because the conference category that sorts to the top of an unfiltered list is the "alt" (alternative) category. "Alt" is unusual among NetNews conference categories in permitting any user who wishes to do so to create a conference without the informal electronic voting procedure normally required in other categories to add new conferences. Not only does this procedure

---

```
Reviewing Titles                                    Line 3072 of 4222
   5659. 5.0794  As:  E-Journal; HyperCard Wksps; Yiddish E-List  28 Mar  1992
   5660. 5.0795  Humanities Computing Position:  King's College   28 Mar  1992
   5661. 5.0796  Qs:  Electronic and Non  (7/104)                 28 Mar  1992
   5662. 5.0797  Rs:  Computer Distribution;  Plagiarism  (2/113) 28 Mar  1992
   5663. 5.0798  Rs:  Gender Diff. in Names;  Angry Student  (4/6 28 Mar  1992
   5664. 5.0799  Internet Mail Extensions  (1/101)                30 Mar  1992

-> Entries in LISTS.HUMBUL
    101. Recent additions to HUMBUL                               30 Mar  1992

-> Entries in LISTS.IOUDAIOS
   2621. Re: Rabbinic beliefs on disease                          6 Mar  1992
   2622. Re: layering of cultures                                 6 Mar  1992
   2623. Re: Rabbinic beliefs on disease                          7 Mar  1992
   2624. Lillith                                                  7 Mar  1992
   2625. Re: Rabbinic beliefs on disease                          7 Mar  1992
   2626. Re: Lillith                                              7 Mar  1992
   2627. Snake bites (Was: Re: Rabbinic beliefs on disease)       7 Mar  1992

1= Help     2= NxTopic   3= Done    4= Cancel    5= Reply    6= ?  PA2= Reset
7= Backward 8= Forward   9= Switch  10= ReadPrev 11= ReadNxt 12= Cursor
====> _
                                                   Macro-read 2 Files

                                                   Mon 30 Mar 07:04
```

Figure 4: A bulletin-board conferencing system: Brown University's Bruno.

produce many bizarre and perhaps unsavory conferences in this category but it also allows users to add fake conference titles as a kind of graffiti.

This particular reader, NewsWatcher, makes a rudimentary effort at filtering some of the noise from a typical news-group listing, showing, for instance, active groups in boldface. This news reader also provides one with the ability to filter news groups interactively; that is, in this case, it only shows the ones that have the text "mac" in the group name. It also has a rudimentary capacity to group by threads. The program does not, however, make very effective use of the hierarchical nature of the group names.

Nuntius, as shown in Figure 6, provides a far more sophisticated interface to the news. Its group list makes some attempt at depicting the hierarchy of news groups, although it does not indicate which ones are active. Its subject list also offers a lot more information than NewsWatcher's, for it groups articles by threads and then indicates both the number of articles in each thread and the number already read. Perhaps most importantly, it shows the name of the author of each article, a real timesaver once one grows familiar with a particular group's dynamics.

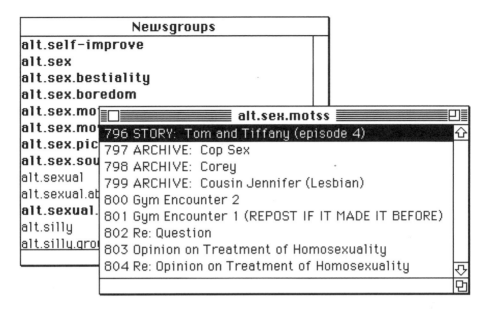

Figure 5: The Netnews reader NewsWatcher, on a Macintosh computer.

Figure 7 gives a more obvious example of how the standard practice of hierarchically naming news groups could be exploited so as to narrow the choices at any given level of the NetNews hierarchy. This is similar to the news reader NewsGrazer, for the NeXT computer. Ideally one would be to able to specify a variety of filters at each of the levels as well as use retrieval techniques to build alternative hierarchies. For instance, one might want to organize the day's viewing by subject line (regardless of conference), by author, and by date. Or one might have the text analyzed and have computed bibliometric relevance coefficients for topics of interest.

These examples show that already an enormous diversity of reading situations exist. Participants in the same conferences have vastly different abilities to manage their participation.

Consequences for Theorizing

Generalizing about computer-mediated communication is very risky business, in part because the range of potential reading environments seems limited only by our imaginations. Many of the apparent social and other characteristics of electronic

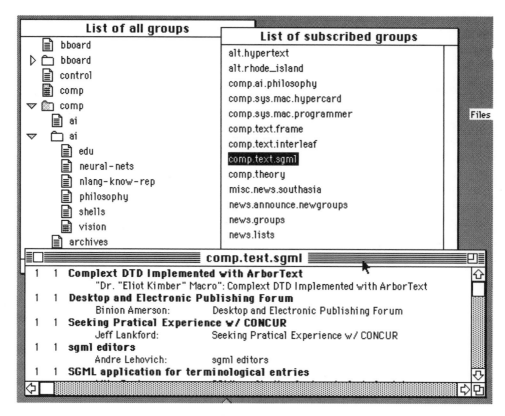

Figure 6: The Netnews reader Nuntius, on a Macintosh computer.

conferencing derive not from computer-mediated communication but from some particular implementation of computer-mediated communication. As technology develops, the range of actual reading environments will become more diverse, as will the range of user attitudes and behavior they can support. Some readers will continue to receive electronic mail and treat each conference as a conversation among friends while others will employ expert system filters and special tools for natural language processing and abstracting to monitor thousands of conferences, preparing summaries of the items that meet specified relevance requirements.

An important corollary is that the experience of computer-mediated communication can differ widely even for members of the same conference. Therefore, participants in what appears to be a single community of interest with a single mode of literacy in fact not only have quite different experiences but cannot make the usual assumptions about the situations of their co-conferencers. No other communication system allows such an extreme degree of variation in the situations of its partici-

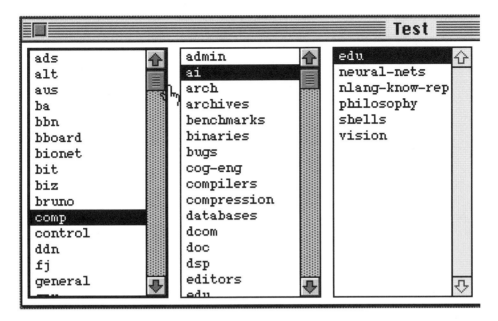

Figure 7. A proposed mechanism for exploiting hierarchical naming.

pants, and in an increasingly electronic world this quality of computer-mediated communication will prove particularly significant to our notions of community and literacy.

Software environments, special tools, and user attitudes of course form only part of the story. Formal procedures for moderation, peer review, and other means of editorial intervention can also provide structure for such conferencing. Here, too, the possiblities are limited only by the imagination of the designer.

Conclusion

Over the next twenty years computer-mediated communication, a protean general-purpose communication technology, will have a profound effect upon the developed world. It will change not only our scholarly and intellectual lives but will, much more importantly, become a prominent feature of our cultural and social lives as well. Its ultimate effects depend upon the forms we evolve to structure our electronic interactions. Some of these forms may imitate traditional nonelectronic ones, but others may shift the dynamic of human interaction radically. To the extent that deliberate innovation and control will influence this development, our difficulty will lie in releasing ourselves from the old forms without losing the myriad possibilities this new technology has to offer.

Effectively exploring these alternative forms requires discovering much more about how we learn, manage information, and communicate. It also requires thoughtful system design and judicious development of the social and economic institutions that will support the new medium. Ultimately, explorations of computer-mediated communication raise fundamental questions about what we really value about knowledge and communication . . . but that is thesis number three.

Notes

1 . In what follows we draw on our experience operating Humanist, a Listserv list devoted to the discussion of humanities computing that has an estimated three thousand readers and includes participants from over forty countries. Humanist was founded In 1987 by Willard McCarty at the University of Toronto. Today, based at Brown University, it is edited by Elaine Brennan and Allen H. Renear.

2 . Making a slightly different, though related point, Pamela McCorduck describes the computer itself as a "Protean Machine" that "moves into the world and, like all artifacts, enters into a delicate reciprocal relationship, imposing shape and giving form back" (105).

3 . From the Usenet Readership Report maintained by Brian K. Reid. Current copies and an explanation of the procedures are available in the NetNews group news.admin.

4 . Donald Wing's short-title catalogue of English books published between 1641 and 1700 dedicates more than twenty-four pages to listing almanacs whereas only half that number of pages is needed to list Bibles and catechisms. See also Bernard Capp.

Bibliography

Bolter, J. David. *Writing Space: The Computer in the History of Literacy*. Hillsdale: Lawrence Erlbaum, 1991.

Capp, Bernard. *English Almanacs, 1500-1800: Astrology and the Popular Press*. Ithaca: Cornell UP, 1979.

Engelbart, Douglas C. "A Conceptual Framework for the Augmentation of Man's Intellect." *Vistas in Information Handling*. Ed. P. Howerton. Washington, DC: Spartan, 1963.

Gibson, William. *Neuromancer*. New York: Ace, 1984.

Harnad, Stevan. "The Post-Gutenberg Galaxy: The Fourth Revolution in the Means of Production of Knowledge." *Public-Access Computer Systems Review* 2 (1991): 39-53.

Heim, Michael. *Electric Language: A Philosophical Study of Word Processing.* New Haven: Yale U P, 1987.

Hiltz, Starr Roxanne, and Turoff, Murray. *The Network Nation: Human Communication via Computer.* Reading: Addison-Wesley, 1978.

_____. "Structuring Computer-Mediated Communication to Avoid Information Overload." *Communications of the ACM* 28 (1985): 680-89.

Kerr, Elaine B., and Starr Roxanne Hiltz. *Computer-Mediated Communication Systems: Status and Evaluation.* Boston: Academic P, 1982.

Kraemer, K. L., and J. L. King. "Computer-Based Systems for Cooperative Work and Group Decision Making." *ACM Computing Surveys* 20 (1988): 115-46.

Landow, George P. *Hypertext: The Convergence of Contemporary Critical Theory and Technology.* Baltimore: Johns Hopkins UP, 1992

Licklider, J. C. R., and Albert Vezza. "Applications of Information Networks." *Proceedings of the IEEE* 66 (1978): 1330-46.

McCorduck, Pamela. *The Universal Machine: Confessions of a Technological Optimist.* New York: McGraw Hill, 1985.

McLuhan, Marshall. *The Gutenberg Galaxy: The Making of Typographic Man.* Toronto: U of Toronto P, 1962.

Malone, T. W., K. R. Grant, R. A. Turbak, S. A. Brobst, and M. D. Cohen. "Intelligent Information Sharing Systems." *Communications of the ACM* 30 (1987): 390-401.

Nelson, Theodor H., *Computer Lib/Dream Machines,* 1974. Seattle: Microsoft P, 1987.

Ong, Walter J. *Orality and Literacy: The Technologizing of the Word.* London: Methuen, 1982.

Quarterman, John S. *The Matrix: Computer Networks and Conferencing Systems World-wide*. Bedford: Digital P, 1990.

Quarterman, John S., and Josiah C. Hoskins. "Notable Computer Networks." *Communications of the ACM* 29 (1986): 932-71.

Sproull, Lee, and Sara Kiesler. *Connections: New Ways of Working in the Networked Organization*. Cambridge: MIT P, 1991.

Vinge, Vernor. "True Names." *True Names and Other Dangers*. New York: Baen, 1987. 49-143.

Wing, Donald G. *Short-Title Catalogue of Books Printed in England, Scotland, Ireland, Wales, and British America, and of English Books Printed in Other Countries, 1641-1700*. 2nd ed. New York: Index Committee of the MLA, 1972-.

Electronic Conferences and Samiszdat Textuality: The Example of Technoculture

George P. Landow
Brown University

Would it be inappropriate to ask that at least some of this writing space initially be devoted to the question of what kind of creature a list like this is? ... I mean to ask (on any number of levels) what the consequences of lists like this are (whether personal, psychological, social, cultural, institutional, technological, ecological, political, etc.)—what is made possible by electronic lists that wasn't possible before? what is made impossible that was possible before? what impossible desires lead to the creation of such lists or cognate technologies? what possible desires lead to such lists or cognate electronic information technologies of writing?
—Richard A. Grusin, Technoculture, 14 March 1992

Before networked computing, scholarly communication relied chiefly upon moving physical marks on a surface from one place to another with whatever cost in time that movement required. Networked electronic communication so drastically reduces the time scale of moving textual information that it produces new forms of textuality. Just as transforming print text to electronic coding radically changed the temporal scale involved in *manipulating* texts, so too has it changed the temporal scale of *communication*. Networked electronic communication has both dramatically speeded up scholarly communication and created new forms of it.

As **Renear and Bilder** point out in this volume, this new form of scholarly exchange exists within a larger network culture, only a very small part of which directly relates to academic or intellectual matters. Nonetheless, however implicated in other concerns this new kind of textuality might be, it clearly has the potential to create new forms of scholarly behavior, and in fact it has already begun to do so. These new electronic forms of scholarly communication deserve inclusion in this particular volume because they raise interesting questions about the nature of textuality itself. The electronic conference, as I shall try to show, produces a multiauthored textuality that the participant experiences as blending important characteristics of speech and writing. In some ways the electronic conference appears closer to speech than to written language, for it possesses the transiency and something of the immediacy of speech. Yet though such conferences seem more distinctly occasional and therefore more ephemeral than writing, they exist in the form of alphanumeric codes and therefore have some of the fixity and potential permanence of any written record. One could describe this mode of communication as a conference that generates its own transcript.

The pages that follow, which will examine some of the issues related to this new form of scholarly textuality that electronic communication has created, draw heavily upon the discussions that took place between March and May 1992 on Technoculture (TNC), an electronic conference founded by Stuart A. Moulthrop, Anne Balsamo, and Richard Grusin at the Georgia Institute of Technology and since handed on to Eric Crump at the University of Missouri.[1] In order to communicate the experience of participating in this electronic community, I shall present the excerpts with a minimum of editorial corrections, and I shall also quote more liberally from TNC than I would if I were quoting from printed materials.

My manner of proceeding in this chapter, as will soon become clear, differs from the usual notions of traditional scholarly method according to which the scholar acts as an uninvolved, supposedly objective observer. As a beginning student of electronic conferences, I found myself in the role of the participant observer, a role that many contemporary anthropologists find inevitable when studying any culture, whether familiar or alien (Geertz). Experiencing an electronic conference like TNC requires that one immerse oneself in the flow of electronic messages that stream through one's mailbox or mail reader. Furthermore, although some members, who occasionally describe themselves as "lurkers," generally prefer to read what others have written, anyone wanting to sense how such a conference differs from sending a letter to the editor of a journal or submitting an article for publication has to engage in the conversation him- or herself. Although the fact might seem obvious, perhaps I had better also mention that downloading, printing out, and then reading all the individual messages that constitute a particular conference, a procedure very easy to carry out, does not produce anything like the effect of encountering it on line. Such downloading, however useful the result might be as a record, translates and hence transforms one kind of textual experience into another.

Electronic textuality demands active, even intrusive observers who affect the very phenomena they wish to observe. For example, readers of electronic hypertext, who choose their paths through a text and thereby in an important sense construct it, not only read in a new and newly active mode but also necessarily participate in producing the text they read. Furthermore, in fully networked hypertext systems in which all readers have the capacity to add links and material as they read, readers become active in a second way since they can always establish new links or paths for others or add new texts in the form of annotation (Yankelovich). In cybertext (the term Espen Aarseth assigns to a form of electronic hypertextuality generated on the fly) readers and critics also necessarily become active participants, for, like the hypertext reader, they influence—they prompt the generation of—the texts they encounter.

At first glance, this role of participant observer or participant reader might not seem characteristic of all forms of electronic textuality, particularly that associated with computer-assisted literary study. How, one might ask, does text-based computing that uses concordances and other forms of searches require such a role? Certainly, one finds it difficult to argue that anyone who applies the methods of **Lancashire** or **Robinson** to a particular text has changed that text itself in any significant way, however much the scholar's relation to the text or ultimate experience of it may have changed. Using TACT, Collate, and other resources of text-based computing does, it is true, demand an active, intrusive reader of the *electronic version* of the printed text. In fact, within this kind of text-based computing readers exist *only* as active manipulators and searchers of an electronic text; that is, one can use such a program only by searching and otherwise manipulating the text in ways not possible with the print original. Nonetheless, the "real text"—what our culture presently defines as the only version of it that counts ultimately—is the printed one. Text-based computing, in other words, blends the textualities associated with electronic and print technology. It converts a manuscript or printed book to electronic form in order more efficiently to examine, manipulate, or transport it, but it does so with the ultimate goal of formatting or publishing a text that exists only in the form of physical markings on a surface. Relying on the enormous power that digitization grants the scholar, text-based computing creates an electronic simulacrum to capitalize on this power, but the printed text itself remains paramount. The kinds of text-based computing associated with computer-assisted literary study therefore blend the textualities and reading modes associated with both electronically and physically instantiated texts.

This discussion suggests something important about electronic textuality in the contemporary world: it exists—and for a long time to come will continue to exist— as a hybrid. Participating in the two worlds of what Jean Baudrillard terms the *tactile* and the *digital*, electronic text bridges textuality based on physical marking with that based on electronic virtuality (115). In electronic conferencing, yet another kind of hybrid textuality appears, one that combines electronic textuality not with print but with speech.

From its earliest days, TNC included discussions and ruminations about its nature and its status in relation to the academic world and to more traditional forms

---

of scholarly and academic text. Early on, Grusin inquired about "what kind of creature a list like this is" and wondered about its various possibilities and consequences (14 March 1992). Realizing that many of the issues under discussion on TNC impinged directly on the question of the nature of this new electronic textuality, I posted the following inquiry, which provoked a great variety of responses. "What," I asked, "is everyone's view of the quotability of statements made on Techcult? I assume that authors of statements MUST be credited, but does everyone believe that one must receive permission from the author before quoting his or her words? I would think attribution would be enough, since one is 'crediting' (or blaming) someone else, but what does everyone else think? I have been thinking about these issues because I wanted to discuss the nature of electronic textuality, scholarly (i.e. academic) communication, and such conferences in an introduction of a book Paul Delany and I are readying for MIT." Is it, I inquired, legitimate—I actually wrote "legit"—to "(a) quote, (b) summarize, or (c) mention statements made on the conference? All of these issues arise again when considering publishing anything based on the conference" (14 April 1992).

This query, which accompanied an invitation for other participants themselves to publish a selection of contributions to the conference, received a wide range of responses. One of the first came from Richard Gess, who commented that the kind of projects proposed "seem perfectly defensible. And do-able without loss of flavor. Now being *quoted* from TNC means that whatever flavor we were when we posted will also flavor the quote" (14 April 1992). As Gess makes clear, he, like many of the participants in TNC, believes that one of the attractions of the electronic conference lies in its having a different tone from conventional, print-based scholarly communications, one more spontaneous, personal, and informal than is possible in books and periodicals. He also recognized that "this might make some uneasy. All of us who've posted may have had moments when we regretted pushing the send key. I share Eric's worry about self-muting. It might be a good idea to ask permission—to have it understood that permission would be asked?—so we can have some say over how our conversation is recycled. Few of us, probably, are loath to be quoted at all, but most of us might want a shot at clarification (or at least doing damage control on our freewritten grammar)" (14 April 1992). Recognizing the different forms of expression appropriate to different communicative spaces or locales—I hesitate to write "different forms of publication" since *publication* decides in advance an important question—Gess proposed that anyone wishing to quote from TNC provide those quoted with the opportunity to revise their remarks. Despite an apparently general acceptance of the idea that contributors should have the chance to accommodate their statements to a new information technology, none of those I have here quoted wished to make any changes, and one person in fact wanted his contribution presented warts and all, with even typographical errors left unchanged.

Although everyone participating in TNC seems to recognize that an electronic conference or bulletin board differs from other forms of scholarly communication, some responded that they had already drawn on electronic communications when preparing materials destined for print or conventional conferences. For example, Crump, who also approved quoting from TNC but with reservations, himself admitted: "I find quoting from list discussions almost irresistible. What am I saying, 'almost'? Every paper I've written in the past year has HAD to include at least one quote from the networks. I'm now more engaged in this conversation than I am in the lumbering print conversation" (14 April 1992).

Not all agreed. Espen Aarseth from the University of Bergen, Norway, made several strong objections to the idea of publishing sessions or portions of the conference:

Why would we do that? Is this the stuff of which articles are made? Sure, it is interesting and all that (I haven't signed off yet), and it could give someone new a faint idea (shadow on the cave wall) about electronic *offentlichkeit*, but it would also be a breach of genre. When I pick up the latest edition of *MacWorld*, I don't want printout of whatever discussions comp.sys.mac has generated lately.

The stuff here is half-baked, fastfoody, and yes, perishable. This is how it should be. When there is an interesting exchange, which indeed there has been more than once, then the involved people should consider joining minds and produce something deeper, such as perhaps an article which could be published, electronically or otherwise . . .

As we have seen, the notion of publishing inevitably brings up the question of editing, and [click, booom] we are back in the chain gang once more . . .

The easy freedom of lists such as these complements the serious heavy academic rituals on which we all depend. Let's keep it distinct.

Don't get me wrong . . . I don't want to spoil everyone's fun and I don't object to publishing this as an experiment, I just have doubts whether it would work if institutionalized. What is the most appropriate medium for the stuff posted here? What are we saying about electronic lists if we want to take it (or some of it) elsewhere? . . . . I understand that discussing tECHnOcULTURE to a large extent means discussing ourselves, but the way we are doing it, *this* is the best place for it.

Technical question: What is the correct formalism when quoting/citing a list posting? (15 April 1992)

This and other responses provoked an intense discussion of the presence (or absence) of conventional, print-based hierarchies of values and power in the world of electronic conferences. Aarseth, like many other members of TNC, believes that this kind of conference enjoys a kind of informality and freedom from the constrictions of conventional print-based communications. Many of his objections seem to arise in a desire not to do anything that might jeopardize something special, something otherwise unavailable—a space in which people with shared interests can quickly receive responses and exchange ideas, a space, as he puts it, whose freedom "complements the serious heavy academic rituals on which we all depend."

Moulthrop, one of the founders of TNC, then, agreeing with Crump, argued that participants should not too sharply oppose the electronic conference to the world of print:

The point that you and very often I and a lot of other people tend to miss is that what we're doing here is print-production. Oh sure there's an element of spontaneity and Glasnost (the Russian term seems just right here) which e-mail has over pageprint. But as you observe, email becomes print by another name, inevitably falling back under some gravitation into value-laden strata. I've come to believe that the "publish or perish" question is really moot. George Landow says he publishes to "convince" and for a week I've been struggling to say that in net exchanges the goal is something different.

But it's not, at least for me. Witness this message.

If it looks like print and it reads like print . . . this is just speedprint, perishable publication, one of those "postmodernisms" that looks very much like the old regime. (22 April 1992)

Moulthrop (and it is interesting to me that in print I feel constrained to call him by his last name whereas on TNC everyone calls everyone else by his or her first name, whether one has met the addressee personally or not) suggested that hypertext nonlinearity might provide one way out of the conventional constraints, and many participants took up this theme for discussion. Others probed Moulthrop's use of the word *glasnost*. David Porush, who in effect repeats Aarseth's perception of TNC as a providing a space outside the academic hierarchy, proposed that "we substitute the more venerable Russian word *samiszdat* for *glasnost*. The former is an underground system of disseminating information that—however structured or statused—still has the air of subversive, unofficial, beneath public notice but known to all, if only unconsciously" (23 April 1992).

At this point, the discussion veered wildly in another direction when Donald Byrd claimed, "We are witnessing the substitution of medium for culture in all the discourses. It is all always there. As people found out with VCRs, there is no point in recording tv. . . . The equivalent to what you recorded is always there" (25 April 1992). This discussion quickly led to exchanges on the nature of knowledge, culture, cultural practice, and the relations that obtain among them by Fred Kemp, Deborah Heath, Henry Jenkins, Martin Rosenberg, Dan Hughes, David Porush, Joe Amato, and Alex Jacobson. I do not propose to follow this or subsequent discussions on TNC over the next month, which, when downloaded to my Macintosh, occupy more than two-hundred single-spaced pages. Instead, I would here like to depart the onward flow of TNC and examine what this last discussion suggests about this kind of textuality.

Although discussion no longer concentrated on the issue of networked electronic text, several things about it become clear when one realizes that the last-named participants sent off their contributions from Texas, Oregon, Massachusetts, Arizona, New York, and Rhode Island. Obviously, such electronic conferencing does, as advertised, make possible and even convenient rapid communication among people spatially distant from one another. The speed with which one can receive a response also makes for a different kind of communication, one closer to a conversation than to a print exchange—even to ones taking place in Letters to the Editor sections of magazines, journals, and newspapers.

Second, a single intervention like Byrd's that can so dramatically change the direction of the conference exemplifies one of the mechanisms that transform this kind of electronic textuality into a discourse without a center, or better, a discourse with a traveling center, one that changes, shifts, disappears, and reappears according to the interventions—the questions and comments—of individual participants. Since at any time any member of TNC or similar electronic conferences can enter or reenter the discussion, its direction and hence its center can swerve unexpectedly.

In this way, the individual contribution to the conference discussion functions much like the link in hypertext, whose readers also encounter a textuality without fixed center or permanent focus. As I have argued elsewhere (*Hypertext*),

> As readers move through a web or network of texts, they continually shift the center—and hence the focus or organizing principle—of their investigation and experience. Hypertext, in other words, provides an infinitely re-

---

George P. Landow   243 centerable system whose provisional point of focus depends upon the reader, who becomes a truly active reader in yet another sense. One of the fundamental characteristics of hypertext is that it is composed of bodies of linked texts that have no primary axis of organization. In other words, the metatext or document set—the entity that describes what in print technology is the book, work, or single text—has no center. Although this absence of a center can create problems for the reader and the writer, it also means that anyone who uses hypertext makes his or her own interests the de facto organizing principle (or center) for the investigation at the moment. One experiences hypertext as an infinitely decenterable and recenterable system, in part because hypertext transforms any document that has more than one link into a directory document, a transient center that one can employ to orient oneself and to decide where to "go" next. (11-12)

Like the individual linked document in hypertext, the individual contribution to an electronic conference has its own order and focus; it has, in other words, a center. Considered as a whole, however, the entire set of words constituting the conference has only the unity implied by its stated subject and it has that unity only as long as the contributors choose to adhere to it and not to some apparently peripheral one.

A third quality of electronic conferences is the unusual degree of democratization, a democratization not apparent in other kinds of scholarly text, that it displays. The same lack of hierarchy that prevents fixed endings or print authority also argues against hierarchies of power. I have observed several undergraduate students in my course on hypertext and literary theory intervening in discussions. Possibly because they did not identify themselves as undergraduates but just had their say, other members of the electronic community treated them not only as equals but even as authorities; that is, when an undergraduate participant had something to report, some reading to suggest, or something to contribute from a nonhumanities discipline, say, economics, other participants asked for clarifications, further information, or suggestions for readings.[2]

I make this observation with cautious optimism and in the face of a significant portion of TNC contributors who remain quite skeptical about the democratizing potential of any technology—even as, it appears, they engage undergraduate students in ways difficult in face-to-face contact. Part of our difference in attitudes lies, I suspect, in what one means by freedom and democratization. Some of those suspicious about the potential of any technology to have positive effects apparently mean by *freedom* and *democracy* some ideal, total abstraction. In contrast, I report only changes in behavior and possibility that suggest greater freedom and democratization relative to behavior in the absence of such technology.[3] Such democratization of scholarly communication, even if only partial or temporary, raises issues of how one relates to the networked electronic text.

As a student of culture concerned with the way people always naturalize technology in crucial ways that concern status and power, I would like to know if this effect is a matter of association and expectation, something intrinsically part of the technology, or something always intrinsically part of the technology in question but only activated in certain situations or under certain conditions. Such questions came to the fore early in the existence of TNC when Anne Balsamo and Angela Wall raised the "issue of situated communication practices, cultural conventions, and forces of determination" and then asked, *"what cultural identities are you screening when you post?* Do you assume the screen is a mirror, reflecting an image of yourself as your ideal reader? What notion of audience is at work here?" (16 March 1992). John M. Unsworth seconded the importance of their inquiry, remarking that the assumptions we make about our audience form "a problematic and somewhat dangerous aspect of networked communication: you don't know who your audience is, so your assumptions are all the more obvious (but always unavoidable: you can't *not* make assumptions about your audience)" (16 March 1992).

These questions arise because electronic conferences have a hybrid nature that combines writing with some of the informality and responsiveness of spoken conversation. Like all writers, contributors to TNC find themselves forced to make assumptions about their audience, and yet unlike the writer of an article, a book, or even a letter to the editor of one's local newspaper, they can receive near-immediate response, much as if they participated in a conversation. At the same time, the cultural identities that play such an important part of one's message in both physical writing and speech here appear garbled, veiled, or simply missing. One often does not know the age, gender, educational status, or area of expertise of other participants, and this lack of knowledge produces a temporary freedom from what Tom Wolfe calls the "statuspheres" (8) in which we exist within our various overlapping social realities. Not surprisingly, some people take the opportunity, as Allucquere Rosanne Stone relates, to try on different identities (82-83).

Balsamo drew attention to this aspect of electronic conferences when she related that she found herself "fascinated by the process whereby people try to disassociate themselves from their institutional e-mail address. This desire to disassociate seems to result from other readers making the assumption that the 'poster's contribution' is somehow tied to the institutional place of posting. What happens, as you all know, is that people start to include all sorts of disclaimers about how their opinions are not necessarily the opinions of the institution they post from." She suggested that "in reading a posting or e-mail message, we do make attributions about the relationship between the posting and the place of communication. And this seems to suggest that an electronic 'writing space' (at least for distributed network exchanges) implicitly contains a notion of 'place.' Where 'place' implies notions of location, identity, and representation, and serves as a gateway to meanings that circulate in social and cultural networks" (17 March 1992). David Durand responded by pointing out that the disclaimers that Balsamo mentioned may serve to "set up one's identity" but also that in the commercial world they serve as company policy to avoid litigation (18 March 1992). Indeed, people who work for corporations rather than universities are much more likely to have disclaimers, such as "The ideas presented above are my own. The X corporation doesn't have any."

Perhaps this partly unknown, often partially masked nature of one's audience explains the fact that one experiences an electronic conference differently from the way one does electronic mail. As I explained on 18 March, the individual e-mail messages directed at me that grew out of the larger discussions felt more comfortable and less ambiguous than did contributions I sent to the conference as a whole: "Perhaps I experience a note addressed just to me as personal, as more informal, as almost more comforting than things encountered in public discussion. There have been several points when my work on Intermedia has been mentioned in ways that might demand some comment. I find it easier to respond to the individual query than to the more public statement for two reasons: first, the private e-mail seems to demand a response whereas the public remark is something one almost overhears rather than finds addressed to one; second, the private response can easily take the form of providing factual information, a friendly gesture, a personal statement of common interest, or the like, whereas a public response seems to require a kind of public rhetoric or display (and we've seen a LOT of plumage thus far). Maybe the problem is that the whole experience is like carrying on a conversation with a group of strangers with apparently common interests that, say, because the lights have gone off, one finds oneself carrying on in the dark."

Michael Blitz emphasized another point about how we confront this electronic text when he astutely remarked that

> it is now possible to imagine our conversations going on "without" us—I am, for example, technically replying to message from days ago because (a) it's the easier way for me to login to these exchanges and (b) I am free to pick up threads as they variously ravel and unravel in the cyber-weave. But it is still difficult to conceptualize what we are/do/ought to work for in the interface between our bodies and this relatively new vocal-textual prosthesis. Having text after text magically appear on my screen every day, some

of them continuing earlier discussions, some of them beginning things I've heard/read nothing about—these incantations have the feel of ghostly voices (my own, partly) rising up from a deep place/situated space, looking for a local human in which to dwell (the Alien theory of e-mail?). And in this sense, the techno-polylog is also monologue as each of us accumulates (or gathers, or quilts together). (19 March 1992)

Any networked text, whether hypertext, e-mail, or portions of an electronic conference, inevitably participates in a docuverse of texts that change the nature of each individual text, which loses its discreteness, its separateness. The authors of a particular bit of text experience it according to different time schemes, depending upon whether they remain in more or less close contact with the changing, enlarging conference discussion or come back to it after many more messages have accrued to theirs—or simply passed them by as the subject under discussion changes. This quality, which permits what Joseph E. McGrath describes as "asynchronous communication" (39), offers one of the great pleasures and great conveniences of electronic mail and electronic conferences: coming and going as one wishes without losing the thread of a conversation or argument.

The electronic conference has the relative informality, rapidity, and spontaneity of a conversation, and one also experiences it as closer to real time with all the strengths and weaknesses that closeness implies. Its potential responsiveness, democracy, and informality seem positive qualities as in certain circumstances are its lack of linearity, unity, and closure. The fact that one can always enter a conversation (as long as someone else responds to one's comments) makes absence of closure a positive quality since a participant, particularly one with something of interest to communicate to others, can always requicken interest in an issue.

Some of these same qualities associated with electronic conferences produce similar problems to those in face-to-face conversations. For instance, the ease of contributing at any point in a discussion, even when it has apparently concluded, tends to produce floods of verbiage, not all of it to every participant's taste or interest. Similarly, as in many oral conversations, class discussions, or meetings when people come together to exchange ideas, the conference easily falls under the control of those who contribute most frequently, even when they babble on or self-indulgently and repetitiously express themselves. Then, too, as Aarseth points out, "The stuff here is half-baked, fastfoody, and yes, perishable. This is how it should be" (15 April 1992).

Finally, the lack of constraint and informality that characterizes electronic communication when combined with its relative anonymity and distance can produce "flaming," the intemperate expression of hostile or critical opinion, usually in the form of ad hominem attacks on some other participant. No one who has ever read the correspondence in *The Times Literary Supplement* or in professional periodicals, particularly those for art historians, believes that scholarly exchange in the humanities always takes the form of temperate, humane statement. Nonetheless, the very informality of electronic conferencing that produces some of the medium's most delightfully unusual and even bizarre communication also produces unpleasant exchanges as well.

As long as a conference like TNC continues, it has a life of its own, and any description of it inevitably takes the form of a narrative, selected and ordered by excluding as well as by emphasizing elements in order to make it fit not only our general purposes but also the general requirements of print medium. As long as it continues, a conference, like an individual life, has no closure.

Notes

1. Technoculture, which apparently takes its name from a volume by Andrew Ross, began with an inaugural message from Stuart A. Moulthrop at 17:45:56 on Friday, 13 March 1992. To join the conference, contact Eric Crump via e-mail at LCERI@UMCVMB.missouri.edu. I would like to thank all those members of the conference who kindly game me permission to quote their contributions.

2. Jeffrey Achter, a mathematics concentrator (major) at Brown, challenged usages of the terms *topology* and *topological* both by other participants in TNC and by literary theorists in general, and he thereby generated an interesting discussion, as did Tom Meyer, who proposed reconceiving the standard conception of hypertext that emphasizes nodes and links joining them. Alexander Jacobson similarly began—and essentially directed—an entire line of discussion when he applied economic theory to the exchange of information. Given my discussion above of the similar ways one experiences hypertext documents and electronic conferences, I find it interesting that all three successfully integrated materials from TNC into hypertext webs (or document sets).

3. For discussions of the political implications and effects of information technology, see Eisenstein 244, 319, 326, Kernan 4-5, Landow 162-90, McLuhan 220, and Miller.

Works Cited

Aarseth, Espen. "Texts of Change: Toward a Poetics of Nonlinearity." Master's thesis. Bergen: U of Bergen Department of Comparative Literature, 1991.

Baudrillard, Jean. *Simulations.* Trans. Paul Foss, Paul Patton, and Philip Beitchman. New York: Semiotext(e), 1983.

Eisenstein, Elizabeth L. *The Printing Press as an Agent of Change: Communications and Cultural Transformations in Early-Modern Europe.* Cambridge: Cambridge UP, 1979.

Geertz, Clifford. *Works and Lives: The Anthropologist as Author.* Stanford: Stanford UP, 1988.

Kernan, Alvin. *Printing Technology, Letters, and Samuel Johnson.* Princeton: Princeton UP, 1987.

Landow, George P. *Hypertext: The Convergence of Contemporary Critical Theory and Technology.* Baltimore: Johns Hopkins UP, 1992.

McGrath, Joseph E. "Time Matters in Groups." *Intellectual Teamwork.* Ed. Jolene Galegher, Carmen Egido, and Robert Kraut. Hillsdale: Lawrence Erlbaum, 1990. 23-61.

McLuhan, Marshall. *The Gutenberg Galaxy: The Making of Typographic Man.* Toronto: U of Toronto P, 1962.

Miller, J. Hillis. "Literary Theory, Telecommunications, and the Making of History." *Scholarship and Technology in the Humanities.* Ed. May Katzen. London: British Library Research/Bowker Saur, 1991. 11-20. (Proceedings of conference held at Elvetham Hall, Hampshire, UK, 9-12 May 1990.)

Stone, Allucquere Rosanne. "Will the Real Body Please Stand Up?: Boundary Stories about Virtual Cultures." *Cyberspace: First Steps.* Ed. Michael Benedikt. Cambridge: MIT P, 1991. 81-118.

Wolfe, Tom. *The Pump House Gang.* New York: Bantam, 1969.

Yankelovich, Nicole, Norman Meyrowitz, and Andries van Dam. "Reading and Writing the Electronic Book." *IEEE Computer* 18 (October 1985): 15-30.

Part IV

Working with Texts

Seeing through the Interface:
Computers and the Future of Composition

Nancy Kaplan
University of Texas at Dallas

Stuart Moulthrop
Georgia Institute of Technology

> *The way we see things is affected by what we know or what we believe.*
> — John Berger, *Ways of Seeing*

In her controversial article "Student Writing: Can the Machine Maim the Message?" Marcia Peoples Halio raises a number of provoking questions. Could the features of particular computer systems, as she claims, affect developing writers in different ways? If so, how should teachers respond or adapt to these differences? These issues beg even more fundamental questions—how does computer-mediated writing differ from conventional, typographic writing, and how should pedagogy take account of these changes? Therefore, they are bound to spark contention at a time when technology has already precipitated an identity crisis in humanities education (see Landow, Lanham, Slatin). This larger arena of controversy involves much more than user interfaces or word-processing software. The features of the Apple Macintosh that Halio believes dangerous—its combination of text and graphics facilities, its direct-manipulation interface, its failure to require special expertise—can also be found in most companies' emerging technologies, from interactive video to hypertext and hypermedia (see Ulmer, Bolter).

Although Halio's article generated intense controversy when it appeared, neither the article nor the heat it engendered would be very significant if Halio's claims had not received uncritical acceptance in some quarters (see Levy). Her conclusions elicited extensive critical response on electronic conferences and in other forums, where specialists in computers and writing contended that Halio's observations were disputable and her claims unwarranted. Even though Halio defended her work at the 1990 Conference on College Composition and Communication, as well as in a special section of a composition journal (Halio, "Maiming Reviewed"; see also Slatin et al., Youra),[1] her defense did not address the methodological inadequacies of her observations. At this writing, Halio's claims have not been confirmed by a properly designed experiment. Meanwhile, the converging evolution of Apple and IBM product lines has rendered her objections moot. Nonetheless Halio's critique of the Macintosh demands reconsideration for two reasons: first, because the flaws in Halio's assertions define methodological problems that all rhetorical researchers need to avoid, and second, because her work illustrates a continuing tension in the composition community between defenders of typographic literacy and those who would more fully explore electronic media (see Moulthrop).

Halio's original article prompted various kinds of critical responses. Some critics questioned the inconsistencies in Halio's stylistic judgments, and not without reason. An unsympathetic reader will notice that although Halio criticizes student prose because she finds it "spiced with slang and colloquialisms" (17), she then complains that when the student uses the Macintosh's "nifty" and "cute" features, he or she turns the word processor into a "pal" (18). A more thoughtful critic might point to Halio's unexamined assumptions about technological agency, as in this sentence: "Indeed, most of us prize our word processors because of the ease they afford us to move text around, delete, insert, correct, and revise, and they produce multiple versions of essays effortlessly" (16). The problems here are not simply technical. The confusing shift of subject between the two parts of this compound sentence ("most of us prize . . . they produce") is less troubling than the implication in the second clause that machines "produce" essays, "effortlessly" or not. Yet such minute criticism is a little unfair. Like any piece of academic argument, Halio's article needs to be understood as the result of a complex process, including the attention—or negligence—of editors and reviewers, the influence of related publications, and the institutional and technological environment in which Halio made her observations.

More productive debate about Halio's claims focuses on the way she presents her observations as if they were answers to the questions she has posed. Those questions still need extensive investigation. But in pursuing this work, investigators must carefully consider the relationship between the nature of their questions and the methods of inquiry used to address them. How we define our questions determines what kinds of answers we find; inquiries that neglect their own grounding assumptions lead to impoverished representations of social reality. At the time Halio's article appeared, we thought that the discussion of interfaces and writing needed a new and more comprehensive agenda, and we believe it still does. A more productive critique must address broad issues involving textual theory, writing pedagogy, and their relationships to technology. But such an examination cannot be conducted within Halio's perspective, which categorizes writing as words on paper, those words either correct or erroneous, and which pits "good" writing technologies against "bad" in a dispute between devoted users of competing computer systems. Such dualisms lead to narrow ways of seeing. Rejecting the specious "Macintosh versus IBM" contention, we explore larger questions about the way technology may influence education and about the growing importance of non typographic conceptions of writing.

Before taking a broader view of the issues, however, we feel it is still necessary to clear up misconceptions about Halio's assertions: Halio's article circulated at some institutions with comments suggesting that its speculations *prove* "friendly" user interfaces have detrimental effects on student writing—even though it proves nothing of the kind. Halio's rhetoric may have led to this misapprehension. Although she acknowledges that her observations were anecdotal and her data inconclusive, Halio nevertheless presents findings based on them—under the heading "Suspicions Confirmed"—and on their strength speculates that teachers may need to be cautioned against the "pitfalls" of oversimplified user interfaces. The validity of the observations reported in the article is highly questionable, but even if they were to be validated, those observations cannot demonstrate any causal relationship between aspects of a computer interface and differences in writing. Her contention that graphic interfaces impair student writing does not stand up to scrutiny. Halio's rush to judgment was both misguided and misleading.

Any critique of Halio's assertions should be balanced by an understanding of the general difficulties of research in this field. Writing research, especially when it is carried out in the classroom, is always beset by complexities. Many quite valuable studies have significant limitations because of difficulties with research design (see Hawisher). Based on the research to date, our understanding of student writing is incomplete. For example, we know very little about the effects on writers of gender, socio-economic status, prior education, or other cultural factors. Although anecdotal or even disputable observations sometimes provide important partial perspectives, we do not yet know enough about writing and technology to draw sweeping conclusions. We need to concentrate instead on framing better questions and on defining forms of inquiry appropriate to them. Seymour Papert has warned against strictly "technocentric" studies, like Halio's, where the researcher concentrates exclusively on the relationship between an isolated user and an isolated machine. We may find an antidote to technocentrism in studies more fully "informed by the interaction of technology with the culture in which it exists" (Hawisher 64). Such studies require us to ask questions other than whether using a particular machine can "maim" a student's writing.

Evaluating Halio's Claims

In order to understand why Halio's conclusions are untenable, we need to examine in some detail the weaknesses in her observations and inferences. There are, as we see it, at least five major problems with her methods.

Establishing Comparable Test Populations

To yield sound data (even in descriptive work), a comparative study must first establish that the test populations have comparable levels of ability before they begin the test conditions. This requirement is especially important when subjects are self-selecting rather than randomly assigned to the treatments (see Slavin). Halio claims that "all students in the computer sections have roughly comparable levels of writing ability" (17), but her methods were inadequate to establish even a rough baseline. Since Halio's test groups were regular classes, their comparability depends on her university's placement system, which assigns students to a "medium writing-ability range" according to verbal SAT scores and a writing sample. Halio gives no account of the range of scores or of the inter-rater reliability for readers of the writing sample, but even had she done so, the SAT scores and writing samples could not have established comparability because the middle group, comprising neither honors nor remedial students, was designed to include the large majority of the university's first-year students.

In his guide to research methods in education, Slavin explains that "so much of the variance [in any study] . . . is explained by student ability or past achievement that treatment effects are almost always small in relation to student-to-student differences" (28-29). In controlled experiments that compare two educational technologies, either the experimental groups are assembled randomly or a single group is introduced to both technologies. This procedure is necessary if the study is to eliminate the influence of social or personal differences—like the contrast between the "childish" attitudes of the Macintosh users and the "businesslike" orientation of the IBM users that Halio posits. With no reliable ways to establish students' abilities at the beginning of the term, Halio could make no valid claims based on differences she saw later.

Determining Comparable Instruction and Practice

Differences in teaching—from organization of the syllabus to the conduct and content of class discussion—can exercise a crucial influence on the writing students produce. In studies in which teachers act as their own controls, comparability is usually confirmed by classroom observation (Slavin). These accounts, vital to case studies, ethnographies, and other forms of descriptive research, portray teachers' attitudes and biases, constructing a picture of the classroom culture. Halio reports no such information, either in her original report or in subsequent defenses. Similar observations are needed to detail students' practices. For example, did students typically compose on paper and then type on a computer or did they tend to compose at the keyboard? Halio claims that because the labs were open the same number of hours, students in both conditions had equal access to machines. But if one type of computer was generally the preferred tool on a particular campus, students may have had more trouble getting enough time on that machine. Students working with the computer less in demand might thus have had longer and more frequent work sessions. Any of these differences might have been confounding factors.

Determining Differences in Performance

Halio used a number of quantitative measures to suggest that writers who use the Macintosh do not write as well as IBM PC users. For a number of reasons Halio's statistics are incomplete and provide inadequate foundations for her claims. First, the results she presents are not subjected to any test of statistical significance, such as the Analysis of Variance (ANOVA), to account for the strength of chance in variations. Second, the sample size (ten essays from each test group) may have been too small to be representative. Halio provides no details on the size and breakdown of the population she observed, but if there were one hundred students using each type of computer and if each wrote five essays during the term (a total production of five hundred samples for each group), then the number of essays evaluated (ten) would represent only 2 percent of the writing. A sample that small *might* be representative, but only if it were carefully controlled for extraneous variations. Were the essays Halio assessed all selected from the same point in the term? Were they written in response to the same assignment? Were the ten in each group selected proportionally from all the test classes—two from each class in each condition—to control for teacher effects? Without controls on these influences we have no way of reliably attributing weaker writing to the use of a particular computer.

Assessing Performances

Halio relied on the Kincaid readability scale incorporated in the Writer's Workbench analysis program to evaluate the importance of the variations in writing she found.

The scores suggest that the Macintosh samples were readable at just below an eighth-grade level and the IBM samples at slightly above the twelfth-grade level. Readability tests rely on quantifiable stylistic measures, such as sentence length and clause type. Halio associates longer and more complex sentences with better writing, but her interpretation may be faulty. In an analysis of topical structure in writing, Witte found texts with *less* complexity and shorter sentences easier to read and understand. Distrusting quantitative methods, many composition specialists prefer evaluations by human raters who can take into account content, purpose, audience, and other features of the rhetorical situation. Even if we accept these stylistic analyses as meaningful, they do not imply, as Halio seems to assume, that Macintosh users are less "mature" than IBM users. Readability scores do not indicate the level at which a writer *reads* but the level at which (in the prose being analyzed) he or she *has written*. A good writer's choice of level is contingent on subject matter, audience, and purpose. Although it takes some effort, even a professor of English can produce copy readable at an eighth-grade level. Readers might not judge this prose weaker than more complex, erudite writing.

Judging Subject Matter

Halio complains that Macintosh writers chose to work not on "serious" subjects like capital punishment, teenage pregnancy, nuclear war, and drunk driving but on "frivolous" topics like graffiti and junk food. Her value judgments here are questionable: many teachers believe that students can write seriously and originally about popular culture, particularly if they are encouraged to think critically. Even more troubling is Halio's suggestion that these choices of topic were influenced by the computer students used, the "toy"-like Macintosh encouraging students to think of writing as "play time," leading them to choose inferior occasions for argument. This claim is entirely a matter of interpretation unsupported by any relevant observations or data. The correlation Halio claims to find between topics and technology may be more related to student attitudes than to computer systems. But in any case, to investigate such a correlation Halio would have needed to conduct a different kind of research altogether, one that measured and analyzed attitudes.

Framing Answerable Questions

Problems in research methods like the ones we have been discussing often result from an approach that lacks a clear vision of causal connections. Research of all sorts begins by noticing something in the course of events that seems unusual or unfamiliar. The observer seeks to verify that the events triggering the inquiry actually exist in a significant way (in other words, that these events do not simply reflect the observer's attitudes or biases), but a researcher cannot proceed without a coherent account of how the events in question might be explained. That account, whether explicit or implicit, guides the study's methodology and provides the theoretical framework for constructing more controlled research.

Even if we suppose that Halio could have demonstrated that students in the IBM sections wrote better essays than students in the Macintosh sections, she has failed to provide a plausible explanatory narrative, one that might serve to inform further research. Suppose then that some well-constructed experiment were to find that writers of equal ability before using a particular computer system became writers of unequal ability after they had worked with different systems for some time. To what factors and influences might we attribute these effects and how might such hypotheses be tested? For example, a researcher might hypothesize that screen size affects writers' work. What elements of writing might be affected? Paragraph length, we might suppose, could be influenced by the amount of text a screen can display. Before testing that proposition, though, the investigator should probably consider whether screen size also interacts with software features, for example whether the word-processing program allows the user to scroll easily or restricts movement within the document to discrete screens (as in page-up and page-down navigation). A combination of factors, rather than an isolated feature, is likely to affect a writer's work (see Carroll).

To study the effects of screen size alone, the researcher should use an experimental design. The study would test two different screens (preferably using the same word-processing software to minimize confounding factors) on the same group of writers, measuring whatever aspect of writers' performance the study was designed to examine. In a study of this type Christine Haas and John R. Hayes compared the effects of large bitmapped displays, small IBM PC displays, and pen and paper on writers' difficulty working with text they had already produced. The study found that the large bitmapped display and pen-and-paper conditions were essentially equivalent whereas writers had more difficulty with the small CRT displays. The study does not make clear whether the bitmapped display alone (holding screen size constant) offers an advantage over the standard CRT, but it does suggest that screen resolution might be as important as screen size in assessing technological effects on writers working on line.

Similarly, what theory would connect a command-driven system with mechanical and grammatical correctness, and how would such a theory be tested? The researcher might hypothesize that a command system demands syntactical accuracy and that there is a transfer effect. In other words, writers would learn that "computer readers" (operating systems or word-processing programs) are inflexible and might come to believe that human readers are similarly exacting. Writers would therefore be more attentive to precise syntax in English. The role of feed-back—immediate machine response to error as opposed to delayed human reader response—might prove crucial here, and the experimental design would have to take into account those factors as well as the substantial differences between artificial command structures and natural languages. The experiment would have to test writers working with command-driven editors, not with programs whose interfaces employ menus or function keys.

Perhaps, as Halio implied, easy manipulation of visual features—everything from fonts and typefaces to full illustrations—affects students' writing on the Macintosh or in other graphic computing environments. The controlling hypothesis might posit that, whether writing on a Macintosh or an IBM, students spend roughly the same amount of time preparing their assignments but that those working on a Macintosh devote less time to text production or revision because they spend more time with visual features. To establish this hypothesis, a descriptive approach would be appropriate. The study would track students' activities and measure the amounts of time writers give to producing words, formatting text, illustrating, and completing the whole task. Any report of this type would certainly have to indicate whether the students composed at the computer or merely typed in already drafted texts before they began to "play" with graphics.

Finally, theories about perceptions and attitudes require careful attention to the entire cultural context (see Kling). As part of this context the hands-on computer training and the documentation students receive may have significant effects on their attitudes and performance. A descriptive approach would be an appropriate way to study cultural context if it includes sufficient and relevant detail not only about computing instruction but also about the more general computing environment at the institution. It is insufficient to note, as Halio does, that students in both test conditions "receive equal amounts of training" (17). This assertion tells nothing about what aspects of the operating systems and available applications the training addressed. If Macintosh instruction included help with fonts, typefaces, imported graphics, and the like, whereas IBM instruction did not, we might expect that students using the one machine would have been more likely to try out such features than students using the other.

Similarly, a user's perceptions of a machine's seriousness and a user's choices as a writer (selecting one topic or target audience rather than another, for example) might be correlated by qualitative methods, including attitudinal surveys and analyses of the physical and instructional settings within which writers work. The researcher would have to determine the origins of features in the computing environment. Here Halio's work reveals important misconceptions. Halio claims that "[students] have nicknamed the printers . . . Happy, Doc, Dopey, Grumpy and

Bashful" (18) and concluded that the names proved students considered the Macintosh a toy. But she was in error. Halio apparently failed to understand that an individual user does not supply the name for the printer: those in charge of networks assign names to printing devices so that the software running the network can differentiate among them.

Managers' attitudes toward machines may influence students' perceptions of their work environment. If supervisors or consultants complain about the "dumbing-down" of the Macintosh interface, some inexperienced users might indeed take the machine less seriously. Likewise, if managers denigrate MS-DOS or UNIX as arcane and authoritarian, users new to these systems could be quick to find them frustrating and constricting. It might be very interesting to study such cultural phenomena, but any study would have to address more than one setting in order to reveal general correlations. Not all institutions and managers hold the same attitudes. The names network managers give devices, for instance, vary considerably from setting to setting. At Cornell and Yale Universities, printers in Macintosh facilities have such prosaic names as Printer A and ImageWriter 6 while at Carnegie Mellon University *all* printers, regardless of which computer system they attach to, have colorful monikers like Maple, Birch, and Dangermouse. These institutional differences suggest that any responsible account of relationships between machines and users' habits must situate the machines and their users in a broadly conceived culture of use.

Some of the tentative narratives we have suggested lend themselves to quantitative and experimental research; others are more appropriately pursued with qualitative and descriptive methods. In the absence of a coherent explanatory narrative, however, it is impossible to construct meaningful studies of either type. Even if we were to construct such studies, however, the results would not necessarily be helpful in guiding technological choices for a writing curriculum. All the approaches we have offered are based on two unstated premises: we all agree on what "writing" is, and our understanding of that activity is not subject to change. As long as these premises remain unchallenged, our perspectives are likely to remain largely technocentric. They may not help us construct the fuller account of communication, technology, and educational goals that we must have if we are to make wise choices.

Reexamining Writing

Taken in context of the debate it engendered, Halio's article clearly indicates that the cultural context of writing is in flux. Halio speculates that elements of graphic communication intrude on the traditional, exclusively *typo*graphic domain of academic writing. When her students used multiple fonts to draw attention to the visual presence of their words or added pictures to their essays, she worried that this "gilding" of the text constituted a frivolous distraction. These activities seemingly diverted students from the "normal discourse" of the writing class, which for Halio consisted of formalized arguments on a predefined range of "serious" issues. Halio implies that graphic interfaces threaten the stability of this discourse, and by extension the ethos of academic high seriousness.

In the earlier version of this essay we defended emerging technologies on the grounds that images and visual features of texts need not undermine the word's traditional authority. We argued that future knowledge workers would need a rhetorical education encompassing many modes of discourse, including visual, aural, and dynamically interactive elements (Kaplan 100). Such arguments have gained force in the two years since we wrote our critique. Recently, industrial researchers—multimedia software developers as well as communications specialists who utilize such software—have emphasized the need for dynamic, flexible, and above all fully integrated information environments. In their descriptions of such environments they include computer-assisted design programs, spreadsheets, project management software, and hypertext linking systems, as well as conventional writing tools like electronic mail and word processors (see Malcolm, Egan, Marshall). Insofar as the writing curriculum serves the interests of employers like Boeing (see Ohmann), our curricular decisions must take into account the needs that industrial researchers articulate.

We do not mean to minimize the importance of industrial or economic considerations, especially at a time when America's competitiveness in the global economy is such a focus of anxiety. Yet most of us work not in industrial-training departments but in colleges and universities, so we must also serve intellectual interests beyond the immediate needs of the marketplace. Precisely because we are not employed by Boeing, we can and should frame more capacious questions. What are texts? Who writes them and for what purposes? What roles do technological constraints and potentials play in framing answers to those questions? By pursuing such issues, we seek to uncover what we teach and why we teach it. Thus many teachers of writing are properly interested not just in practical applications of writing technologies to traditional constructions of the essay or the business memo but in theories of reading and writing—formalist, cognitivist, response-based, feminist, poststructuralist, historicist, and cultural-materialist. Because technological systems necessarily embody only some visions of what a text is or of who an author is, these theories do not operate in abstraction from technological practice. Theories of reading and writing actually inform the systems technologists build. As a number of commentators

(Bolter, Landow, Poster) have recently pointed out, current electronic information systems seem in many ways to realize propositions about texts and reading put forward by literary theorists in the last thirty years.

Theory and practice are not incommensurable or separate, nor should they be. Communications technologies are evolving more complex and powerful forms of systematic representation—what cultural theorists call hyperreality and what one computer scientist has called mirror reality (see Baudrillard, Gelernter). If David Gelernter is right, technology will grow considerably more important as we evolve "mirror worlds" or "software models of some chunk of reality" (3). As we come to live in increasing intimacy with electronic simulations, the thinking and planning behind these systems becomes tremendously important—too important, Gelernter says, to leave to the computer scientists alone. "The intellectual content, the *social* implications of these software gizmos make them far too important to be left in the hands of the computer sciencearchy" (5). Rhetoricians and communication theorists should certainly be enfranchised in the decision making about what sort of mirror realities to build, but perhaps this participation cannot be left to the guardians of traditional rhetoric. For in Halio's view, no form of signification other than unadorned words has merit in the composition classroom—or, by implication, in the educated world. As Halio sees it, any technology that might introduce "a drastic change from the type of discourse that has long been valued in the academic world" must be carefully controlled. Young writers, those especially vulnerable to pernicious cognitive effects, must be kept within the bounds of traditional literate culture.

In our view, part of Halio's distress arises from a wider cultural anxiety about iconic representations. We have tended to forget that *graphic* comes from a Greek root meaning "to inscribe or write." As W. J. T. Mitchell argues, there is no inherent difference between depiction and description. Yet despite their inseparability and despite centuries of productive combinations, words and images have always been the scene of intense ideological struggle. Since the beginning of the print revolution, publications have incorporated graphic elements not merely as decorative illustrations but as substantive and irreplaceable content. In addition to such visual conventions as titles and subheadings, maps and diagrams have always "gilded" the printed page, especially in technical and scientific subjects. Perhaps because graphics have always been more expensive to publish, however, they have never occupied the central position that words have held. Before mechanical reproductions of texts, writers could illustrate their texts with relative facility (though dissemination remained a problem). This ease changed with the advent of mechanical writing systems. A pen can be used to draw as well as to write, but a typewriter cannot. But technologies now emerging allow the writer to control both the final appearance of the text and many other forms of graphic expression: line drawings and graphs as well as digitized photographs, video images, animations, and multimedia presentations. So the struggle between iconic and verbal expression has just now spilled over into curricular debates because technologies enabling graphic and typographic representations to co-exist in a student writer's work are just now becoming available.

This development raises new questions about what counts as knowledge and what sorts of representations certain kinds of knowledge might require. Composition teachers like Halio seem to believe that illustrations have no role in serious intellectual matters, but a research chemist would surely disagree. In one key research task in chemistry—finding what chemists call an analogous transformation—visual representations of molecular structures convey more meaning than the accompanying text. In fact, students in one study trying to complete this task were always unsuccessful unless they found the correct illustration in the materials through which they were searching (Egan). Advanced work on visualization of data also belies the logocentric viewpoint so evident in much discussion of the writing curriculum. In these cases, writing—by which we mean the interpretation and representation of ideas—necessarily involves more than mere words (Landow 49-52).

Not surprisingly, Halio has taken up arms on the side of the verbal, at the expense of the iconic, just at the moment when the evolution of electronic technology may enable valuable combinations of words and images, to say nothing of sounds and simulations. Hypertext and hypermedia systems have come into widespread use, and now software and hardware designers plan to add facilities for interactive video. In technical fields, graphic visualization programs for calculation and design have become important educational resources. Some technological forecasters see these tools as the primitive elements of Gelernter's artificial reality, or as some call it, cyberspace (see Benedikt). But in what sense are the objects produced by these technologies still texts? To what extent are we still discussing writing?

Perhaps the communications activities we have described are indeed not "writing" since they are not purely typographic or even alphabetic. But we maintain that the representation of ideas through advanced technologies still requires the production of text; it is still *composition*. This type of composition situates language—spoken, written, and iconographic—in a much richer context than the typed or word-processed essay can provide. A course in multimedia composition would still do the work of rhetoric, the critical study of semiotics in action, but it would do so in a broader technological context.

Composition, as we envision its future, involves more than words plus pictures, or video, or three-dimensional modeling programs and the like. As Jay David Bolter argues, writing is and has always been "topographic"—it is speech made visible and then *arranged* in a mental space. But until graphic-user interfaces for computers became available, writers could not fully exploit the spatial and visual dimensions of texts. Computer-mediated technologies like hypertext allow creators of texts to construct their discourses in multiple dimensions, exploring alternative pathways for traversal and development. This is the feature of hypertext that makes its spatiality most apparent. Working in a hypertextual writing space, an author employs visual as well as verbal codes to structure and represent knowledge. The arrangement of topics, their order and their relations to one another, can be mapped on a plane, displayed as a hierarchical tree, or represented in some other scheme. At least one researcher argues that this graphic schematization augments textual communication: "integrating additional information about the author's intentions and knowledge structure. . . . [i]mplies that documents produced with [hypertext] tools keep authors' knowledge structures alive by preserving their argumentation and rhetorical structures which then can be used for subsequent processing" (Streitz 343).

"Subsequent processing," however, implies that the knowledge structure revealed in topographic writing is neither definitive nor static, and this implication has important consequences for the future of composition. Although it is possible to conceive of hypertext conservatively as a simple extension of book technology (see Bolter), the more interesting and relevant applications, from the viewpoint of many professional communities, belong to what one theorist calls "constructive hypertext," a class of texts that allow collaboration and dynamic revision (Joyce 11). These texts blur or collapse altogether the distinction between reading and writing, defining the knowledge worker as always both a producer and a consumer of textual information. Although this collapse of distinctions has long been a concern of literary theory (see Barthes, Iser, Landow), it has recently become a key issue for nonliterary practice. Reviewing the applicability of hypermedia products, a team of industrial researchers contends that "a larger role for hypermedia requires eliminating the distinction between authors and readers. We assume that all members of engineering teams will be able to create and access information in a shared, distributed environment" (Malcolm 15). The kinds of electronic texts envisioned by these researchers resist the closure and the formality that have characterized printed texts. Always open to further interventions and to new arrangements and relationships, such texts require us to rethink what we mean when we say "text," suggesting that what we mean is less an object than an articulated social practice. This difference in conception would require corresponding differences in our idea of rhetoric. All this will mean rethinking the project of writing education.

None of this will happen without controversy. We can dismiss Halio's claims because they lack valid support, but we cannot so easily dispense with her underlying argument. Emerging technologies will always have their critics. Relying on well-designed empirical research, more careful investigators might conceivably argue against communication systems capable of integrating print with other media (see Charney). But in doing so, they would have to articulate a theory of writing, or of knowledge representation, that privileges the static and objectified features of print over the complexity and flux of newer media. This sort of claim implies a narrowly essentialist view of communication, one that sees print as an adequate and necessary medium for the expression of discrete, specific cognitive structures (see Turner). This view defines texts not as dynamic networks of social discourse but as repositories of established truth.

Although such approaches may seem attractive in the short run, particularly at moments when technology calls into question received cultural truths, in the long run they provide no foundation either for academic institutions or for the society those institutions serve. As Shoshana Zuboff explains, the nature of production in an information society demands a rethinking of textual work: "The textualization process moves away from a conception of information as something that individuals collect, process, and disseminate; instead, it invites us to imagine an organization as a group of people gathered around a central core that is the electronic text. . . . In such a scenario, work is, in large measure, the creation of meaning, and the methods of work involve the application of intellective skill to data" (394). Essentialist approaches to communication, including a restrictive definition of text as printed writing, cannot help us understand notions like Zuboff's central core of electronic text—or, for that matter, the distributed hypermedia system called for by the knowledge engineers at Boeing.

Thinking about the Bottom Line

The argument we have engaged in here is far from a merely theoretical dispute over approach or method in the teaching of composition. It has real implications for the directions institutional planning might take in this decade. If teachers of rhetoric and communication embrace an exclusive, old-time print literacy, we could see the computer put to work in writing courses as little more than a rather expensive typewriter. Since all major computer vendors have now implemented graphic interfaces and multimedia systems, the logical extension of this position would have teachers of writing prefer older or more limited personal computers (like the early Apple II, the original IBM PC, or its surviving clones) over the more sophisticated computing environments now available. This preference might well appeal to some administrators and managers of technology resources. After all, writing programs typically serve *all* an institution's students, making these courses a notably expensive enterprise. If only because of the scale involved, it would no doubt be cheaper to supply the writing program (and the humanities faculty in general) with outdated or low-grade technology and to delay or limit their access to newer equipment.

A print-only approach would also have dangerous consequences for our intellectual development as a profession. If as teachers of literacy we allow ourselves to be defined in terms of one narrowly conceived skill, we shall be opting out of an important set of cultural transformations. Bound to antique machines and procedures, we shall be unable to change our pedagogies and curricula to accommodate new ideas, approaches, and practices. Such conservatism means relegating ourselves to the study of the past and the instruments of the past—a reckless policy. Technological change calls for ways of seeing that are broad, not narrow. Gelernter points out that the new world of textualized work and "mirror reality" requires the critical engagement of both technologists and users of technology. The current state of communications systems presents both an opening and a challenge. As Lanham points out, technology often presents an opportunity to redefine an enterprise— sometimes with substantial penalties for rejecting that opportunity: "Newspapers had to decide whether they were in the information business or only the newspaper business; most who chose the newspaper business are no longer in it" (270). This logic may apply just as well to the knowledge business.

In our study of this emerging rhetoric of machine-mediated communication we need to reveal (or invent) ways in which a technological culture can envision and revision the multitude of messages it produces. Our project calls for culturally and historically situated research encompassing both textual theory and practice. We need to see through all the interfaces that mediate knowledge—typographic, topographic, iconographic, and perhaps even holographic. We must also learn to see ourselves reflected in those surfaces, defined and defining, both shaping and shaped by our means of text production. As John Berger says of seeing in general: "We only see what we look at. To look is an act of choice. . . . We never look at just one thing; we are always looking at the relation between things and ourselves."

Notes

1. An earlier version of this chapter appeared along with Halio's response as "Computers and Controversy: Other Ways of Seeing" in *Computers and Composition* 7 (1990): 89-102.

Works Cited

Barthes, Roland. *S/Z: An Essay*. Trans. Richard Miller. New York: Hill and Wang, 1974.

Baudrillard, Jean. *Simulations*. Trans. Paul Foss, Paul Patton, and Philip Beitchman. New York: Semiotext(e), 1983.

Benedikt, Michael, ed. *Cyberspace: First Steps*. Cambridge: MIT P, 1991.

Berger, John. *Ways of Seeing*. New York: Viking, 1973.

Bolter, Jay David. *Writing Space: The Computer, Hypertext, and the History of Writing*. Hillsdale: Lawrence Erlbaum, 1991.

Carroll, John M., and Wendy A. Kellogg. "Artifact as Theory-Nexus: Hermeneutics Meets Theory-Based Design." *CHI '89 Conference Proceedings*. Ed. Ken Bice and Clayton Lewis. New York: ACM, 1989. 7-14.

Charney, Davida. "The Impact of Hypertext on Processes of Reading and Writing." *Literacy and Computers*. Ed. S. Hilligoss and C. Selfe. New York: MLA, forthcoming.

Egan, Dennis E., and Michael E. Lesk, R. Daniel Ketchum, Carol C. Lochbaum, Joel R. Remde, Michael Littman, and Thomas K. Landauer. "Hypertext for the Electronic Library? CORE Sample Results." *Hypertext '91 Proceedings*. New York: ACM, 1991. 299-312.

Gelernter, David. *Mirror Worlds; or, The Day Software Puts the Universe in a Shoebox . . . How It Will Happen and What It Will Mean*. New York: Oxford UP, 1992.

Haas, Christine, and John R. Hayes. "What Did I Just Say? Reading Problems in Writing with the Machine." *Research in the Teaching of English* 20.1 (1986): 22-35.

Halio, Marcia Peoples. "Maiming Re-Viewed." *Computers and Composition* 7 (1990): 103-07.

_____. "Student Writing: Can the Machine Maim the Message?" *Academic Computing* January 1990: 16-19, 45.

Hawisher, Gail. "Research and Recommendations for Computers and Composition." *Critical Perspectives on Computers and Composition Instruction*. Ed. G. E. Hawisher and C. Selfe. New York: Teachers College P, 1989: 44-69.

Iser, Wolfgang. *The Act of Reading: A Theory of Aesthetic Response*. Baltimore: Johns Hopkins UP, 1978.

Joyce, Michael. "Siren Shapes: Exploratory and Constructive Hypertext." *Academic Computing* November 1988: 10-13, 37-42.

Kaplan, Nancy, and Stuart Moulthrop. "Computers and Controversy: Other Ways of Seeing." *Computers and Composition* 7 (1990): 89-102.

Kling, R. "Social Analyses of Computing: Theoretical Perspectives in Recent Empirical Research." *Computing Surveys* 12 (1980): 61-110.

Landow, George P. *Hypertext: The Convergence of Contemporary Critical Theory and Technology.* Baltimore: Johns Hopkins UP, 1992.

Lanham, Richard. "The Electronic Word: Literary Study and the Digital Revolution." *New Literary History* 20 (1989): 265-90.

Levy, Steven. "Does the Macintosh Make You Stupid?" *MacWorld* November 1990: 69-72, 74, 78.

Malcolm, Janet C., Steven E. Poltrock, and Douglas Schuler. "Industrial Strength Hypermedia: Requirements for a Large Engineering Enterprise." *Hypertext '91 Proceedings.* New York: ACM, 1991. 13-24.

Marshall, Catherine C., Frank G. Halasz, Russell A. Rogers, and William C. Janssen, Jr. "Aquanet: A Hypertext Tool to Hold Your Knowledge in Place." *Hypertext '91 Proceedings.* New York: ACM, 1991. 261-75.

Mitchell, W. J. T. *Iconology: Image, Text, Ideology.* Chicago: U of Chicago P, 1986.

Moulthrop, Stuart. "Beyond the Electronic Book: A Critique of Hypertext Rhetoric." *Hypertext '91 Proceedings.* New York: ACM, 1991. 291-98.

Ohmann, Richard. *English in America: A Radical View of the Profession.* New York: Oxford UP, 1976.

Papert, Seymour. "Computer Criticism vs. Technocratic Thinking." *Educational Researcher* 16 (1987): 22-30.

Poster, Mark. *The Mode of Information: Poststructuralism and Social Context.* Chicago: U Chicago P, 1990.

Slatin, John M. "Reading Hypertext: Order and Coherence in a New Medium." *College English* 52 (1990): 870-83.

Slatin, John M., Trent Batson, Robert Boston, Michael E. Cohen, Louie Crew, Lester Faigley, Lisa Gerrard, Gail Hawisher, Edward M. Jennings, Michael Joyce,

Nancy Kaplan, Stuart Moulthrop, Rose Norman, John O'Connor, Cynthia Selfe, Geoff Sirc, Michael Spitzer, Patricia Sullivan, Robert Woodward, and Art Young. "Computer Teachers Respond to Halio." *Computers and Composition* 7 (1990): 73-79.

Slavin, R. E. *Research Methods in Education: A Practical Guide*. Englewood: Prentice-Hall, 1984.

Streitz, Norbert A., Jörg Hannemann, and Manfred Thüring. "From Ideas and Arguments to Hyperdocuments: Travelling through Activity Spaces." *Hypertext '89 Proceedings*. New York: ACM, 1989. 343-64.

Turner, Mark. *Reading Minds: The Study of English in the Age of Cognitive Science*. Princeton: Princeton UP, 1991.

Ulmer, Gregory. *Teletheory: Grammatology in the Age of Video*. New York: Routledge, 1990.

Witte, Stephen P. "Topical Structure and Revision: An Exploratory Study." *College Composition and Communication* 34 (1983): 313-41.

Youra, Steven. "Computers and Student Writing: Maiming the Macintosh (A Response)." *Computers and Composition* 7 (1990): 81-88.

Zuboff, Shoshana. *In the Age of the Smart Machine: The Future of Work and Power*. New York: Basic Books, 1988.

Redefining Critical Editions

Peter M. W. Robinson
Oxford University

Critical editions are easy to recognize. They are usually heavy, thick, impressively bound books. They may be found massed with their confrères, identical in binding and substance, in scholarly series along library shelves. Their titles resonate with authority—the *Works of Shakespeare*, the *Centenary Edition of the Works of Nathaniel Hawthorne, Piers Plowman: The A Version*—as if the act of making such a book lifted it above the struggling herd of texts into the Canon. Open a critical edition and it declares itself: after copious introductions a thin trickle of text emerges and flows over layer on layer of footnotes, its progress obstructed by marginal annotations and ingenious typographic devices, until it is brought to a dead stop by a wall of commentary, glossaries, endnotes, and appendices. Everything says, This is a Serious Book.

From the fifteenth century until the present day, major critical editions have been among the most complex of all books, in terms of the quantity and variety of the information packed on the page. The first part of this essay explains why the production of a critical text is such a complicated process, one that can occupy the whole of a scholar's working life. The second part discusses how the computer is revolutionizing both the work of establishing a critical text and the presentation of the results of that work.

It is easier to describe and recognize critical editions than it is to define them: to the casual eye, at least, they are defined by their presentation. Alternatively, they might be defined by the methods used in their production, and thus the attractively simple definition offered by the introductory statement of the Center for Scholarly Editions (CSE): critical editions are "editions in which every word of the text is subject to the critical scrutiny of an editor" (583). However, there are many kinds and degrees of "critical scrutiny." The CSE introductory statement implicitly acknowledges this fact, and the whole of this document amounts to a definition of just what "critical scrutiny" is in the context of critical editions and a series of recommendations about how the results of this critical scrutiny are to be presented.

Thus, critical editing is both a method and a presentation. The method lies in gathering, collating, and weighing all the witnesses to the text being edited. The presentation is the final printed book, containing the edited text itself and an account (in the form of apparatus, introductions, commentaries, and endnotes) of how this text was arrived at. This is the model of critical editing that has obtained for some three hundred years, at least since Bentley declared himself willing to overturn the authority of a hundred manuscripts for "ratio et res ipsa" (Kenney 71-74). With that proclamation, the concept of editing shifted decisively from educated reprinting of actual texts toward critical reconstruction of the ideal text, with the stages of the reconstruction documented in complex apparatus.[1]

This model of editing has come under wide attack in the last decade. Central here is the frank disbelief in the notion that for any one work there must be just one "text," an ideal text that can be fixed by an editor armed both with full knowledge of all the witnesses and with the correct method for sorting these witnesses one from another. First, there is dispute on just what this "ideal" text ought to represent. Should it represent the editor's conception of the author's intentions (whether "final" or "last" or arrived at while in the grip of a primary artistic impulse), or the text as it left the printing house for the final edition supervised by the author in his or her lifetime, or the hypothetical archetype of a manuscript tradition, or some other formulation—even, perhaps, Hans Walter Gabler's "emended continuous manuscript text at its ultimate level of compositional development" (3: 1903)?[2] Second, there is no agreement on what method editors should use to arrive at the distillation of this ideal text (however conceived) from the available evidence. What weight should be given to authorial revisions, in manuscript, in proof, and in subsequent editions? How does one select a "copy-text"? In a manuscript tradition what use should be made of derivative, apparently unauthoritative manuscripts that nevertheless include some excellent readings? Furthermore, an editor brings to the task the baggage of preconceptions, at the least a set of critical preferences: no two editors will produce the same text.

Such considerations lead Peter Shillingsburg to declare: "The word *definitive* should be banished from editorial discussion. Scholarly editions can be no more than valuable access routes to the work of art" (93). But if the work of art is not itself a single definitive text, just what do these access routes lead to? In the same discussion, Shillingsburg argues that the edited work of art consists not just of *text* but *process*. This view of a text as not simply a realized object but a series of definable events, a process of becoming, is most clearly enunciated in Jerome J. McGann's work. His *Social Values and Poetic Acts* seeks to establish a broad view of texts: there is not one text but the many texts produced by the author in the process of composition and the many texts produced by printers and others in the process of publication. Indeed, McGann shows that a text may take different meanings from the occasion of publication even though the words remain the same: thus with various printings of Byron's "Fare Thee Well" ("Critical Editing"). The words *textual indeterminacy, fluidity,* and *instability* run through McGann's *Social Values* (see, for example, 182-83).

At least two other influential critics have—apparently quite independently—arrived at conclusions similar to McGann's. Bernard Cerquiglini, from his account of the problems of editing medieval French texts (including a chapter entitled "Gaston Paris et les Dinosaurs") concludes that "l'écriture médiévale ne produit pas des variantes, elle est variance" (111).[3] D. F. McKenzie, in a series of lectures and articles over the last two decades, has shown how texts reshape themselves according to their readers and their age. He speaks of a "sociology of texts," of texts as "open, unstable and indeterminate," and argues that "any history of the book must be a history of misreadings" (16, 50). In this context the existence of differing versions of a text has taken on new meaning: such cases as the two versions of Wordsworth's *Prelude* no longer appear as exceptions to the rule of "one work, one text" but as dramatic illustrations of the general rule of textual variation.

McGann (*Social Values* 193) quotes with approval Christine Froula's specification for an edition of Pound's *Cantos* that "we must reconceive the text not as an object which the editorial project aims to perfect but as the trace of a temporal process which . . . is neither contained and bounded by the author during his life nor concluded and closed off by his death." Not only are we obliged to present the variant versions as documentation of the process but these variant versions of a text may be worthy of publication in their own right. Thus the decision of the editors of the Oxford Shakespeare to print both the Folio and Quarto texts of *King Lear*: "Each version has its own integrity, which is disturbed by the practice, traditional since the early eighteenth century, of conflation" (Taylor 1025).

Even if the literary value of a particular variant text is minimal, it may be of interest for other reasons. Most of the forty-six manuscripts of the Old Norse narrative sequence *Svipdagsmál*, written largely in Iceland between 1670 to 1830, are descended from just two manuscripts and, therefore (by the strict canons of the recensionist method), of no critical worth. But these manuscripts are of considerable historic interest, documenting a fragment of the cultural history of Iceland—especially that country's relations with its Danish rulers. Many of the manuscripts were written specifically for sale to Danish collectors: these are splendid coffee-table books, embellished with illustrations and with forests of marginal variants. The manuscripts written by Icelanders for their own use are much less grand but show their scribes grappling with the meaning of this rather obscure narrative as the coffee-table productions do not. Some scribes make intelligent use of words and phrases of the poetic Edda (the poems collected in the famous Codex Regius) in attempting emendation: a sign of the increasing confidence of Icelanders in their own powers and culture, a confidence that would finally issue, almost two centuries later, in full independence from Denmark. A traditionally constituted critical edition would have no use for this information, as irrelevant to the "ideal text" of *Svipdagsmál*. But it would find a natural home in an edition embodying the "renovated historical criticism" advocated by McGann (*Social Values* 124).

Even if one were to reject the arguments of McGann, Shillingsburg, and others about the editorial task, traditional critical editions would still be vulnerable. I stated above that critical editing is both a method and a presentation. The two stages should be properly separated: for the method, the operations of the editor's system should be explicit and accessible to the reader at every stage; for the presentation, all the data about all the variants in all the witnesses should be accessible to the reader. As a minimum, each reader should be able to reconstruct the full text of each witness from the apparatus as presented. The relationship among the various actual texts of actual witnesses and that given by the editor (whether "ideal" or not), with all its complex stages of reconstruction, should be completely clear, with readers able to follow every step of the editorial process.

The Printed Edition: Chaucer and Langland

Let us test the two most important editions this century of the two most important of all Middle English works, the John M. Manly and Edith Rickert edition of Chaucer's *Canterbury Tales* and the editions of George Kane and E. Talbot Donaldson of Langland's *Piers Plowman*, against this standard.[4] The importance of both works warrants editions of grand scale, editors of great knowledge and percipience, and labors of Herculean length, intensity, and consistency. These editions have all that; the care and intellect embodied in them makes them monuments of human endeavor. In the courts of scholars, these editions have been approved; the work of Manly and Rickert has guaranteed the pre-eminence of the Hengwrt manuscript for two generations of Chaucer scholars, and Kane's and Donaldson's work has provoked a reassessment of editorial attitudes that has spread beyond Middle English studies.[5]

Neither edition, however, meets either part of the standard I have outlined for critical editions. First, for all the immensity of the apparatus given in these editions, one cannot reconstruct the full text of each witness from them. In both editions the spelling is normalized before collation: the record of variants one finds in the apparatus is not always the "actual" spelling, or at least a diplomatic of the manuscript spelling, but the editor's normalization of it. Thus information about the differing abbreviations, letter forms, and morphemic and punctuation variants found in any manuscript is discarded; one can reconstruct the manuscripts as they have been normalized but not the texts themselves. The scholar seeking information about the development of the language, or about changes in scribal practices over the hundred-year span of these manuscripts, will not find it in these editions.

The justification for exclusion of all this information is that the editors are primarily interested in "substantive" variants, that is, variants that are textually or historically significant. This assertion rests on editorial confidence that "substantive" variants can be identified at every stage of the collation—even in the collation of the very first manuscripts, before all the variants are known. I cannot subscribe to this confidence. I give two examples for my lack of such confidence. The first relates to the very first word of the Wife of Bath's Prologue. In most of the manuscripts (some forty of the fifty-one that have this line), this is "Experience." Ten manuscripts have, remarkably, "Experiment" (the good wife as a scientific experimenter in marriage!); one manuscript alone, Rawlinson Poetic 149 (Ra^2), has the nonsensical "Eryment." This Ra^2 reading is most likely to have arisen from a manuscript that either had "Experiment" with the common abbreviation for "per" (p with a bar through the descender) or had "Experiment" with a y, or both. But one cannot determine from Manly and Rickert just which of the ten manuscripts with the normalized "Experiment" had just what spelling. A fragment of information possibly linking Ra^2 to other manuscripts has been lost, and with it possibly crucial information about the development of the manuscript tradition.[6]

The second example concerns the two primary manuscripts of the *Canterbury Tales*, the Hengwrt manuscript (favoured by the Chaucer Variorum editors and others, since the publication of Manly and Rickert) and the Ellesmere manuscript (favoured by most editors before Manly and Rickert). It is not too much to say that the relationship between these two manuscripts and among these two and all the other manuscripts are the most important textual issues facing any editor or reader of the *Canterbury Tales*. I shall discuss here the relationship between these two manuscripts; the relationship among these two and other manuscripts I discuss below. Hengwrt and Ellesmere are so alike in orthography that they are commonly (but not universally) believed to have been written by the same scribe.[7] My transcriptions of the Wife of Bath's Prologue in these two manuscripts and the consequent collation of these two transcriptions have shown a remarkable dichotomy. The collations done so far of Ellesmere and Hengwrt against each other and against other manuscripts show that these two manuscripts agree, over and over again, against all other manuscripts in what editors call "accidentals": fine points of punctuation and choices of letter form. Yet Ellesmere and Hengwrt disagree, over and over again, on what editors call "substantive variants": in just the first lines, experience is sufficient authority "to" the good wife in Ellesmere, "for" her in Hengwrt, "sith" she was twelve in Ellesmere, but "sith that" in Hengwrt; she had five husbands "at chirche dore" in Ellesmere but "at the chirche dore" in Ellesmere, "for" she could be married that often in Ellesmere against "if" she could be married that often in Hengwrt, with Hengwrt here introducing a note of doubt absent from Ellesmere. One gains no inkling of the collision between this extraordinary agreement of the two manuscripts in "accidentals" and their equally extraordinary disagreement in "substantives" from Manly and Rickert simply because their collation discards all the accidentals. Yet one cannot sensibly discuss the relationship between Hengwrt and Ellesmere—and the possibility of the two manuscripts' representing different versions by Chaucer himself—without taking this into account (Manly 2: 495-518).

It is revealing that in the discussions I have read of Manly and Rickert, many of them far from uncritical, no scholar has ever criticized them for collating "normalized" texts, with the consequent loss of information.[8] Kane and Donaldson's normalization is lighter than that of Manly and Rickert and accordingly preserves considerably more information about variant spellings and orthographies than do Manly and Rickert. Thus the apparatus "records all substantive variants which may possibly be substantive, the majority of grammatical variants, the majority of dialect variants, and a great many orthographical variants" (Kane, *A Version* 170). Punctuation variants and many "accidentals" are therefore excluded. But for these editions based on many manuscripts the consensus seems to be that these editors had no choice: including every variation of spelling, every scrap of information about punctuation and word forms for all these manuscripts would have over-burdened the collations and rendered the editions unmanageably bloated. I collated the manuscripts of *Svipdagsmál* both in normalized spelling and in unnormalized spelling: the unnormalized collation was approximately five times as large as the normalized collation. On this scale the four volumes of Manly and Rickert's collation would have swollen to twenty volumes. No publisher would print all this. Nor would any scholar possibly be able to absorb all this information from a printed edition; better far then to normalize, sifting out (one hopes) the wheat from the chaff.

Thus problems with a particular mode of presentation (the reluctance of publishers to print such a full collation, the inability of readers to absorb so much information) have come to determine a key scholarly decision of method. The decision about what is, and what is not, a "significant" variant is determined, at least in part, by the scholar's perception of what can be published and what could be usefully read in a printed book. Method is decided by presentation; the presentation is itself incomplete.

Manly and Rickert also fail the second part of the standard I outlined above for critical editions: the steps by which they reach their conclusions concerning the relationships between the manuscripts, conclusions fundamental to their espousal of Hengwrt, are far from clear.[9] The foundation of the method by which they grouped the manuscripts is their statement that "the law of probability is so steady in its working that only groupings of classificatory value have the requisite persistence and consistency to be taken as genetic groups" (1:22). They do not say just what law of probability they mean; they give no examples of its working; they do not discuss just how one identifies "persistence and consistency." It appears that they distinguish three types of variant groups: "acco," that is, manuscripts that agree by simple coincidence; "ctm," that is, manuscripts that agree by deliberate contamination; and "genetic groups," manuscripts that agree because they are related by direct copying. They do not say just how these three groups are to be discriminated one from another. After all this work, at the end of two decades of debilitating collation, they could classify only a third of the manuscripts into "constant groups" effective throughout the *Canterbury Tales* and based on the "genetic groups" of variants characteristic of them. In their defense, my own work with the manuscripts of the Wife of Bath's Prologue so far suggests that their analysis may be far more accurate than the scanty explanation in their introduction suggests. The later stages of their edition were done under great difficulty: Edith Rickert died before it was published, John Manly soon after. If they had been given good health and favorable circumstances, the introduction might have been worthy of their work.

Not only is the presentation of their method and its application defective, one must suspect that the tools they had, for all their heroic application of them, were simply not adequate to cope with the immense problems of the *Canterbury Tales*. Let us return to the Hengwrt and Ellesmere manuscripts, and the problem of their relation with all the other manuscripts of the *Canterbury Tales*. Again, the Wife of Bath's Prologue provides a battleground: there are five passages not found in Hengwrt but accepted by many editors into the text, thirty-two lines in all; four of these passages are in Ellesmere as well as in other manuscripts. Including or excluding these passages might significantly alter our perception of the Wife. It is in one of these passages (lines 619 to 625) that she says, according to the text of F. N. Robinson's edition:

"I ne loved nevere by no discrecioun,
But evere folwede myn appetit,
Al were he short, or long, or blak, or whit;
I took no kep, so that he liked me,
How poore he was, ne eek of what degree"

—a statement of promiscuity one cannot parallel from the rest of her prologue. Did Chaucer write these lines? If he did, why are they not in Hengwrt but in Ellesmere? Manly and Rickert suggest that these passages were all inserted into "some one MS": Hengwrt then represents an earlier state of the text, the manuscripts with the five passages a later state. But much is obscure: it is not explained why Ellesmere has only four of the five passages (a third state of the text?). Above all, Manly and Rickert do not relate these additions to the many other differences among Hengwrt, Ellesmere, and the other manuscripts. If these lines represent different authorial versions, might not other lines, other readings, also represent different authorial versions? But there is no discussion of this issue, and the reason emerges as one reads through Manly and Rickert's account: the quantity of variation is so great, the overlappings of variant groups with variant groups so subtle, so multifarious, that hypotheses erode even as they are framed. The discussion of the important Cambridge manuscript Dd.4.24 (2: 208-09) is a paradigm of the indecision so produced. Their practice of referring to variants by simple line number does not help; it is a lengthy task to check that a variant actually is a variant and not, for example, an archetypal reading and hence valueless for analysis.

Over the twenty thousand lines and the eighty-three manuscripts of the *Canterbury Tales* one might expect several hundred thousand variants even in a normalized collation. Such are the operations of coincident variation and contamination that all these variants will not neatly sort themselves into groups corresponding to the groups of manuscripts and reducible to a single stemma. An unhappy lesson of Manly and Rickert's work is that, with the tools available to them, analysis then becomes so complex that even if it is achieved, lucid explanation may be impossible. Kane and Donaldson's meticulous researches into the manuscripts of Langland's *Piers Plowman* and their attempts to reduce their relations to a single stemma led them to conclude that the relations between manuscripts are so tangled that the presence or absence alone of any one reading in any one or more manuscripts is of no value in determining the authenticity of that reading. Kane states that "the genetic history of the A manuscripts is not recoverable in any form useful for the editorial process of recension" (*A Version* 112-13); similar statements are made about the B manuscripts (*B Version* 54, 62).

Hence, Kane and Donaldson decided that the only test of the originality of any reading is the editor. In both introductions page after page shows the editors in judgment of the merits of this reading or that, giving their choice of the "original" text and explaining just how the degenerative forms actually found in the manuscripts arose from this "right" reading.[10] The manuscripts may confirm an editor's choice, or they may offer lessons in the varieties of corruption, lessons the editor may apply as he or she works back to the "original." This approach implicitly asserts there was just such a single original (not the least disturbing feature of these editions is the editors' willingness to import from the A version into the B version, for example, readings found in no B-version manuscript) and that the editors can indeed recreate it from the *disjecta membra* of many manuscripts—or from no manuscript at all, if none are satisfactory. It asserts too a perfect confidence in the editor's ability to distinguish the merely "scribal" from the "authorial."[11]

Of the B-version text produced by this process, D. C. Fowler remarked, "I am convinced that in large part it is a text that never existed in the fourteenth century." In their introduction Kane and Donaldson consider this issue directly: "There remains the question whether we have not constructed an 'ideal text.' If this implies that a part of our editorial thinking was to measure the readings of the manuscripts against our *idea* of how the poet would write we have certainly done so: we would not know how else to edit" (213). Thus, despite the immense apparatus of historical collation in their editions Kane and Donaldson stand foursquare for the "ideal text," against all the movement toward a "renovated historical editing" I noted above. The chaos of the manuscripts permits no ordered historical reconstruction; the knowledge and intuition of the editors are our only guides through the dark.

Accordingly, the sole historical responsibility of editors is to show how the various supposed corruptions might have arisen from the reading they bless as "right." They have no responsibility to show the stages of transmutation from one actual text to another because, indeed, these stages cannot be discovered. Kane's and Donaldson's failure to determine any historical reconstruction of the development of the *Piers Plowman* tradition is central to their assertion that their method of editing was the only one available to them. A "historical" text, or texts, is nonsense; only an "ideal" text is possible. In all the discussion of Kane's and Donaldson's work the necessity of this failure has not been questioned. E. G. Stanley accepts "the impracticality amounting to impossibility" of recension, and he even suggests that historical reconstruction of manuscript traditions will be impossible for any medieval vernacular text surviving in many manuscripts. But Kane's and Donaldson's failure does not mean that such a historical reconstruction is impossible: different tools might produce a different result.

Essentially they sorted all the variant groups according to the number of manuscripts in each: groups with two manuscripts agreeing against all others, groups with three manuscripts against all others, groups with four manuscripts against all others, and so on. They then attempted to construct the "genetic groups" on the theory (based on Paul Maas) that, for example, for a genetic group of two manuscripts (such as the manuscripts R and F discussed in *B Version* 25-32) there would be an overwhelming number of variants found in just those two manuscripts and very few, or no, cases where either of those manuscripts agreed in error against the other. They did not find this situation: even though there are indeed many cases in which R and F agree in error against all other manuscripts, there are also many in which F agrees with some other manuscript against R, and some in which R agrees with some other manuscript against F. The larger the manuscript groups became, the worse matters became, as hypotheses involving groupings of three, four, or more manuscripts disappear in storms of conflicting counterexamples.

The major weakness of this procedure is the practical restriction by which, when searching for evidence of a group of, say, eight manuscripts, one is restricted to looking at the various variant groups of just eight manuscripts. Now, it is to be expected that there will be many occasions when a member of the group is absent at a particular variant (perhaps for no more reason than loss of a manuscript page), or it might be that another manuscript joins the group, perhaps through occasional contamination or simple accident. In these cases one would find evidence of the existence of the group of eight not in variant groups involving just eight manuscripts but in groups with seven and nine manuscripts, respectively—or in groups of six or ten and so on. Because of the method of hand-sorting Kane had to use, it was very difficult for him to gain answers to such questions as how many variants are there on which seven of these eight manuscripts agree against all others? When I attempted to use this same procedure in analysis of the forty-six manuscripts of the *Svipdagsmál* tradition, I found that just as it failed for Kane, it failed for me: it did not produce unambiguous evidence of even the most clearly marked groups, groups whose existence was confirmed by external evidence ("Icelandic Manuscripts" 175). But other methods did produce better results; see below.

The Computer and Editions of Medieval Authors

Both of these editions, that of Langland and that of Chaucer, are limited by the forms of presentation and the methods available to their editors. But neither of these editions could have been other than they are; one can only work with what is available. But an editor beginning work now would have very different resources available. This discussion has not yet mentioned the words *computer, hypermedia,* or *electronic publication.* But everything I have said of these editions has been conditioned by the great advances made in the past decade in these areas. It would have been pointless to remark a few years ago that these editors might have transcribed, collated, and published the un-normalized texts: until very recently, this process was unthinkable. I believe that the impact of these advances on the scholarly business of critical editing will be at least equal to that of the recensionist method associated with Karl Lachmann on nineteenth-century (and later) editors, and perhaps as great as that of the invention of printing itself.

Redefining Critical Editions

Let us look forward to see how an edition of something like the *Canterbury Tales* might use the methods and modes of presentation now becoming available. First, it would begin with transcription of all the manuscripts into the computer. Many decisions will have to be made about this transcription: it is simply impossible, certainly unnecessary (as we shall see) and perhaps even undesirable, to try and capture everything—every dot, every mark on the page, every slight variation in every letter form—in the transcription. One will need to determine in advance the likely uses of the transcription and then seek to include in the transcription all the information relevant to these uses. For example, in the transcription I am currently supervising of the fifty-eight manuscripts of the Wife of Bath's Prologue, our first priority is production of collatable texts. Because of my conviction that the distribution of certain features traditionally normalized out of the collations of medieval English texts—especially punctuation, abbreviations, certain spellings, and tailed final letters—might be of genetic significance in tracing the history of the tradition, we seek to retain all information about these in the transcriptions: they will be "unnormalized" to this extent at least. Our second priority is production of texts that will be useful to people studying the language of the manuscripts. Thus, we seek to preserve all information about the actual spelling of the words themselves (not, indeed, just that fraction likely to be of collational, genetic significance): from our transcriptions, one can tell whether a scribe uses *non* or *noon* or *none*. Our third priority is production of texts that will be useful to people studying the orthography of the manuscripts. Our transcription distinguishes certain letter forms traditionally leveled by editors: we separate three forms of lower-case *r*, for example (beside our standard *r*, there is round *r*, rather like a modern *z* with a curly descender, and long-tailed *r*, like modern *r* but with an elongated descender). We have not attempted to discriminate all different forms of every letter, but we have at least tried to be consistent about those we do separate so that paleographers might confidently use this information. We do not record detail of the physical appearance of the manuscript, beyond its page, column, and line division and occasional notes on holes, marks, and the like.

Transcriptions such as these might be worthy of publication in their own right. Publication in electronic form (on CD-ROM, or whatever) is preferable to traditional "paper" form, both because it is far cheaper and because it will permit scholars to use various computer tools to search, concord, or index the transcriptions in any way they wish. Also, the utility of the transcriptions will be greatly increased if one can compare them directly to facsimiles of the originals. One could include digitized facsimiles of every page of every manuscript alongside the transcription. Computer software might also be included so that scholars could use image-enhancement techniques on a difficult-to-read passage, expanding it on the screen or viewing it with different "filters" (compare Kiernan). Hypertext software could also be provided, so that the scholar could read several different transcriptions and facsimiles at once, with the software scrolling the transcriptions and facsimiles all in synchrony with one another. Provision of the facsimiles themselves would obviate the need to include everything any scholar might need in the transcription. Scholars interested in our Chaucer manuscripts as specimens of artistic history could add the information they want to the transcriptions (a much easier process than creating transcriptions ex nihilo) and then distribute these in turn.

If an edition of the *Canterbury Tales* did no more than this, it would meet a primary aim of historical editing: the provision of access to the text of the original witnesses. But it would reduce the editor to a compiler of texts and a distributor of computer programs. There is a school of thought that would welcome this interpretation of the editor's function (see White), but it is likely that readers will want more of editors than just this. After the initial excitement of having every manuscript of the *Canterbury Tales* available for inspection, readers are soon likely to feel lost in so many manuscripts, so many pages, so many words. They will need guides through the labyrinth. They will ask, what are the relationships among all these manuscripts? What is the evidence for these relationships? Which manuscripts appear closest to what Chaucer actually might have written? What is the evidence for this belief? How do the differences among manuscripts show the development of the language in the century after Chaucer's death? After all, what is Chaucer most likely to have written? These are difficult and legitimate questions, just the questions that scholars with special training and special intimacy with the material are best placed to answer.

The tools now available to editors promise answers to these questions of a precision not previously available and supported with a clarity not previously available. First, one can collate all the transcriptions with a program that permits simultaneous regularization and collation and that permits endless experimentation with different regularizations: my own Collate program was written for just this purpose. Second, one can import the collation output, with all its information about the patterns of agreements and disagreements between and among manuscripts, into a database and then use the database facilities to get immediate answers to questions like those that Kane's method could not easily answer: how many variants are found in any seven of a group of eight manuscripts, and only in these, and what are these variants and what other variants occur at those points? Interestingly, close reading of Manly and Rickert's discussion of the tradition of particular tales (but not reading of their introduction) shows them asking just this sort of question; essentially, they were using database techniques without a database to assist them. To have got as far as they did is indeed a cause to wonder.

This kind of database analysis of the *Svipdagsmál* tradition permitted me to construct a coherent and probable account of the history of the text ("Icelandic Manuscripts" 174-81).[12] Third, as well as direct database interrogation of the corpus of variants, one could use computer methods to analyze the patterns of agreements and disagreements between and among the manuscripts and to construct from these patterns alone a reconstruction of the history of the tradition. Over the last thirty years evolutionary biologists have developed a range of methods for use in reconstruction of the descent of related species, a situation directly analogous to that of reconstruction of the descent of related manuscripts. With Robert J. O'Hara of the Philosophy Department of the University of Wisconsin I have used one of these methods, cladistic analysis, with astonishing success on the manuscripts of the *Svipdagsmál* tradition. For example, for fifteen of the forty-six manuscripts I had certain external evidence of just which of these fifteen manuscripts were copied from which. The evolutionary tree produced by O'Hara with the cladistic analysis program PAUP placed these fifteen in exactly the relations to one another that I knew to be correct from external evidence (see Swofford). It took me much effort and travel to gather that evidence: he, knowing no Old Norse and nothing of the manuscripts, did it in minutes.[13] Cladistic analysis has now been tested on three complete manuscript traditions, together comprising some one hundred and thirty manuscripts, and also on parts of four more traditions, comprising a further eighty. In each case, the method has shown its power to confirm the perceptions of editors; in some cases it has also pointed to significant relations between and among manuscripts that had escaped editorial notice.

In my work with the Wife of Bath's Prologue I expect to run through this cycle of regularization/collation/database and cladistic analysis not once but many times. Each time, as I learn more of the relationships among the manuscripts, I shall adjust the regularization and the collation itself so that, for example, instances of spellings that appear to have survived from copy to copy against the grain of scribal practice will appear in the collation. As different recensions become more clearly identified as present in particular manuscripts, I shall collate just these manuscripts against their reconstructed subarchetype, to try and identify more accurately subgroups within these manuscripts. The final "edited" text may be not one text but a series of texts, each representing a particular moment in the text's history. Some of these texts might represent Chaucer's own revisions; some of them will represent revisions by other hands. A single "ideal text" might be constructed from these texts, if the editor wished. My aim is rather to recover the history of the expression of the text through the manuscripts, a necessary step before any "ideal text" could be made.

Thus, our hypothetical edition of the *Canterbury Tales* might consist of a series of texts, giving the editor's reconstruction of the historic stages through which the text passed into all the surviving manuscripts. By providing all the transcriptions of all the manuscripts upon which the reconstruction is based (transcriptions that can be checked against the images of the manuscripts also provided), by providing also a record of the final collations and analyses that support the reconstruction, the reader will be able to follow every stage of the editorial process. Hypertext software will again facilitate this progression, permitting easy movement from hypothesis to analysis to evidence and back again. Further, the reader's activity need not be restricted just to tracing what the editor has done: collation, database, and cladistic-analysis software could all be included with the edition so that the reader could redo any part of or all the editor's work—even make his or her own edition based on differing assumptions.

The relationships among the text, the reader, and the editor in an edition such as this will be very different from that obtaining in a printed text. Traditionally, the text is a single, fixed object; the editor is the master of the text, controlling every detail of its realization; the reader is the editor's client, seeing just those things the editor shows. In the electronic edition here outlined the text itself is fluid: it may be a series of linked texts, transmuting from version to version; it might be a stack of differing views of the one text, for example, varying regularizations of a manuscript; it might be the reader's own creation from the supplied materials. The privilege of the editor, of exclusive access to materials (manuscripts, transcriptions, collation cards) of which the reader sees only what the editor chooses to reveal, is removed. Editor and reader are now partners in the quest for understanding: both have access to the same materials; both may use the same tools. Indeed the spread of electronic networking may make the partnership an actuality; the electronic edition might be held centrally, with scholars accessing it from remote terminals all around the world; scholars could communicate mistakes in transcriptions and differing collations back to the central repository where they could modify the edition for all who use it.

This concept of fluid editions, reshaping themselves in use, offers a way around one of the most difficult problems facing editors. The problem is this: one wishes to edit a single work, representative of a larger body of works—one play by Shakespeare or one of many Elizabethan English dramatists or only the dramatic works in the literature of Elizabethan England. As one edits that single work, one finds that all the ancillary reference tools giving access to the surrounding work—the dictionaries, the concordances, the word lists, and so on—are based on outdated editions, multiplying many times the difficulty of using them. In extreme cases, to edit this single work successfully, one will first have to reedit all the surrounding work, then update all the compilations of materials based on it.

Old Norse skaldic poetry is such an extreme case. It could be argued that it constitutes the single most remarkable and original cultural achievement of the medieval Germanic peoples. Yet since the completion of Finnur Jónsson's massive *Skjaldedigtning* in 1915, with two volumes presenting diplomatic texts and two presenting a normalized, emended text with a Danish translation, editing of skaldic poetry has stopped dead. Skaldic verses have been edited where they occur in the sagas, a few anthologies and surveys have appeared, and the poems have been reedited purely from Finnur's own diplomatic transcriptions; that is all.[14] Major poets, poets of European importance such as Egill Skallagrímsson and Sighvatr Þórðarson, await their first editor. The inactivity has spread to secondary literature: Roberta Frank observes that compared to the progress in Old English scholarship in the last century, "skaldic research has stood almost still" (165).

One reason for this inactivity is that the major resources for the study of skaldic poetry form a perfectly self-sustaining closed unit. Beside Finnur's *Skjaldedigtning*, the scholar must use Finnur's own dictionary to the skaldic and eddic poetry, naturally based on his own editions (*Lexicon Poeticum*), and Rudolph Meissner's indispensable index to the kennings, itself based on the first, 1916, edition of Finnur's *Lexicon Poeticum* and, once more, on Finnur's own texts. As it stands in printed form, this is a "hermeneutic circle" (Frank 163), at risk of collapse if one removes a single stone. Matters need not be so; one can now conceive an electronic edition of skaldic poetry in which the texts are linked both to manuscript images and transcriptions and to dictionaries, concordances, and indices by links that fashion themselves anew as texts are edited and reedited. One could reform the corpus from within by the incremental editing activity of many scholars, rather than by a single heroic assault by a single scholar such as that of Finnur in the first decades of this century. Thus, a literature that has been progressively marginalized by scholarly neglect might claim due attention at last.

There has been much talk, on electronic bulletin boards, in articles, and at conferences and indeed where any two scholars gather together with a computer, of editions like these outlined in the last few pages; as yet, no such edition has actually appeared.[15] In part this delay is due to the newness of the technology. In part the delay itself reflects the enormous impact these methods will have on editing. It will not be enough just to republish existing editions in electronic form, as might be done with an archive of photographs or newspapers. Every stage of the editing process must be rethought and redone. Most of all, the delay between the desire for such editions and their realization reflects uncertainty about standards. Just how should we encode our transcription of a manuscript? How do we represent different manuscript characters or features such as lacunae or scribal additions or deletions? What assurance do we have that the system of transcription we adopt can be read by computers in five, ten, a hundred years' time? Because electronic editions of medieval texts, at least, will rest on a base of transcriptions of manuscripts, production of electronic editions is dependent on progress toward standards of transcription. I estimate that transcription of the manuscripts of the Wife of Bath's Prologue will require about nine hundred hours of work; all the manuscripts of the *Canterbury Tales* might require twenty thousand hours. If these transcriptions remain in use for centuries, passing through many different forms as computers and scholarly fashions change, then this expenditure will be very cheap. But if they have to be discarded within a few years, then it will be very expensive. Encoding for the sake of encoding, like electronic editions for the sake of electronic editions, will be profligate.

Great progress has been made on these issues in the last few years as scholars have come to realize that the costs of the maintenance and use of electronic texts in incompatible formats threaten to strangle all enterprise in this direction. The Text Encoding Initiative (TEI) has done much to release scholars from dead-end discussions of this computer or that software (see Burnard). Although at the time of writing, commonly accepted protocols remain still some distance away, enough has been done for scholars to proceed with their own transcription projects, using their own systems of encoding, with reasonable certainty that it will be possible to translate files from their own private encodings to a future, universal TEI standard. I am confident, for example, that there is nothing in the transcription system we are using for the Chaucer manuscripts that cannot be translated into the likely TEI format.

There are considerable difficulties ahead and problems and dangers in store we cannot yet imagine. But the possible rewards are great: the access of many more scholars to materials long unobtainable, not to mention a clearer understanding of how some of the most important texts in our culture were shaped by their authors and received by their readers. Above all, our view of what text is and what we do as readers and editors will change. John of Salisbury said that if we see further than our giant predecessors, it is because we can stand on their shoulders, a cliché deftly reversed by Joseph Harris reviewing the past century of Old Norse scholarship: it seems at times as if the giants are standing on us (126). To help us see further, we may now stand on computers as well—but we should beware that the computers do not stand on us.

Notes

1. This discussion of the "ideal text" draws on the chapter "Ideal Texts" in Shillingsburg.

2. Gabler's edition of *Ulysses* has itself become an arena for fierce conflict about the theory of critical editions: see, for example, reviews by Anthony Hammond and McGann (*Social Values* 173-94), and Bruce Arnold.

3. The impact of Cerquiglini's work can be gauged from the devotion of the entire January 1990 number of *Speculum* to articles advancing a "New Philology" built upon his ideas. A special number of *Romance Philology* 54 (August 1991), in press at the time of writing, has been publicized as a counterpoise to this "New Philology."

4. An edition of the C version is in preparation.

5. In this way we have the acceptance by the editors of the *Variorum Chaucer* of the authority of Hengwrt; see the introductions by D. C. Baker, A. I. Doyle, and M. B. Parkes. McGann places Kane's and Donaldson's work among the few "seminal works" about which modern textual studies orient themselves, raising "a serious theoretical challenge... against certain prevailing editorial and textual views" (*Social Values* 173-74).

6. In fact, of the ten manuscripts, two (Ld^1, Sl^2) have plain "Experiment," four (Bw, La, Mm, Ry^1) have the abbreviation for "per," but with two of these (Mm and Ry^1) having final "e"; one manuscript alone (Sl^1) has "Experyment"; I have not yet seen the other three manuscripts. I give a remarkable instance of the survival of an "accidental" variant in the Old Norse *Svipdagsmál* tradition through some seven stages of copying in the first of my two articles in *Literary and Linguistic Computing* describing the *Svipdagsmál* work. See also Donaldson 119-20, where his discussion of the phrase "in parfit wys" of line 117 of the Wife of Bath's Prologue is inhibited by the lack of information in Manly and Rickert's collation concerning the exact spellings of this phrase in the manuscripts.

7. See Doyle's and Parkes's introductions to the Hengwrt facsimile, Baker xix-xx. This point is disputed by R. V. Ramsay in "Hengwrt and Ellesmere Manuscripts" and "Palaeography."

8. The closest approach to such a criticism is Dorothy Everett's review, regretting the exclusion of information possibly useful in establishing Chaucer's own spelling and punctuation—not, however, the spelling and punctuation of all the manuscripts. For criticism of Manly and Rickert on other grounds, see Kane, *Editing Chaucer* 207-29.

9. See, for example, Germaine Dempster's report of, and attempts to answer, criticisms of Manly and Rickert (especially 411-15) and Kane's article in *Editing Chaucer*.

10. For example, the discussion of the proposed reading "wy" at 3: 95 in *A Version* 164.

11. At least one reviewer, T. Turville-Petre, registered incredulity at this claim. See also L. Paterson. Gabler claims to be able to distinguish "scribal" from "authorial" even when scribe and author are both James Joyce: "In copying, he was both author and scribe. As author, he composed and revised unceasingly, but as scribe he was simultaneously prone to inattention and oversight" (3: 1864).

12. Similar methods were used by Didier Xhardez in his analysis of the tradition of Gregory of Corinth's treatise on Greek dialectology, surviving in more than fifty manuscripts.

13. The results of this analysis were presented at the joint conference of the Association for Computing and the Humanities and of the Association for Literary and Linguistic Computing in Oxford, England, in April 1992 and at the International Medieval Congress in Kalamazoo in May 1992.

A fuller report will appear in P. M. W. Robinson and R. J. O'Hara, "Cladistic Analysis of an Old Norse Manuscript Tradition," *Research in Humanities Computing,* ed. Nancy Ide and Susan Hockey, Oxford: Oxford UP, forthcoming.

14. Anthologies include Jón Helgason and E. O. G. Turville-Petre. E. A. Kock reedits the poems from Finnur's transcriptions.

15. For example, the discussion on the ANSAXNET bulletin board in October and November 1991 concerning electronic editions. A plenary session at the 1991 conference of the Society for Textual Scholarship was devoted to editing and new technologies; see too my forthcoming article in *Text.*

Works Cited

Arnold, Bruce. *The Scandal of Ulysses.* London: Sinclair-Stevenson, 1991.

Baker, D. C., A. I. Doyle, and M. B. Parkes. Introductions. *The Canterbury Tales: A Facsimile and Transcription of the Hengwrt Manuscript with Variants from the Ellesmere Manuscript.* Ed. P. G. Ruggiers. Norman: U of Oklahoma P, 1979.

Burnard, Lou, and C. Michael Sperberg-McQueen. *Guidelines for the Encoding and Interchange of Machine-Readable Texts.* Draft Version 1.0 (TEI P1). Chicago: TEI, 1991.

"The Center for Scholarly Editions: An Introductory Statement." *PMLA* 92 (1977): 583-97.

Cerquiglini, Bernard. *Éloge de la Variante: Histoire Critique de la Philologie*. Paris: Éditions du Seuil, 1989.

Dempster, Germaine. "The Early History of the Canterbury Tales." *PMLA* 61 (1946): 379-415.

Donaldson, E. Talbot. *Speaking of Chaucer*. London: Athlone, 1970.

Everett, Dorothy. Review. *Review of English Studies* 18 (1942): 93-109.

Fowler, D. C. Review. *Yearbook of English Studies* 7 (1977): 23-42.

Frank, Roberta. "Skaldic Poetry." *Old Norse-Icelandic Literature: A Critical Guide*. Ed. C. J. Clover and J. Lindow. Ithaca: Cornell UP, 1985.

Gabler, Hans Walter, Wolfhard Steppe, and Claus Melchior. *Ulysses: A Critical and Synoptic Edition*. 3 vols. New York: Garland, 1984.

Hammond, Anthony. Review. *Library* 8 (December 1986): 382-90.

Harris, Joseph. "Eddic Poetry." *Old Norse-Icelandic Literature: A Critical Guide*. Ed. C. J. Clover and J. Lindow. Ithaca: Cornell UP, 1985.

Helgason, Jón. *Skjaldevers*. Oslo: Dreyers forlag, 1962.

Jónsson, Finnur. *Lexicon Poeticum*. 2nd ed. Copenhagen: S.L. Møller, 1932.

Kane, George. *Editing Chaucer: The Great Tradition*. Norman: Pilgrim, 1984.

_____. *Piers Plowman: The A Version*. London: Athlone, 1960.

Kane, George, and E. Talbot Donaldson. *Piers Plowman: The B Version*. London: Athlone, 1975.

Kenney, E. J. *The Classical Text*. Berkeley: U of California P, 1974.

Kiernan, K. S. "Digital Image Processing and the *Beowulf* Manuscript." *Literary and Linguistic Computing* 6 (1991): 20-27.

Kock, E. A. *Den Norsk-isländska Skaldedikningen*. Lund: Gleerup, 1946-50.

Maas, Paul. *Textual Criticism*. Trans. B. Flower. Oxford: Clarendon P, 1958.

Manly, John M., and Edith Rickert. *The Text of the Canterbury Tales*. 8 vols. Chicago: U of Chicago P, 1940.

McGann, Jerome J. *Social Values and Poetic Acts*. Cambridge: Harvard UP, 1988.

_____. "What Is Critical Editing?" *Text* 5 (1991): 15-29.

McKenzie, D.F. *Bibliography and the Sociology of Texts: The Panizzi Lectures 1985*. London: British Library, 1986.

Meissner, Rudolph. *Die Kenningar der Skalden*. Rheinische Beiträge und Hülfsbücher zur Germanischen Philologie und Volkskunde 1. Bonn: K. Schroeder, 1921.

Paterson, L. "The Logic of Textual Criticism and the Way of Genius." *Textual Criticism and Literary Interpretation*. Ed. Jerome J. McGann. Chicago: U of Chicago P, 1985.

Ramsay, R. V. "The Hengwrt and Ellesmere Manuscripts of the *Canterbury Tales*: Different Scribes." *Studies in Bibliography* 35 (1982): 133-54.

_____. "Palaeography and Scribes of Shared Training." *Studies in the Age of Chaucer* 8 (1986): 107-44.

Robinson, Peter M. W. "The Collation and Textual Criticism of Icelandic Manuscripts. (1): Collation. (2): Textual Criticism." *Literary and Linguistic Computing* 4 (1989): 99-105, 174-81.

_____. "Collation, Textual Criticism, Publication and the Computer." *Text*, forthcoming.

Robinson, F. N. *The Works of Geoffrey Chaucer*. 2nd ed. London: Oxford UP, 1957.

Shillingsburg, Peter. *Scholarly Editing in the Computer Age: Theory and Practice*. Athens: U of Georgia P, 1986. 79-95.

Stanley, E. G. Review. *Notes and Queries* 221 (October 1976): 435-47.

Swofford, D. L. *PAUP: Pylogenetic Analysis Using Parsimony, Version 3.0.* Computer program. Champaign: Illinois Natural History Survey, 1991.

Taylor, G., and S. Wells. *William Shakespeare: The Complete Works.* Original-spelling edition. Oxford: Clarendon P, 1986.

Turville-Petre, E. O. G. *Scaldic Poetry.* Oxford: Clarendon P, 1976.

Turville-Petre, T. Review. *Studia Neophilologica* 49 (1977): 153-55.

White, Patricia S. "Black and White and Read All Over: A Meditation on Footnotes." *Text* 5 (1991): 81-90.

Xhardez, Didier. "Computer-Assisted Study of a Textual Tradition." *Research in Humanities Computing.* Ed. Susan Hockey and Nancy Ide. Oxford: Oxford UP,

Computer-Assisted Critical Analysis: A Case Study of Margaret Atwood's *Handmaid's Tale*[1]

Ian Lancashire
University of Toronto

Computer-Aided Criticism

John B. Smith defines Computer Criticism as using the computer for two activities: first, "to gather [*retrieve*] the information the critic asks for, [and] to *display* or present the information," and second, "to apply some analytic *model* to the information" ("Criticism" 339; emphasis added). Studies that employ this methodology include Smith's own *Imagery and the Mind of Stephen Dedalus*; Nancy M. Ide, one of his students, extends his methods statistically in her article on William Blake. Text-retrieval software displays selected words from the text according to their nondebatable characteristics, such as spelling, frequency, and position. Critics in this way view the text from some nonlinear but critically neutral perspective. The second activity, modeling, starts with an interpretation or hypothesis. It then applies statistical tests to frequency or positional data and reorganizes them into secondary displays. These lists, graphs, and maps show to what extent the data fall into a pattern at some "level of significance": this occurs when words selected randomly from the text fail the so-called null hypothesis and do *not* "behave" randomly.

Are the results of this second step—the modeling—true patterns in the text, comparable to structures seen by literary critics or preferable to his or her work because these results can be repeated by others and so "falsified"? How a reader answers this question depends on what the act of reading is conceived to be. Computer Criticism is a separate school in literary studies, related to structuralism and Marxism, because computer analysis treats words as quasi-material objects, fundamental particles of text, so to speak.[2] Most critics, however, discuss a text differently, sometimes as if it were an active player in the society for which it was written, other times as if it were an unpredictable recreation of the mind of the individual reader. The moment a text interacts with history, other forms of communication (for example, film), political movements, or the "common reader," that text cannot be studied only as a closed system of particles. It is not surprising, then, that computerized content analysis has had only a marginal influence on literary criticism. Readers normally interact with the texts they read.

Yet computer tools can be employed, independently of modeling, much as translation software can help human translators. Computer-assisted critical analysis uses displays of textual phenomena (that is, lists, indexes, tables, graphs, and maps) without separating patterns into the statistically "significant" and "insignificant." Users of these displays need make no theoretical assumptions, least of all that it is possible that texts are randomly organized.

For the past thirty years, automatic-index and concordance software has displayed word-frequency and keyword-in-context lists (Lancashire, "Back to the Future"). These reorganize the vocabulary of a text "vertically" so that every instance of any word can be found quickly under either its spelling or lemmatized (dictionary) word form. WordCruncher, Oxford Concordance Program, MacConcordance, and TACT all generate keyword-in-context (KWIC) concordances (Lancashire, *Humanities Computing Yearbook*).

In the past ten years, position-based displays have become possible. These reorganize the words of a text "topographically" so that we can see where the words do and do not occur. WordCruncher and TACT allow for this display. These positions may be within chapters, scenes or speeches, next to specified words, and so on. Displays may take the form of distribution graphs marking the presence or absence of those words in segments of the text.[3] Another application of position-based analysis is to study word associations or collocational patterns. These displays take the form of tables showing which collocates occur with the specified word or words, inside a context that may "span" any number of words but usually is the sentence.

Critics may use all these displays to find citations of words and to characterize how one part of a work, or one word, differs from another. Text-retrieval tools are, then, checkers of the memory of the critic in regard to where a subject or a word is mentioned. Computers also assist critics as they do lexicographers, by quickly assembling all sentences in which a word is used, or by listing word associations that suggest semantic fields.

The program I use is TACT (version 1.2), which runs under MS-DOS. It has been developed at the Centre for Computing in the Humanities in Toronto since 1984 as part of an IBM Canada-University of Toronto cooperative in the humanities and has been made freely available throughout the world.[4] Copying is encouraged, although the program is itself copyrighted to its developers, John Bradley and Lidio Presutti. Briefly, to use the software, a researcher turns a plain text file into a text database with a program called MAKBAS and then runs inquiries on the resulting database file with the TACT program itself. Making an inquiry has two steps: selecting the word or words from a frequency list (word patterns, collocations, phrases, and inquiries by frequency number are also allowed) and then displaying it in one of five forms. These are the full text, a one-line KWIC, an adjustable-context KWIC, a distribution graph, and a table of collocates. A session with TACT can also be recorded and played back. Several ancillary programs work off a TACT text database. COLLGEN generates all repeated phrases in the text, TACTFREQ does batch-frequency files, and ANAGRAM finds all possible anagrams in the text for a given word. I have also developed programs that, working with TACT, lemmatize English text and produce a new display that I call a phrasal repetend graph. TACT has a graphical interface with drop-down menus. It can generate a text database on any tagged or untagged text, both in modern European languages and in Greek.

Using displays asks for common sense. A content word with a high frequency need not be important. The word *time,* for instance, occurs among the most often-used nonfunction words. Low-frequency or nil-frequency words may well be more crucial, and authors sometimes expect readers to infer theme by indirection or from negation. For example, the word *dystopia* does not occur in *The Handmaid's Tale* at all, yet most readers agree that Margaret Atwood has written a dystopian tale (see Malak).

Displays also need never appear in a critical essay. In this paper I show where they can affect understanding of a controversial issue: to what extent Atwood's *Handmaid's Tale* and its narrator, Offred, are "feminist." Displays enlarge the common ground for all critics in debating the hard issues that make literary study exciting for succeeding generations of students.

The Handmaid's Tale: An Overview

The Handmaid's Tale resembles an ideological simulation. Starting with only a few assumptions, Atwood devises a new America where people have lost their freedom because severe environmental pollution rendered much of the population sterile. After the birthrate plummeted, extreme Christian fundamentalists seized power, first assassinating the president and members of Congress, then systematically imposing an Old Testament kind of surrogate motherhood. This code reduces everyone to a social type: the men to commanders, "eyes," "angels," guardians, and soldiers; the women to wives, "aunts," "marthas," "econowives," "unwomen," and handmaids (the surrogates). Atwood defines Gileadean men by their power over others, women by their role in child-bearing. She fixes on information technology—the replacement of money by computer credit and identity cards—as the main tool of the enslavers. Gilead thus begins like the computer game Life (which projects the survivability of atomistic life forms by beginning with a few assumptions about birthrate, deathrate, and food supply). It operates predictably once a few initial parameters are set. Religious wars, a secret police, the erasure of sexuality, the absence of rape, a new security for women to walk the streets, the computerization of prayer, and public executions for "gender treachery," among other things, follow naturally as corollaries from these "settings."

Yet Gilead is only the context of the novel. Its "text" is Offred herself and her oral history.

Powerful men name both the heroine and her confessions. The thirty-three-year-old woman who in Gilead is surrogate breeder for Commander Fred and his wife Serena Joy acquires a name, Offred (Of-Fred), when she enters his household. She never tells us what her real name is. Two professors from the future, Wade and Pieixoto, "edit"—transcribe, section, sequence, and name—her partial oral autobiography; in doing so, they make her tale theirs, after their image and name, as Fred in naming Offred takes possession of her. In homage to Geoffrey Chaucer they call the text "The Handmaid's Tale." The self-revelations in the thirty unnumbered audio tapes Offred used recall the confessional nature of tales by three well-known characters in *The Canterbury Tales*, the Wife of Bath, the Pardoner, and the Canon's Yeoman. They reveal both good and bad about themselves in stories as much about their professional occupations as about their inner selves. Chapter headings of Offred's story also hint at her occupational life as a handmaid—"Shopping," (the doctor's) "Waiting Room," "Nap," "Household," "Birth Day" (for Janine's baby), "Soul Scrolls" (the computerized prayer store), "Jezebel's" (the nightclub for commanders and their mistresses), and "Salvaging" (the handmaids' execution of wrongdoers)—leaving only the seven interwoven chapters entitled "Night" for her innermost thoughts and feelings.

Atwood's epigraphs to *The Handmaid's Tale*, from Genesis 30.1-3, Jonathan Swift's *Modest Proposal*, and Sufi proverbial wisdom, leave no doubt about her attitude concerning Gilead. Swift's "proposal," to feed the poor Irish by selling their babies as food to the rich English, ironically succeeds Rachel's poignant cry, "Give me children, or else I die." The Sufi epigraph, "In the desert there is no sign that says, Thou shalt not eat stones," quietly underscores the fact that absurdities should not be entertained just because they are not forbidden. Gilead buys more children death than life.

Atwood's tale is enriched by the tension between the *context* that is Gilead, an ideological simulation, and Offred's confessional *text*. The content of the first is horrific, of the second, at times monotonous. Offred herself acknowledges this contrast in iterating the word *context*. The first of the four occurrences I found in my TACT text database occurs when she sees mundane reminders of her old life, such as a dishtowel in a kitchen, "out of context." She is shocked by the difference between the then and the now (58). The appalling normality, the alien routine, first dawn on her at this time. Her "minimalist life" (as she calls it)[5] is filled with domestic routines like lying on a bed looking at the ceiling, walking down stairs, and calculating how to walk to a food store or what to say to the servants. In this context, reading from old magazines and playing Scrabble (forbidden pastimes that Commander Fred secretly enjoys with Offred) are revolutionary. The "trivia" and "time to be endured," the daily-ness, are appalling just because they sharply contrast with their context, what Offred calls "these red events, like explosions" (279). These are the changes in social order that account for the Particicutions, the hangings, and Offred's silence and dissimulation.

Later Offred twice echoes Edgar's "Ripeness is all" (*King Lear* V.ii.11), and perhaps Hamlet's "Readiness is all" (V.ii.211),[6] in saying "Context is all" (154, 202). She first appeals to "context" to explain the Commander's forbidden rendezvous with her, arranged only in order to play Scrabble; but her later repetition of the sentence "Context is all; or is it ripeness?" clearly echoes Edgar's mild rebuke to his blind father Gloucester for his fatalistic gloominess. Edgar's brother Edmund earlier mocked Gloucester in the play: "when we are sick in fortune, often the surfeits of our own behavior, we make guilty of our disasters the sun, the moon, and stars; as if we were villains on necessity" (I.ii.116-18). Offred wonders here whether "you can help how you behave," questioning how she can accept so readily the loss of her former husband, daughter, identity, job, and freedom. Does her own lack of "ripeness," rather than political, religious and social regimentation, explain her slavery? Offred's repeated allusion to *King Lear* crystallizes her dilemma. Is she free and responsible for her minimalist life, as Edgar would have it? Or is she a pathetic puppet of Gilead, reluctant to accept responsibility for herself?[7]

The hard question in *The Handmaid's Tale* is how to interpret Offred, not Gilead.

Three years ago Lucy Freibert proposed one way. Her article argues that Offred embodies all those "aspects of French feminist theory that offer women a measure of hope."[8] Freibert says that "Atwood demonstrates through Offred that women, able to take risks and to tell stories, may transcend their conditioning, establish their identity, joyfully reclaim their bodies, find their voices, and reconstruct the social order" (285). The recent film of the novel, scripted by Harold Pinter, reinterprets the

---

novel in this light. He makes Offred, played by Natasha Richardson, just as much of a hero as Sigourney Weaver in *Aliens* and Linda Hamilton in *The Terminator*, two contemporary popular science-fiction films of a similar kind. The film has events never hinted at in the book. Natasha Richardson helps her friend Moira escape, becomes pregnant by Nick, assassinates Fred, helps precipitate a revolt against Gilead, and vows (like the heroine in *Aliens*) to find her lost daughter again as she (like the heroine in *The Terminator*) takes up a rebel's base in the mountains. Pinter turns Offred into a feminist fighter. He perhaps takes advantage of an intuition that Offred, in her own inactivity, has heroic qualities. A critic, Roberta Rubenstein, has a more moderate view of Offred's virtues but all the same sees her through "two of the most persistent clusters of theme and imagery . . . nature and nurture" (which she glosses as motherhood and procreation).

Professor Pieixoto, the twenty-second-century critic whose analysis Atwood gives in an appendix to the novel, interprets Offred differently. He selects Offred's sexual relations, her "tail" (313), jokingly as a key to her character. Unsurprisingly, Pinter excludes him from the screenplay. Barbara Hill Rigney assesses Offred in a balanced way, yet shares Pieixoto's skepticism: "Offred values her own physical survival above sisterhood, and in so doing sacrifices her own integrity, that which is, for Atwood, more crucial even than life" (116).

In the light of these very different views, what is the critic to do? Does the tension between the horrific context—which makes women the victims of a patriarchal tyranny—and the self-deprecating confessions of Offred really allow for so much variation in what we ought to think of her?

Offred's Self-Characterization

Computer tools will not decide one way or the other, but in my experience they highlight enough neglected material from the book to qualify both positions and perhaps suggest a perspective truer to Atwood's.

Selecting the words *joy* and *risk*—keys to a feminist interpretation of Offred—from the complete vocabulary of the novel produces two KWIC displays in TACT. The words *joy* (forty-four occurrences), *joys* (one), and *joy's* (six) never refer to Offred. Instead of "joyfully reclaiming her body," Offred remembers Nick's body (281). The same proves true of her *risk*-taking (Figure 1).[9] Offred takes risks only when ordered to do so by others: Fred makes her his concubine; Serena Joy pushes her to take Nick as a lover; Ofglen leads her to speak frankly about Gilead; and Nick stage-manages her escape from Fred's household. As she walks with the second Ofglen at the end of the novel, Offred says, "I should not be rash, I should not take unnecessary risks" (296).

Computer-Assisted Critical Analysis: Atwood's Handmaid's Tale

04-28	keep walking. He's just taken a	> risk,	but for what? What if
04-29	more than name. I can't take the	> risk.	'The war is going well,
04-32	would not want to take the	> risk	of looking inside,
07-49	to the world of fact, which is	> riskier,	more hazardous: who
11-71	to me, his services, at some	> risk	to himself. 'I hate to
11-71	I've given no trust, taken no	> risk,	all is safe. It's the
14-90	would be an illusion, and too	> risky.	My hands stay where
17-109	far. Too much trust, too much	> risk,	too much already. 'I was
17-110	bad, for him, that he'd take the	> risk	of coming to my room at
19-122	Wringing her hands. It's a	> risk	you're taking, said Aunt
19-122	territory. The greater the	> risk	the greater the glory.
20-130	my mother said. It was a	> risk,	you could have been
27-176	for the first time. There is	> risk,	suddenly, in the air
29-196	It can't be only a joke. Have I	> risked	this, made a grab at
31-216	She does want that baby. 'It's a	> risk,'	I say. 'More than that.'
36-243	told that what he's proposing is	> risky,	for him but especially
37-252	around: no sign of it. Nor can I	> risk	getting up and walking
38-257	any more. It was getting far too	> risky.	'So I tried to recall
38-258	me to another house. They hadn't	> risked	phoning. 'The other house
38-259	that these other people were	> risking	their lives for you
40-274	no heroics. It means: don't	> risk	yourself for me, if it
45-281	like that would be too great a	> risk;	so I have to make do
44-296	I should not take unnecessary	> risks.	But I need to know. I
46-306	Possibly he will be a security	> risk,	now. I am above him,

Figure 1: KWIC index of *risk**.

Events show that Offred does not measure up to other aspects of a feminist ethic. Atwood has said, "There was a risk that it [the novel] would be thought feminist propaganda of the most outrageous kind, which was not really what I intended" (Hancock 140). Although Offred tells "herstory" in her own voice, she fails to sign it. She dictates her identity but never names it. She accepts all that happens to her. Her position in Fred's house is her third posting; she knows what she signed up for. Fear genuinely rules her. Only when Serena Joy encourages her to become impregnated by Fred's chauffeur, Nick (after it becomes clear Fred is sterile), does Offred go to Nick. Ashamed though she is to describe the Particicution in which she took part—the handmaids' barbaric dismemberment of a soldier falsely accused of rape—Offred says that the experience made her hungry and excited. All she asks of the Commander in return for her illicit company is hand lotion. When Offred dresses as a prostitute for Fred at Jezebel's, an illegal nightclub and brothel, she feels degraded and miserable, but she confesses herself happily willing to do the same for Nick if he asked her. Her friend Moira engineers a violent escape from the handmaids' school, and her friend Ofglen kills herself before the secret police, the Eyes, can take her away. Offred thinks about escape and suicide but does neither. At the end she surrenders herself to "the hands of strangers, because it can't be helped" (307).

Yet TACT listings show evidence that Atwood was likely thinking about feminist hopes when she wrote the novel, assuming that Atwood, like Freibert, associated feminist virtues with risk-taking, story-telling, a woman's joy in her body, and so on. There is one woman associated ironically with joy, Serena Joy; and the handmaids' formulaic reply, "Which I receive with joy," links them with her. Although Serena and many of the handmaids take little joy from anything, including their own plight, Serena's name—a gift of men in Gilead, like Offred's—gives her ironic feminist associations. She takes risks, however joylessly, and dominates those around her. Handmaids like Ofglen and Moira also risk their lives to rebel and escape. Under tyrannicide, the story may say, feminism reveals itself in neither joy nor a public identity but rather in matriarchal politics for Serena, underground revolt for Ofglen, and simulation and silence for Offred. Of these three, only Offred, the meekest, survives.

Text-retrieval software highlights aspects of the text *in which the critic is already interested and of which indeed he or she probably already has an interpretation.* It might be said that by serving up these contexts of *joy* and *risk,* TACT gives the critic an opportunity to reconsider.

Other critical views fare no better than Freibert's. Forms of the word *tail* occur just six times, once when Offred thinks of looking at pictures of eunuchs waving peacock tails, several times when she sees women at Jezebel's in animal costumes with tails, and finally when she owns that she would willingly wear a rabbit tail for Nick. Yet Offred's love of Nick and her diary do not characterize a "playmate," Pieixoto nothwithstanding. Likewise, Rubenstein's theme words *nature* (six occurrences), *nature 's* (three), and *natural* (three) (Figure 2) have more to do with male promiscuity and female power over men than they do with motherhood. Her term *nurture* does not occur at all. TACT displays show that these generalizations are tied to the text they describe, but too slenderly to be themes.

How then does a critic choose what is important? I believe high-frequency content words are remarkably accurate first guides.

TACT gave me the option of looking at Atwood's own overall word usage and selecting the most frequent content (rather than function or grammatical) words she employs. First, I listed all words with a frequency of over 100 (see Figure 3). After function words are ignored,[10] the high-frequency words fell into six types:

1. People (aunt, commander, Moira, woman, women, Lydia, man/men)
2. The house (door, room)

---

3. The human body (eyes, face, hands, head)
4. Colors (red, white)
5. Time
6. Cognition and sensation (feel, know, look, see, think, thought, want)

The two young Guardians salute us, raising three fingers to the rims of their berets. Such tokens are accorded to us. They are supposed to show respect, because of the nature of our service. ('Shopping,' p. 31 [Offred])

It's not the husbands you have to watch out for, said Aunt Lydia, it's the Wives. You should always try to imagine what they must be feeling. Of course they will resent you. It is only natural. Try to feel for them. ('Waiting Room,' p. 56 [Lydia])

Men are sex machines, said Aunt Lydia, and not much more. They only want one thing. You must learn to manipulate them, for your own good. Lead them around by the nose; that is a metaphor. It's nature's way. It's God's device. It's the way things are. ('Night,' p. 153 [Lydia])

Those years were just an anomaly, historically speaking, the Commander said. Just a fluke. All we've done is return things to Nature's norm. ('Jezebel's,' p. 232 [Bald Commander])

"Don't gawk,' says the Commander. 'You'll give yourself away. Just act natural.' ('Jezebel's', p. 247 [Commander])

As we know, the sociobiological theory of natural polygamy was used as a scientific justification for some of the odder practices of the regime, just as Darwinism was used by earlier ideologies. ('Historical Notes,' p. 318 [Pieixoto])

I wait for him to elaborate on this, but he doesn't, so I say, 'What does that mean?' 'It means you can't cheat Nature,' he says. 'Nature demands variety, for men. It stands to reason, it's part of the procreational strategy. It's Nature's plan.' (Jezebel's,' p. 249 [Commander])

The Nature Walk and Outdoor Period-Costume Sing-Song have been rescheduled for the day after tomorrow, as we are assured by our own infallible Professor Johnny Running Dog of a break in the weather at that time. ('Historical Notes,' p. 307 [Maryann Crescent Moon])

Once we had the transcription in hand and we had to go over it several times, owing to the difficulties posed by accent, obscure referents, and archaisms - we had to make some decision as to the nature of the material we had thus so laboriously acquired. ('Historical Notes,' p. 314 [Pieixoto])

Supposing, then, the tapes to be genuine, what of the nature of the account itself? ('Historical Notes,' p. 315 [Pieixoto])

Figure 2: Concordance of *natur**.

Repeated references to people by name or role (type 1) come with the story; so do ones to time (it would be hard to find a novel without this word in its high-frequency word profile). Words of cognition and sensation (type 6) belong to a confessional work told in the first person. References to the human body, to the house, and to colors stand out. Why not words of violence, sex, tyrannicide, corruption, animality? Some readers see these as crucial to the novel.

5166	the
3284	i
2291	to
2132	a
2111	of
1926	it
1821	and
1561	in
1252	s [i.e. 'is' in 'it's']
1184	she
979	that
968	is
912	her
906	t [i.e. 'not' in 'don't', etc.]
905	he
834	on
831	they
819	was
791	you
750	we
735	for
710	my
699	me
660	with
643	as
631	be
618	there
608	but
592	at
589	have
572	like*
564	this
530	what
516	not
513	or
459	are
436	one
429	can
420	said*
398	if
379	them
376	out
370	from
354	were
350	would
339	all
335	up
326	his
314	no
310	been
303	say*
294	says*
287	could
281	so
273	now
272	an
271	know*
269	about
265	him
262	time*
259	us
257	by
256	too
255	do
252	had
239	d [i.e. 'would' in 'you'd']
229	don [i.e. in 'don't']
222	some
215	then
214	when
211	their
209	back
202	down
199	into
198	m [i.e. 'am' in 'I'm', etc.]
196	see*
194	who
193	here
189	must
188	go*
188	more
187	our
186	way*
185	think*
183	over
179	something
174	will
168	even
164	get
163	aunt*
163	look*
162	has
159	which
158	room*
153	other
152	where
151	only
148	women*
144	how
144	want*
142	things*
142	ve [i.e. 'have' in 'I've', etc.]
139	before
139	re [i.e. 'are' in 'you're', etc.]
137	feel*
136	any
136	through
135	around
134	after
133	ll [i.e. 'will' in 'I'll', etc.]
130	commander*
130	still
129	Moira*
128	did
128	two
127	didn [i.e. in 'didn't']
127	just
125	used
122	am
122	eyes*
122	once
121	off
119	little*
116	woman*
114	your
112	much
112	red*
110	door*
108	because
108	face*
107	hands*
107	right*
107	thought*
105	Lydia*
103	white*
102	head*
102	make*
101	away
101	though

Figure 3: High-frequency words (100+).

Of types 2, 3, and 4, words for the body (type 3) proved most numerous. Atwood mentions almost every part of the body (except for spleen, liver, kidneys, intestines, jaw, and navel), but of about 195 different words in the group, most refer to the head (707 occurrences) and the arms (368 occurrences); and, of these, the eyes (169 occurrences) and hands (211 occurrences) turn up most often. No one among the half-dozen critics whose work I read mentions that *The Handmaid's Tale* might be about something as self-evident as a woman's body, yet of course this follows directly from Atwood's first epigraph, from Genesis. When Rachel tells Jacob, her husband, "Give me children, or else I die," he angrily replies that she owes the barrenness of her womb to God, not to him. Resigned to the failure of her body, Rachel then asks Jacob to take her maid's body as if it were her own: "Behold my maid Bilhah, go in unto her; and she shall bear upon my knees, that I may also have children by her." Atwood's novel hinges on whether Offred's body can succeed where Serena's failed.

No one can interpret text on the basis of a word-frequency list. Meaning only arises when words cohere by means of syntactic relationships and proximity. Word lists cannot be used to discuss what a work means because meaning inheres in larger units. For this reason critics faced with quantitative data often fail to see what it has to do with their work.

Semantic Profiles

Accordingly, I turned to a neglected quantitative measure, phrasal *repetends*. Repetends are any repeated textual unit, from syllable to sentence, but phrasal repetends comprise specifically (1) fixed-order word sequences and (2) collocations, that is, words that occur near to one another (the context normally is a sentence) but may be in any order.[11] Unlike single words, phrasal repetends reflect the constituent structures within sentences, which is to say, meaningful units. Both proximity and syntactic relationships bind the parts of a phrasal repetend together. That association gives a semantic field of reference for given words.

For example, the words *men* and *women* often co-occur, either in sequences such as "men and women" and "women and men," or in collocations, before or after one another in a variety of sentences. Twenty sentences in the novel have both words. The exact phrase "men and women" occurs three times (60-61, 65, 68), the variant phrase "women and the/some men" three times (66, 189, 261), and other examples are collocations. As I read them, the passages contrast the past, when men loved, played with, and assaulted women, with the present, when the sexes skirt each other, unable to touch, always expectant. A précis like this helps interpretation but is tedious to do repeatedly. It would be helpful if software could display a "semantic" profile of collocating words.

A TACT ancillary program called COLLGEN, operating on a TACT text database, makes a start on this goal. It lists all fixed-order phrasal repetends in a text, of whatever length or frequency. The "collocate" display of the TACT retrieval program itself displays all co-occurring words (or collates) for any word, sorted in descending order of association, strong first. Combining data from each, I can list all phrasal repetends in a text succinctly *without interpretation*. These may then be combined into "semantic networks" by linking repetends that share the same content word. Both the profile of phrasal repetends and the networks that they form "generalize" about the text. It is unclear whether they have a role in authorship attribution, but they do crystallize out iterated motifs of that text. The collocational display and the COLLGEN output also prove easier to use than a one-line index or a five-line KWIC concordance. In them the large number of contexts makes comparison of many word contexts difficult.

Collocational displays were devised in the early 1970s by a computational linguist who used a simple statistical measure to list collocates of any given keyword, that is, words found within, say, the same sentence as it, according to how far from randomness the linkage seemed (Berry-Rogghe).[12] The working concept is not hard. A reader first identifies a node word or word group (such as *eye* and *eyes*) that represents an idea or object and then collects all words within a given span of each occurrence of the node words. The collected contexts are called the minitext. Then the reader produces a word-frequency list for this minitext. This list includes all the collocates of the node words. Next, by comparing the number of times each collocate is expected to occur within the minitext with the number of times it actually does occur there, one has a measure of collocate-node attraction. The assumption is that any collocate is "expected" to spread out randomly through the text. If a collocate occurs more often in the minitext than it should, on average, an association with the node word is said to exist; if less, the two words are less well connected than they should be, on average.

Figures 4 and 5 (the singular and plural forms of *woman* and *man)* combine lists of both fixed phrases and collocations into a new kind of display, the phrasal graph. This connects word nodes by arcs or pointers so as to schematize all phrasal repetends containing a given word. Like all graphs, this display condenses information into a tight diagrammatic form that can be easily grasped. The legend explains the syntax of this graph. Words within rectangular boxes, connected by pointers, represent fixed phrases. Words collected within a larger circle or "cloud" are the unfixed collocates for a given word.

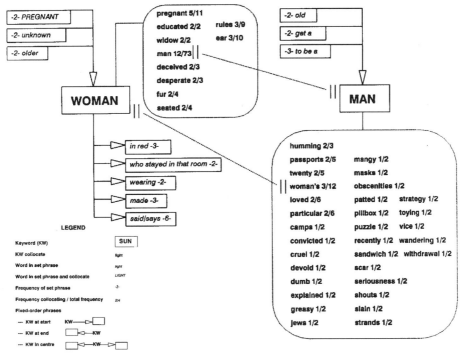

Figure 4: Phrasal repetends of *woman* and *man*.

This graph does not give dictionary definitions, or thesaurus synonyms, for the node word (synonyms in fact seldom co-occur). The graph also does not denote: it knows nothing of the world. Instead, phrasal graphs shed light on word connotation and implicature, both clearly important to literary studies. Most people know the general "meaning" of words from childhood, and reference or historical dictionaries describe the widest range of senses for any word, as if every-person were the speaker. Phrasal graphs distinguish how one person, the writer, uses a word.

Figures 4 and 5 show Atwood's main semantic connotations for each gender. Highest among collocating terms for women are *pregnant* and *reproductive*, exactly the bodily role Gilead prescribes for the sex. Subservience and confinement, expressed in bodily positions, appear in phrases like "woman who stayed in that room," "women kneeling on the floor," and "women are sitting." Women's bodies are also shown covered up with clothes, in phrases like "woman in red" and "woman wearing" and in collocates like *fur* and *shawls*. In contrast, the words *man* and *men* collocate with terms of action and movement, not confinement—*passports, driven, cars, road*—and they are *standing*, not seated. Woman is associated with the collocates *deceived* and *desperate;* man, with *loved, cruel,* and *sexually.*

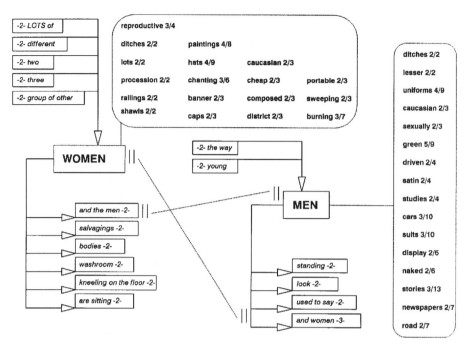

Figure 5: Phrasal repetends of *women* and *men*.

"Semantic cloud" rather than "motif" or "image" may capture best what phrasal graphs imply about the fictional state of a word, although content analysts would want to select the collocating keywords in such clouds more rigorously (with statistical tools) than I do. By limiting word associations to fixed phrases and collocations *occurring at least twice*, I also do not take account of (1) motifs expressed once, but each time in different words, or (2) images occurring once only or represented by collocating terms that do not stand out as unusual. Repetition reveals something static in an author's thinking or imagination, what does not change from one chapter to another. Phrasal graphs, then, describe *ongoing conditions or states*. For that reason they prove a useful check on critics who make sweeping generalizations about the content of a text.

Graphs show that Atwood depicts her gender as clothed bodies, held in positions of rest, awaiting impregnation. Graphs for the words *hand* (Figure 6), *head*, *face* (Figure 7), and *eye* (Figure 8) give a little more detail to this representation of gender. The hands of a handmaid are raised over the mouth, held behind the back, gloved, clasped, or folded in the lap or on an apron. Women's hands appear constrained, concealed, and passive; they are associated with nerves, awkwardness,

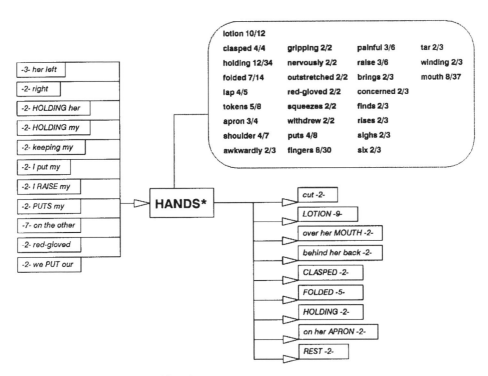

Figure 6: Phrasal repetends of *hands**.

and pain. Remarkably, their closest link is to lotion, which makes them appear younger than they are. Handmaids do not use their hands; they reserve them. The head is turned, kept down, lowered, bent, and bowed in submissiveness. The female face is unmoving, painted with cream or powdered (as the hands are covered with lotion), and surrounded by the handmaid's "wings"; the male face cannot be seen because the woman's look (her face, her head) is averted, not because men hide their stares.

The focal points of both head and face, the eyes, have especially rich associations. By using TACT's interactive concordance display, I examined each context in turn. Their dominant state is closed or blind, the handmaid's vision restricted by the wings that surround her head. Atwood links the blindered gaze of a woman's eyes to the name of the male organization that enforces the male tyranny over women. *Eyes* is a word for members of the team of Gilead secret police, and their black vans are also repeatedly described as having a "winged eye in white on the side" (31, 178, 305). The printing machines in Soul Scrolls also use an eye-wing insignia. These eyes watch, control, and oppress. Handmaids like Offred greet one another with the formal saying, "Under His Eye" (54, 297). She has a small tattoo on her ankle, "Four

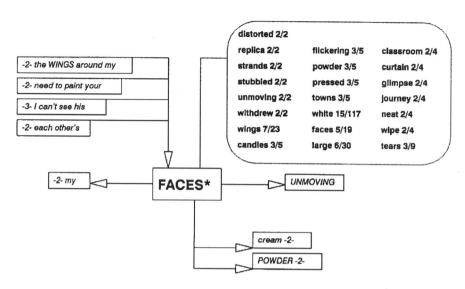

Figure 7: Phrasal repetends of *faces**.

digits and an eye" (76). It is not surprising that they are associated more with men than with women. When Offred lies in bed, she looks upward to the ceiling, where she sees a relief ornament with a "blind plaster eye" in the center space, "like the place in a face where the eye has been taken out" (17, 46, 61, 108). Handmaids must keep their eyes closed during sexual intercourse with their commanders and during childbirth, just like the eyeless plaster relief. (Only when Offred lies with Nick does she open her eyes [281].) The commander, on the other hand, stares as he moves above the handmaid. Finally, Atwood employs an extraordinary metaphor for the commander's penis: it is "his delicate stalked slug's eye" (98). When the commander watches Offred reading in his room, she thinks that his "watching is a curiously sexual act" (194). Normally handmaids cannot look at others, especially at men, because their white wings act as blinders.

We might expect that a handmaid would be at "hand" to do something. In Atwood's imagination, male heads, faces, and eyes greet others, but not the handmaids' heads, faces, and eyes. They are disabled. Only the men of Gilead act and look. The boldness of the Guards' eyes in scanning the handmaids as they walk by establishes their power, "standing on the corner, watching all the girls go by," as the popular song says. In bodily ways, then, Atwood's handmaids—and their gender—are disabled as autonomous individuals; they await commands that only come from others. An entire gender is decommissioned from the world so that it can function as a passive garden, like the one Serena Joy ironically tends.

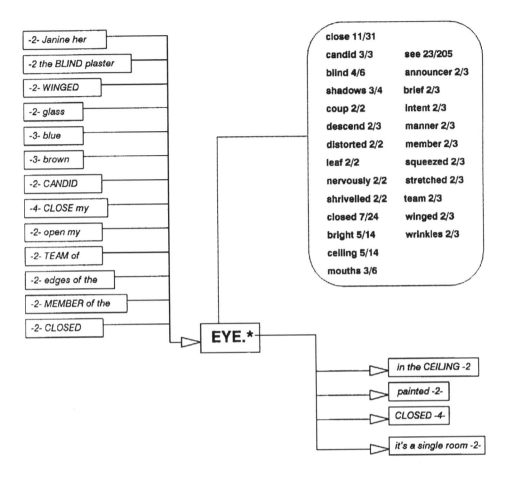

Figure 8: Phrasal repetends of *eye**.

These semantic focuses belong to the core of Atwood's novel. They should have played a large part in what critics said about it, but often they did not.

Offred Herself

Computer tools can also provide evidence for the study of a specific character, by doing a phrasal graph of her name and by studying her vocabulary. Pieixoto describes Offred's name as a patronymic but misses the point: Fred is not her father. Her name indicates possession, not descent. Pieixoto's guess makes the naming more familial and proper than it really is; Offred belongs to Fred, not to Fred's "blood" or to his "household." Because Offred never tells us her real name, readers have assumed that it is June, which seems likely enough from the very first chapter. The nameless narrator describes a night lying in bed side by side with the other handmaids-in-training in the old gymnasium. There they engage in a forbidden act, lipreading their barely whispered names as they touched hands. "In this way we exchanged names, from bed to bed: Alma. Janine. Dolores. Moira. June" (14). The reader can rule out all but one of these women from being the handmaid to be known as Offred. Alma had the bed next to Offred, and still another Alma attended the delivery of Janine's baby. Janine's occupational name was Ofwarren. Dolores had the bed next to Janine (143) and was punished for wetting the floor (82). Since Offred candidly describes most other aspects of her life, it does not make sense that she should disguise this embarrassment if she were Dolores. The lesbian Moira, Offred's oldest friend, has a streak of rebelliousness that lands her in the classy brothel-nightclub called Jezebel's. By process of elimination, June is left. Possibly Aunt Lydia refers to this name when she accuses the girls of "mooning and June-ing around" when they daydream of love, because one of Offred's night thoughts is that "It's lack of love we die from" (113). If Offred's name is June, then Atwood's irony appears again, for June is the month of weddings.

Atwood's skill as a poet, however, gives Offred's name several other meanings. One of TACT's functions, a similarity index, lists other words in the vocabulary of the novel that resemble *Offred* according to a "percentage" of likeness (where zero percent would include all words and one hundred percent would exclude all words). Another searches for word patterns, such as *of*r.** or *of.** | *r.**[13] These searches associate "Offred" with "offered" or "of red" or even "off-red." All seem apt. Offred is "offered" by the state to Fred for procreation. Her garments are made of red material: as she says, "we might be bundles *of red* cloth" or "a wraith *of red* smoke" (137, 219; emphasis added). Yet as a friend of Moira and the first Ofglen, as a secret concubine for Fred and lover of Nick, Offred is less of a handmaid than she is supposed to be. Her appearance, a "shape, red with white wings around the face" (28), also makes her off-red. She is not the fully committed handmaid that Janine-Ofwarren is, her person dazed and submerged in her role. Offred wakes up during the nights.

The words for the colors *white* and *red* (type 4 of the most frequent content words), then, indirectly describe Offred herself. Phrasal graphs for those two words associate red with Offred's clothing, her dress, habit, skirt, gloves, and veil, as well as with the brick walls that confine the society much as clothing does Offred and with the tulips in the garden that Serena grows. The phrase "woman in red" resonates with associations we have seen before with words for *woman* and *women* and with the head, face, eyes, and hands. White, in contrast, belongs to the clothes she wears at night in her bedroom (the cotton nightgown) and to the wings that make her "off-red," different from the others. The collocates of *white* sometimes suggest freedom from constraint.

Concording the word pattern *nam.** *(name, naming, names,* and the like) elaborates this point. Offred meditates on her name, and what she says tells us more about it than does the possibility it is June:

> My name isn't Offred, I have another name, which nobody uses now because it's forbidden. I tell myself it doesn't matter, your name is like your telephone number, useful only to others; but what I tell myself is wrong, it does matter. I keep the knowledge of this name like something hidden, some treasure I'll come back to dig up, one day. I think of this name as buried. This name has an aura around it, like an amulet, some charm that's survived from an unimaginably distant past. I lie in my single bed at night, with my eyes closed, and the name floats there behind my eyes, not quite within reach, shining in the dark. (94)

Offred rationalizes her loss—"I tell myself it doesn't matter, your name is like your telephone number, useful only to others"—and connives with a repression that she knows is wrong. As Rigney emphasizes, when the handmaids accept the loss of their names, they forfeit their identity (116). Despite her rationalizations, Offred wants to be told the name as a "reminder of what she was" (108) and repeats it to herself alone and gives it to Nick once he is her lover. Her reason is to make herself "known" (282). There is a quiet pride in this act, although neither Ofglen nor Alma (134) nor her readers and editors discover her real name. She admits, "Attaching a name attaches you to the world of fact, which is riskier, more hazardous: who knows what the chances are out there, of survival, yours?" (49). To survive in a society where the alternatives to being a handmaid amount to serving in a brothel (like Moira), or fighting in the underground and committing suicide when discovered (like Ofglen), or dying of radiation poisoning in the waste lands, Offred gives up her name. At the end, when Nick tells her to go from Fred's house with Mayday, the rebels' movement, he calls her by her "real name" (305). This comes as an invitation to resume her true self, because once out of Fred's household she gives up all rights to *that* name, or so we learn from Pieixoto, who says, "Such names were taken by these women upon their entry into a connection with the household of a specific Commander, and relinquished by them upon leaving it" (318). When Nick whispers her name at the end, then, we might expect the woman who was Offred to reclaim her original name. Yet the audio-taped confessions that she dictates in hiding after her escape from Fred's house are not "signed" with her "shining name."

Rather she selects "authentic period labels"—one might say tags—for her confessions. These disguise her authorship under the names of others. Pieixoto explains the "camouflage":

> The labels on the cassettes were authentic period labels, dating, of course, from some time before the inception of the Early Gilead era, as all such secular music was banned under the regime. There were, for instance, four tapes entitled "Elvis Presley's Golden Years," three of "Folk Songs of Lithuania," three of "Boy George Takes It Off," and two of "Mantovani's Mellow Strings," as well as some titles that sported a single tape each: "Twisted Sister at Carnegie Hall" is one of which I am particularly fond. (314)

Offred chooses labels that travesty her self and her book. Most belong to male performers. She takes a man's name and can be said to "perform." Her confessions are like the songs of common people from a country under repression, and like Boy George she does "take it off." Her night thoughts of Luke and love of Nick resemble mellow "strings," and she is conscious of their mawkishness. Pieixoto's favorite, "Twisted Sister at Carnegie Hall," parodies the self-abasing public performance of her own faults, not the least of which, her part in the Particicution, she describes honestly.

By using TACTFREQ once more, I made a second word-frequency list, this time only for the chapters entitled "Night," where Offred speaks of herself. Among function words, the first-person pronoun, as expected, increases from 2.98 percent in the daytime chapters to 3.61 percent in the night chapters. Content words change predictably, as Figure 9 shows. Reported conversation diminishes in the night sections (see the words *say, said,* and *says*). Offred's thoughts turn on her mother, her lover, Nick, and her husband, Luke, not on Moira, the Commander, or the aunts. She speaks of her nighttime surroundings: "bed," "pictures," "window," and things normally hidden, like "face," "arms," and "hair." The word *want*, expressing unfulfilled desire, decreases, as words of personal knowledge (especially *believe, need, remember, meant,* and *mean*) increase. Offred thinks less about red and white, the colors of her clothing that define her to others, and more about light and darkness, symbolizing her hope for freedom from the present. The word *hope* grows; the word *think* lessens. Verbs in the past tense tend to characterize night sections; verbs in the present tend to dominate the rest. The word *story* occurs more often: in dictating the confessions, Offred rebuilds her self. She is a different person. Although four words for the human body that touch on the core of the novel—*hands, hand, eyes,* and *head*— vary little between day and night chapters, enough variation appears to show Offred's complexities.

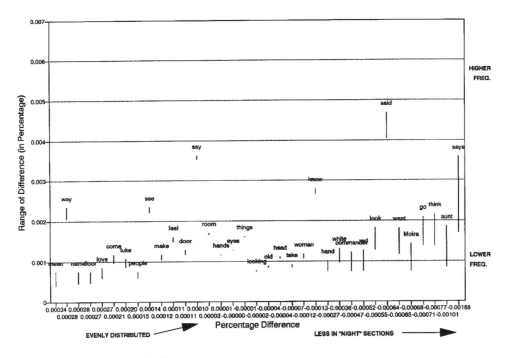

Figure 9: Comparing Offred's night and day sections.

My final list, the fifty-six phrasal repetends of six words and more in the novel, shows how well Atwood fuses Offred and her text. About a quarter of these long repetitions (thirteen, actually) occur together on the same page—a deliberate stylistic device (Atwood has good control over haphazard echoes). Another four of the fifty-six are quotations: three from the first epigraph ("am I in God's stead," "give me children," and "she shall bear upon"), and one from Milton ("they also serve"). Although clichés are few ("as far as I could see" and "at one and the same time"), Atwood invents several formulas for life in Gilead ("blessed be the fruit," "don't let the bastards," "I don't want to be telling," "no preliminaries he knows," and "who can do what to whom"). Although neither true linguistic habits nor a fictional idiolect ties the fifty-six fragments together, the first-person pronouns do: *I* (twenty-seven occurrences among them), *me* (six), and *my* (five). Figure 10 gives these in one summary phrasal graph. This, a profile of Offred's mind, dwells on surrogate childbearing, blindered vision, yearning for love, and determination to survive intact ("what I have on him is," "don't let the bastards," "I don't want to be telling," "I think about how I could"). When Atwood repeats herself, she has a good reason for doing so.

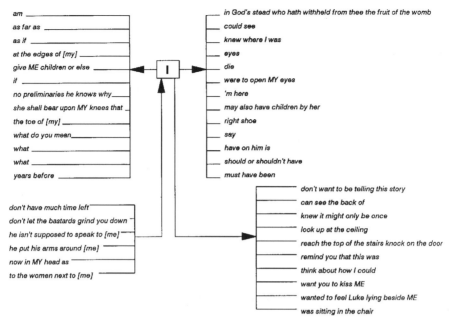

Figure 10: *I, me,* and *my* in phrasal repetends of six words and more.

Conclusion

Harold Pinter, who wrote the screenplay of the film version of the novel, and Professor Pieixoto, who named it, rendered Offred in entertaining and absurdly different ways. Freibert, Rubenstein, Rigney, and other critics have only a some-what larger common ground. Computer-assisted analysis suggests that each has a claim to part of the truth about her.

The opening words of the novel, "We slept . . . ," hint at a personal horror behind the namelessness of the heroine and her work. Offred surrenders her public, daily selfhood when she gives up her name into the hands of others whose ends will determine what she becomes. "I have given myself over into the hands of strangers, because it can't be helped" (307). Daytime will be for walking to the grocer's with another handmaid to do shopping, praying and reading scriptures with Fred and the household, watching as Ofwarren-Janine gives birth, visiting the prayer factory Soul Scrolls, witnessing hangings and—as one of many handmaids—tearing an accused rapist to death. Offred condemns herself in a way consistent with Pieixoto's scorn. Yet when Offred closes her eyes at night, the self submerged beneath her occupational role comes out. It is filled with vivid memories of the husband and the daughter from whom she has been separated, her remembered mother, absent friends like Moira, lost job, lost possessions, and obscured personal names and surnames.

This double self comes out in the novel's first pages. During the first "Night," Offred (yet unnamed) describes sleeping in the once-gymnasium-now-school-for-handmaids. Everything recalls a past no longer with her. She speaks of "games that were formerly played there," the "afterimage" of sweat, chewing gum, and perfume, and a sense of lingering music ("a palimpsest of unheard sound"). Most of all she remembers their longing for the unknown future. She says:

> There was old sex in the room and loneliness, and expectation, of something without a shape and a name. I remember that yearning, for something that was always about to happen and was never the same as the hands that were on us there and then, in the small of the back, or out back, in the parking lot, or in the television room with the sound turned down and only the pictures flickering over lifted flesh.

Here she introduces the public Offred, the tart that Pieixoto mocks. This nameless narrator and her friends expect "something without a shape and a name" as they did before in romantic longings that intercourse lacked. This "something" will not be what they have now but rather an unfocused "yearning" for an immanent change. Atwood implies that this change may be themselves, shapeless under the red cloak, nameless except as property, engaging in a "Ceremony" that has nothing to do with imagined eroticism or love or even, as Offred later says, "copulation." The confessions of the woman known as Offred tell us about the consequences of accepting a definition of selfhood from others.

Frequency lists and phrasal graphs clearly identify this character but do so in a context charged by Atwood with feminist terms, for Offred has different, far more personal night thoughts. She may not take risks in the day, but at night she does tell her own story. Awake, her every movement and posture are confined, but after dark she walks abroad in her imagination with alert eyes. The something without a shape and a name that the handmaids expect at the start is themselves, dehumanized by their reproductive occupation, but it is also an unseen woman who speaks her thoughts at night and creates a titleless book of her own in a room of her own. We do not know her real name, and she gave her story no title, but to say it lacks a quiet heroism would be wrong.

Computerized text-retrieval and analysis have an enduring role to play in critical thinking. Like spelling and grammar checkers, they cannot read or choose readings. Like checkers, they work invisibly in the study, prompting the critic to read more carefully. When electronic editions become available, they will help critics to be accurate and fair to the author's text. In 1986 Margaret Atwood complained about deconstructionism: "What it . . . means is that the text is of no importance. What is of interest is what the critic makes of the text. Alas, alack, pretty soon we'll be getting to pure critical readings with no text at all" (Hancock 133). Critics with electronic texts at hand might well be held accountable for their readings. Then more, not less, attention will be paid to what the author writes. That is the spirit in which computer-assisted criticism ought to be practiced.

Notes

1. I would like to acknowledge the support of the Social Sciences and Humanities Research Council of Canada for this research, as well as my colleagues at the Universities of Edinburgh, Lund, and Stockholm (especially Jonquil Bevan, Jan Svartvik, and Magnus Ljung), who invited me to give lectures on earlier versions of this paper and gave me both encouragement and helpful comments.

2. Barbara Stevenson points out the following difficulty with modeling: "Stylometry's null hypothesis assumes that no significant difference exists between the writing style of two texts, and, consequently, this lack of difference supposedly proves that the same person produced both texts. The null hypothesis rests upon an unproven assumption that word position and collocations do differ among writers. Because of the unproven assumption, it is impossible to interpret the results. Ideally the null hypothesis should not rest on any unproven assumptions" (63).

3. These words are sometimes called plus or minus words. They occur either more or less frequently at one location than they do at other locations.

4. A manual and diskettes are available at cost from TACT Distribution, Centre for Computing in the Humanities, Robarts Library, University of Toronto, Toronto, Ont., Canada M5S 1A5 (416-978-4238). TACT may also be obtained by FTP. For information on how to log on to the CCH mainframe and transfer the programs at no cost, send an electronic-mail message to CCH @ EPAS.UTORONTO.CA with the subject line "FTP TACT Distribution."

5. "The minimalist life. Pleasure is an egg. Blessings that can be counted, on the fingers of one hand. But possibly this is how I am expected to react. If I have an egg, what more can I want?" (120).

6. Shakespeare, *Complete Works*.

7. Offred's final use of *context* occurs when she asks Fred the meaning of a Latin sentence, "Nolite te bastardes carborundorum" ("Don't let the bastards grind you down"), written in small print by the handmaid who preceded her in Fred's house and who eventually hanged herself. Offred thinks to herself, truly, that in the context of her situation the sentence is "neither prayer nor command, but a sad graffiti, scrawled once, abandoned" (196).

8. Janet L. Larson takes a different feminist perspective by relating the novel to "the history of women's biblical hermeneutics" (36).

9. The words concerned are *risk* (sixteen occurrences), *risked* (two), *riskier* (one), *risking* (one), *risks* (one), and *risky* (three).

10. The word *like* (over 570 occurrences) signals Atwood's similes and so can be regarded as a function word.

11. Lucy B. Palache defines *repetend* in *The Princeton Encyclopedia of Poetry and Poetics* as "A recurring word, phrase, or line . . . usually . . . a repetition occurring irregularly rather than regularly within a poem, or to a partial rather than a complete repetition" (699).

12. The collocational display compares one node-collocate relation with another node-collocate relation by means of what is called a z-score. The higher the z-score above about 2.75, the stronger the word association. Any z-score above 4.0 is well worth thinking about.

13. Here * means any number of instances, from zero up, of the previous character; . means any character, except a word separator; and | means "followed by."

Works Cited

Atwood, Margaret. *The Handmaid's Tale.* Toronto: McClelland and Stewart, 1985.

Berry-Rogghe, G. L. M. "The Computation of Collocations and Their Relevance in Lexical Studies." *The Computer and Literary Studies.* Ed. A. J. Aitken, R. W. Bailey, and N. Hamilton-Smith. Edinburgh: Edinburgh UP, 1973. 103-12.

Freibert, Lucy M. "Control and Creativity: The Politics of Risk in Margaret Atwood's *The Handmaid's Tale.*" *Critical Essays on Margaret Atwood.* Ed. Judith McCombs. Boston: G. K. Hall, 1988. 280-91.

Hancock, Geoff. "An Interview with Margaret Atwood." *Canadian Fiction Magazine* 58 (December 1986): 113-44.

Ide, Nancy M. "Meaning and Method: Computer-Assisted Analysis of Blake." *Literary Computing and Literary Criticism: Theoretical and Practical Essays on Theme and Rhetoric.* Ed. Rosanne G. Potter. Philadelphia: U of Pennsylvania P, 1989. 123-41.

Lancashire, Ian. "Back to the Future: Literary and Linguistic Computing 1968-1988," *Computers in Literary and Linguistic Research. Literary and Linguistic Computing 1988*. Ed. Yaacov Choueka. Paris-Genève, 1990. 36-47.

_____.*The Humanities Computing Yearbook 1989-90: A Comprehensive Guide to Software and Other Resources*. Oxford: Clarendon P, 1991. 438-39, 486-88, 495-96.

Larson, Janet L. "Margaret Atwood and the Future of Prophecy." *Religion and Literature* 21.2 (Spring 1989): 27-61.

Malak, Amin. "Margaret Atwood's *The Handmaid's Tale* and the Dystopian Tradition." *Canadian Literature* 112 (Spring 1987): 9-15.

Palache, Lucy B. "Repetend." *The Princeton Encyclopedia of Poetry and Poetics*. Princeton: Princeton UP, 1974. 699.

Rigney, Barbara Hill. *Margaret Atwood*. London: Macmillan Education, 1987.

Rubenstein, Roberta. "Nature and Nurture in Dystopia: *The Handmaid's Tale*." *Margaret Atwood: Vision and Forms*. Ed. Kathryn Van Spanckeren and Jan Garden Castro. Carbondale: Southern Illinois UP, 1988. 101-21.

Shakespeare, William. *The Complete Works*. Rev. ed. Ed. Alfred Harbage. Baltimore: Penguin, 1969.

Smith, John B. "Computer Criticism." *Style* 12.4 (Fall 1978): 326-56.

_____. *Imagery and the Mind of Stephen Dedalus: A Computer-Assisted Study of Joyce's "A Portrait of the Artist as a Young Man."* Lewisburg: Bucknell UP, 1980.

Stevenson, Barbara. "Adapting Hypothesis Testing to a Literary Problem." *Literary Computing and Literary Criticism: Theoretical and Practical Essays on Theme and Rhetoric*. Ed. Rosanne G. Potter. Philadelphia: U of Pennsylvania P, 1989. 61-74.

Beyond the Word:
Reading and the Computer

David S. Miall
University of Alberta

Text Analysis and Coleridge's Fiend

Occasionally, while walking home as a child, I would become convinced that someone was dogging my footsteps. Afraid to look around, I would eventually snatch a glance but see only the empty path behind me, with perhaps a scatter of dead leaves being blown across it. Even so, the sense of being pursued would sometimes persist. Coleridge makes effective use of this common experience toward the end of his poem "The Rime of the Ancient Mariner" (written in 1797-98). To gain a better understanding of one of the words that occurs in this passage, one could find it helpful to turn to the computer.

The moment at which Coleridge introduces the experience seems an odd one, if one considers the shape that the Mariner's story has taken up to this point: he has done penance for shooting the Albatross, the curse that had been laid upon him seems to have been lifted, and he is on his way back to his home country. Yet something is still pursuing the solitary Mariner:

> And now this spell was snapt: once more
> I viewed the ocean green,
> And looked far forth, yet little saw
> Of what had else been seen —
>
> Like one, that on a lonesome road
> Doth walk in fear and dread,
> And having once turned round walks on,
> And turns no more his head;
> Because he knows, a frightful fiend
> Doth close behind him tread.

(lines 442-51)

The poem contains several other alarming figures: Death and Life-in-Death, who appear on the skeleton ship; the Polar Spirit, who seeks vengeance for the shooting of the Albatross, and the spirits whose voices the Mariner hears debating his fate. Yet nowhere else in the poem is the "frightful fiend" mentioned. The implications of the fiend are left to resonate with no further elucidation, perhaps partly because his presence is figurative rather than actual: he is introduced as a simile: "Like one, that . . . . "

Thus at this point in the poem a reader might raise the question of what Coleridge meant by "the fiend." The question could be explored by means of a text-analysis program. Are there other contexts within which Coleridge uses the word *fiend* with similar implications? A concordance of the poetry for *fiend* and *fiends* yields nineteen instances. Several of the examples turn out to be rather conventional: the fiends are mostly from hell (Milton seems responsible for some of these) or they are figurative representations of evil. But two of the examples seem more relevant. In "Religious Musings" the notion of pursuit is also present, but here the church provides a refuge (for an allegorical personage called Fear):

> God's altar grasping with an eager hand
> Fear, the wild-visag'd, pale, eye-starting wretch,
> Sure-refug'd hears his hot pursuing fiends
> Yell at vain distance. Soon refresh'd from Heaven
> He calms the throb and tempest of his heart.
>
> (lines 68-72)

The fiends are not further described, but they appear to be the earthly powers that are inimical to religion. An interesting footnote to line 89, however, also implies that the fiends may be our "evil Passions." Since Fear is a personification, these fiends, like the one in "The Mariner," are also figurative.

The second reference is to an earlier poem, the sonnet "Pantisocracy" (1794). Here Coleridge imagines the ideal colony to which at that time he intended to emigrate. Once there, he says, tears of sorrow will turn to tears of joy:

> Eyes that have ach'd with Sorrow! Ye shall weep
> Tears of doubt-mingled joy, like theirs who start
> From Precipices of distemper'd sleep,
> On which the fierce-eyed Fiends their revels keep,
> And see the rising Sun, and feel it dart
> New rays of pleasance trembling to the heart.

Unlike the majority of fiends elsewhere in Coleridge's poetry, the fiends in this poem are explicitly internal: they inhabit a dream landscape from which the sleeper awakens with relief. These too are figurative: they could be construed as the evils of his home country from which the emigrant has escaped, but placing them in the world of sleep gives them a more disturbing and less explicable power (we do, after all, have to sleep again). In this respect they seem closer to the arbitrary world of the Mariner.

Pursuing these instances is quickly done with a concordance program, such as the OCP, WordCruncher, or TACT. Unlike the printed concordance to Coleridge's poetry, which has long been out of print and is hard to obtain, the second and third of these programs also allow us to view the complete text of the references on screen, making evaluation of their relevance to the original query an easier undertaking. The programs have other advantages, however, that take the reader beyond this simple concordance operation. The two additional references to fiends that I have cited provide some clues to Coleridge's usage in "The Mariner." The Mariner's fiend may, like those in "Pantisocracy," be internal, an agent beneath the consciousness known only from dream states or other unconscious promptings. This interpretation would help elucidate the obscure lines that introduce the simile, where the Mariner says he "looked far forth, yet little saw / Of what had else been seen." "Pantisocracy," in other words, helps to gloss the Mariner's comment: it suggests that what he would have seen if he had looked in the right place (within instead of "far forth") would have been something like a pursuing fiend. Is the fiend then a part of the self? The structure of connotations that now begins to surround the word can itself be explored through the computer. The method I will show is drawn from TACT, and it illustrates a line of inquiry that would not be feasible by conventional means but which the computer makes readily available.

One of the connotations concerns the meaning of feelings and passions, and in particular a fear of what lies within. TACT makes possible a search for collocations that combine two lists of words, so what I request now are instances in which any of the words for feeling (*feels, felt,* and the like, and *passion, passions,* and so on) occur with such terms as *within, below,* or *beneath.* I create two categories containing these terms, then write a rule that searches for all instances that occur within a context of five lines. The search produces eleven instances, among which I find such lines as "Naked, and void, and fixed, and all within / The unquiet silence of confuséd thought / And shapeless feelings" ("The Destiny of Nations"); "Perhaps 'tis tender too and pretty / At each wild word to feel within / A sweet recoil of love and pity" ("Christabel"); and these lines from a poem of 1810, "The Visionary Hope," which also, it is interesting to note, refers to dreams:

An alien's restless mood but half concealing,
The sternness on his gentle brow confessed,
Sickness within and miserable feeling:
Though obscure pangs made curses of his dreams,
And dreaded sleep, each night repelled in vain,
Each night was scattered by its own loud screams .

(lines 9-14)

Other relationships implied by terms used in the three fiend passages also yield suggestive passages in other poems (by trying different combinations of the terms for feeling, sleep, pursuit, dread, and so on). A tentative conclusion on what Coleridge's fiend in "The Mariner" may mean becomes possible. The Mariner remains in a state of enthrallment to which the moral categories of guilt, penance, or forgiveness seem inapplicable: they do not reach the core of dread before which the Mariner is "Naked, and void, and fixed." The variety of poems given by this series of searches also indicates certain underlying similarities in the lexical resources drawn upon by Coleridge: they point to a predicament Coleridge seems increasingly to be aware that he shares with his fictional Mariner, as later poems such as "Pains of Sleep" (1803) and "The Visionary Hope" (1810) testify. Even in the earlier poems the accounts of dread seem over-determined, as if Coleridge were already witnessing to some intractable feeling beyond the reach of the moral framework that was the reason for introducing it. Whether in "Pantisocracy," "The Destiny of Nations," or "The Mariner," the unconscious fiend seems to call into question Coleridge's announcements of redemption or his attempts to nurture hope or love.

This example from Coleridge is based on one that I offer when teaching text analysis in an undergraduate class on romantic poetry. It suggests how the examination of a particular word can, with some care, lead to identifying a significant concept within a given corpus of texts. The method has certain strengths and limitations, which can readily be pointed out.

The use of text-analysis methods, of the kind just illustrated, remains marginal among literary scholars; even fewer seem to have the inclination or opportunity to incorporate such methods into their regular teaching. It might be argued that this situation is unlikely to change until more sophisticated technologies become available. Current text-analysis facilities, exemplified by the OCP, WordCruncher, or TACT, are primarily concordance-based systems, oriented toward counting words or finding specified collocations. One condition of their use is that the user must already have some hypothesis about what would be worth examining, as I have shown in the case of Coleridge's fiend.

The amount of material offered by a concordance (over eleven thousand word types in the case of Coleridge's poetry) is overwhelming without some initial point of entry. But once I have formulated a question, the software is then adept at supporting certain kinds of inquiry, simply by giving immediate access to the nearly five hundred pages of Coleridge's complete poetry.

Text-analysis inquiries of this kind can readily be integrated into regular undergraduate courses in literature. But as this example implies, their inclusion requires a shift toward student-initiated questions. Once students have been shown how to use a tool such as TACT (which I undertake to teach in two fifty-minute sessions), students are then able to define their own questions and work singly or collaboratively on projects that make effective use of the computer as an investigative tool. In the process, however, students become more aware of their own reading process and more aware of the dialogic nature of literary texts (the Miltonic fiends in Coleridge offer a useful example).

The computer provides a resource that can broaden students' understanding of interpretive problems as well as facilitate their grasp of the stylistic and structural aspects of the texts they study. In some respects the computer provides a more rigorous approach to certain types of evidence often cited in discussions about the meaning of texts. Current text technology can thus play an important part in helping to redesign classroom practice.

The computer resources readily available to us, however, can see only words and can handle only rather elementary patterns of collocations among words. As such, it could be argued that the focus the programs offer is at too low a level, providing little access to texts at the level of concepts, themes, and figures, which is where the reader's main interest is located. For instance, although I might wish to find further examples of the situation presented in the fiend passage, unless other instances actually use one or more of the same significant words, the computer will be unable to see them. In *The Prelude* (1805) Wordsworth describes how, when a child, he stole birds from traps that he had not set. Afterward he is haunted in a way that has strong similarities to Coleridge's fiend passage:

> and when the deed was done
> I heard among the solitary hills
> Low breathings coming after me, and sounds
> Of undistinguishable motion, steps
> Almost as silent as the turf they trod.
>
> (1.328-32)

But the two passages have no significant words in common, thus no computer-based search for this theme in romantic poetry would produce results.

Although more sophisticated approaches to examining literary texts have been devised, as I shall mention, such methods are still word based, and most depend on rather special research skills (often statistical in nature) which seem unlikely to find their way into the repertoire of the literary scholar or undergraduate. More advanced computer methods of this kind thus seem likely to remain without serious influence, on the periphery of literary scholarship.

Such arguments have been put forward by several critics recently, and I shall be concerned to evaluate their validity. The issues raised seem to fall into three main areas: first, the level at which readers engage with literary texts (to what extent this goes beyond the word); second, the affective component of response (which would appear to be beyond what computers are able to do with words); and third, the type of discourse that takes place about a text (including what readers say they are doing as they work toward an interpretation). It has been argued that computer-based methods of literary study are at best inadequate—and at worst misleading. Underlying each of these problems lies a more basic problem: the theoretical positions that might support a more productive engagement with texts are conspicuously absent from the computer domain. These are genuine and important concerns, but as I shall argue, the case for using existing text analysis and other readily available computer methods is not invalidated. I shall point to two different domains in which computing finds an important place, one available immediately, the other only slowly being developed and dependent on some basic research in the domain of artificial intelligence.

The Limitations of Textual Computing

Although discussion of the problems I have outlined seems to have become more frequent within the last two or three years, the issue is not a new one. In 1978 Susan Wittig commented that the text analysis scholars, whose work was currently available in the humanities computing journals and discussed at conferences, were dependent on an outdated and restrictive view of the literary text. In brief, she argued that computer scholars treated the text as a linear string, as complete and unalterable (ignoring the choices made by the author during the process of composition), and as autonomous, as though a text could be understood with no reference to its context or other texts. She located these assumptions within the now-suspect approach of the New Criticism. She argued for a redirecting of computer work to align it with reader-response criticism, referring to studies of the affective and associational responses to language, such as Osgood's semantic differential; these would enrich our understanding of how particular words or groups of words are understood. Such research would ask how "the text is fulfilled with meaning by its readers" (214), although Wittig offered no discussion of how the studies she envisaged would be carried out.

In the same year Klaus Schmidt also attacked the main body of computer-based work up to that time, in remarks that continue to hold a certain validity. Given that content or meaning has been the principal aspect of interest for the great majority of literary scholars, the main tool in use, the concordance, had contributed little of value to the analysis of the content of literary texts. Not only does the user of the concordance have to know exactly what he is looking for, said Schmidt, but a thorough knowledge of the text is indispensable to evaluating what he finds. Studies based on counting word frequencies and collocations tended to produce only vague or trivial results, and too many studies concentrated on methodological issues rather than substantive results. Schmidt's own approach, which he has continued to pursue in studies of medieval German poetry, recommends an alternative grasp on the analysis of content: the conceptual glossary or thesaurus, in which search words are grouped by common meanings (an early and influential example being the General Inquirer [see Stone]). This tool allows a more precise and productive grasp on the lexicon of the literary text, although Schmidt's work makes it clear that in order to yield significant results, such a tool requires redesigning with each major corpus of texts to allow for historical shifts and changes in word meaning.

Ten years later the same problems still seem to beset the field of literary computing. Willie Van Peer has argued that the focus on the text as a string of words, which is basically all that current technology allows, has tended to reify its object: the student of literary texts is reduced to counting words ("Quantitative Studies"). Echoing Karl Kroeber's reservations twenty years ago about the destructive effect of quantitative research on the object being studied, Van Peer argues that "in the very act of transforming textual qualities into counts, their essentially process-like character is irretrievably lost." The elimination of the figurative is Van Peer's paradigm case, but much else in the way of verbal nuance is also eliminated, thus undermining the literariness of the texts that are being studied. Although computer methods may be rather successful in the case of phonetic and grammatical features, the meaning and the illocutionary force of texts that are their most characteristic features remain beyond quantitative study. Such methods, says Van Peer, are "trapped in the levels of grammar and lexis" (305). Progress beyond this point will only come when researchers interested in using the computer shift their focus to the quantifiable aspects of text that can be shown to have a relationship with readers' responses. He cites his own studies on the effect of foregrounding (see *Stylistics)*, and a study of readers' subjective estimates of sentence length, where the findings in both cases were related to identifiable features of literary texts. (Van Peer's recent study "Measurement of Metre" provides another productive example of such research.) Van Peer also calls for greater interchange between quantitative studies and the theory of literature. Both would benefit from the exchange: theoretical studies would gain by the greater rigor of quantitative studies, and quantitative studies would be drawn in from their current peripheral status ("Quantitative Studies" 306).

An earlier article by John B. Smith, recently reprinted, would appear to offer the kind of meditation on computing and literary theory that Van Peer seeks. Smith attempted to argue the case for seeing Computer Criticism as a comprehensive approach, able eventually to subsume a range of existing non-computer-based theoretical methods. How the theoretical procedures of a Barthes (*S/Z* is cited) were to be made computable, however, was not clear. The methods of Tzvetan Todorov or Paul De Man do not seem readily amenable to computation with present-day technology.[1] Nevertheless, Smith looked forward to the paradigm shift that would be represented by the success of Computer Criticism in his terms. Smith's focus on structuralist models now looks somewhat dated: the early claims to "scientific" status of this type of literary theory were premature and no longer seem so credible. Its more recent examples are written off, indeed, in Paul Fortier's article in the same collection.

In his article Smith also reported, as an example of what Computer Criticism could achieve, a study of his own in which such themes as fire and water were mapped in Joyce's *Portrait of the Artist as a Young Man* (this work continues his earlier, more detailed study of the novel). But the example, although sophisticated in computer techniques, provides little support for Computer Criticism as a new paradigm. R. A. Zwaan argues that Smith's approach was a circular one: having noticed a set of words that embody a major theme, the computer was used only to map the presence and distribution of the words. Such studies are undoubtedly helpful in providing confirmation of a critical idea, and Zwaan certainly underestimates their value; but they do not show the computer as a tool of discovery, able to put the critic in possession of findings that would be impossible without it.

Critics of computing, from Wittig to Van Peer, thus call into question the use of counting—whether words, collocations, word distributions, or stylistic features. As the Coleridge example will have suggested, however, the basic concordance, for all its limitations, is not without some power, provided the user has an initial conception worth pursuing by computer. The lexical and grammatical studies criticized by Van Peer can, with care, produce important and persuasive results. Forming an impression of a stylistic feature, which is all that most literary critics are able to do, is a different matter from obtaining sufficient statistical evidence to prove its presence. Robert Allan, for example, is able to show by statistical methods how an author's style is characterized by the presence of certain words whose occurrence differs markedly from their frequency of use in a comparable body of other prose (his studies are of nineteenth-century French novelists)—an example of research that begins to realize Riffaterre's notion of stylistic context. The accounts of Carlyle's prose style reported by Robert Oakman offer another convincing example.

Oakman is also well aware of the limitations of computer methods: indeed, his paper offers a review of some criticisms leveled at computer stylistics. But Oakman then proceeds to describe his own study of Carlyle and to integrate with it the results of two other computer-assisted studies of aspects of Carlyle's prose where different aims were pursued. The three studies were concerned with relating Carlyle's style to Scottish associationist rhetoric, with German prose style, and with other Victorian prose writers. The studies involved sampling passages from Carlyle's texts and counting a range of stylistic features, from alliteration to sentence structure. The effect of Carlyle's interest in German prose, for example, is seen in the high incidence of inversions, parentheses, and appositives in his prose. Much of Oakman's own work was dependent on sophisticated techniques for the automatic parsing of a sample of Carlyle's sentences.

The three studies discussed by Oakman are in general agreement. After counting the frequency of various features of the prose, it was shown that Carlyle's style progresses through four stages: from an eighteenth-century, Johnsonian style, then to a Germanic style, followed by a more efficient and dramatic style, and finally to an irregular or eccentric style. The summary of his comparative study offered by Oakman is persuasive:

> Stylistic features discovered independently in three separate computer studies are candidates for stylistic "universals" of Carlyle's prose. All have been validated by computerized analysis of surface features combined with statistical and contextual criticism. The weight of all this evidence lends precision to critical conjectures of earlier scholars about Carlyle's style with a profusion of detail and a statistical measure of generality never before possible. (283)

In the study of Carlyle, then, the computer is being used to confirm insights on a scale and with a detail not previously attainable. Several of the studies in Rosanne Potter's collection provide other persuasive examples: Fortier's work on modern French novels, Goldfield's study of Gobineau, Ide's account of the structure of

Blake's *Four Zoas*. Each is able to show the computer extending and developing the critic's original hypotheses and making genuine advances in understanding. In one case, indeed, in Fortier's study of Robbe-Grillet, the critic is able to report, "The machine furnished overwhelming evidence that my original approach and hypotheses were dead wrong" (90-91).

Each of these studies, however, makes sophisticated use of statistical techniques, from the Chi-square to Fourier analysis. The great majority of literary scholars are unlikely to wish to employ such measures, or even to be in a position to estimate where they might be relevant. Most of the studies also required advanced computer skills in programming and data handling (not to mention earlier scholars' wrestling with recalcitrant mainframe computers in the first, heroic phase of literary computing). Research of this kind may support the case for scholars' acquiring relevant computing and statistical skills, but at the moment it still leaves the computer-assisted study on the periphery. Without the support of statistics, nevertheless, there is still much that can be done with the standard concordance software and databases. For all its limitations, judicious use of the computer will make it an important tool to support many kinds of textual research. The case of Coleridge's "Mariner" suggests another example.

Did Coleridge Become the Mariner?

It was shown above that by following the implications of Coleridge's use of the word *fiend*, a sense of dread beyond any moral framework could be found operating in Coleridge's poetry, both early and late. It could also be proposed that once Coleridge had tapped this dread in "The Mariner" in 1797-98, its implications would surface more openly and more disturbingly in his subsequent poetry. As several commentators have pointed out, Coleridge came increasingly to identify his own predicament with that of the Mariner.

This idea can be posed as a question amenable to computer study. To what extent do the themes of Coleridge's "Mariner," as suggested by the fiend passage, appear in subsequent poetry? In the printed text, edited by E. H. Coleridge, in which the poems are organized chronologically, "The Mariner" occurs a little before the halfway point in the book: it occupies pages 186 to 209 in the 492-page collection (Coleridge wrote half his poetry before 1799; a considerable diminution in his productivity as a poet took place over his remaining years up to 1834). My computer text of Coleridge's poetry is based on this edition. TACT enables word distributions to be graphed in a simple histogram, where the text can be divided into segments by percentage; the number of search words in each percentile is shown as well as the bar. A graph for "The Mariner," in fact, shows that the poem occurs in the 38 to 44 percent segment. But the histogram can now be used to see how certain key words are distributed across the text as a whole.

Taking certain themes represented in the fiend passage, we can see how often the words representing them occur before and after "The Mariner." The "lonesome road" simile is a reminder that the Mariner also complains of being "Alone, alone, all, all alone, / Alone on a wide wide sea!" (lines 232-33). The word *alone* occurs six times altogether in the poem. In the poetry prior to "The Mariner" it occurs nine times, but this figure is potentially misleading: in several of these instances the word means "only," as in "Shall France alone a Despot spurn?" ("Destruction of the Bastile"); four of the instances have the meaning "solitary." In the poetry following "The Mariner," by contrast, there are no fewer than twenty-two occurrences that mean solitary. If the word were distributed evenly across the text (ignoring "The Mariner"), one would expect to find ten instances before and sixteen instances after "The Mariner." This distribution indicates that Coleridge is more concerned with states of solitude in the later poetry (a Chi-square test, incidentally, shows this difference to be statistically significant).

The fiend passage also suggests that the moral categories may carry less weight in the later poetry (Coleridge, it may recalled, himself commented that "The Mariner" had too much moral in it). Testing this suggestion with the words *evil* and *sin* (including such forms as *evils* and *sinful*), and dividing the poetry into two equal halves, shows that there are twenty occurrences in the earlier poetry but only twelve in the later. Despite Coleridge's later explicit adherence to Anglicanism, his poetry seems to show a greater caution in dealing with moral issues. These simple examples of word counts in Coleridge's poetry serve to test an idea based on a single passage in one poem. Even though the method used lacks the technical sophistication of the Oakman or the Fortier studies, the implications of the findings are potentially far-reaching for the view of Coleridge's poetic concerns that they provide. The only tool needed for this inquiry has been the concordance program TACT, but it is easy to implement and is now becoming more widely available. I have made a point of introducing students to the basic facilities offered by TACT in my regular undergraduate courses, which has meant making available electronic texts of the major romantic poets and several British texts of modernist fiction, from Conrad to Joyce.

One difficulty in the use of concordance techniques was shown in the case of the word *alone*. Here it was necessary to distinguish instances meaning "solitude" from other meanings: although various advanced techniques are being developed to enable different meanings to be discriminated automatically, TACT allows instances to be assigned manually to one or more categories, thus giving the user control over the instances that should appear in a concordance or be considered during a collocation search. Some analysis of word use requires a more careful and elaborate handling of the nuances of meaning and their implications, however, and for this purpose it is possible to use a database. This database use provides another effective and often powerful application of the computer to support study of a text.

Simple Databases and Textual Study

It is quite feasible to export concordance data from TACT in a form that can be imported to a database. The technique is not difficult, although it requires an intermediate stage in which data exported from the INDEX display of TACT is edited with a word processor to produce fields for each record. After importing the records to a new database file and adding two or three further fields, the records are now ready to be annotated. Each line of extracted text can be elaborated by categorizing it, entering interpretive comments, or recording syntactic information. With some planning and care, a combination of TACT and a simple flat-file database enables quite advanced studies of textual features to be carried out, including several of the types of analysis described by Fortier in his study of French fiction, or Oakman on Carlyle's stylistic development (albeit by undertaking manual rather than automatic parsing).

Another use also exists for the database alone, which enables the computer to act as an analytical tool for textual study. When teachers or their students are examining a text in some detail, they might make use of marginal notes in the text or take extensive notes on paper. The equivalent labor spent on compiling a database file may often be more productive. For example, a database that I compiled to accompany study of Conrad's *Heart of Darkness* and several other texts was made available through Reflex (Borland's database program) in a computer lab open to students of English who were taking a modernism course with me. The records each had seven fields: Author, Text, Aspect, Instance, Quotation, Comment, and Reference. The Aspects field contained some of the standard approaches to the analysis of fiction, such as setting, character, theme, structure. Each Aspect could then be further subdivided into appropriate categories. The aspect Language, for example, included a range of Instances in which language itself occurs as a theme. In the two examples shown below some of the troubling questions about the status of language raised by the novella are apparent:

```
AUTHOR:    Conrad
TEXT:      Heart of Darkness
ASPECT:    lang
INSTANCE:  empty word
```

```
QUOTE:      the Kurtz whom at the time I did not see . . . He was just
            a word for me. I did not see the man in the name any more than
            you do.
COMMENT:    talk doesn't give the reality
REF: 172


AUTHOR:     Conrad
TEXT:       Heart of Darkness
ASPECT:     lang
INSTANCE:   explanatory
QUOTE:      I listened on the watch for the sentence, for the word, that
            would give me the clue to the faint uneasiness inspired by
            this narrative
COMMENT     frame narrator requiring the speakable
REF: 173
```

A significant advantage for the student who has developed a system of this kind is the ability conferred by the database program to search and sort the material. If the student elects to write an essay on the theme of language in several modernist texts, the database can readily bring together all the entries concerned with language and sort them by instance. A part of the labor of organizing the material is thus already done within two or three seconds. The rigour of the database method also encourages the user to make more systematic and comprehensive notes while reading (although the widespread use of the computer for such purposes will have to wait until more students have their own readily accessible computers: reading for long periods in the computer lab is not likely to prove congenial). The database acts as a powerful tool for categorizing and sorting research notes. A far-reaching defense of database principles in literary study is offered by Lynette Hunter, who notes that not only is there no necessary connection between computer use and quantification but also that adoption of the computer as a tool invites a rethinking and refinement of the methods characteristically used in the humanities.

The computer methods discussed so far have involved the pursuit of questions about texts that, for the most part, are already in the mind of the student or researcher. Thus, having read "The Mariner," I formulate a question about the meaning of the fiend, which I can explore by means of the concordance, collocations, and counting word frequencies. For more elaborate studies of vocabulary where classifying and annotating occurrences are required, I can export concordance entries to a database. Studies of this kind are able to go beyond the level of the word, and they are able to do so because the user of the computer exercises the same care and caution in judgment that the literary scholar would normally use in making interpretations of texts. Interpretations reached with the help of such computer methods, however, are likely to be more firmly grounded in evidence: counting words does make a difference. Occasionally a computer study can serve to show that traditional scholarship has resulted in false conclusions, as Ian Small's study of Pater has demonstrated. Two earlier critics proposed that Pater's distinctive style came from his frequent use of a few characteristic words, but their claims could not be sustained by the evidence: objective counts of Pater's word use showed a different set of words to be the most frequent.

Studies of stylistic features, word use, themes, and text structure, may all be facilitated by the careful use of the computer. The lack of influence of such studies so far has been noted most recently by Tom Corns: he observes that almost no computer-assisted studies are apparent in the main journals concerned with literature in English.[2] But this situation may be due as much to the lack of user-friendly software and machine-readable texts as to the kind of inherent limitations of literary computing identified by Kroeber or Van Peer. Both of the practical limitations are now being overcome: the release of OCP to run on personal computers and the development of WordCruncher and, in particular, TACT, to a high level, are making accessible to scholars literary computing with minimal technical demands; and extensive literary text bases are now being developed that will place the Canon of literary texts on the scholar's computer in the near future (for texts in English, Oxford University Press and Chadwyck Healey have announced major projects that will achieve this end). One of the points I have wanted to stress in this chapter is that much significant work can be done already with the resources now available, such as TACT and database programs: standard undergraduate courses in literature can be enhanced if the texts being studied are accessible on computer and if learning methods encourage students to formulate their own inquiries as a part of regular course work.[3]

The concern remains, however, that the computer is peripheral to the study of literature. Although it provides a hitherto unparalleled command over texts considered as data, offering scholarship much in the way of efficiency and reliability, it provides no new principles when the methods of textual study are considered. The literary scholar who uses the computer is still doing what such scholars have traditionally done, although with a new tool. Moreover, this scholar also generally continues to work alone, pursuing interpretive ideas about texts, relying on intuition and various theoretical perspectives; surprisingly little collaborative work has taken place among computer-assisted scholars. The multiplication of interpretive ideas about the major texts, of which Jean-Claude Gardin has complained, shows no signs of abating. The computer is not yet being used appropriately to model and test interpretation in the spirit of John B. Smith's call for a general theory of Computer Criticism. To overcome this limitation, one direction proposed by several of the critics of literary computing would lie in broadening the computer approach to embrace the study of reading. What are the conditions under which readers arrive at interpretations? Can our existing explanations, whether based on traditional or computer sources of evidence, account for how readers actually come to understand texts (readers, that is, who are not professors of literature)?

Thus Wittig called for studies of how readers endow texts with meaning; Van Peer argued for research that would focus on quantifiable aspects of response, pointing to his own studies, including his ground-breaking study of responses to foregrounding. Zwaan is less interested in the use of the computer to study actual readers: he suggests the development of programs for simulating the reading process that would test alternative theoretical models of reading. A related proposal by Jean-Claude Gardin calls for the modeling of interpretive arguments about literature, on the lines of the logicist approach that has yielded important results in archaeology (see "On the Way"). In the last part of this chapter, I shall outline some principles that would enable progress to be made in this direction.

Artificial Intelligence and Literary Response

Empirical studies of reader response are still uncommon while studies that attempt to capture information about the process of response are particularly rare. Although reader-response issues have staged a major resurgence among students of critical theory—the most frequently cited names being Jonathan Culler, Stanley Fish, and Wolfgang Iser—such theorists carry out no empirical work to validate their claims. Since the theories are by no means convergent, showing numerous points of disagreement and conflict, it seems probable that empirical studies would at least have the virtue of helping to establish which aspects of which current reader-response theories appear to merit acceptance and which should be discarded for lack of evidence (before professional interest turns elsewhere—an event that, to judge by Elizabeth Freund's account, may already be in prospect). It should be possible to gather empirical data and analyze it in a consistent and rigorous form to test existing theoretical ideas and perhaps to discover new ones, but for this endeavor neither text-based computing, as discussed so far, nor the experimental method commonly used to study human behavior in the social sciences provides an adequate methodology, although they may both provide elements of such a method. For this purpose only methods being developed in artificial intelligence (AI) will be adequate.

Substantial advance in understanding literary response will come from processing information about readers' responses within a knowledge-based system. Evidence that has been systematically gathered is maintained in consistent form within a complex database, which provides the basis for deriving inferences and formulating rules about specific procedures during reading. Existing AI systems that model comprehension of discourse are unlikely to provide a suitable foundation for this project: their emphasis, with some minor exceptions (for example, Lehnert, Dyer), is on cognitive forms of representation and on a limited set of plans and goals.[4] It is unlikely that literary response will be effectively modeled in any current or future AI system of this kind. An adequate system will need to account for the place and function of affect in the response process.

Enough is now known about literary response as a process to begin to sketch what the elements of such a system might be. I shall mention three aspects that have been a primary focus in my own research in this area. First, it is evident that literary texts possess a linguistic property generally absent from other kinds of texts: foregrounding. Certain features of the language of a text stand out as deviating in some significant respect from the normal nonliterary uses of the language. Such deviations are manifested at the phonetic level (such as assonance, meter, and rhyme), at the grammatical level (ellipsis, inversion), and at the semantic level (irony, metaphor). All readers who are competent speakers of the language of the text in question seem to be sensitive to this aspect: no differences have been found between readers with literary training and those without (see Van Peer, *Stylistics* 120).

The most advanced work in understanding diction began with the Russian Formalist theorists and continued with a number of significant studies of Czech and other literatures by the Prague structuralists, among whom Mukarovsky was the best known. Computational stylistics already offers the possibility of automating to some degree the identification of the lower levels of foregrounding. Jiri Levy, for example, showed the feasibility of (1) estimating the probabilities of different phonemes in a language and the extent to which their use in verse deviates from the norm, (2) estimating the choices available for rhyme words in several languages, hence the degree of surprise provided by a given rhyme, and (3) calculating the distribution of stresses in verse and hence accounting for the effect of metrical deviation. Each of these approaches provides a context or norm,[5] either for the language as such or for the text being studied, against which we can measure the deviations that we postulate that readers will notice.

Second, we have found in our own studies that a primary component of the response to foregrounded language is affect. Readers find such features more striking or arresting, and they report a greater affective response (see Miall et al.). Moreover, several of the studies have indicated that affect may be the main vehicle for channeling the reader's experience into the act of interpretation, connecting different parts of the text, and facilitating anticipations of the text's overall meaning

(Miall, "Affect" and "Responses"). Third, studies of response have indicated an emergent process wherein a focus on lower-level details of the text gradually gives way to high-order concepts, accompanied by a shift from a primarily affect-based and private response to a predominantly cognitive one, capable of being expressed and shared (Miall, "Authorizing").

A consideration of each of these aspects suggests that to a significant degree a set of responses to a text will show systematic features in common. Even though readers will bring their own experience and backgrounds to bear on interpreting the text, the process of response will be determined in part by foregrounding and by connections and anticipations that readers make as a result of the common effects of foregrounding and other textual features. It should therefore be possible to detect beneath the range of individual variance in interpretations systematic rules shaping the process of response: the knowledge-based approach will enable response data to be collected and analyzed for the common elements within the response process and for this information to be matched with information about the text (foregrounding, structure, and the like). The rule set that emerges will, among other things, provide scholars with a practical demonstration of alternative interpretations for the text under study, allowing them to trace sources and implications. The rules will also provide a test of existing, theoretical reader-response positions, by informing us about what aspects of text readers actually pay attention to and what constructive processes they then bring to bear on the text as they work toward an interpretation.

Various algorithms for achieving such an outcome already exist in the expert systems devised by knowledge engineers. The key to the inductive process lies in the set of probabilities contained within a group of responses to a given text: certain lines of a poem or phrases in a story, because of foregrounding, will receive more attention than others; a majority of readers relate two or more specific phrases as they work toward an interpretation; a certain group of ideas is consistently mentioned as readers think aloud about the meaning of a part of the text. From these and other regularities within the response data a map of the pathways taken by readers can be plotted, with probabilities attached to the steps of each pathway. In addition, a knowledge base of the kind being described will be provided with information about the personalities, gender and literary backgrounds of the readers. The latter information will put scholars in a position to assess the degree to which the various literary competencies (as proposed by Culler) interact with specific response processes and at what points on the interpretive path they make a difference to the outcome.

It cannot be said that AI has, as yet, made any decisive advances that would assist the development of the system outlined here. The experimental programs usually mentioned, said to foreshadow the type of text-analysis facility that would interest some literary theorists, are located in the story-grammar tradition (compare Ide and Véronis). I have argued elsewhere that such grammars are based on models of text structure that are inappropriate for the study of literary response ("Beyond the Schema"). Other developments in the machine-learning domain, and in the study of medical expertise, point to more fertile ground for development.

The attempt to automate learning by computer has led a number of AI workers to analyze the aspects and stages of learning. R. S. Michalski, for example, reviews three main types of learning that have been studied. First, he outlines a set of deductive processes in which the learner draws inferences from existing knowledge (in AI terms, backward chaining); second, he looks at inductive processes, in which the learner generalizes from input and selects a plausible result for further testing (forward chaining); the third process is analogical, the finding of a common substructure in two domains, enabling one structure to be mapped upon another. Of these three types, two of the forms of induction described by Michalski seem particularly relevant: learning from examples or learning by experimentation, in which either from observation or from discovery the learner is able to generalize from instance to class or from part to whole. Such processes can be detected in response protocols, when readers are invited to think aloud as they read a literary text. In this respect coming to understand a poem or a novel seems to embody some of the processes of learning now being studied in machine form.

Given that some readings of a text seem more competent and thorough than others, another domain of research that seems relevant is that relating to expertise. Studies of experts and novices in medicine have begun to identify the features of the diagnostic process that distinguish an expert. In fact, the earliest expert systems were built in order to capture medical expertise, but recent research has shown that the principles of such early systems were incomplete in significant ways. Thus V. L. Patel and G. J. Groen, in studies of diagnosis by cardiologists, showed that the most effective diagnoses used pure forward chaining, not the backward chaining of hypothesis testing, as implemented in expert systems such as MYCIN. Novices, by contrast, tended to use a mixture of forward and backward chaining that involved trying out different high-level hypotheses. The expert would make a closer examination of the data of the case being presented, formulate several tentative hypotheses, and postpone closure on a given diagnosis while seeking further information. A similar process among readers of literary texts has also been noticed: the studies of Patrick Dias and Michael Hayhoe, for example, led them to contrast readers who impose a prefabricated meaning on a text (whom they call allegorizers or thematizers) with those who begin by looking carefully and repeatedly at details and arrive at an interpretation only later (called problem-solvers). The "expert" readers (in this case, upper-level school students) spent more time looking at phrases and dealing with the images, concepts, or affects that occurred in response to the local detail of a poem whereas poor readers tended to neglect the details of the text and their own responses and to use mainly backward chaining, deducing meaning for the poem from an initial idea or feeling and then imposing it on the details of the text.

It has also been shown by A. Lesgold and his colleagues that medical experts have more highly responsive and accurate perceptual processes than novices. Expert behavior is characterized by a rapid recognition skill that involves an interaction between lower and higher levels of representation, which is neither purely top-down nor purely bottom-up (once again, this contrasts with the "hypothetico-deductive" model). The novice is constrained by the immediate perceptual evidence to construe what he sees. Thus a novice reader may see a poem as being "about" its literal subject matter, rather than wait to see if the text is symbolic or ironic in some way. Experts also make more inferences from relevant material, and they are more able to identify what is relevant. As Lesgold and friends say, "The expert spends proportionally more time building up a basic representation of the problem situation before seeking for a solution"; the expert is then more flexible in entertaining several schemata, testing them against the data, and tuning a schema to match the specifics of the case being examined to determine if he or she has invoked the correct one. This process, again, seems to match rather well the evidence from studies of literary protocols. The expert reader will, for instance, be more aware of foregrounding and spend longer examining the text to explore its meanings at the detailed level. Such a reader will also then try out several different configurations of meaning in order to see which one best fits the evidence provided by the text.

These considerations show that reading a literary text is analogous to the learning of the child rather than of the adult. Lesgold and his colleagues observe that their findings on expertise "are better accommodated by developmental psychology" than by standard learning theory. Thus the main task facing readers of a literary text lies in creating schemata to account for the world of the text, rather than in instantiating their existing schemata. The same point is made by W. John Harker: the reader, he says, "must learn conceptually to inhabit the literary text in a manner similar to the way he has learned conceptually to inhabit the world of everyday experience." In this respect the reader is obliged to go beyond the medical expert: whereas the expert cardiologist knows that his diagnosis will eventually issue in the recognition of a known pathology, the reader creates a meaning that is distinct to him or her and is important precisely because it is new and because it calls into question previous knowledge. It is this creativity within the response process that makes a strictly information-processing analysis problematic; but a model that also incorporates the constructive processes of affect may succeed where previous models have proved inadequate.

This project will involve the application of the computer in an unfamiliar domain, and one of the problems in carrying it out will be its methodological challenge. Zwaan's discussion of the prospects for AI in advancing literary research pointed to the two main genres of AI programs: those that operate in the performance mode and those that operate in the simulation mode. The first type of program is designed to produce results, based on analysis of data and rules that determine how data is managed; expert systems now provide the most familiar examples. Zwaan points out, probably correctly, that such programs have little or nothing to offer literary research. The simulation program, by contrast, is not primarily intended to produce results but to model some aspect of human information processing. Simulation programming is advocated by recent psychological theorists, such as Philip Johnson-Laird, for their value in forcing the theorist to specify all the features of the process being studied in order to get a model of it to run on a computer; Zwaan argues that simulation programs hold potential value for modeling the cognitive processes of literary reading. The system for studying literary response described above, however, fits neither mode. Although it borrows features from both, it can perhaps more appropriately (if figuratively) be described as a symbiotic model.

In true symbiosis, which involves two living systems, both organisms in the partnership require the presence of the other for survival and both benefit from the relationship. In the literary response system the partners are the computer program and the literary theorist: each has an essential contribution to make to the joint labor of analyzing literary response. At the initial stage, when configuring the program to accept data about a given text and a set of readers, the theorist provides a detailed knowledge of the text, comprising such matters as foregrounding (until more of this work has been automated), text structure (episodes, plot), and information about the readers. During the operational stage the theorist must also provide protocols in coded form and infer some of the initial rules that will be represented by the computer. Finally, the theorist has a role in adjusting and fine-tuning the methods of analysis that the system will use. The system in its turn makes available inferential powers over a large body of data that lie beyond the reach of human analysis. Through its speed of processing and through its ability to manage far more comparisons and evaluations of data points than would be accessible to the human eye, the computer offers a tool for discovery: as a result patterns and relationships in the data will be apparent which no noncomputer analysis could produce. This systematicity, inferred from clusters of probabilities, forward chaining, pattern matching, and the like, forms the theorist's primary data for theory building. In what ways does foregrounding exert a systematic influence on the reading process? Is affect predictive of schema change? Is effective reading characterized by the maintenance of several candidate schemata during interpretation? These questions, and others that are topics of dispute in the current reader-response debate, will be arbitrated by the help of a knowledge base system of the kind I have been describing, grounded on the analysis of protocols from actual readers. Some of the elements of the system will be based on existing algorithms, developed in both performance- and simulation-mode AI programs, but the system itself constitutes a development of AI that seems distinct, offering new powers and new potential. Given the scale and complexity of the issues it is intended to illuminate, this expansion is perhaps to be expected.

In conclusion, it seems likely that text-based computing as we have known it for forty years or more, centered on the concordance, will soon be seen as just one method for understanding literary texts. Some of the stylistic aspects of literature, known as foregrounding, seem closest to computational analysis, and many important and productive methods already exist beyond this one for thematic and structural study where the computer offers valuable tools for both quantitative and qualitative research. But the major challenge facing literary scholarship, partly anticipated by Gardin's far-sighted analysis ("Interpretation"), is to understand how readers arrive at interpretations. Here the most advanced level of computing methods will be required, in combination with careful empirical studies and the insights of several disciplines from cognitive science to reader-response theory. It may be possible to claim, ten or twenty years from now, that the computer provided the workbench upon which the conflicting theories of interpretation currently dividing scholars were tested and a new, well-founded science of literature came into being.

Notes

1. For an interesting computational approach to Todorov, however, see Jim Doran.

2. Compare with Rosanne G. Potter, "Literary Criticism."

3. For a more detailed examination of the issues, see Miall, "Rethinking English Studies." For examples of the OCP in undergraduate projects, see Howard Jackson.

4. A critical discussion is provided by Nancy M. Ide and Jean Véronis.

5. Compare Riffaterre, who finds the notion of a norm unacceptable. He proposes an Average Reader as a test of what stylistic devices are noticed in a text.

Works Cited

Allan, Robert F. "The Stylo-Statistical Method of Literary Analysis." *Computers and the Humanities* 22 (1988): 1-10.

Corns, Tom N. "Computers in the Humanities: Methods and Applications in the Study of English Literature." *Literary and Linguistic Computing* 6 (1991): 127-30.

Culler, Jonathan. *Structuralist Poetics*. London: Routledge, 1975.

Dias, Patrick, and Michael Hayhoe. *Developing Response to Poetry*. Milton Keynes: Open UP, 1988.

Doran, Jim. "A Distributed Artificial Intelligence Reading of Todorov's *The Conquest of America*." *Interpretation in the Humanities: Perspectives from Artificial Intelligence*. Ed. Richard Ennals and Jean-Claude Gardin. London: British Library, 1990. 143-68.

Dyer, M. G. "The Role of Affect in Narratives." *Cognitive Science* 7 (1983): 211-42.

Fortier, Paul A. "Analysis of Twentieth-Century French Prose Fiction: Theoretical Contexts, Results, Perspectives." Potter, ed., 77-95.

Freund, Elizabeth. *The Return of the Reader: Reader-Response Criticism*. London: Methuen, 1987.

Gardin, Jean-Claude. "Interpretation in the Humanities: Some Thoughts on the Third Way." *Interpretation in the Humanities: Perspectives from Artificial Intelligence*. Ed. Richard Ennals and Jean-Claude Gardin. London: British Library, 1990. 22-59.

____. "On the Way We Think and Write in the Humanities: A Computational Perspective." Paper. The Dynamic Text: ALLC-ACH Conference. Toronto, June 1989.

Groen, G. J., and V. L. Patel, "The Relationship between Comprehension and Reasoning in Medical Expertise." *The Nature of Expertise*. Ed. M. T. H. Chi, R. Glaser, and M. J. Farr. Hillsdale: Lawrence Erlbaum, 1988. 287-310.

Harker, W. J. "Information Processing and the Reading of Literary Texts." *New Literary History* 20 (1989): 473.

Hunter, Lynette. "Fact—Information—Data—Knowledge: Databases as a Way of Organizing Knowledge." *Literary and Linguistic Computing* 5 (1990): 49-57.

Ide, Nancy M., and Jean Véronis, "Artificial Intelligence and the Study of Literary Narrative." *Poetics* 19 (1990): 37-63.

Jackson, Howard. "OCP and the Computer Analysis of Texts: The Birmingham Polytechnic Experience." *Literary and Linguistic Computing* 5 (1990): 86-88.

Johnson-Laird, Philip N. *Mental Models*. Cambridge: Cambridge UP, 1983.

Kroeber, Karl. "Perils of Quantification: The Exemplary Case of Jane Austen's *Emma*." *Statistics and Style*. Ed. Lubomir Dolezel and Richard Bailey. New York: American Elsevier, 1969. 197-213.

Lehnert, W. G., and E. W. Vine. "The Role of Affect in Narrative Structure." *Cognition and Emotion* 1 (1987): 299-322.

Lesgold, A., H. Rubinstein, P. Feltovich, R. Glaser, and D. Y. Klopfer. "Expertise in a Complex Skill: Diagnosing X-ray Pictures." *The Nature of Expertise*. Ed. M. T. H. Chi, R. Glaser, and M. J. Farr. Hillsdale: Lawrence Erlbaum, 1988. 311-42.

Levy, Jiri. "Mathematical Aspects of the Theory of Verse." *Statistics and Style*. Ed. Lubomir Dolezel and Richard Bailey. New York: American Elsevier, 1969. 95-112.

Miall, David S. "Affect and Narrative: A Model of Response to Stories." *Poetics* 17 (1988): 259-72.

_____. "Authorizing the Reader." *English Quarterly* 19 (1986): 186-95.

_____. "Beyond the Schema Given: Affective Comprehension of Literary Narratives." *Cognition and Emotion* 3 (1989): 55-78.

_____. "Readers' Responses to Narrative." *Poetics* 19 (1990): 323-39.

_____. "Rethinking English Studies: The Role of the Computer." *Humanities and the Computer: New Directions*. Ed. David S. Miall. Oxford: Oxford UP, 1990. 49-59.

Miall, David S., and Don Kuiken, "Foregrounding, Defamiliarization, Affect: Response to a Short Story." Manuscript. U of Alberta, in progress.

Michalski, R. S. "Understanding the Nature of Learning: Issues and Research Directions." *Machine Learning: An Artificial Intelligence Approach*. Ed. R. S. Michalski, J. G. Carbonell, and T. M. Mitchell. Los Altos: Morgan Kaufmann, 1986. 2: 3-25.

Oakman, Robert L. "Computers and Surface Structures in Prose Style: The Case of Carlyle." *Computers in Literary and Linguistic Computing*. Ed. Jaqueline Hamesse and Antonio Zampolli. Paris: Champion-Slatkine, 1985. 277-85. (Proceedings of the Eleventh International Conference Université Catholique de Louvain, 2-6 April 1984).

Patel, V. L., and G. J. Groen. "Knowledge Based Solution Strategies in Medical Reasoning." *Cognitive Science* 10 (1986): 91-116.

Potter, Rosanne G. "Literary Criticism and Literary Computing: The Difficulties of a Synthesis." *Computers and the Humanities* 22 (1988): 91-97.

_____, ed. *Literary Computing and Literary Criticism: Theoretical and Practical Essays on Theme and Rhetoric.* Philadelphia: U of Pennsylvania P, 1989.

Riffaterre, Michael. "Criteria for Style Analysis." *Word* 15 (1959): 154-74.

Schmidt, Klaus M. "Conceptual Glossaries: A New Tool for Medievalists." *Computers and the Humanities* 12 (1978): 19-26.

Small, Ian. "Computational Stylistics and the Construction of Literary Readings." *Prose Studies* 7 (1984): 250-60.

Smith, John B. "Computer Criticism." Potter, ed., 13-44.

_____. *Imagery and the Mind of Stephen Dedalus: A Computer-Assisted Study of Joyce's Portrait of the Artist as a Young Man.* Lewisburg: Bucknell UP, 1980.

Stone, Philip J., Dexter C. Dunphy, Marshall S. Smith, Daniel M. Ogilvie, et al. *The General Inquirer: A Computer Approach to Content Analysis.* Cambridge: MIT P, 1966.

Van Peer, Willie. "The Measurement of Metre. Its Cognitive and Affective Functions." *Poetics* 19 (1990): 259-79.

_____. "Quantitative Studies of Literature: A Critique and an Outlook." *Computers and the Humanities* 23 (1989): 301-07.

_____. *Stylistics and Psychology: Investigations of Foregrounding.* London: Croom Helm, 1986.

Wittig, Susan. "The Computer and the Concept of Text." *Computers and the Humanities* 11 (1978): 211-15.

Zwaan, R. A. "The Computer in Perspective." *Poetics* 16 (1987): 557-58.

Notes on Contributors

Geoffrey Bilder (gbilder@brownvm.brown.edu) is Academic Projects Coordinator for Computing and Information Services at Brown University. He received his AB from Bowdoin College in 1988 and his MA in history from Brown University in 1989. He is the author of a number of academic-computing applications, including the hypermedia-authoring system Abulafia, and has collaborated on the design and development of large hypermedia systems and client-server network applications.

Jeremy H. Clear (jclear@oup-uk.uucp) is Corpus Project Manager for Oxford University Press. He worked at Birmingham University on the COBUILD project in computational corpus-based lexicography from 1980 to 1988 and was Senior Computing Officer from 1985. During 1986-87 he was engaged on a project funded by IBM to work on the development of a corpus-based grammar for speech recognition, spending three months at the IBM Watson Research Center at Yorktown Heights, NY. He was Chief Lexical Systems Analyst for Collins Reference Division for a year before joining Oxford University Press in 1989.

James H. Coombs (jazbo@brownvm.brown.edu) is Research Scientist at the Institute for Research in Information and Scholarship (IRIS), Brown University. A former Mellon Fellow, he holds a PhD in English literature and an MA in Computational Linguistics from Brown University. The chief editor of *A Pre-Raphaelite Friendship: The Correspondence of William Holman Hunt and John Lucas Tupper* (1985), he has published articles on poetics as well as computing. The creator of IRIS InterLex, an on-line dictionary integrated into Intermedia, he also created the full-text search application for this hypertext system.

Paul Delany (delany@sfu.ca), Professor of English at Simon Fraser University, is author of *D. H. Lawrence's Nightmare: The Writer and His Circle in the Years of the Great War* and *The Neo-pagans: Rupert Brooke and the Ordeal of Love*. He has been involved with computers and the humanities for the past twelve years and co-edited with George P. Landow *Hypermedia and Literary Studies*. A former Guggenheim Fellow, he has also taught at Columbia University and the University of Waterloo. He is currently working on two projects: a collection of essays on Vancouver as a postmodern city and a study of English literature and the financial culture.

Steven J. DeRose (sjd%ebt-inc@uunet.uu.net) is Senior System Architect for Electronic Book Technologies, maker of DynaText, an SGML-based browsing, navigation, and retrieval system for delivering very large hypertextual documents on line. His research interests include linguistics and computer science, particularly where these intersect in providing tools for scholarship in the humanities and the social sciences. His work with literary hypertext systems began at Brown University in 1979, when he joined the FRESS project, a hypertext/hypermedia system begun around 1969. He has published papers on descriptive markup theory, SGML, artificial intelligence, natural language processing, corpus linguistics, hypertext, and other topics. He was a co-founder of Brown's Computing in the Humanities Users' Group (CHUG), is the biographer for the on-line forum Humanist, and is a member of the Text Encoding Initiative. He has contributed to several academic and commercial software systems.

Nancy Kaplan is Associate Professor and Director of Writing in the College of Arts and Humanities at the University of Texas at Dallas. Along with articles on electronic writing, Kaplan is co-author of PROSE (Prompted Revision of Student Essays, McGraw-Hill, 1987), software that won the EDUCOM/NCRIPTAL award for best program in writing. In 1992, Kaplan and Moulthrop won the Ellen Nold Award for best essay in computers and writing for their work on interactive fiction.

Ian Lancashire (ian@epas.utoronto.ca) is Professor of English and Director, Centre for Computing in the Humanities, University of Toronto. His books include *Two Tudor Interludes* (1980), *Dramatic Texts and Records of Britain* (1984), and *The Humanities Computing Yearbook* (1991). Recently he also guest-edited the first volume of the *Research in Humanities Computing* series (1991).

George P. Landow (gplandow@brownvm.brown.edu) is Professor of English and Art, Brown University, where he is Faculty Fellow at the Institute for Research in Information and Scholarship (IRIS). He has taught at Columbia University, the University of Chicago, and Brasenose College, Oxford, and his books include *The Aesthetic and Critical Theories of John Ruskin* (1971), *Victorian Types, Victorian Shadows: Biblical Typology and Victorian Literature, Art, and Thought* (1980), *Images of Crisis: Literary Iconology, 1750 to the Present* (1982), *Ruskin* (1985), *Elegant Jeremiahs: The Sage from Carlyle to Mailer* (1986), and *Hypertext: The Convergence of Contemporary Critical Theory and Technology* (1992). Since 1985, he has worked as a member of the IRIS team that developed Intermedia. *The Dickens Web*, a selection of Intermedia materials, won the 1990 EDUCOM/NCRIPTAL award for most innovative courseware in the humanities. Eastgate Systems has recently published Storyspace editions of both the Dickens materials and *The "In Memoriam" Web*, which he created with Jon Lanestedt.

Alan T. McKenzie (vyc@mace.cc.purdue.edu) is Professor of English and Director of Graduate Studies in English at Purdue University and the author of *Certain, Lively Episodes: The Articulation of Passion in Eighteenth-Century Prose* (1990), a forthcoming collection of essays on eighteenth-century correspondence, and an MLA book on word processing.

David S. Miall (dmiall@vm.ucs.ualberta.ca) is Associate Professor of English at the University of Alberta. He was educated in Britain and taught at Cheltenham for ten years before moving to Canada in 1989. His published articles include work on Coleridge, reader-response studies, classroom method, and literary computing. He is director of the biannual Coleridge Summer Conference in Somerset, England.

Stuart Moulthrop (sm51@prism.gatech.edu) is Assistant Professor of Literature, Communication, and Culture at the Georgia Institute of Technology. He has published several articles on hypertextual theory, rhetoric, and pedagogy, as well as Victory Garden (Eastgate Systems, 1991), a novel-length interactive fiction. In 1992, with Kaplan, Moulthrop won the Ellen Nold Award for best essay in computers and writing for their work on interactive fiction.

Allen H. Renear (allen@brownvm.brown.edu) is Planning Analyst, Computing and Information Services, Brown University. He received his AB from Bowdoin College and an MA and a PhD from Brown, specializing in logic and epistemology. Prior to holding his current position, he taught philosophy and held a variety of computer-consulting and user-services positions. Renear has consulted on many large text-base projects and publishes regularly on theoretical topics in text encoding and humanities computing. He is co-editor of Humanist and represents the American Philosophical Association on the advisory board of the Text Encoding Initiative.

Peter M. W. Robinson (peterr@vax.ox.ac.uk) is Research Officer for the Computers and Manuscripts Project, within the Oxford University Computing Service. He has edited Old Norse poetic texts, is chair of the Textual Criticism working group of the Text Encoding Initiative, and is the developer of Collate, a computer program widely used in collation of variant texts.

Sue Stigleman (stigle@cs.unca.edu) is currently studying computer science at the University of North Carolina at Asheville and writing about text management. She was previously Information Management Education Librarian at the Health Sciences Library University of North Carolina at Chapel Hill. She also held positions as Systems Librarian and Information Services Librarian at the same library. She received a BS in zoology from Northern Arizona University and an MA in dance and a master's in library science from the University of California at Los Angeles.

Christinger Tomer is Assistant Professor, School of Library and Information Science, University of Pittsburgh. Tomer was educated at the College of Wooster and Case Western Reserve University and has taught previously at Case Western Reserve University, Slippery Rock University of Pennsylvania, and Notre Dame College of Ohio. His professional research interests include computer networking and network-resource management, alternative software development in the MS-DOS and UNIX environments, and computer-mediated conferences. He is a member of the American Library Association, the American Society for Information Science, and the Association of Library and Information Science Educators.

Jacques Virbel (virbel@irit.fr) is at the Institut de Recherche en Informatique de Toulouse, Université Paul Sabatier. A linguist and computer scientist, his interests lie in the analysis and management of text bases, artificial intelligence, and cognitive science. His current research focuses on the modeling of written communication, the conception and formalization of annotation languages, the definition of the Bibliothèque de France reading station, and the impact of new computerized resources on written communication.

Mark Zimmermann (science@oasys.dt.navy.mil) received his BA (1974) from Rice University and his MS (1976) and PhD (1980) in physics from the California Institute of Technology. He works for the United States Government and in his spare time enjoys writing computer software to help people.

Index

Association for Literary and Linguistic
    Computing (ALLC), 155, 288
Association Française de Cybernètique et
    Technique, L' (AFCET), 44
Association of American Publishers (AAP), 99,
    102, 113, 122, 125
AT&T Bell Laboratories, 174, 186
Atkinson, Steven D., 141
attribute lists, 122
Atwood, Margaret, 295
Augment, 127
Austen, Jane, 207
Australian National University, 139
authorial property, 6

Babbage, Charles, 3, 24
Baecker, R., 41
Baker, D. C., 287
Balsamo, Anne, 238, 245, 246
BARTON, 139
Barron, Billy, 143, 144
Barthes, Roland, 265, 326
Baudrillard, Jean, 7, 10, 239, 263
Benedikt, Michael, 5, 18, 264
Bentley, Richard, 24, 272
Bérard, Victor, 191
Berger, John, 253, 267
Berry-Rogghe, G. L. M., 304
Bevan, Jonquil, 316
Bible, The, 224, 234
    Greek New Testament, 132
    King James, 62, 132
    Old Testament, 295
        Hebrew, 155
        Genesis, 303
bibliographic-file management software, 77
bibliography
    formatting, 69
    generators, 77
    software, 77
Bibliothèque de France, 11, 19, 22, 31-43
Bibliothèque Nationale, 31
BibTex, 77
BiB/SEARCH, 77
Bilder, Geoffrey, 15, 237
biomedical research, 140
Biosis, 160
bitmaps, 121
BITNET, 20, 154,159, 203, 204, 205, 208, 214, 215,
    219, 221
Blake, William, 293, 328
    Four Zoas, 328

Blitz, Michael, 246
Boeing Aircraft Co., 266
Bolter, J. David, 6, 7, 16, 218, 253, 263, 264, 265
Bookends, 77
Book of Mormon, The, 154
Borland, 330
Bormouth, John R., 11
Boston Library Consortium, 139
Bouf, P., 44
Bradley, John, 295
Brain and Behavioral Sciences, 224
British Lending Library, 155
British Library, 11, 167
British National Corpus, 19, 167, 170, 185
    criteria, 168-169
    availabilty of, 169
Brennan, Elaine, 9, 234
Brown University, 96, 127, 129, 228, 230, 234
Browning, Robert, 155
Browser, 61
Brunner, Theodore, 197
Bruno, 230
Burkowski, Forbes J., 125
Bush, Vannevar, 6, 24, 85, 113, 127
Buxton, W., 45
Byrd, Donald, 243

cable-TV connection, 224
Cadigan, Pat, 12
California, University of, 139, 206, 215
CALS, see Computer-aided Aquisition and
    Logistics Support
Cambridge University Press, 114
CANCOPY, 18
Candide, 41
canon, literary, 271
Canter, D., 40
Capp, Bernard, 234
Cardbox, 75
CARL system, 156, 158, 192, 198
Carlyle, Thomas, 327, 330
Carmody, Steven, 113, 114, 115, 126
Carnegie-Mellon University, 65, 261
    OPACS, 145, 156
Carroll, John M., 259
Carroll, Lewis, 154, 155
    Alice's Adventures in Wonderland, 154, 213
    Hunting of the Snark, The, 213
Caruso, Denise, 193-194
CATALIST, 145
Catano, James, 126

dot commands, 90
Doyle, Sir Arthur Conan, 154
  Adventures of Sherlock Holmes, The, 154
  Sign of Four, The, 154
  *Study in Scarlet, A,*154
Doyle, A. I., 287
Drucker, Peter F., 85, 113
DTI, see Department of Trade and Industry
Duggan, Richard H., 145
Durand, David, 246
Dyer, M. G., 334

EARN, 159, 193
Edda, 274
editing
  accidentals, 276
  electronic, 281, 284
  reconceiving process, 285
  structure-oriented, 108, 110, 112, 115
  see also critical editions
editor's privilege, 284
education, influence of technology on, 255, 262
EDUCOM, 204
Egan, Dennis E., 262, 264
Ehrlich, Heyward, 195, 198
Eighteenth-Century Short-Title Catalogue, see
    Donald Wing
Eisenstein, Elizabeth, 6, 248
EJournal, 210
electronic bulletin boards, 285
electronic conferencing, 218, 247
  see also computer-mediated communication,
    Technoculture (TNC)
  blends speech and writing, 237, 239
  cultural identity, 245
  democratization, 244
  electronic mail, compared to, 246
  generates own transcript, 238
  hypertext-like, 244
  informality, rapidity, and spontaneity, 247
  lack of linearity, unity, and closure, 247
  list etiquette, 227
  lurkers, 238
  multiauthored textuality, 237
  nothing alien to, 219
  self-presentation on, 245-246
electronic mail, 159, 211, 218, 228, 246, 247
Electronic Manuscript Project, 99
electronic publication, 280
electronic style sheets, 114
element recognition, 103, 104, 106

Ellmann, Richard, 197
Elm, 212
emacs, 209
Encyclopaedia Britannica, The, 154
English, William K., 85, 113, 115
English Poetry Full-Text Database, 191-92
EndNote, 77
Englebart, Douglas C., 85, 113, 115, 127, 226
ergonomics, 31
ERIC system. 143
Ertel, Monica, 67
Ethernet, 65, 174
Ethnograph, 79
Etude, 95
European Economic Community, 129, 167
European Refernce Corpora, 185
Evans, Nancy H., 139
Everett, Dorothy, 287
Evrard, F., 41

facsimile machine, 123, 197
Farrell, David, 140, 141
Fast indexed word lists, 53
Febvre, Lucien, 24
Federalist Papers, The, 154
Feiner, Steven, 134
feminism, 299, 300, 315
Fetch, 24, 203
fields, 125
File Manager 80
File Retrieval and Editing System (FRESS), 96,
    126, 127, 159
file transfer protocol (FTP), 20, 142, 203
filing software, 77
Fish, Robert S., 39
Fish, Stanley, 23, 333
Fitzgerald, F. Scott, 154
  Great Gatsby, The, 154
Flores, Fernando, 39
Fogel, Earl, 144
FOLIO, see Princeton University
FolioViews, 81
foreign language alphabets, 71
Forth, 61
Fortier, Paul, 326, 328, 330
Fourier analysis, 328
Frank, Roberta, 285
Frantext, 43, 189
Free Software Foundation, 65
FreeText, 53-67
Freibert, Lucy, 297, 314

FRESS, see File Retrieval and Editing System
Freund, Elizabeth, 333
Froula, Christine, 273
Frye, Northrop, 207
FTP, see file transfer protocol

G. & C. Merriam, 154
Gabler, Hans Walter, 272, 287, 288
Gardin, Jean-Claude, 332, 333, 339
Garfinkel, Simson L., 20
Garg, Pankaj K., 40
Garreau, Joel, 197
Garside, Roger, 173, 181
Gator, 79
Geertz, Clifford, 238
Gelernter, David, 263, 267
General Inquirer, 325
General Markup Language (GML), 87, 92, 93, 113
Georgia Institute of Technology, 238
George, Boy, 312
Georgetown Center for Text and Technology, 43, 154, 155
Gess, Richard, 240
Getty Art and Architecture Thesaurus, 33
gIBIS, 39
Gibson, William, 12, 18, 219, 221
Giffard, A., 44
Gilbert, Jody, 24
Glushko, Robert, 16, 17
GML, see General Markup Language
GNU Emacs, 65, 159
Gobineau, Arthur de, 327
Gofer, 74
Goldfarb, C. F., 85, 92, 108, 113, 114, 115
Goldfield, Joel D., 327
Gopher, 20, 54, 151, 152, 153, 157, 159, 193, 203
Gordon, George, Lord Byron, 273
Gore, Senator Albert, 153
GOVDOC-L, 143
grammar correctors, 89, 113, 184
Graphical User Interface (GUI), 174, 215
Gregory of Corinth, 288
grep command, 80
Grice, Roger A., 40
Groen, G. J., 336
Grolier's Encyclopedia, 156
Gross, M., 36
group decision-making, 218
Grusin Richard A., 237, 238, 240
GUI, see Graphical User Interface

Guide, 78
Guttenberg, Johannes, 5, 6, 224

Halio, Marcia Peoples, 253-267
  no explanatory narrative, 259
  judgments of subject, 258
  sample size, 257
  test population, 255
  ignores effects of gender,255
  ignores socio-economic status, 255
  ignores prior education, 255
Hall, Stephen C., 20, 198, 204
Hamilton, Linda, 298
Hammond, Anthony, 287
Hancock, Geoff, 315
Harker, W. John, 337
Harnad, Stevan, 223, 224
Harris, Jospeh, 286
Hart, Michael, 25, 154
Harvard University, 139, 129
Harvard On-Line Library Information System, 139, 142, 206
Haas, Christine, 259
Hayes, John R., 259
Hayhoe, Michael, 336
Hawisher, Gail, 255
Hawthorne, Nathaniel, 271
Heath, Deborah, 243
Heather, M., 40
Heim, Michael, 13, 218
Helgason, Jón, 288
HES, see Hypertext Editing Systems
High-Performance Computing Act of 1989, 153
Hiltz, Roxanne, 217, 218, 225, 226, 227
histogram, 328
Hofmann, Martin, 40
HOLLIS see Harvard On-Line Library Information System
Homer, 14
Howard, Tharon, 215
Howard-Hill, T. H., 82
Hughes, Dan, 243
Humanist, 207, 208, 209, 234
Humanities Computing Facility, 215
Hunter, Lynette, 331
HyperCard, see Apple Computer
hyper-islands, 128
hypermedia, 13, 24, 66, 77, 124, 126, 129, 195, 197, 266, 280; see also hypertext
Hypermedia and Literary Studies, 9, 24, 78, 197
Hyperpad, 78

Hyperrez, 144
HyperScribe, 127
hypertext, 6, 13, 15, 24, 40, 61, 69, 77, 81, 126-129,
    131, 144, 160, 238, 244, 247, 264, 265, 281,
    284; see also Augment, Fress, Guide,
    Hypercard, Hypertext Editing Systems,
    hypermedia, Hyperties, Intermedia,
    Storyspace
  models
      algebraic, 40
      electronic book, 40-41
      first-order logic, 40
      hypergraphs, 40
      Petri networks, 40
Hypertext '87, 126
Hypertext Editing Systems (HES), 114
Hyperties, 78
Hytelnet, 144
HyTime, 130

IBM, see International Business Machines
IBMNEW Forum, 154
IdeaList, 75, 78, 80, 81
Ide, Nancy M., 293, 327, 336, 339
ILLINET On Line, 206
Illinois Benedictine University, 25, 154
Illinois, University of, 154, 206
image-enhancement, 281
IMSS, see Information Management System for
    Scholars
index, 14, 24, 35, 73, 77
indexing
    computer-assisted indexing, 281
    and retrieval, 74
    software, 74, 75, 77
Indiana University, 207
information environments, need for integrated,
    262
Information management System for Scholars
    (IMSS), 115
information-management software, 75
information overload, 227
information retrieval,
    in manuscripts, 6
    software, 75
    stemming, 56
    stop words, 56
    see also text retrieval
information systems, 31
informatique, l', 4
informatization, 11

INFOTRAC, 158
INFOTRAX, 139
Ingres, 54
Innovative Interfaces system, 158
Integrated Services Digital Network (ISDN), 20,
    25
Interactive ELectronic Technical Manual, 123
interfaces
    command-driven, 259
    context views, browsing-oriented, 53
    and copyright, 17
    current, 228
    user, 141, 147
    visual, 260
InterLeaf, 93, 95
Intermedia, 78, 246
Internal Revenue Service, 102
International Business Machines (IBM), 114, 115,
    174, 254, 255, 260, 266, 294
    Grand conferencing system, 228
International Medieval Congress, 288
International Organization for Standardization
    (ISO), 128, 130, 133
    ISO Formal Public Identifiers, 132
    ISO 10646, 133
International Unabridged Dictionary, 154
Internet, 9, 20, 67, 68, 120, 123, 128, 129, 139, 140-
    145, 147, 151, 152, 154, 157, 158-159, 193,
    203, 204, 205, 208, 214, 215, 219
Internet-wide information servers (IWIS), 21,
    193
Internote, 39
intertextuality, 15
ISBN, 131
ISDN, see Integrated Services Digital Network
Iser, Wolfgang, 265, 333
Island Write, 42
ISO, see International Organization for
    Standardization
Isys, 74, 81
Ivins, William M., 6
IWIS, see Internet-wide information servers
IZE, 75

Jackson, Howard, 339
Jacobson, Alex, 243, 248
James Joyce Quarterly, 190
Jamet, D., 31
JANET, see Joint Academic Network of the
    United Kingdom
JANUS, 158

Mukarovsky, 334
multilanguage database, 66
multilinear reading paths, 13
multimedia, 5, 43
Murray, John J., 22
Mutual Information (MI), 178-181
MYCIN, 336

National Center for Machine-Redable Texts In the Humanities, 154
National Center for Text and Technology, 154
National Digital Library, 153
National Endowment for the Humanities, 129
National Research and Education Network (NREN), 20, 153, 159, 204, 221
National Science Foundation, 147, 149, 203
natural language processing (NLP), 169
  economic, social, and political benefits of progress in, 184
n.b.Ibid (see also Nota Bene), 77, 80
Nelson, Theodor H., 6, 15, 85, 113, 115, 123, 127, 131, 226
NetNews, 218, 221, 222, 229, 231, 234
NetNorth, 159
networks, 4, 7, 15, 69, 120, 121, 139, 140, 142, 148-150, 154, 158-159, 212, 247
  campus-wide, 152
  definition of, 201
  disorientation on, 204-5
  and docuverse, 190
  high-capacity, 31
  high-speed, 12, 139
  Petri, 40
  semantic, 304
  text on, 210
  see also BITNET, Internet, Joint Academic Network of the United Kingdom, National Research and Education Network, NSFNET, Research Library Information Network
New Criticism, 324
New English Dictionary on Historical Principles, 154
New Mexico, University of, 143, 145
NeWS, 174
NewsGrazer, 212
NewsWatcher, 229, 230, 231
Newton, Sir Isaac, 224
NeXT Computers, 24, 42, 145, 151, 212, 214, 231
  Digital Librarian software, 61
  NewsGrazer, see NewsGrazer

NeXTMail facility, 24
NeXT OS, 151
Nielsen, Jakob, 37, 78
NLP, see natural language processing
Nora, Simon, 19
North Texas, University of, 143
Nota Bene, 75, 80, 92, 95
Notebook II ,75, 80
note managers, 75
NOVEL: A Forum on Fiction, 102
NREN, see National Research and Education Network
nroff/troff, 90
NSFNET, 151
Nuntius, 230, 232
Nutshell, 75

Oakman, Robert, 327, 330
object-oriented design, 122
object-oriented languages, 40
OCLC, see Online Computer Library Center
OCP, 321, 322, 332
OCR, see Optical character Recognition
Office Document Architeture (ODA), 128
O'Hara, Robert J., 283, 288
OHCO, see ordered hierarchy of content objects
Ohmann, Richard, 262
Olsen, Mark, 15, 22, 23
Ong, Walter J., 218
Online Computer Library Center (OCLC), 160, 192
on-line help, 203
Online Journal of Current Clinical Trials, 156
on-line public access catalog (OPAC), 139, 140, 144, 156, 158, 160, 202, 205, 215
OPAC, see on-line public access catalog
Operation Desert Storm, 207
Optical Character Recognition, 44, 100, 101, 170, 192, 195, 198
optical disks, 4
Oracle, 54
ordered hierarchy of content objects (OHCO), 7
Oregon, University of, 145, 158, 159
OUCS, see Oxford University Computing Services
OUP, see Oxford University Press
outlines, 110, 115
Owens, Larry, 24
Oxford Advanced Learners Dictionary, 181
Oxford Concordance Program, 79, 294
Oxford English Dictionary, 19, 129, 164

Oxford Text Archive, 43, 81, 154, 155, 185, 213
Oxford University Computing Services (OUCS), 167
Oxford University Press (OUP), 114, 163, 167, 171, 273, 332

packet assembler dissasembler (PAD), 206
PACS-L, 143, 144
PAD, see packet assembler dissasembler
page fidelity, 124
page-layout tools, 121
Pagemaker, see Aldus Pagemaker
Paine, Tom, 154
    Common Sense, 154
Palache, Lucy B., 317
Paperless Library, see Advantage Foundation's Paperless Library Program
Papert, Seymor, 255
Papyrus, 77
PARA discussion group, 68
parallel text servers, 151
parallel processing, 153
Parkes, A., 41, 287
parsers,
    grammar, 113, 184
    Standard General Markup Language, 102
    syntactic tree, 170
PARTS, 181, 182
Pascual, E., 41
Pasquier-Boltuck, Jacques, 40
Pat, 79
PAT, 42, 186
Patel, V. L., 336
Pater, Walter, 332
Paterson, L., 288
Patrologia Latina, 191
PAUP, 283
PC-Hypertext, 78
Peck, Rodney II, 65, 67
Pennsylvania, University of, 213
Perez, Ernest, 69
performance optimization, 103
PERL, 159
Perseus Project, 14, 129, 195
Peter Pan, 154
Peters, Paul E., 20
Peters, Thomas, 156
Petersons College Database, 213
philology, 164
Philosophy and Phenomenological Research, 102
phrasal graphs, 15, 310, 315
    check generalizations, 306

describe conditions or states, 306
    shed light on word connotation, 305
phrasal repetends, 303, 305-309, 313
Phrasea, 41
Pinter, Harold, 297, 314
Pittsburgh, University of, 140
    OPAC, 142, 145
Plato, 5
Polo, Marco, 41
portability of documents, 120, 121
Porush, David, 242, 243
Postmodern Culture, 211
PostScript, 100, 121, 124, 143
poststructuralism, 10
Potter, Roseanne G., 78, 79, 327, 339
Pound, Ezra, 273
Prague structuralists, 334
Pre-Raphaelite Friendship, A, 96
Presley, Elvis, 312
Presutti, Lidio, 295
Princeton University, 154
    FOLIO service, 147
print literacy, 166
print-only approach to education, 267
print technology, 6
    adds fixity, 6
    deficiencies, 6
    invention of, 280
    movable type and, 6
    multiplicity and, 6
    steam-driven, 6
Pro-Cite, 77
Procomm, 214
Prodigy, 221, 224
professional readers, 31
program documentation, 105
Project ATHENA, 44
Project Gutenberg, 25, 149, 154, 155, 213
Project Whirlwind, 3
protocols, 202
Providence Journal-Bulletin, The, 221, 223
Prusky, John, 114, 126
PSYCOLOQUY, 224
publication, 240
Purtopoi, 215
Pynchon, Thomas, 207

qualitative-analysis software, 79
quantitative research, 325, 326
    effects, 325
    opposition to, 325, 326

text (cont.)
  containment and, 125
  debate about, 262
  defined, 7
  environments, 5
  hand-sorting, 280
  ideal, 283, 287
  interlinear manipulation, 81
  need to preserve unnormalized, 281
  literary, 334
  as ordered hierarchy of content objects, 7
  rethinking work with, 266
  see textuality
text analysis, 69
  collocational patterns, 294, 295
  displays, 295
  distribution graphs, 294
  frequency lists, 315
  keyword-in-context (KWIC), 36, 60, 67, 79,
    170, 174, 175, 294, 295, 298, 304
  keyword-out-of-context (KWOC), 79
  methods, 322
  marginality among literary scholars, 322
  software for, 320
  word associations, 294
  see also Computer Criticism and TACT
text base, 4, 7, 17, 31, 37, 39, 108, 110, 163-185,
    202, 213, 331, 332
  programmable, 189
  rigour of, 331
text-based computing, 239
  blends textualities, 239
  database managers, 75
  environment, 4
  formerly centered on concordance, 339
  management, 69
    effects of, 195
    freeform, 75
    systems for (TBMS), 75
text corpora, see text base
text database, see text base
Text Encoding Initiative (TEI), 19, 43, 128, 154,
    155, 170, 286
text-management software, 15, 69-81
text processing, 6, 110, 217
text retrieval 36
  displays, 53
  fuzzy-proximity-neighborhood subsets, 53,
    57-59, 67
  prompts careful reading, 315
  tools, 294
  highlights interests of critic, 300

software, 69, 74, 75, 151
stemming, 56
stop words, 56
  see also information retrieval, searching
TEXTNET, 39
text-oriented database managers, 75
TEXTPACK, 79
Textpro, 78
textual information management systems
    (TIMS), 74
textuality
  electronic, 4, 196, 201, 240
    demands active readers, 238
    fluidity of, 284
    as intermediate, 273
    partial, 189
    temporary, 189
    virtual, 7, 189
  on network,
    ownership, 210
    privacy, 210
    copyright, see copyright
  new conceptions of, 196
  retrieval, software for, 69, 75
  visual features of, 262
  written, two-level hierarchy, 14
Thesaurus Linguae Graecae, 185, 191
thesaurus programs, 113
Thinking Machines, Incorporated, 21, 147, 148,
    151, 193
Thom's Dublin Directory, 191
Þórðarson, Sighvatr, 285
Times Literary Supplement, The, 247
TIMS, see textual information management
    systems
TNC, see Technoculture
Todorov, Tzvetan, 339
Tomer, Christinger 21, 193
Tompa, Frank W., 40, 129
Toolbook, 78
Toronto corpus of Old English, 185
Transmission Control Protocol/Internet
    Protocol (TCP/IP), 142, 151, 152, 159, 203
Treasury of the Greek Language, 42
Très Grande Bibliothèque (La TGB), 43
Trésor de la Langue Française, 185
Trigg, Randall H., 39, 40, 113
TRSDOS, 214
t-score, 178-181
Turner, Mark, 266
Turoff, Murray, 217, 218, 225, 227
Turville-Petre, T., 288

Writer's Assistant, 39
WriterStation, see Datalogic's WriterStation
Writer's Workbench system, 39, 257
WYSIWYG, see What You See Is What You Get

Xedit, 115
Xerox Bravo, 93, 95
xerography, 194
Xhardez, Didier, 288
X-Windows, 174
XyWrite, 92, 93, 95x

Yale University, 261
Yankelovich, Nicole, 39, 40, 85, 113, 239

Zampolli, Antonio, 11
Zimmermann, Mark, 7, 9, 36, 195
ZyIndex, 74, 80
Zuboff, Shoshana, 266
Zwaan, R. A., 326, 333, 338

The MIT Press, with Peter Denning as general consulting editor, publishes computer science books in the following series:

ACL-MIT Press Series in Natural Language Processing
Aravind K. Joshi, Karen Sparck Jones, and Mark Y. Liberman, editors

ACM Doctoral Dissertation Award and Distinguished Dissertation Series

Artificial Intelligence
Patrick Winston, founding editor
J. Michael Brady, Daniel G. Bobrow, and Randall Davis, editors

Charles Babbage Institute Reprint Series for the History of Computing
Martin Campbell-Kelly, editor

Computer Systems
Herb Schwetman, editor

Explorations with Logo
E. Paul Goldenberg, editor

Foundations of Computing
Michael Garey and Albert Meyer, editors

History of Computing
I. Bernard Cohen and William Aspray, editors

Logic Programming
Ehud Shapiro, editor; Fernando Pereira, Koichi Furukawa, Jean-Louis Lassez, and David H. D. Warren, associate editors

The MIT Press Electrical Engineering and Computer Science Series

Research Monographs in Parallel and Distributed Processing
Christopher Jesshope and David Klappholz, editors

Scientific and Engineering Computation
Janusz Kowalik, editor

Technical Communication and Information Systems
Edward Barrett, editor